A Social History of Ottoman Ista

Using a wealth of contemporary Ottoman sources, this book recreates the social history of Istanbul, a huge, cosmopolitan metropolis and imperial capital of the Ottoman Empire. Seat of the sultan and an opulent international emporium, Istanbul was also a city of violence, shaken regularly by natural disasters and by the turmoil of sultanic politics and violent revolt. Its inhabitants, entertained by imperial festivities and cared for by the great pious foundations which touched every aspect of their lives, also amused themselves in the numerous pleasure gardens and the many public baths of the city. The authors capture the lives of those who lived in this vibrant, violent, luxurious and cosmopolitan city through intimate portraits. While the book focuses on Istanbul, it presents a broad picture of Ottoman society, how it was structured and how it developed and transformed across four centuries. As such, the book offers an exciting alternative to the more traditional histories of the Ottoman Empire.

EBRU BOYAR is Assistant Professor in the International Relations Department at the Middle East Technical University, Ankara. Her previous publications include *The Ottomans and Trade* (edited with Kate Fleet, 2006) and *Ottomans, Turks and the Balkans: Empire Lost, Relations Altered* (2007).

KATE FLEET is Director of the Skilliter Centre for Ottoman Studies at Newnham College, University of Cambridge, and Newton Trust Lecturer in Ottoman History in the Faculty of Asian and Middle Eastern Studies at the University of Cambridge. Her previous publications include *The Ottoman Capitulations: Text and Context* (edited with Maurits van den Boogert, 2003) and *The Cambridge History of Turkey, Vol. I. Byzantium to Turkey, 1071–1453* (ed., Cambridge, 2008).

A Social History of Ottoman Istanbul

Ebru Boyar

and

Kate Fleet

CAMBRIDGE UNIVERSITY PRESS
Cambridge, New York, Melbourne, Madrid, Cape Town, Singapore, São Paulo, Delhi

Cambridge University Press
The Edinburgh Building, Cambridge CB2 8RU, UK

Published in the United States of America by Cambridge University Press, New York

www.cambridge.org
Information on this title: www.cambridge.org/9780521136235

First published 2010

Printed in the United Kingdom at the University Press, Cambridge

A catalogue record for this publication is available from the British Library

ISBN 978-0-521-19955-1 Hardback
ISBN 978-0-521-13623-5 Paperback

Contents

Illustrations

All illustrations, unless otherwise stated, are from the collection of the Skilliter Centre for Ottoman Studies, Newnham College, Cambridge. The authors would like to express their gratitude to the Skilliter Centre for permission to reproduce the images.

Maps

Acknowledgements

This book is dedicated to the memory of Susan Skilliter, Lecturer in Turkish Studies at Cambridge University and Fellow of Newnham College, who on her death in 1985 left her books and money to found a centre for research in Ottoman studies. It was Dr Skilliter's foresight, together with the imagination and strength of Sheila Browne, then Principal of Newnham College, which resulted in the establishment of the Skilliter Centre for Ottoman Studies, an institution to which we are both grateful. We are also dedicating this book to the memory of Julian Chrysostomides, an inspirational supervisor and truly generous person who lives on through the many, many students she inspired, cared for and intellectually reared.

This book grew out of a series of lectures we gave in September 2005 on the Skilliter Centre tour of Istanbul, Bursa and Edirne. The tour was for us a most enjoyable experience and we learnt a great deal both from preparing and giving the lectures and from the questions, interest and enthusiasm of those with whom we travelled. We should like to thank in particular all those who took part in the tour and who stimulated us to consider writing this book in the first place.

We should also like to thank Rebecca Gower, the Librarian of the Skilliter Centre, for her help with the illustrations and editing. Her calmness and ability are considerable assets for the Centre. We are also most grateful to Dr Tuba Çavdar, who was instrumental in procuring the cover illustration for us, to Marigold Acland, Jo Breeze and Sarah Green at Cambridge University Press, and to our copy-editor Alison Thomas. Our thanks are also due to the staff of the University Library, Cambridge, the library of the Middle East Technical University, Ankara, the library of the Turkish Historical Association, Ankara, the Principal, Fellows and Members of Newnham College, Cambridge, the Middle East Technical University, Muharrem Özsait and the Boyar family.

Chronology

1421–44, 1446–51	Murad II
1453	Ottoman conquest of Constantinople
1444–46, 1451–81	Mehmed II
1481–1512	Bayezid II
1512–20	Selim I
1520–66	Süleyman I
1566–74	Selim II
1574–95	Murad III
1595–1603	Mehmed III
1603–17	Ahmed I
1617–18, 1622–23	Mustafa I
1618–22	Osman II
1623–40	Murad IV
1640–48	İbrahim
1648–87	Mehmed IV
1687–91	Süleyman II
1691–95	Ahmed II
1695–1703	Mustafa II
1703	Edirne incident
1703–30	Ahmed III
1730	Patrona Halil revolt
1730–54	Mahmud I
1754–57	Osman III
1757–74	Mustafa III
1774–89	Abdülhamid I
1789–1807	Selim III
1807–08	Mustafa IV
1808–39	Mahmud II
1839–61	Abdülmecid
1861–76	Abdülaziz
1876	Murad V
1876–1909	Abdülhamid II

1908	Young Turk Revolution
1909–18	Mehmed V (Reşad)
1918–22	Mehmed VI (Vahdeddin)
1919–22	National Liberation War
1923	Creation of the Republic of Turkey
1923	Declaration of Ankara as capital of the Republic

Who's who

Abdi Wrote a short account of the 1730 Patrona Halil revolt, of which he was a contemporary.

Abdülaziz Bey (Abdülaziz İbn Cemaleddin) Born Istanbul 1850, died Istanbul 1918. Writer and poet who worked in various government offices and was a member of a wealthy and well-established Istanbul family. Wrote his memoirs of the late nineteenth century, which were not published until the 1990s.

Ahmed Cavid Born Istanbul, died 1803. Into palace service in 1787. Held high office and was close to Selim III.

Ahmed Cevdet Paşa Born Bulgaria 1822, died Istanbul 1895. Prominent statesman, court historian, author of a 12-volume Ottoman history.

Ahmed Midhat Efendi Born Istanbul 1844, died Istanbul 1912. Writer, novelist, newspaper proprietor. Known as close to Abdülhamid II, he taught at the Darülfünun.

Ahmed Rasim (1865–1932) Writer, journalist, librettist and composer. Wrote for various newspapers and was an MP between 1927 and 1932.

Alus, Sermet Muhtar (1904–52) Writer and journalist, satirist, painter, caricaturist. Wrote many newspaper articles about old Istanbul.

Aşıkpaşazade (*c.*1400–after 1484) Ottoman chronicler, author of an Ottoman history to 1484.

Badoaro, Andrea Venetian ambassador extraordinaire to Istanbul in 1572.

Balıkhane Nazırı Ali Rıza Bey Born Istanbul 1842, died 1928. Worked in government service until 1910. From 1919 to 1925, published various newspaper articles about life in late Ottoman Istanbul.

Barbaro, Nicolò Venetian surgeon, wrote a diary of the siege of Constantinople in 1453, of which he was an eyewitness.

Basiretçi Ali Efendi Born Istanbul 1838. Prominent nineteenth-century Ottoman journalist, owner and chief writer of the important newspaper *Basiret*, which became very influential between 1870 and 1878. Exiled in 1878, he returned to Istanbul in 1908 and died soon afterwards.

Basmajean, Grigor Yakob Born Edirne 1853. Converting to Protestantism aged 18, he became a priest and went to the United States in 1886.

Bassano, Luigi Born Zara *c.* 1510. He was in the Ottoman empire probably between 1532 and 1540.

Beyatlı, Yahya Kemal Born Skopje 1884, died 1958. Poet, politician, diplomat. Into exile in Paris under Abdülhamid, he stayed nine years, returning to Istanbul in 1913. Considered one of the greatest poets of the early Republican era.

Bon, Ottaviano (1551–1622) Venetian ambassador 1604–08 and wrote an account of the Ottoman court.

Brassey, Anna (1839–87) Made various voyages with her family in their yacht between 1874 and 1887. Was in Istanbul in 1874 and 1878; wrote an account of her time there.

Broquière, Bertrandon de la Travelled in Anatolia 1432–33, leaving Constantinople in January 1433 for Edirne.

Busbecq, Ogier Ghiselin de (1522–92) Austrian ambassador to Süleyman I, in Istanbul 1554–62.

Cabi Ömer Efendi Cabi (revenue collector) of Ayasofya mosque complex. Active in reigns of Selim III, Mustafa IV and Mahmud II. Wrote an account covering 1788–1814, which is particularly detailed on the period 1808–14 and contains much gossip. Some of his information comes from his close contacts with people in bureaucratic circles.

Cafer Efendi Active in the late sixteenth/early seventeenth centuries. Author of an account of the life and works of the imperial architect Mehmed Ağa, who built the Sultan Ahmed mosque complex.

Careri, Giovanni Francesco Gemelli (1651–1725) Italian traveller, in Istanbul at the end of the seventeenth century.

Cemal Paşa (Ahmed Cemal) Born Mitylene 1872, assassinated Tiflis 1922. Prominent politician and member of the Committee of Union and Progress, navy minister, and commander-in-chief of the Ottoman army in Syria during the First World War.

Cemil Paşa (Topuzlu) Born Istanbul 1866, died Istanbul 1958. Famous doctor, taught in various medical schools and set up the medical faculty at Istanbul University. Mayor of Istanbul in 1912 and 1919.

Çeşmizade Mustafa Reşid Born Istanbul, died 1770. Poet, and court historian 1766–68. A member of the *ulema*, he taught in *medrese*s and held high office.

Chishull, Edmund (1671–1733) English clergyman, chaplain to the English factory at İzmir to 1702, he was in Istanbul in 1699.

Contarini, Alvise Venetian ambassador 1636–41.

Courmenin, Louis Deshayes, Baron de Born end of sixteenth century, executed 1632. Sent by the French king to Istanbul 1621.

Covel, John (1638–1722) Chaplain to the English embassy in late 1670, and in sole charge of the embassy from the death of the English ambassador Sir Daniel Harvey in 1672 to the arrival of the new ambassador Sir John Finch in 1674. In Istanbul to 1677.

dei Crescenzi, Crescenzio Author of a letter from Istanbul in 1615 describing the wedding of the daughter of Ahmed I.

La Croix, Sieur de Died 1704. Secretary to the French ambassador, in the Levant 1670–80.

Dallam, Thomas (*c.*1575, d. *c.*1630) Commissioned by Queen Elizabeth I to construct and deliver a mechanical organ and clock for the Ottoman sultan. In Istanbul 1599–1600.

Defterdar Sarı Mehmed Paşa Born Istanbul between 1655 and 1658, executed 1717. Held many high offices 1703–17. Author of a history covering 1656–1704.

Destari Salih Author of an account of the 1730 Patrona Halil revolt of which he was a contemporary. Known to have been close to the palace.

Domenico (Domenico Hierosolimitano) (*c.*1552–1622) Third physician to Murad III, probably in Istanbul between 1578/79 and 1588/89.

Doukas Died post 1462. Byzantine historian, author of history of Byzantines and Turks from 1204 to 1462.

Dwight, Harrison Griswold (1875–1959) American journalist and writer.

Ebussuud Efendi Born İskilip 1490, died 1574. Taught in many *medrese*s and served as *kazasker*. 1545 became *şeyhülislam* and held the position until his death. One of the most famous *şeyhülislam*s.

Eremya Çelebi Kömürcüyan Born Istanbul 1637, died 1695. Close to the grand vezir Köprülü Fazıl Ahmed Paşa. Opened a printing press. Wrote a contemporary account of Istanbul.

Erimez, Salih Born Istanbul 1901, died 1974. Caricaturist, educated in Vienna, published caricatures in many journals and newspapers, famous for his caricatures of Ottoman life.

Evliya Çelebi Born Istanbul 1611, died Egypt post 1683. Traveller, wrote extensive account of his travels. Held various government posts.

Fontmagne, Louisa, Baronne Durand de Died 1867. In Istanbul after the Crimean War, in 1857–58.

Forbin, Louis Nicholas Philippe Auguste, comte de (1777–1841) French painter, travelled in the Ottoman empire 1817–18.

Foscarini, Pietro Venetian ambassador to Istanbul, 1634–37, sent as ambassador extraordinaire in 1640–41.

Fresne-Canaye, Phillipe du Accompanied the French ambassador to Istanbul in 1573.

Galland, Antoine (1646–1715) Was attached to French embassy in Istanbul in 1670.

Garzoni, Costantino Accompanied the Venetian ambassador extraordinaire Andrea Badoaro to Istanbul in 1572.

Gelibolulu Mustafa Ali Born Gelibolu 1541, died Jedda 1600. Poet, historian and author of many works; he held high office and took part in many campaigns.

Georgievitz, Bartholomeus (*c.*1510–66) Captured at the battle of Mohács 1526.

Gerlach, Stephan (1546–1612) Protestant priest attached to the Habsburg embassy 1573–78.

Grelot, Guillaume-Joseph Born *c.*1630. French artist and traveller, in Istanbul 1670–72.

Gürpınar, Hüseyin Rahmi Born Istanbul 1864, died Istanbul 1944. Journalist, novelist and short story writer, MP 1936–43. His stories are known for being reflective of Istanbul and *mahalle* life.

Hasanbeyzade Ahmed Paşa Died 1636 or 1637. Author of an Ottoman history from 1520 to 1635. Entered palace service in 1591. Held many high offices both in Istanbul and in the provinces, and was present on various campaigns.

Hayrullah Efendi Born Istanbul 1818, died Tehran 1866. A doctor from an influential medical family, he taught in medical schools, wrote an Ottoman history, was briefly minister of education and opened schools for girls. Went to Europe for medical treatment in 1863. Published his account of his visit to Europe in 1864. Appointed envoy to Tehran in 1865.

Heberer, Michael Born between 1555 and 1560. From Bretten near Heidelberg. Captured by the Ottomans in the Mediterranean, he became a galley slave between 1585 and 1588.

Hoca Sadeddin Efendi (1536/37–99) Member of the *ulema*, teacher of Murad III and Mehmed III, and became *şeyhülislam* in 1598.

Hovhannesyan, Sarkis Sarraf Born Istanbul 1740, died Istanbul 1805. Historian, teacher, author of a history of the Ottoman empire and of Istanbul.

Ibn Battuta Born Tangier 1304. Arab traveller who was in Anatolia in the 1330s.

İbn Kemal (Kemalpaşazade) Born 1468 or 1469 in Edirne, died 1534. Came from an eminent family, became a member of the *ulema*. Held many high positions. Became *şeyhülislam* in 1526 until his death.

İbnülcemal Ahmed Tevfik Author of memoirs of his bicycle journey from Bursa to Istanbul in 1900.

Karaosmanoğlu, Yakup Kadri Born Cairo 1889, died Ankara 1944. Writer, diplomat, politician. Wrote for *İkdam* newspaper during the National Liberation War.

Karay, Refik Halit Born Istanbul 1888, died Istanbul 1965. Writer, journalist, known for his stories about Anatolian life. Opponent of the

National Liberation War, fled to Beirut in 1922, returning to Istanbul in 1938.

Katip Çelebi Born Istanbul 1608, died 1657. Writer and historian, held various government posts and went on many campaigns.

Kritoboulos Died post 1467. Byzantine, probably from Imbros. Went into the service of Mehmed II shortly after the conquest of Constantinople in 1453 and was later appointed governor of Imbros 1456–66.

Kydones, Demetrios (*c.*1324–*c.*1397). Byzantine scholar, statesman and theologian. Served John VI Kantakouzenos, John V Palaeologos and Manuel II.

Lacroix, Frédéric Died 1864. Wrote a guide book to Istanbul.

Lane, Edward William (1801–76) Lived in Cairo 1825–28, 1833–35 and 1842–49.

Latifi Born Kastamonu *c.*1490–91, died *c.*1582–83. Worked in the bureaucracy.

Leyla (Saz) Hanım Born Istanbul 1845, died Istanbul 1936. Composer, writer, poet. Spent early childhood in the harem of Çirağan palace. Published her memoirs of that period in *Vakit* newspaper between 1920 and 1922.

Lithgow, William (1582–*c.*1645) Traveller. In Istanbul 1610–11.

Ludovisi, Daniello de' Venetian envoy to Istanbul 1533–34.

Lütfi Paşa Born 1488, died Didymoteichon 1553. Came from the *devşirme* (the collection of Christians boys). Grand vezir 1539–41.

Mehmed Enisi (Yalkı) Born *c.*1870. Intern in the French navy 1895. Wrote his memoirs of his time in France.

Menavino, Giovanantonio Captured by the Ottomans *c.*1501, escaped after battle of Çaldıran 1514.

Mihailović, Konstantin Serb captured in battle, served in the Ottoman army as janissary 1455–63.

van Millingen, Alexander (1840–1915) Son of the Istanbul doctor Julius van Millingen, and professor at Robert College, 1879–1915.

Mimar (Ahmed) Kemaleddin Bey Born Istanbul 1870, died Ankara 1927. Famous architect and pioneer of Turkish national architecture.

Montagu, Lady Mary Wortley (1689–1762) Accompanied her husband Edward when he was sent as ambassador to Istanbul in 1716. In Istanbul 1717–18.

Moro, Giovanni Venetian ambassador to Istanbul 1587–90.

Morosini, Gianfrancesco Venetian ambassador to Istanbul 1582–85.

Müneccimbaşı Ahmed Dede (1631–1702) Chief royal astrologer from 1668. Exiled to Egypt on death of Mehmed IV in 1687. Mevlevi *şeyh* in Mecca from 1694, then in Medina. Died in Mecca.

Murad Efendi (Franz von Werner) Born Vienna 1836, died The Hague 1881. Writer, diplomat. Around 1854 escaped to the Ottoman empire, served in Ottoman army and went into diplomatic service.

Naima (Mustafa Naima Efendi) Born Aleppo 1655, died 1715. From janissary family. To Istanbul in the 1680s, and into palace service. *c.*1702 became court historian.

Navagero, Bernardo Venetian ambassador to Istanbul 1549–53.

Nedim (1681–1730) One of the most famous Ottoman poets, court poet of Ahmed III.

Nicolay, Nicolas de (1517–83) Accompanied the French ambassador to Istanbul in 1551.

Oğulukyan, Georg Armenian from Istanbul. Worked in the mint and had close contacts with people in the palace. Wrote an account of the events of 1806–10.

Orga, İrfan Born Istanbul 1908, died UK 1970. Writer and novelist. Wrote biographical work about his childhood.

Peçevi İbrahim (Peçeylu İbrahim) Born Pec 1574, died Budin 1650. Into army service in 1593; also served in various chancery positions.

Pertusier, Charles (1779–1836) Attached to the French embassy; in Istanbul 1815.

Promontorio, Jacopo de Genoese merchant at the courts of Murad II and Mehmed II.

Quiclet, M. Travelled to Istanbul 1657. His account of Istanbul was published in 1664, after his death.

Rashid Rida (1865–1935) Prominent Arab journalist and thinker; in Istanbul 1910.

Recaizade Mahmud Ekrem Born Istanbul 1847, died Istanbul 1914. Writer, journalist, novelist, poet, teacher, founder of the *Edebiyat-ı Cedide* (New Literature). Held various government positions.

Roe, Sir Thomas English ambassador to Istanbul 1621–29.

Sadri Sema (Mehmet Sadrettin Aydoğdu) Born Istanbul 1880, died Istanbul 1964. A government official, retired in 1933. Wrote many articles about late Ottoman and early Republican Istanbul, published in *Vakit* newspaper between 1955 and 1959.

Safveti Ziya Born Istanbul 1875, died Istanbul 1929. Playwright, novelist and short story writer; worked in the foreign ministry.

Salahaddin Enis (1892–1942) Journalist, novelist, short story writer, poet. Held various government posts.

Sanderson, John (1560–1627) English merchant, attached to the English embassy in Istanbul 1584; returned to Istanbul 1592–97, and was sent to Istanbul again in 1599 as consul and treasurer. Left 1601.

Sandys, George (1578–1644) Writer and traveller, in Istanbul in 1610.

Santa Croce, Aurelio In Istanbul with Venetian ambassador Marcantonio Barbaro, 1567–73.

Schweigger, Salomon (1551–1622) German Protestant priest attached to the Habsburg embassy 1578–81.

Selaniki Mustafa Efendi Held various important positions, including high office in the chancery, and attended various campaigns. Author of detailed history from 1563 to 1600.

Şerafeddin Mağmumi Born Istanbul 1869, died Cairo 1927. Doctor and founding member of the Committee of Union and Progress. Spent some years under Abdülhamid II in exile, first in Paris, and from 1901 in Cairo. Returned briefly to Istanbul in 1908, but then went back to Cairo.

Seyid Vehbi Died 1736. Important poet during the reign of Ahmed III.

Simavi, Lütfi Chief secretary of Mehmed V, 1909–12 and of Mehmed VI (Vahdeddin), 1918–19.

Smith, Albert (1816–60) Writer, public lecturer, mountaineer. Travelled to Istanbul in 1849.

Solakzade Mehmed Hemdemi Died 1657/58. Close to Murad IV, and served İbrahim and Mehmed IV. Author of an Ottoman history to 1657.

Spandounes, Theodore (Teodoro Spandugino) Born probably in Venice, died post 1538. He was sent as a young boy to live with his great-aunt Mara, widow of Murad II, in Macedonia. Seems to have visited Istanbul in 1503.

Spataris, Haris Born Istanbul 1906. Left Istanbul 1922. Wrote his memoirs about Istanbul, published in Greek in 1988.

Spon, Jacob (1647–85) French doctor, travelled with Sir George Wheler in the Levant 1675–76.

Tacizade Cafer Çelebi Executed 1515. Poet and writer. Held various high government positions during the reigns of Bayezid II and Selim I.

Talu, Ercümend Ekrem Born Istanbul 1886, died Istanbul 1956. Son of Recaizade Mahmud Ekrem. Worked in different government positions. Taught in universities and in Galatasaray. Wrote novels and short stories about life in old Istanbul.

Tanpınar, Ahmet Hamdi Born Istanbul 1901, died Istanbul 1962. Well-known writer and literary historian of the early Turkish Republic.

Tavernier, Jean-Baptiste (1605–89) French traveller, in Istanbul 1631–32.

Tevfik Fikret Born Istanbul 1867, died Istanbul 1915. Famous poet, journalist, thinker.

Thévenot, Jean de (1633–67) French traveller, in Istanbul 1655–56.

Tokgöz, Ahmet İhsan Born Erzurum 1868, died İzmit 1947. Publisher, writer, translator, owner of *Servet-i Fünun*.

Topçular Katibi Abdülkadir Efendi Active late sixteenth/first half of seventeenth century. A janissary; wrote a contemporary history.

Tournefort, Joseph Pitton de (1656–1708) French botanist; in Istanbul 1701.

Tursun Bey Born after 1425, died after 1491. Chancery official during Mehmed II's reign.

Ubicini, Jean Henri Abdolonyme (1818–84) French political writer and historian; in Istanbul in 1848.

al-'Umari (1300–84) Arab chronicler; wrote history, including section on Anatolia.

Wheler, Sir George (1650–1723) English botanist, travelled with Jacob Spon in the Levant 1675–76.

Wratislaw, Baron Wenzel (Vratislav Václav von Mitrović) (1576–1635). In Istanbul with the Habsburg embassy 1591.

Wraxall, Sir Frederic Charles Lascelles (1828–65) Writer; in Istanbul 1856.

Yirmisekiz Mehmed Çelebi Born Edirne towards the end of the 1660s, died Cyprus 1732. A janissary, he then went into the upper echelons of government, undertook diplomatic missions, and was Ottoman ambassador to France 1720–21.

Zarifi, Yorgo L. Born Istanbul 1881, died Athens 1943. Grandson of Yorgo Zarifi; known as the banker of Abdülhamid II.

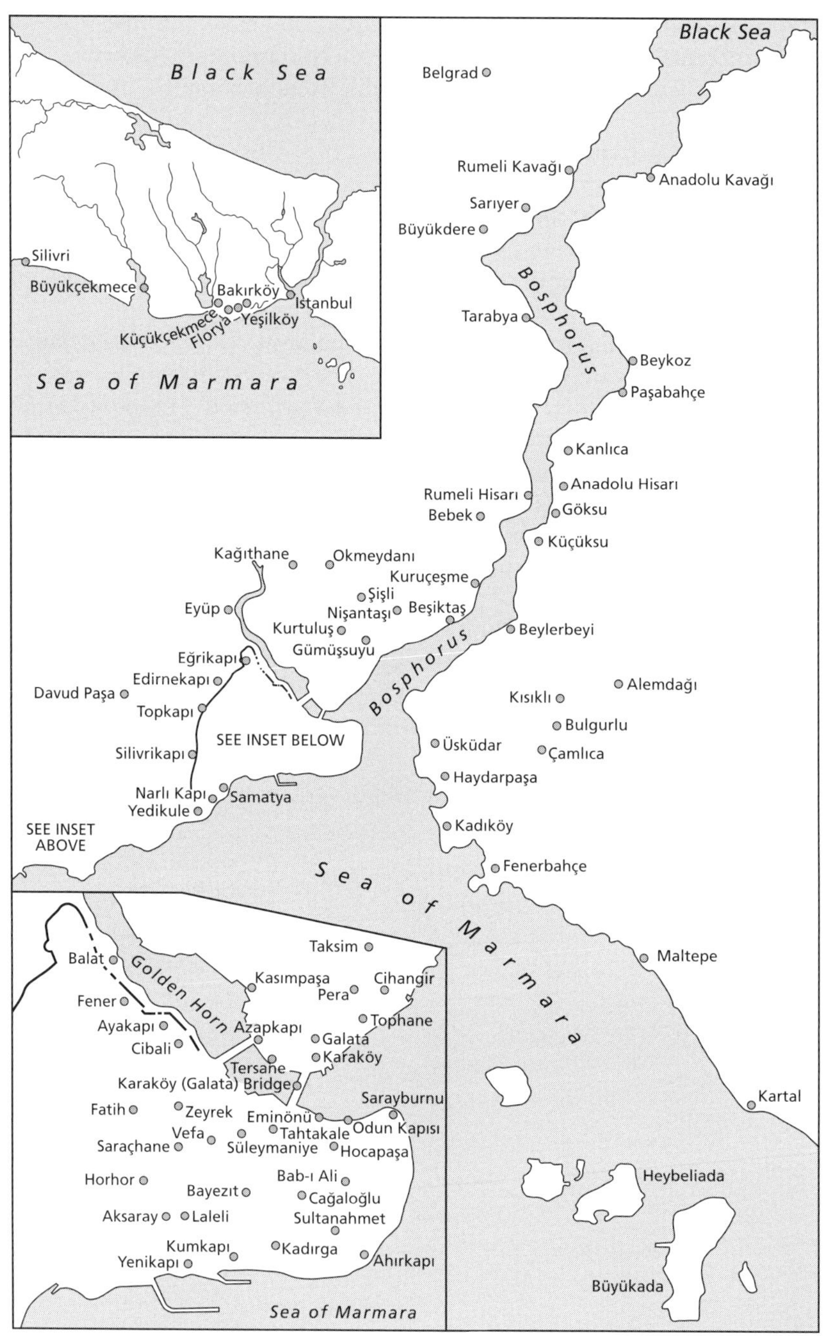

1 Istanbul and its environs

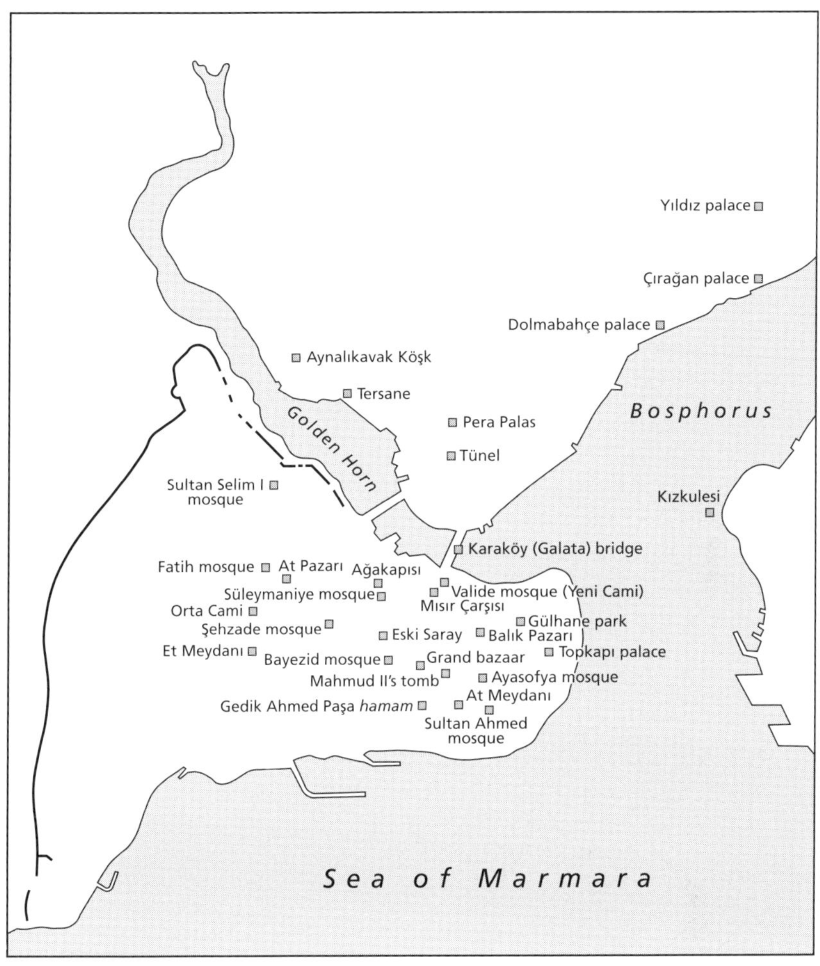

2 Locations within the city

Introduction

I looked at you yesterday from a hill, oh beloved Istanbul
I saw no place which I have not wandered through and loved
As long as I live, use my heart as it pleases you
Just to love one neighbourhood is worth a lifetime.

Many splendid cities exist in the world
But it is you who have created enchanted beauties
For those who have lived many years in you, died in you and lie buried in you
I say that they have lived in a beautiful and everlasting dream.[1]

For 470 years Istanbul was the capital of the Ottoman empire, which at its heyday stretched from Morocco to Ukraine, from the borders of Iran to Hungary. This was the artistic and intellectual centre of the Ottoman world, a commercial magnet for merchants from across the globe and the political piston of the empire. Its citizens lived surrounded by the pageantry of power and spectacle, caught up in the violence of the capital, and sustained by the enormous web of welfare that kept the city together. Our book offers a social portrait of this vibrant, violent, dynamic and cosmopolitan capital.

Captured in 1453 by Mehmed II (1444–46, 1451–81), known in Turkish as the conqueror, Istanbul became the capital of an ever-expanding empire as Mehmed II's successors, Bayezid II (1481–1512), Selim I (1512–20) and Süleyman I (1520–66) – the magnificent for the West, the lawgiver for the Ottomans – expanded the frontiers, conquering eastern Anatolia, parts of Iran, Syria, Egypt, the North African coast to Morocco, Rhodes, much of the Balkans, and reaching as far west as the gates of Vienna, which was besieged twice but not taken. Under succeeding sultans, the expansion was to slow, but territory did continue to fall to the Ottomans, with Süleyman I's successor Selim II (1566–74) taking

[1] Yahya Kemal, *Aziz İstanbul* (Istanbul, 1989), p. 4.

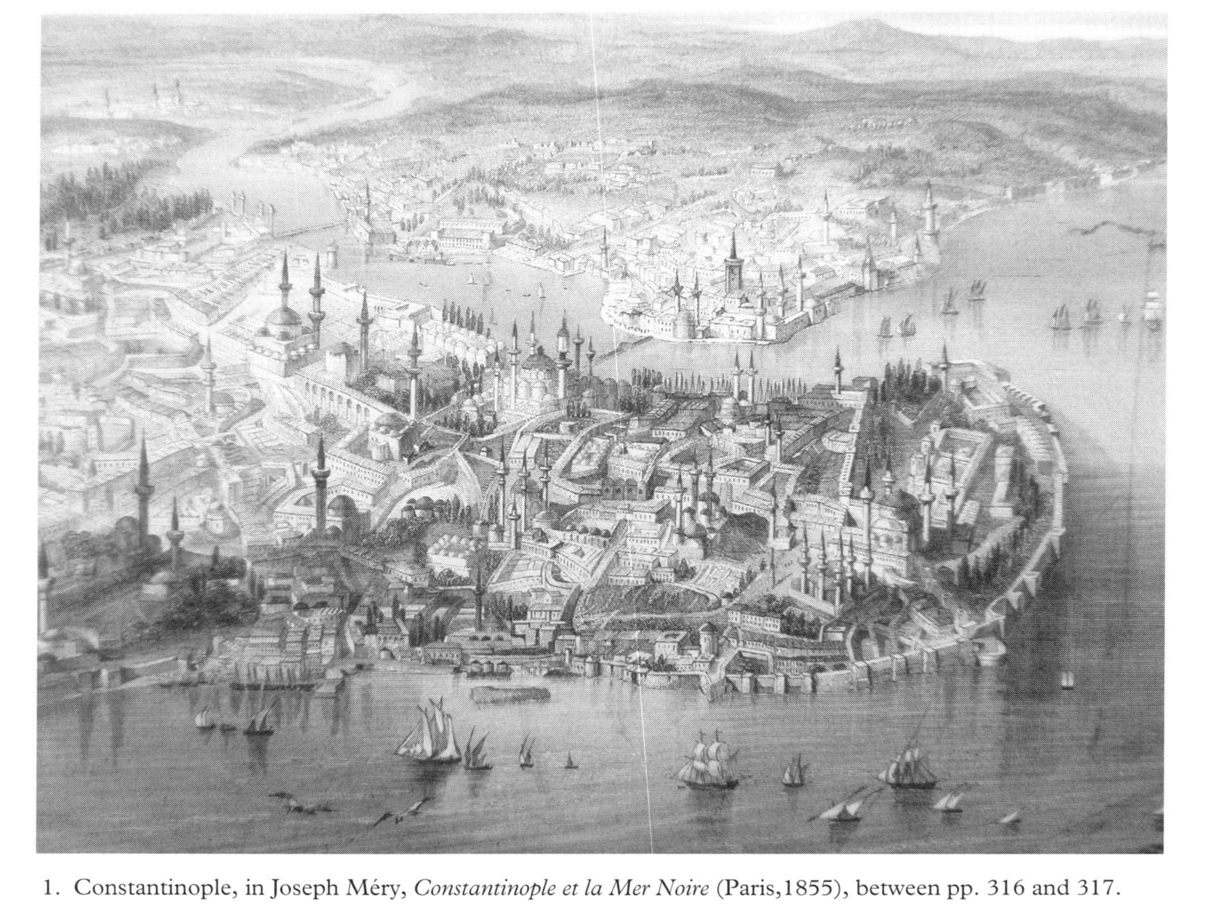

1. Constantinople, in Joseph Méry, *Constantinople et la Mer Noire* (Paris,1855), between pp. 316 and 317.

Cyprus in 1570. The last major territory in the West to be captured by the Ottomans was Crete in 1669.

Under Selim II's successors, Murad III (1574–95), Mehmed III (1595–1603) and Ahmed I (1603–17), the city was hit by economic problems as the empire struggled with the influx of silver from the New World and the difficulties of maintaining the value of its currency. This period also saw destructive wars with the Safavids in Iran and major upheavals in Anatolia, the Celali rebellions, which caused population movements into the city and disrupted its food supplies.

Economic difficulties continued during the reign of the following sultans: Mustafa I (1617–18, 1622–23), Osman II (1618–22), Murad IV (1623–40) and İbrahim (1640–48). The city was the setting for great political upheavals, with the accession to the throne of the mentally incapable Mustafa I and the deposition and murder of Osman II. This was the period known as the sultanate of the women, when the role of the women of the harem (private quarters) in politics was particularly influential. Kösem Sultan, the mother of Murad IV and İbrahim, was a key figure in the running of the state.

In the second half of the century, this influential role was to be taken over by the Köprülü family, which produced a series of grand vezirs. Militarily the period was dominated by wars with the Habsburgs. During this time, the sultans Mehmed IV (1648–87), Süleyman II (1687–91), Ahmed II (1691–95) and Mustafa II (1695–1703) spent an increasing amount of time away from the capital in the empire's second city, Edirne, until, by the reign of Mustafa II, Edirne had become their de facto residence. This was bitterly resented by Istanbul's population, which revolted, demanding the return of the sultan in what was known as the Edirne incident (1703).

Ahmed III (1703–30) therefore came to the throne in Istanbul. His reign was to usher in the Lale Devri (the Tulip Age), a period of extravagant display and cultural effervescence, which highlighted Istanbul's return to its central position as capital of the empire. Ahmed's reign came to an abrupt halt in 1730 with the Patrona Halil revolt, which saw the sultan deposed and the grand vezir murdered.

Under Ahmed III's successors, Mahmud I (1730–54), Osman III (1754–57), Mustafa III (1757–74) and Abdülhamid I (1774–89), the empire suffered a series of military defeats against the Russians, loss of territory and further economic difficulties. Istanbul was hit by great waves of immigration, which threatened the stability and internal order of the city. The coming to the throne of Selim III (1789–1807) marked the beginning of a major movement of reform, as the sultans grappled with military defeat and loss of central control over the provinces. Selim's attempts to restructure the army eventually led to his overthrow in 1807 and his subsequent murder in 1808. He was very briefly followed by Mustafa IV (1807–08), in a period of political upheaval during which the capital witnessed great violence and a total lack of political authority as factions jostled for power. Removed from the throne in 1808, Mustafa was replaced by Mahmud II (1808–39), who, after bringing the violence in the city under control and after a long and careful process of preparing the ground, introduced a series of very firm and far-reaching changes, which ushered in immense reforms in the empire over the following decades. He was unable, however, to prevent further loss of territory. Serbia gained its full autonomy in 1829 and Greece became independent in 1830, due to the support of the Great Powers who were to interfere more and more in the internal affairs of the empire as the century wore on. Mahmud also lost de facto control of Egypt, invaded briefly by Napoleon in 1798, although it was technically to remain Ottoman territory until the First World War.

In 1839 the *Tanzimat* began. This was a period of reforms in which the direction of the state was largely in the hands of three bureaucrats, Mustafa Reşid Paşa (d.1858), Ali Paşa (d.1871) and Fuad Paşa (d.1869), and the sultans Abdülmecid (1839–61) and Abdülaziz (1861–76) were less politically significant. Economically the empire became more and more enmeshed in a series of loans, and more and more entangled in the tentacles of imperialism, until the state eventually went bankrupt in 1875. In 1881 the Public Debt Administration – a European body headed alternately by the British and the French – was set up to ensure repayment of the many loans the empire had taken out. By the beginning of the twentieth century, this body was to control a considerable section of the empire's economy, in effect reducing it to a semi-colony. The empire also suffered territorial loss, with much of its Balkan territory becoming independent or autonomous under the Treaty of Berlin in 1878. This triggered a wave of migration into the city, to be repeated after the Balkan Wars in 1912–13, when Istanbul received thousands of Muslim refugees fleeing the aggression of the Balkan states.

After the brief reign of Murad V, declared mad and removed a few months after his accession in 1876, Abdülhamid II (1876–1909) came to the throne and, despite the great vicissitudes of the period, the hostility of the Great Powers and the development of a very hostile opposition movement, the Young Turks, managed to stay there for over thirty years, being deposed only in 1909, to be succeeded by Mehmed V (Reşad) (1909–18), who was in turn followed by Mehmed VI (Vahdeddin) (1918–22). By this time, however, power was in the hands of the Committee of Union and Progress (CUP), which had orchestrated the Young Turk Revolution in

1908 and which, under the triumvirate of Enver Paşa, Talat Paşa and Cemal Paşa, was to run the empire until its collapse after the First World War and the defeat of its ally Germany.

The nineteenth century saw many changes as the Ottomans engaged dynamically with Europe, importing much from the West and adapting or rejecting it. Much changed as new concepts of the role of the state, new political theories and ideas of identity were discussed. Fashions changed, the novel was introduced and the position of women was revolutionised. By the outbreak of the First World War the city was a very different one from that which had ushered in the previous century.

After the First World War the city was occupied by the victorious Allies and the British took control. The CUP leaders fled to Berlin, to be assassinated shortly afterwards – Talat Paşa in Germany in 1921, Cemal Paşa on his way to Moscow in 1922, and Enver Paşa dying the same year in Çeğen in Tajikistan, still dreaming of a comeback. The last sultan, Mehmed VI (Vahdeddin), was a mere cipher in the hands of the new British masters, agreeing unconditionally to whatever demands were made. Under the Treaty of Sèvres drawn up in 1920, the Allies carved up the Middle East between them, assigning a small, rump state to the Turks in the north-west of Anatolia, with Istanbul under Allied control and the Straits turned into a consortium-controlled waterway. Acceptable to the sultan – a puppet in the hands of the British, who had no interest in seeing a strong, independent Turkish state and who largely orchestrated the unsuccessful Greek invasion of Anatolia in 1919–22 – the treaty was rejected by the Turkish resistance movement which developed under the leadership of Mustafa Kemal Atatürk and which set itself up in Ankara in the heartland of central Anatolia. After a gruelling war with the Greeks, this movement successfully regained territory, expelled the foreign powers and forced a new treaty on the Allies, the Treaty of Lausanne, signed in 1923. The new Turkish Republic was established with its capital at Ankara, the only country to arise in the Middle East from the ashes of the First World War as an independent nation state.

1 Conquest

On 29 May 1453 Mehmed II wrenched out 'one of the two eyes of the church'.[1] The Christian West watched aghast as this 'new Caligula', this figure 'crueller than Nero' and 'more dangerous than a wild beast',[2] seized the city of Constantinople from the weakened and desperate hands of the last Byzantine emperor, Constantine XI, and plunged this once great seat of learning into ruin. The glorious capital which had reigned supreme for more than a thousand years was now lost to the Turks, 'the most despicable people ever, barbarous, lecherous and ignorant enemies of civilisation'.[3] This, needless to say, was the view of the Latins, for whom the fall of the city, a totally predictable event, but one they had done very little to prevent, was a catastrophe of immense proportions. Indeed it was of such magnitude that the hand of Enea Silvio Piccolomini, later Pope Pius II, trembled as he wrote of it.[4]

The fall shook the West, which reverberated with reports of Turkish atrocities performed in the fallen Byzantine capital. Latin accounts talked vociferously of the rivers of blood[5] which poured through the streets of the fallen city and flowed like rainwater in the gutters after a sudden storm.[6]

1 Enea Silvio Piccolomini, 'Lettera al cardinale Nicola di Cuesi', in Agostino Pertusi (ed.), *La caduta di Costantinopoli* (Milan, 1999), II, p. 56.

2 Niccolò Tignosi, 'Expugnatio Constantinopolitana', in Agostino Pertusi, *Testi inediti e poci noti sulla caduta di Costantinopoli*, posthumously ed. Antonio Carile (Bologna, 1983), p. 108; Theodore Spandounes, *On the Origin of the Ottoman Emperors*, trans. and ed. Donald M. Nicol (Cambridge, 1997), pp. 53, 54; Fra Girolamo da Firenze, 'Lettere al cardinal Capranica', in Pertusi, *Caduta*, II, p. 34; Jacopo Tedaldi, 'Informazioni sulla conquista di Costantinopoli', in Pertusi, *Caduta*, I, p. 186; Jacopo de Promontorio, *Die Aufzeichnungen des Genuesen Iacopo de Promontorio-de Campis über den Osmanenstaat um 1475*, ed. Franz Babinger (Munich, 1957), p. 92.

3 Piccolomini, 'Lettera a Nicolò V', in Pertusi, *Caduta*, II, p. 46; 'Lettera al cardinale Nicola di Cuesi', pp. 52, 54.

4 Piccolomini, 'Lettera a Nicolò V', p. 44.

5 Piccolomini, 'Lettera al cardinale Nicola di Cuesi', p. 52.

6 Nicolò Barbaro, 'Giornale dell'assedio di Costantinopoli', in Pertusi, *Caduta*, II, p. 35; Nicolò Barbaro, *The Diary of the Siege of Constantinople 1453*, trans. J. R. Jones (New York, 1969), p. 67.

Corpses floated out to sea like melons along a canal;[7] religious relics were plundered, tombs were pillaged and the bones of emperors and saints were thrown to the pigs and dogs.[8] Much-venerated religious images were shattered and trampled underfoot by the Turkish soldiers.[9] A distressed Bishop of Caffa, the Dominican Giacomo Campora, described the Turkish pillaging and the slaughter of the faithful. Bursting into the sacred places, the Turks

> dragged from the tombs and reliquaries the bodies of the saints who had slept in peace in their sepulchres and their caskets where they had been conserved with devotion and with their hands still dripping in blood ripped out and shamelessly possessed the jewels and gold ornamentation with which the holy reliquaries were adorned. The bones, stripped of their ornaments, were thrown away, some into the sea, some scattered over the squares and streets to be crushed underfoot.[10]

It was not only the religious relics but also books that were desecrated. For Latin contemporaries, the Turkish conquest spelt the destruction of a great seat of learning and the end of Greek letters,[11] one contemporary estimate placing the number of lost volumes at 120,000.[12] 'What can one say', wrote Piccolomini, 'of the books which were there in very large numbers and still not known to us Latins?',[13] a sentiment echoed by the noted intellectual and merchant Lauro Quirini, who felt himself 'destroyed by grief, and by pain and by sadness to such a point that, to use a Greek proverb, I have sweated blood':[14]

> Who could be so unpolished and so insensitive that he does not feel tears welling in his eyes? We have lost those works which gave splendour to the whole world, which created the sacred philosophy and all those other beautiful arts through which human existence was able to make progress.[15]

The fall, a second death for Homer, a second passing for Plato, brought at one and the same time the destruction of faith and of culture.[16] The Turks, about whom Piccolomini had nothing good to say, these enemies

[7] Barbaro, 'Giornale', p. 35; Barbaro, *Diary*, p. 67.
[8] Giacomo Campora, 'Orazione al re Ladislao d'Ungheria', in Pertusi, *Caduta*, I, p. 194; Piccolomini, 'Lettera a Leonardo Benvoglienti', in Pertusi, *Caduta*, II, p. 62; Enrico di Soemmern, 'Come la città di Costantinopoli fu conquistata e saccheggiata dai turchi', in Pertusi, *Caduta*, II, pp. 82–6.
[9] Enrico di Soemmern, 'Città', pp. 82–6. [10] Campora, 'Orazione', pp. 192, 194.
[11] Piccolomini, 'Lettera al cardinale Nicola di Cuesi', p. 52.
[12] Lauro Quirini, 'Epistula ad beatissimum Nicolaum V pontificem maximum', in Pertusi, *Testi*, p. 74.
[13] Piccolomini, 'Lettera a Nicolò V', p. 46. [14] Quirini, 'Epistula', p. 66.
[15] Quirini, 'Epistula', p. 74.
[16] Piccolomini, 'Lettera a Nicolò V', p. 46; Piccolomini, 'Lettera al cardinale Nicola di Cuesi', p. 54.

of Greek and Latin letters, which they held in arrogant contempt, had now imposed their ignorance through destruction.[17] Not only had the Turks taken the imperial capital, devastated the churches and polluted what the Byzantines held sacred, but they had also conducted a massacre of the entire population and thus wiped out the very name of the Greeks.[18]

The Latins trembled not merely at the thought of all this barbarism, but also at the more immediate terror of the Turkish advance. Many feared that the Turks were on their way to the very heart of the Christian world and would speedily be riding into Rome itself,[19] for Mehmed was said to be boasting publicly that he would be in Rome, conquer Italy and destroy the Christian faith the following summer.[20] 'The air', as Piccolomini noted, 'was full of the fear of war'.[21] Contemporaries predicted that this 'horrible, cruel, mad and malignant Turk', as the Genoese merchant Jacopo de Promontorio called him,[22] would be in Italy within eighteen months and would exterminate the Christians,[23] for whom he was said by Enrico di Soemmern to have such a strong loathing that if he saw one he would immediately cleanse his eyes as if contaminated.[24] This was presumably something of an exaggeration, for he had several at his court, including Chiriaco di Ancona and another Italian who read to him daily from the works of Laertius, Herodotus and Livy,[25] as well as two very competent doctors – one Latin, one Greek – from whom he learnt ancient history and whom he treated with great friendliness.[26]

The Ottoman ruler certainly did have expansionist ambitions. This ferocious enemy considered himself much more powerful than Caesar or Alexander and aimed, in the estimation of several Latin contemporaries, at world domination,[27] an ambition to which he directed every thought and action.[28] The world had now changed, and in future advance would be

17 Piccolomini, 'Lettera al cardinale Nicola di Cuesi', p. 54. 18 Quirini, 'Epistula', p. 74.

19 Paolo Dotti, 'Missiva sull'espugnazione di Costantinopoli', in Pertusi, *Caduta*, II, p. 14; Lampo Birago, 'Trattato di strategia contro i turchi', in Pertusi, *Caduta*, II, p. 114; Leonardo Benvoglienti, 'Dispaccio da Venezia alla Signoria di Siena', in Pertusi, *Caduta*, II, p. 109; Franco Giustiniani, in Pertusi, *Testi*, p. 104; Piccolomini, 'Lettera al cardinale Nicola di Cuesi', p. 56, Enrico di Soemmern, 'Città', pp. 90, 96; Birago, 'Trattato', p. 124; 1453.vi.30, in Pertusi, *Testi*, pp. 20, 22.

20 Enrico di Soemmern, 'Città', p. 92.

21 Piccolomini, 'Lettera a Leonardo Benvoglienti', p. 66.

22 Jacopo de Promontorio, *Aufzeichnungen*, p. 81. 23 Benvoglienti, 'Dispaccio', pp. 110–11.

24 Enrico di Soemmern, 'Città', p. 92.

25 Giacomo Languschi, 'Excidio e presa de Costantinopoli nell'anno 1453', in Pertusi, *Testi*, pp. 172–3.

26 Nicola Sagundino, 'Orazione al re Alfonso V d'Aragona', in Pertusi, *Caduta*, II, pp. 130, 132.

27 Benvoglienti, 'Dispaccio', p. 109; Tignosi, 'Expugnatio', p. 108.

28 Sagundino, 'Orazione', p. 132.

from East to West and not from West to East, as before. The world would have one empire, one faith and one sovereign.[29] Although already master of a considerable realm, Mehmed was not satisfied with what he had.[30] Instead he spent his time planning conquests in emulation of the Alexanders, Pompeys and Caesars of history.[31] His eye was certainly on the West, as many Latins feared, for he spent much time studying the position of Italy and in learning the situation in Europe.[32]

Not only was Mehmed ambitious, but he also had a stratagem, for he was cunning and shrewd, and had been 'since before he was born, a wolf putting on sheep's clothing'.[33] His cunning was clear to Konstantin Mihailović, a Serb captured in battle who then served in the Ottoman army as a janissary between 1455 and 1463.

> The Emperor ordered a great rug to be brought as an example and to be spread out before them [the lords with him], and in the center he had an apple placed, and he gave them the following riddle, saying: 'Can any of you pick up that apple without stepping on the rug?' And they reckoned among themselves, thinking about how that could be, and none of them could get the trick until the Emperor himself, having stepped up to the rug took the rug in both hands and rolled it before him, proceeding behind it; and so he got the apple and put the rug back down as it had been before. And the Emperor said to the lords: 'It is better to torment the *kaury* [i.e. infidel] little by little than to invade their land all at once. For we are so insecure that if we had a small setback there, then all our lands that we have conquered from the *kaury* would be against us and rebel.' And one lord named Essebek Awranozowicz said: 'Fortunate Lord, they have long said of this Roman Pope that he means to march against us with all Christendom. If he were riding on a pig he would have been here long ago. Therefore, as you picked [the apple] up before you, do the same to the *kaury*. Pay no heed to the news.' And so they all praised his speech and the Emperor's example.[34]

Mehmed's troops did arrive in Italy, but not until 1480, when Ottoman forces landed at Otranto, only to evacuate the following year on the death of the sultan.

While Piccolomini's hand trembled as he wrote of the disastrous fall of the city and the Latins watched in dread from the precincts of Rome, the Byzantine historian Doukas was struck dumb by the calamity. 'My tongue', he wrote, 'is stuck fast in my larynx. I am unable to draw breath

[29] Languschi, 'Excidio', p. 174.
[30] Kritoboulos, *History of Mehmed the Conqueror. By Kritovoulos*, trans. C. T. Riggs (Westport, 1954), 22, pp. 13–14.
[31] Kritoboulos, *History*, 22, pp. 13–14. [32] Languschi, 'Excidio', p. 173.
[33] Doukas, *Historia Byzantina*, ed. I. Bekker (Bonn, 1843), p. 231; Doukas, *Decline and Fall of Byzantium to the Ottoman Turks*, trans. H. J. Magoulias (Detroit, 1975), p. 191.
[34] Konstantin Mihailović, *Memoirs of a Janissary*, trans. Benjamin Stolz (Ann Arbor, 1975), pp. 145, 147.

through my sealed mouth'.[35] However sharply Piccolomini and many other Latins may have felt the fall, their pain, experienced at a safe distance, was not as acute as that of the Byzantines, for whom Mehmed, Doukas's 'truly flesh-bearing demon',[36] spelt the end of their world. The sight of the massed Ottoman forces before the city struck terror into their hearts, leaving them as if 'half-dead, unable to breathe either in or out'.[37] The defenders fought hard, employing lead balls as small as Pontic walnuts which could kill several soldiers at one time, provided they were standing one behind the other.[38] Grimly the Byzantines hung on, but to no avail, for they were unable to prevent the collapse of the walls and the entry of the Turkish troops. Many were slaughtered, Turkish soldiers later complaining to Doukas that had they known there were so few Byzantine soldiers in the city they would not have killed them so liberally, but would have sold them all like sheep.[39]

The Turks poured into the city, rampaging through the streets, breathing fire, their hands bloodstained with murder.[40] The religious relics were pillaged and the remains of venerated men were torn apart and 'made the sport of the wind'.[41] The great church of Hagia Sophia fell, to become the Ayasofya mosque, and those who had taken refuge there were led out in chains.

> Who can recount the calamity of that time and place? Who can describe the wailing and the cries of the babes, the mothers' tearful screams and the fathers' lamentations?... The infinite chains of captives who like herds of kine and flocks of sheep poured out of the temple sanctuary made an extraordinary spectacle! They wept and wailed and there was none to show them mercy.[42]

The Turks triumphed and the city was left 'desolate, lying dead, naked, soundless, having neither form nor beauty'.[43] For the Byzantines, the destruction of their capital was absolute. The once beautiful city was

> emptied and deserted, despoiled and blackened as if by fire. One might easily disbelieve that it had ever had in it a human dwelling or the wealth or properties of a city or any furnishing or ornament of a household. And this was true although the city had been so magnificent and grand. There were left only ruined homes, so badly ruined as to cause great fear to all who saw them.[44]

[35] Doukas, *Historia*, p. 292; Doukas, *Decline*, p. 227.
[36] Doukas, *Historia*, p. 232; Doukas, *Decline*, p. 191.
[37] Doukas, *Historia*, p. 281; Doukas, *Decline*, p. 221.
[38] Doukas, *Historia*, pp. 226–7; Doukas, *Decline*, p. 212.
[39] Doukas, *Historia*, pp. 287–8; Doukas, *Decline*, pp. 224–5.
[40] Kritoboulos, *History*, 241, pp. 72–3.
[41] Kritoboulos, *History*, 244, p. 73.
[42] Doukas, *Historia*, pp. 291–2; Doukas, *Decline*, p. 227.
[43] Doukas, *Historia*, p. 306; Doukas, *Decline*, p. 235.
[44] Kritoboulos, *History*, 254, p. 76.

While Piccolomini's hand trembled and Doukas was unable to breathe, the Ottoman chronicler Aşıkpaşazade remained calm and unmoved by the momentous events of 1453. Writing his history of the Ottomans towards the end of the fifteenth century, Aşıkpaşazade described how Mehmed II crossed the Straits from the Asian section of the state soon after the death of his father Murad II in 1451, and set up camp on the European shore opposite Akçahisar, modern Anadolu Hisarı. 'Here', he told Halil Paşa, his former tutor, 'I need a castle'.[45] He summoned Akçaylıoğlu Mehmed Bey, ordered him to begin the siege of the Byzantine capital and announced that he would be in Constantinople that summer.[46] The Ottoman forces gathered and the siege commenced.

They besieged the castle by land and by sea with ships. There were four hundred ships on the water. Seventy ships opened their sails from above Galata, from the land. The warriors rose, they unfurled the banners, they came and entered the sea at the base of the castle. They made a bridge over the water. For fifty days they fought day and night. On the fifty-first day the *Hünkar* [the ruler Mehmed] gave permission for pillaging. They attacked. On Tuesday the city was taken. Valuable plunder was seized. Gold, silver, jewels and all kinds of cloth poured onto the markets, and they began to trade. They enslaved the people, they killed the *tekfur* [the Byzantine ruler], the warriors embraced the young beauties... On the first Friday after the conquest, prayer was held in Ayasofya. The *hutbe* [sermon delivered after Friday prayer] was read in the name of Sultan Mehmed Gazi... This conquest was made by Mehmed Han Gazi in the year 857.[47]

The motivation for the conquest

For the Ottomans, this conquest – the death and destruction of the known world for the Latins and Byzantines – was not an extraordinary event, nor was it portrayed as a victory of unprecedented proportions. It does not appear in Ottoman writings as the overriding conquest that would seal Mehmed's ambitions or set the Ottoman empire at the centre of the world. Nevertheless, 1453 has since became a '1066 date', a date which everyone knows and whose significance as a turning point in history is unquestioned. This is very much related to the psychological impact of the conquest in the West, and the horror over the fall of the Byzantine empire. The idea of an Ottoman empire also has a part to play in this, for it forms a convenient point at which to date the beginning of the empire. Its significance, however, was symbolic and represented no

45 Aşıkpaşazade, *Die Altosmanische Chronik des Ašıkpašazade*, ed. Fredrich Giese (Leipzig, 1929, reprinted Osnabrük, 1972), *bab* 123, p. 131.
46 Aşıkpaşazade *Chronik*, *bab* 123, pp. 131, 132.
47 Aşıkpaşazade, *Chronik*, *bab* 123, p. 132.

dramatic shift in power or turning point in the course of history. The Byzantine empire had become a city, the city had shrunk to a faded and sorry reflection of past glories, 'no longer a city but surviv[ing] only in name',[48] and the shadow of the desolation referred to by Doukas already hung over it. For the Ottomans, its conquest, though symbolically important, was no more than another in a long string of victories, no more or less significant than the fall of Thessalonike in 1430. While 1453 is usually taken by scholars as representing the beginning of an empire, the creation of a new, imperial image, and the transforming of an Ottoman warlord into a world-dominating sultan, Mehmed's attitude to the city, its conquest and his subsequent actions in his new capital do not demonstrate anything other than a gradual evolution in Ottoman rule. They form a natural development, which continued, with various reversals and shifts in direction and emphasis, after his death into the reign of his successor Bayezid II, and on through the reigns of succeeding sultans.

Regardless of any lack of imperial significance, however, Mehmed II was certainly determined to take the city. Its conquest was always 'in his dreams... and the thought of conquest never left his tongue'.[49] Indeed, apparently he thought of very little else, for 'night and day the ruler's only care and concern, whether he was lying in bed or standing on his feet, or within his courtyard or without, was what battle plan and stratagem to employ in order to capture Constantinople'.[50] His reasons for wishing to conquer the city were economic and strategic rather than imperial. Constantinople's location allowed it to control the Straits, the 'throat'[51] between the Black Sea and the Mediterranean, and the crossing from Europe to Asia. This throat of water, 'greater than the Nile and mightier than the Danube',[52] was of such beauty that it brought 'relief to a man's heart'.[53] For a ruler of a state with lands on both sides of the Straits, freedom of passage was clearly imperative, and inability to control the waterway effectively had caused the Ottomans considerable difficulties in the past. On several occasions they had had to rely on the Genoese for assistance to ship them across the Straits, as Mehmed's father Murad II had done in 1422 and 1444, or as Murad's uncle Süleyman had done in 1402 – at least according to hostile Venetian sources. Such strategic control had allowed the Byzantines the opportunity to pressure the

48 Kritoboulos, *History*, 66, p. 27.
49 Tursun Bey, *The History of Mehmed the Conqueror by Tursun Beg*, ed. Halil İnalcık and Rhoads Murphey (Minneapolis and Chicago, 1978), f. 31a.
50 Doukas, *Historia*, p. 252; Doukas, *Decline*, p. 201.
51 Tursun Bey, *Tarih-i Ebü'l-Feth*, ed. Mertol Tulum (Istanbul, 1977), p. 41.
52 Tursun Bey, *Tarih*, p. 41. 53 Tursun Bey, *History*, f. 32a.

Ottomans. Mehmed was keenly aware of this inconvenience and knew well the problems this had caused in the past. According to Kritoboulos, it had almost caused them to abandon the European section of their territory.[54]

As part of the aim of cutting the Byzantine maritime stranglehold and in preparation for his siege of the city, Mehmed had the shining idea[55] of building the castle of Rumeli Hisarı on the European shore, a counterpart to the castle of Anadolu Hisarı built by his great grandfather on the Asian side of the Straits.[56] With these two castles facing each other at the narrowest point of the waterway, Mehmed was now unquestionably in charge of the Straits.[57]

Control of the water was not only strategic but also commercial. The new castle enabled Mehmed to dominate shipping to and from Constantinople and to and from the Black Sea, from the important trading settlements in the Crimea, the Genoese settlement at Caffa (modern Feodosia) and the Venetian settlement at Tana. It was an active trade artery, for it was one of the main slave trading routes, carrying slaves from the Crimea to the Mediterranean and, in particular, to the Mamluk sultanate in Egypt – a trade largely dominated by the Genoese. Many other items were shipped through it, wheat from further North, metals to and from the Black Sea coast of what is now Turkey, alum from the alum mines of northern Anatolia, silks and luxury items from further East, from Iran and beyond. Mehmed, ever focused on commercial opportunities, was keen to benefit from the revenue potential of his newly established dominance and he issued instructions that all ships, flying whatever flag – Genoese, Venetian, Constantinopolitan or Ottoman, or from Caffa, Trabzon, Amasra or Sinop – of whatever class – trireme, bireme, barque or skiff – were not to pass through the Straits without paying customs duties. Any ship that did not comply was to be sunk.[58] Firuz Ağa, to whom he entrusted the command of the castle, was well equipped to carry out these instructions, for Mehmed had fitted his new 'Frankish'[59] fortress with cannon like dragons,[60] whose cannonballs skipped along the surface of the sea as if they were swimming,[61] and whose sound when fired made the sky and earth resound.[62] When fired the cannonballs were so numerous that they seemed to those who saw them to form a bridge across the water.[63]

[54] Kritoboulos, *History*, 31, p. 16. [55] Tursun Bey, *History*, f. 31b.
[56] Aşıkpaşazade, *Chronik*, *bab* 123, p. 131. [57] Kritoboulos, *History*, 30, p. 16.
[58] Doukas, *Historia*, p. 246; Doukas, *Decline*, p. 199. [59] Tursun Bey, *History*, f. 35a.
[60] Tursun Bey, *History*, f. 35b. [61] Kritoboulos, *History*, 50, p. 21.
[62] Tursun Bey, *History*, f. 35b. [63] Tursun Bey, *History*, f. 35b.

With Rumeli Hisarı constructed and the Straits so tightly shut that not even a bird could fly from the Mediterranean to the Black Sea,[64] Mehmed turned his sights to Constantinople, which lay as 'a scar in the midst of Ottoman lands'.[65] In a speech attributed to him by Kritoboulos, Mehmed explained to his followers that the matter was a very simple one. If they took the city, then Ottoman lands would be secure and the way to further conquests guaranteed. If they did not, they would be constantly at risk and any further advance would be jeopardised. The hard-pressed Byzantines could even turn to another, stronger power, for help. In these circumstances they would be constantly under threat or at war, and would suffer ruinous expense.[66]

Constantinople also represented a considerable commercial prospect. Although greatly impoverished and in ruins, as Aşıkpaşazade noted,[67] it had been, and could soon be again, a thriving commercial centre at the hub of the trading networks of the eastern Mediterranean and the Black Sea. Mehmed liked to see money coming in, and liked to follow it assiduously. Indeed, at the very beginning of his reign he had gone through the finances carefully, questioning the tax officials closely and checking their accounts. He was annoyed to find that much revenue was being squandered and wasted to no good purpose,[68] a situation he set to putting right, thereby recovering about one-third of the annual revenues for the royal treasury, according to Kritoboulos. Not only did he streamline, sacking many financial officials and bringing in others, but he also increased the revenues. In this he apparently differed in approach from his father Murad II, who, in Kritoboulos's phrase, 'had dealt with such matters in a much more hit-or-miss manner'.[69] Money meant power, and it was to his constant use of money that Mehmed owed his ascendancy, according to the Genoese merchant Jacopo de Promontorio, who was active at Mehmed's court.[70]

The Ottomans as an economic power

One of the more commonly held myths about the Ottomans is their disinterest in economic matters. This was not the view held by Greek contemporaries, however, for whom the Turkish 'nation' was, in Doukas's words, 'a lover of money'.[71] For the Ottoman chronicler

[64] Tursun Bey, *History*, f. 35b. [65] Tursun Bey, *History*, f. 34a.
[66] Kritoboulos, *History*, 73, p. 29. [67] Aşıkpaşazade, *Chronik*, *bab* 124, p. 133.
[68] Kritoboulos, *History*, 27, 28, p. 15. [69] Kritoboulos, *History*, 27, 28, p. 15.
[70] Promontorio, *Aufzeichnungen*, p. 84.
[71] Doukas, *Historia*, p. 287; Doukas, *Decline*, pp. 224–5.

Aşıkpaşazade, too, the first Ottoman ruler took commerce seriously. Although Aşıkpaşazade was writing considerably later, in the late fifteenth century, his account represents something of perceived Ottoman economic policy in the early period of their rule. According to Aşıkpaşazade, the eponymous founder of the state, Osman,

> had a market built in the Hamam quarter of Eskişehir. Even the infidels of the surrounding region would come and buy and sell there. From time to time the people of Germiyan [another small Turkish state] would also frequent the market. One day, infidel traders came from Bilecik. The infidels in Bilecik produced good jugs and, loading them up, used to come to the market to sell them. A man from Germiyan bought a jug but did not pay for it. The infidels therefore came and complained to Osman Gazi. Osman Gazi had the man... brought before him. He punished him and gave his rights to the infidel. He severely forbade the injuring of the infidels of Bilecik. Because commerce was thus conducted justly and the situation progressed well, even the women of the infidels of Bilecik came to the market at Eskişehir, and did their shopping and came and went and carried out their business in safety. The infidels of Bilecik trusted greatly in Osman and they said 'This Turk behaves very honestly with us'.[72]

Far from being disinterested, the early Ottomans were economically motivated and the routes of their conquest were to some extent dictated by economic considerations. Ottoman advance in northern Anatolia, for example, was connected with the desire to take over the mines in the region. The Ottomans used their control of commodities such as alum as leverage in their relations with the city-states of Venice and Genoa, with whom they developed close commercial relations. Murad I, for example, imposed restrictions on alum export after his conquest of the alum-producing region of Kütahya in 1381, forcing Venice into negotiations over alum prices and export.[73] It was commercial motivation that was behind the close Ottoman-Genoese relationship, a mutually profitable relationship, dating from the very early days of the Ottoman state, which both sides took care to cultivate. Genoese commercial agents worked for the Ottomans and the value of an alliance with the Ottomans was acknowledged by the Genoese. Orhan's 'merits and services'[74] were recognised by the Genoese authorities and various treaties were concluded between them, one in the winter of 1351–52 and one in 1387,[75]

[72] Aşıkpaşazade, *Chronik*, *bab* 9, pp. 14–15.

[73] G. Thomas (ed.), *Diplomatarium Veneto-Levantinum*, 2 vols. (Venice, 1890–99), II, no. 116, p. 194 (1384.vii.22).

[74] Archivio di Stato di Genova (henceforth ASG), San Giorgio Manoscritti Membranacei IV, ff. 304v–305r (1356.iii.21); L. T. Belgrano, 'Documenti riguardanti la colonia genovese di Pera', *Atti della Società Ligure di Storia della Patria* 13 (1877–84), no. 18, pp. 126–7.

[75] Kate Fleet, 'The Treaty of 1387 between Murad I and the Genoese', *Bulletin of the School of Oriental and African Studies*, 56/1 (1993), pp. 13–33.

under the terms of which the Genoese benefited from special arrangements when trading in Ottoman territory and the Ottomans received preferential treatment in the Genoese settlement of Pera, opposite Constantinople. By the end of the fourteenth century, there was a constant exchange of envoys and ambassadors between the Ottoman court of Bayezid I and the Genoese at Pera, also known as Galata.[76] The account books of the Genoese note expenses such as sugar and other confectionaries for visiting Turkish envoys, and for cloth, given as a gift to Turkish envoys or for robes for the Genoese officials sent to the Ottoman court.[77]

This close relationship continued into the fifteenth century, with Genoese, such as the merchant Jacopo de Promontorio, established at the Ottoman court. It was this closeness that led the Genoese merchants to complain to Ottoman officials when a Genoese ship, at anchor at Galata, fully loaded and about to leave for Italy, was mistakenly sunk by the Turks during the siege of Constantinople. The Turks apologised, explaining that 'we did this not knowing that the ship was yours but thinking that it belonged to the enemy. Take courage, however, and pray that we take the city. This task is already at hand and the time is near. You will then be indemnified for every injury and loss sustained'.[78] Praying for an Ottoman conquest of the city was probably within the range of Genoese ability, for they managed to maintain relations with both sides throughout the siege, supporting the Byzantine defenders and negotiating with the sultan, providing soldiers for the city and oil for the Turkish cannon, appealing to the Doge in Genoa and slipping news of a Genoese scheme to burn the Turkish ships to Mehmed.[79] What upset them were the irritating implications of an interruption of trade. As one Genoese merchant, Aron Maiavello, gloomily noted during the Turkish bombardment of the ships anchored at Constantinople, the situation was not good. 'I am afraid', he remarked, 'that we shall lose the ship'.[80]

It was this realisation of commercial potential that propelled Zaganos Paşa hotfoot to Galata during the siege. Zaganos was one of Mehmed's close advisors and it was to him that the sultan had entrusted the siege of

[76] ASG, San Giorgio, Sala 34, n. 590/1304, ASG, Antico Comune 22 and ASG, Archivio Segreto 498.

[77] ASG, San Giorgio 34, n.590/1304, f. 25v (1390.iii.31); ASG, Antico Commune 22, ff. 70, 192 (1391.xii.19); ASG, Antico Commune 22, ff. 74, 193 (1392.i.16); ASG, Antico Commune 22, ff. 76, 193 (1392.ii.24); ASG, Antico Commune 22, ff. 78, 196 (1392.v.23); ASG, Antico Comune 22, ff. 88, 175 (1392.x.15).

[78] Doukas, *Historia*, pp. 278–9; Doukas, *Decline*, p. 219.

[79] Doukas, *Historia*, pp. 265, 267, 275, 277; Doukas, *Decline*, pp. 211, 212, 217, 218.

[80] Ausilia Roccatagliata, *Notai genovesi in Oltremare. Atti rogati a Chio (1453–1454, 1470–1471)* (Genoa, 1982), doc. 65, p. 101 (1453.xii.31).

the Galata region,[81] an area full of Christians which had long been 'part of Frengistan', the land of the Franks.[82] It was from here that, thanks to the great number of small barques and rowing boats, a person could cross from Rumeli (the European section of the Ottoman empire) to Frengistan and from Frengistan to Rumeli for only one *mangır*, a copper coin, the smallest denomination of Ottoman money.[83] With the city falling around them, the Genoese merchants hurried with their wives and children to the shore in search of boats in which they could row out to the ships and sail safely away. Zaganos Paşa

> rushed to Galata, shouting, 'Do not depart'. Swearing an oath on the head of the tyrant [i.e. the Ottoman ruler], he assured them, 'Be not afraid. You are the ruler's friends, and your city will suffer no injury. Furthermore, you will receive better treaties than your former treaties with the emperor and with us. Do not be concerned with anything else lest you move the ruler to wrath'. With these words Zaganos was able to restrain the Franks of Galata from leaving.[84]

Reassured, the Genoese promptly handed over the keys of the town to Mehmed, who 'received them gladly and dismissed the Galatinians with cheerful words and countenance'.[85] An *amanname*, an imperial decree, was immediately issued, on 30 May 1453, granting the Genoese various commercial concessions, and, once the city had fallen, the merchants returned rapidly to their trade.[86] What mattered for the Genoese was not who ruled the city but that they should be able to trade with them. Early in 1454, two Genoese ambassadors, Luciano Spinula and Balthasaro Marrufo, were dispatched to the Ottoman court to arrange a resumption of commercial relations. Underlining that the current situation suited neither side, the ambassadors were to emphasise that both would profit from the presence of a flourishing Genoese trading community in the city.[87]

Very shortly after the surrender of Galata, the Turks launched a final offensive against Constantinople. Soldiers moved against the city like a flood, and the sound of the drums and the *ney* (a flute-like wind instrument) 'brought down the heavens and blasted the earth into the sky'.[88] So much booty poured from the palaces of the ruler and the nobles, and from the houses of the rich, that silver, fine pearls and brilliant rubies were sold for the price of beads and glass, while gold and silver went for the price of

81 Kritoboulos, *History*, 117, p. 41.
82 Tursun Bey, *History*, f. 33b.
83 Tursun Bey, *History*, f. 33b.
84 Doukas, *Historia*, p. 297; Doukas, *Decline*, p. 230.
85 Doukas, *Historia*, p. 297; Doukas, *Decline*, p. 230.
86 Belgrano, 'Documenti', no. 148, pp. 226–9 (1453.v.30).
87 Belgrano, 'Documenti', no. 154, pp. 265–7 (1454.iii.11).
88 Tursun Bey, *History*, f. 39a.

copper and tin, precipitating many instantly from poverty to riches.[89] The plunder was so great that it became a byword for later generations; according to Tacizade Cafer Çelebi (d.1515), it was 'still now an example for the people. If somebody begins to be a little too extravagant and profligate they say did you take part in the plunder of Istanbul?'[90] İbn Kemal, too, remarks that the plunder was an example for the common people. Someone who did not work but had money would be asked if he had obtained it from the booty of Istanbul.[91] The great city now fell and the Byzantine empire was no more.

The Ottoman-Byzantine relationship

A further common misconception of the early Ottoman state is that it was merely a fighting machine, that the Ottoman was first and foremost a soldier and that the state was in essence an army. Without military success and skill the early Ottoman state would clearly not have succeeded as it did. But there is far more to the early state than just military might. Apart from being aware, and acute, economically, Ottoman rulers were also adept at political manipulation and diplomatic manoeuvring, as was to become apparent in their dealings with the Byzantines.

The Ottoman-Byzantine relationship, which stretched back over a century and a half to the very beginnings of the Ottoman state, was by no means merely one of conflict. The Ottomans initially followed an alternating policy of conquest and co-operation and, from the middle of the fourteenth century, even became allies of the new Byzantine emperor. From this point on, Ottoman diplomatic relations slipped into Ottoman political dominance of internal Byzantine affairs, as the empire slid further and further into what amounted to a vassal relationship with its Ottoman neighbours. Not only economically minded and able to use their economic muscle to their advantage in their relations with the city-states of Venice and Genoa, the Ottomans also adopted a policy of co-operation with the Byzantines when expedient. Osman, the eponymous founder of the state, certainly did inflict many defeats on the Byzantines, and the first recorded contact between them was in battle in the early fourteenth century.[92] Under his leadership the small state expanded from its base

89 Tursun Bey, *History*, f. 49a.

90 Tacizade Cafer Çelebi, *Mahsure-i İstanbul Fetihnamesi*, İstanbul Üniversitesi Kütüphanesi, T 2634, f. 21b.

91 İbn Kemal, *Ibn Kemal Tevârih-i Âl-i Osman, VII. Defter*, ed. Şerafettin Turan (Ankara, 1991), p. 75.

92 Pachymeres, *George Pachymérès Relations Historiques IV. Livres X–XIII édition, traduction française et notes*, ed. Albert Failler (Paris, 1999), pp. 358, 366–7.

round Söğüt in north-western Anatolia into Byzantine territory, spreading along the Sakarya river westwards towards the sea of Marmara. At the same time, however, he also advocated diplomatic relations, at least according to later accounts. While his brother Gündüz adopted the somewhat unsubtle approach of total destruction of the enemy, proposing that they should attack and destroy the area, Osman disagreed. 'This', he told his brother, 'is a bad idea', for plundering and devastating the region round Karacahisar, their latest conquest, would simply ensure that the town would not thrive and develop. Therefore, Osman argued, 'the first thing which should be done is to get on well with our neighbours and be their friends'.[93]

In accordance with this policy, Osman had very good relations with the local Byzantines when he came to the throne (according to Aşıkpaşazade), and a long-standing friendship with the Byzantine ruler of Bilecik,[94] to whom he gave presents of fine carpets and rugs, cheese and clotted cream.[95] It was to the ruler of Bilecik that Osman turned for help when his followers were continuously attacked as they migrated between the winter and summer pastures. Osman asked for, and received, permission to leave goods at Bilecik for safekeeping.

> Whenever Osman Gazi went to the summer pastures, they loaded all their goods onto oxen and sent them with the many women to the *tekfur* [Byzantine ruler]. They left them in the castle. When they returned from the summer pastures, they brought gifts of cheese, carpets, rugs and lambs. They took back what they had entrusted to them and left. These infidels' trust in them was great.[96]

No doubt more pragmatic than sincere, such relations were very useful for the survival of a small state in a hostile environment, and the policy of 'dissimulation' was praised by Aşıkpaşazade.

> Cheat your enemy that you may in the end win
> If you find an opportunity, do not draw back from taking his head
> Feed him on good food and let him drink sweet wine
> Let this weaken him while you grow strong
> But do not be careless, think that he can cheat you
> If in the end you suffer, regret will be useless.[97]

This ability both to conquer and to cohabit was one of the reasons for Ottoman success. Diplomatically and economically shrewd and militarily highly effective, the Ottomans emerged above the other small Turkish

[93] Aşıkpaşazade, *Chronik*, *bab* 9, p. 14.
[94] Aşıkpaşazade, *Chronik*, *bab* 3, pp. 8–9.
[95] Aşıkpaşazade, *Chronik*, *bab* 9, p. 14.
[96] Aşıkpaşazade, *Chronik*, *bab* 3, p. 9.
[97] Aşıkpaşazade, *Chronik*, *bab* 9, p. 15.

states in Anatolia to become the dominant power in the region by the end of the century. They were also helped in this by the luck of location, for they were neither bordered by powerful Turkish states such as Germiyan or Karaman, initially much more important than the Ottomans, nor by the sea, as was the case with the successful commercial states of Aydın and Menteşe, whose territorial expansion was blocked by the Aegean. The Ottomans were further fortunate in that the early rulers (Osman (d. *c.*1324), Orhan (*c.*1324–62), Murad I (1362–89) and Bayezid I (1389–1402)) reigned for comparatively long periods and were not apparently troubled by succession struggles. Religious war (the *gaza*), so commonly used to account for Ottoman success, was probably not a significant factor. *Gazi* (fighter in *gaza*) was not apparently a term used in the early fourteenth century, and when it was later adopted it did not carry any religious significance, but meant rather 'hero' or 'warrior'.[98] In any case, *gaza* was a factor common to all the small Turkish states and cannot therefore satisfactorily explain the rise of one state in particular. This also applies to the role of the dervishes (the sufis), whose presence was influential in easing the path of Ottoman expansion, offering a spirituality which made Ottoman rule more palatable and was more appealing to the conquered Orthodox population than a strict orthodox Islam would have been. Dervishes, however, were not peculiar to the Ottomans, but an integral part of the fluid frontier world of fourteenth-century Anatolia.

The importance of military success cannot, of course, be underestimated. Military victories brought land, booty and followers, and Ottoman forces soon began to lay siege successfully to Byzantine towns. Under Osman's son and successor, Orhan, the Ottomans took Prusa (Bursa) in 1326.[99] The city had been put under a siege so tight that 'an infidel could not even extend a finger out of the castle'.[100] It was to be the Ottoman capital and it was here that the bodies of the sultans were brought for burial. Further Byzantine cities followed: Nikaia (İznik) fell in 1331, and Nikomedia (İzmit) in 1337. By this time Orhan was an established military leader of many forces, according to the Arab chronicler al-'Umari.[101] For

[98] Colin Imber, 'What does *ghazi* actually mean?', in Çiğdem Balım-Harding and Colin Imber (eds.), *The Balance of Truth. Essays in Honour of Professor Geoffrey Lewis* (Istanbul, 2000), pp. 174, 177.

[99] Gregoras, *Nicephori Gregorae Byzantina Historia*, 3 vols., ed. L. Schopeni (Bonn, 1829), I, p. 384.

[100] Aşıkpaşazade, *Chronik*, *bab* 18, p. 23.

[101] Al-'Umari, 'Notice de l'ouvrage qui a pour titre Masalek alabsar fi memalek alamsar, Voyages des yeux dans les royaumes des différentes contrées (ms. arabe 583)', in E. Quatremère (trans.), *Notices et Extraits des mss. de la Bibliothèque du Roi*, XIII (Paris, 1838), p. 336.

the famous Arab traveller, Ibn Battuta, who was in Anatolia in the 1330s, Orhan was

> the greatest of the kings of the Turkmens and the richest in wealth, lands, and military forces. Of fortresses he possesses nearly a hundred, and for most of his time he is continually engaged in making the round of them, staying in each fortress for some days to put it in good order and examine its condition. It is said that he has never stayed for a whole month in any one town. He also fights with the infidels continually and keeps them under siege.[102]

In the middle of the fourteenth century, the Ottoman-Byzantine relationship was to move from conquest and cohabitation to firm diplomatic and family ties, for, as a result of the civil war which broke out in Byzantium in 1341, both John V, the infant emperor, and his mother Anna, and John Kantakouzenos, the Grand Domestic, sought Turkish allies. Kantakouzenos secured the support of Orhan, to whom he married his daughter Theodora, in what the Greek chronicler Doukas described as an 'abominable betrothal'.[103] The arrangement was very much to Orhan's liking and he was as 'a bull which had been parched by the burning heat of summer, and was with mouth agape drinking at a hole filled with the coldest water but unable to get his fill'.[104] This was not the only marriage alliance concluded by the Ottomans with neighbouring Christian powers. An asset in furthering Ottoman expansion, it was used by Murad I when he married Thamar, the sister of Šišman of Tarnovo, by Bayezid in his marriage to the daughter of the countess of Salona, and by Murad II in his to Mara, the sister of George Branković, despot of Serbia. The alliance between Orhan and Kantakouzenos continued until Kantakouzenos's abdication in December 1354.

While Ottoman troops were active in Europe as Kantakouzenos's allies, their permanent settlement in 1354 was due to divine rather than Byzantine intervention. Gallipoli (modern Gelibolu), which was to become the major Ottoman naval base and 'the Muslim throat that gulps down every Christian nation',[105] was badly damaged in an earthquake. Süleyman, Orhan's son, moved in swiftly to occupy it and, despite Byzantine pressure, never moved out. The Ottomans were to remain on European soil for the next five and a half centuries.

For the next hundred years the Byzantines were to turn repeatedly and unsuccessfully to the West for help. The West, however, made promises

102 Ibn Battuta, *The Travels of Ibn Battuta*, 3 vols., trans. and ed. H. A. R. Gibb (Cambridge, 1958–71), II, pp. 451–2.
103 Doukas, *Historia*, p. 34; Doukas, *Decline*, p. 73.
104 Doukas, *Historia*, p. 33; Doukas, *Decline*, p. 73.
105 Doukas, *Historia*, p. 155; Doukas, *Decline*, p. 144.

but gave no concrete aid, as John V's friend and advisor Demetrios Kydones was well aware. This was a situation pleasing only to the Turks, who had, Kydones noted bitterly, already begun to laugh.[106]

The reign of Murad I, Orhan's son and successor, was one of rapid expansion, both in Anatolia and in the Balkans. Around 1369 Adrianople (modern Edirne) fell. It now became the next Ottoman capital. A crushing defeat of the Serbs in 1371 on the Maritsa river opened up Bulgaria to Ottoman forces. Deciding that caution was the better part of valour, the Bulgarian ruler Šišman 'wound a shroud around his neck and... prostrated himself before the feet of the sultan's horse',[107] not once but twice, for he was forced into a similar performance not long afterwards when it became ever clearer that the Ottomans were there to stay. Murad was killed at the famous battle of Kosovo in 1389, stabbed to death, according to some accounts, by a Serbian deserter in what Doukas describes as 'an unexpected and novel deed'.[108] Although this battle was to have much resonance in Serbian history and be a rallying cry of Serbian nationalism under Slobodan Milošević 600 years later, it was not the turning point for Ottoman advance in the Balkans. In this respect the battle of the Maritsa was of much greater significance.

As the Ottoman star ascended, Byzantine power declined ever further, and the Byzantines became increasingly enmeshed in their own power struggles and more and more caught in the trap of Ottoman interference in their internal affairs. In the struggle for the Byzantine throne, the Ottomans played one claimant off against another, backing Andronikos against his father John V, only to switch their support to John in 1379. It was Ottoman backing that put Andronikos IV's son John VII on the throne in 1390. By now Ottoman support was a decisive factor in Byzantine power struggles. 'Everyone admits', Kydones wrote, 'that whomever the barbarian supports will prevail in the future'. This did not stop the infighting over the 'shadow of power'. The Byzantines had been reduced to the role of vassal and were 'forced to serve the barbarian'.[109] Manuel II, who was to become emperor in 1392, spent six months of 1391 serving miserably in the Ottoman army.

Only three years later the Byzantine capital went under Ottoman siege. The new ruler Bayezid I, known as Yıldırım (the thunderbolt) for the

[106] R.-J. Loenertz (ed.), *Demetrius Cydones' Correspondence*, 2 vols. (Vatican City, 1956, 1960), I, letter 93, pp. 126–7.
[107] Neşri, *Čihannüma die Altosmanische Chronik des Mevlana Mehemmed Neschri*, 2 vols., ed. Franz Taeschner (Leipzig, 1951), I, p. 69; Neşri, *Kitab-i Cihan-nüma*, 2 vols., ed. Faik Reşit Unat and Mehmet A. Köymen (Ankara, 1949, 1957), I, p. 250.
[108] Doukas, *Historia*, p. 15; Doukas, *Decline*, p. 61.
[109] Loenertz, *Cydones*, II, letter 442, p. 407.

speed at which he crossed between the Asian and European sections of his state, mopped up opposition in Anatolia and advanced in Europe, dominating Serbia and Bulgaria and moving forward through Epirus, Albania and the Peloponnese. In 1396 he smashed an army made up of various European forces under King Sigismund of Hungary. The European troops fled from the battlefield in disarray, many rolling down the banks of the Danube into the water, which turned red with the blood of the dead and dying. Some clung in desperation to the sides of the ships, already overloaded with the fleeing. Those on board slashed at the grasping hands of their fellow soldiers and hacked them off at the wrists.[110] By the end of the battle, the ground was strewn with the corpses of the European army, and the Ottoman troops were victorious. The captives were lined up and either executed or, if rich, put aside for ransom. Many nobles and knights were ransomed at considerable cost to their families, and at considerable profit for the Ottoman coffers.

By 1400, the Ottoman state had grown from a small, insignificant state in north-western Anatolia to an imposing enemy, with lands stretching across much of Anatolia and over large areas of the Balkans. The Byzantines had been reduced to what amounted to vassal status and their capital was under Ottoman siege. In Bursa, Bayezid, in contrast, 'enjoyed the many fruits of good fortune and revelled in the daily homage of many nations either in animals or in metals or anything of pleasing aspect, given by God to the world; all were to be found in his treasuries'.[111]

What saved Constantinople and the Byzantines was not help from the West, vainly sought by the Byzantine emperor Manuel II, who slipped out of Constantinople in 1399 on an unsuccessful begging trip around the various capitals of Europe, but another enemy from the East. Timur, known in the West as Tamerlane, swept out of central Asia and moved southwards against the lands of the Mamluk sultanate. In 1400 he took Damascus, slaughtering, pillaging and burning, 'the flames almost mount [ing] to the clouds' as a result of the high winds.[112] After his sack of Aleppo, 'bodies lay on the ground, overspreading it like a carpet', the city left 'a desert waste darkened by fire, a lonely solitude where only the

[110] Johann Schiltberger, *The Bondage and Travels of Johann Schiltberger, a Native of Bavaria, in Europe, Asia and Africa, 1396–1427*, trans. and ed. J. Buchan Telfer (London, 1879), p. 4.

[111] Doukas, *Historia*, p. 59; Doukas, *Decline*, pp. 87–8.

[112] Ibn Taghribirdi, *History of Egypt 1382–1469. Part II, 1399–1411 A.D. Translated from the Arabic Annals of Abu l-Mahasin ibn Taghri Birdi*, trans. and ed. William Popper (Berkeley and Los Angeles, 1954), p. 50; Ibn Taghribirdi, *Al-Nujūm al-Zāhira fī mulūk Misr wa al-Qāhira* (Cairo, 1389/1970), XII, p. 245.

owl and the vulture took refuge'.[113] By 1402 he had swerved round, and instead of attacking the Mamluk sultan al-Nasir Faraj, quivering in Cairo, he moved his forces northwards and entered Anatolia. In June his army met that of the Ottomans in battle near Ankara on the central Anatolian plains. Bayezid was captured, his sons fled and his state collapsed headlong into a decade of internecine fighting.

It was not until 1413 that the Ottoman state emerged from the ashes of destruction after the battle of Ankara. Mehmed I, a man 'virtuous in character and gentle', who 'truly despised warfare and loved peace',[114] gradually reassembled Ottoman power, carefully building up relations with his neighbours, including the Byzantines, with whom he sought to maintain a peaceful relationship. He also cultivated his relationship with Venice, with whom he concluded a treaty in 1419.[115] Militarily, too, he made advances and his conquest of Valona (Vlorë) gave him access to the Adriatic. Mehmed's position was not an easy one, however, for he was faced with internal opposition. Two revolts broke out in 1416 which he put down with difficulty.

In 1421 Mehmed died. Far from profiting from the golden opportunity of Ottoman disarray presented to them in 1402, the Byzantines and the various European states had failed to unite in any effective way or to prevent the re-emergence of a vibrant Ottoman state. In part this was due to the commercial considerations of major powers such as Venice and Genoa, whose interest in a hostile alliance against the Ottomans was always balanced against trade concerns and their own commercial rivalry, which resulted in two wars between them in the course of the fourteenth century. Genoa was even excommunicated several times as punishment for its preference for commercial gain to spiritual duty. The Byzantines were eventually to receive some assistance, after John VIII agreed at the Council of Florence in 1439 to accept the supremacy of the Pope, a condition that was not popular in the empire. The assistance secured was, however, too little, too late.

Apart from their attempt to elicit support from the West, the Byzantines also tried to destabilise the Ottomans as much as possible, releasing Ottoman pretenders who had taken refuge in Constantinople. On Murad II's accession to the throne in 1421, the Byzantine emperor Manuel II released Mustafa, brother of Mehmed I. Known as Düzme (False) Mustafa in Ottoman tradition, he had unsuccessfully attacked Mehmed and had subsequently been held on Lemnos by the Byzantines

[113] Ibn Taghribirdi, *History*, part II, p. 39; Ibn Taghribirdi, *Al-Nujūm al-Zāhira*, XII, p. 225.
[114] Doukas, *Historia*, pp. 203, 228; Doukas, *Decline*, pp. 173, 189.
[115] 1419.xi.6 = Thomas, *Diplomatarium*, nos. 172 and 173, pp. 318–30.

in return for payment by the Ottomans. At first successful, taking both Gelibolu and Edirne, Mustafa, whose behaviour was 'like a prancing and snorting horse',[116] wasted his opportunity with his 'fatuous conduct'.[117] Having advanced towards Bursa, he was met by the forces of Murad II and fled back westwards 'like a plucked jackdaw'.[118] He was caught and hanged at Edirne. The releasing of Mustafa had been a mistake and Constantinople went briefly under Ottoman siege in June 1422.

For the next twenty years, Murad II built on the foundations his father had carefully laid. Defeating a further revolt against him – this time by his brother Mustafa, who was captured and killed in early 1423 – Murad secured the Ottoman position in Serbia and Albania. In 1430 he took Thessalonike, which the Byzantines, unable to protect it, had ceded to Venice in 1422. Despite the initial success of John Hunyadi, the *voyvoda* of Transylvania, in the early 1440s, and the campaign of 1443 which left Serbia devastated, Sofia 'a black field' and its villages like 'black charcoal',[119] in 1444 Murad inflicted a crushing defeat on the combined forces of Hunyadi, Vladislav I, the King of Hungary and George Branković, the Despot of Serbia.

Murad sought to secure his military successes by making alliances. In 1424 he concluded a treaty with the Byzantines whereby the emperor ceded cities on the Black Sea and agreed to payment of a large tribute. In 1430, after the Ottoman conquest of Thessalonike, he made a treaty with his 'brother the Doge' of Venice which ensured peaceful relations, secured commerce and guaranteed various territorial arrangements.[120] He concluded the treaty of Edirne with Vladislav, Branković and Hunyadi in 1444, and a treaty with the state of Karaman in the same year. At this point this 'very humane, gentle and liberal'[121] leader abdicated, a decision possibly related to the death the year before of his son Alaeddin. His abdication was seen by Vladislav and Hunyadi as an opportunity to attack. The new, and very young, sultan, Murad's son Mehmed, was distinctly insecure in his new role. Called back from retirement to lead the troops against the attack in the Balkans, Murad defeated the forces of Hunyadi and Vladislav at the second battle of Kosovo in November 1444. 'Heads

116 Doukas, *Historia*, p. 166; Doukas, *Decline*, p. 151.
117 Doukas, *Historia*, p. 166; Doukas, *Decline*, p. 151.
118 Doukas, *Historia*, p. 177; Doukas, *Decline*, p. 158.
119 Halil İnalcık and Mevlud Oğuz (eds.), *Gazavât-ı Sultân Murâd b. Mehemmed Hân. İzladi ve Varna Savaşları (1443–1444) Üzerine Anonim Gazavâtnâme* (Ankara, 1978), f. 15a; Colin Imber, *The Crusade of Varna, 1443–45* (Aldershot, 2006), p. 56.
120 1430.ix.4 = Thomas, *Diplomatarium*, no. 182, pp. 343–5.
121 Promontorio, *Aufzeichnungen*, p. 80.

rolled like pebbles on the battlefields',[122] in particular that of Vladislav, who was killed in battle. Hunyadi fled. Although saved by this victory, Mehmed's position remained weak. He was toppled two years later by a janissary revolt and 'the world was in chaos'.[123]

Any chaos, however, was short-lived. Murad returned from retirement and promptly defeated Hunyadi at the second battle of Varna. Greece came increasingly under attack, Arta falling in 1449. The Ottomans were also active at sea, attacking Aegean islands and Negroponte. By the time of Murad's death in February 1451, the Ottoman state had fully recovered from the devastating setback of 1402 and was poised to become one of the great empires of the world.

The Ottoman city

Ambitious, determined, tireless and shrewd,[124] Mehmed II was back on the throne. Two years later Constantinople had fallen and Mehmed could turn his deep and lively intelligence[125] to the rebuilding of his new capital. 'What', Aşıkpaşazade asks, 'did Sultan Mehmed Han Gazi do in Istanbul?'

> He built eight schools, in the middle [of the city] he built a Friday mosque, and opposite the mosque a soup kitchen and to the side of it a hospital. Behind each school there was another school preparing for higher education ... Apart from this he built a soup kitchen, a school, and mosque for Hazret-i Eyüb el Ensari and a large tomb for him.[126]

He also built a covered market,[127] *hamam*s (public baths) and aqueducts.[128] Immediately after the conquest he adopted a policy of enforced repopulation of the city[129] and was

> solicitous to work for the repeopling of the City and to fill it with inhabitants as it had previously been. He gathered them there from all parts of Asia and Europe, and he transferred them with all possible care and speed, people of all nations, but more especially of Christians. So profound was the passion that came into his soul for the City and its peopling, and for bringing it back to its former prosperity.[130]

[122] İnalcık and Oğuz, *Gazavât*, f. 57a; Imber, *Crusade*, p. 99.
[123] Oruç Bey, *Oruç Beğ Tarihi*, ed. A. Nihal Atsız (Istanbul, 1972), p. 98.
[124] Sagundino, 'Orazione', p. 128; Languschi, 'Excidio', p. 173.
[125] Sagundino, 'Orazione', p. 128. [126] Aşıkpaşazade, *Chronik*, *bab* 123, p. 131.
[127] Doukas, *Historia*, p. 340; Doukas, *Decline*, p. 258.
[128] Kritoboulos, *History*, 55, p. 105.
[129] Aşıkpaşazade, *Chronik*, *bab* 124, pp. 133–4; Neşri, *Čihannüma*, p. 181; Neşri, *Kitab-i Cihan-nüma*, II, pp. 708–10; Tursun Bey, *History*, f. 53a-55b; Kritoboulos, *History*, 280–283, p. 83; 56, p. 105.
[130] Kritoboulos, *History*, 56, p. 105.

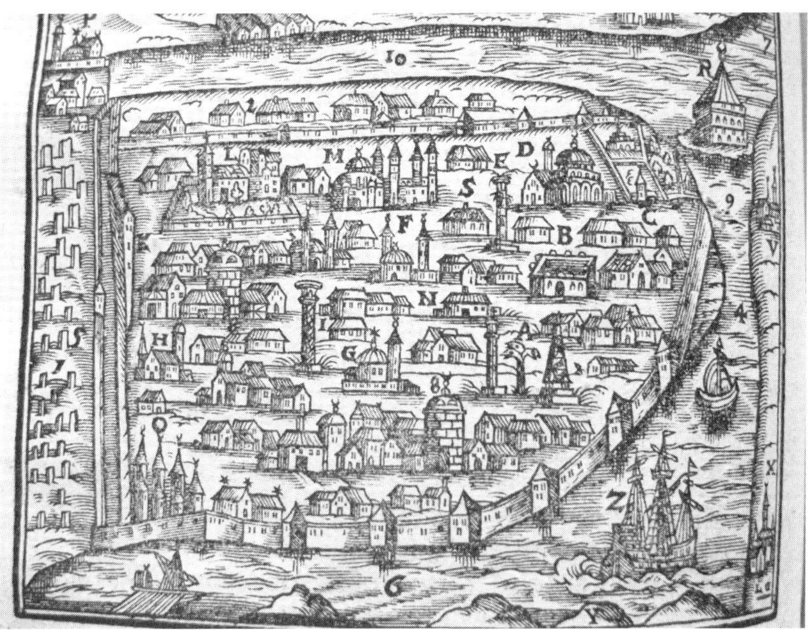

2. Constantinople, in Salomon Schweigger, *Ein newe Reyssbeschreibung auss Teutschland nach Constantinopel und Jerusalem* (Nurnberg, 1639), p. 102.

The city was resurrected and within a few years was 'prosperous, ornamented and well-organised':[131]

> Every corner, a paradise, every garden an Eden
> Every fountain a water of Paradise, every river, a river of honey.[132]

Mehmed thus set out to stamp the city with the seal of his power. His aim was undoubtedly to create a capital that would impress both Ottomans and foreigners with its magnificence and dazzle them with the might of his empire. It was also to be a capital of wealth, thriving and prosperous and bringing much revenue into the Ottoman treasury. It was this capital that was to be the centre of the empire for the next five and a half centuries. And it was from here, from the palace of Topkapı, that this empire was to be governed.

[131] Tursun Bey, *History*, f. 63a. [132] Tursun Bey, *History*, f. 63a.

2 The palace and the populace

The acquisition of the great Byzantine capital spurred Mehmed II on to a great effort of revitalisation: encouragement of commerce, transfer of population to the city, and a major building programme. One of his first actions was to build a palace, later to be known as the Eski Saray, almost immediately superseded by the imposing palace of Topkapı, erected on rising ground in the centre of the city overlooking the sea and dominating the landscape. From here the sultans were to run the affairs of state until the mid nineteenth century, when they transferred to the palace of Dolmabahçe, which they considered at that time more suited to the modern age. The sultans who ruled from here were the focal point of power, their lives a reflection of the magnificence, wealth and power of the empire. They embodied the prestige of that empire and their imperial pomp sustained it. The populace approved of, admired or were dissatisfied with their sultans. Greatly respected, Süleyman I's death in 1566 provoked deep distress and the people were much moved by the elegy composed for him by the great poet Baki.[1] The execution of his son Mustafa, much loved both by the common people and by the upper echelons of society,[2] caused great grief and the production of many poems written in his memory;[3] while the crowds for the funeral of Murad IV (1623–40) were so great that it was difficult to clear a pathway to the grave, and the day of his death was one of such grief that it was like doomsday.[4] Murad III's (1574–95) greeting of the Muslims with 'total respect and indisputable humility' at the crowded Friday prayer in Ayasofya in December 1574 was greeted with a great roar of approval,[5]

[1] Selaniki Mustafa Efendi, *Tarih-i Selânikî*, 2 vols., ed. Mehmet İpşirli (Ankara, 1999), I, p. 53.

[2] İbrahim Peçevi, *Peçevî Tarihi*, 2 vols., ed. Murat Uraz (Istanbul, 1968), I, p. 18.

[3] Peçevi, *Tarihi*, I, pp. 162–3.

[4] Topçular Katibi Abdülkadir Efendi, *Topçular Kâtibi 'Abdülkādir (Kadrî) Efendi Tarihi (Metin ve Tahlil)*, 2 vols., ed. Ziya Yılmazer (Ankara, 2003), II, p. 1143.

[5] Selaniki, *Tarih*, I, p. 104.

his fame as a generous, just, fair and wise ruler noted by Gerlach, a priest with the Habsburg embassy.[6]

It could perhaps be argued that the presentation of such popular sentiment should simply be disregarded as eulogistic rhetoric in official chronicles or acts of flattery aimed at attaining concrete reward – an island governorship in the case of Kritoboulos, the author of a history of Mehmed II. But such judgements also appear in anonymous chronicles not so inclined to sycophancy and much more given to critical comment, or in western sources, such as Gerlach's comment on Murad III, where the influence of the court was not involved. Such opinions were important, for an Ottoman sultan could not rule in Istanbul by ignoring its people. The relationship between the sultan and the city was a symbiotic one: the city was the capital because of his presence, and his power as a successful sultan was influenced by his reception by its populace. To this end, all sultans invested heavily in pageantry and display, in being both seen and accessible, a source of justice and of reassurance of success for the people of the city and of the empire as a whole.

The omnipresent sultan

It has often been argued that with the conquest of Constantinople and the acquisition of a traditional imperial capital, the Ottoman ruler became more remote, withdrawing behind the high walls of the Topkapı palace and adopting a style of regality which emulated in part the Byzantine tradition of an inaccessible and distant caesar.[7] The person of the sultan himself became less important, and as the symbolic role of the house of Osman took over, the significance of the individual sultan decreased.

This presumption may come, at least in part, from the many western observers' accounts which, from the fifteenth century onwards, present the Ottoman sultan as a distant and secluded figure who rarely left the sanctuary of his palace or appeared in public. That this was the case is, interestingly, contradicted by Luigi Bassano, himself a westerner present in Istanbul in the 1530s, who commented that the sultan processed to the Friday prayer each week, appearing before the people and greeting

6 Stephan Gerlach, *Türkiye Günlüğü 1573–1576*, 2 vols., trans. Türkis Noyan (Istanbul, 2007), I, p. 359.

7 See, for example, Nicolas Vatin and Gilles Veinstein, *Le Sérail ébranlé. Essais sur les morts, dépositions et avènements des sultans ottomans XIVe–XIXe siècle* (Paris, 2003), p. 35; Suraiya Faroqhi, 'Crisis and change, 1590–1699' in Halil İnalcık and Donald Quataert (eds.), *An Economic and Social History of the Ottoman Empire*, 2 vols. (Cambridge, 1994), II, p. 616.

Le sultan se rendant à la mosquée.

3. The sultan going to the mosque, in Edmondo di Amicis, *Constantinople* (Paris, 1883), p. 213.

them: 'Thus the Gran Turco is seen every Friday, in contrast to the liars who say that he never lets himself be seen'.[8]

This view of an increasingly distant and remote ruler does not represent the reality of sultanic power as displayed in Istanbul or reflected in the Ottoman accounts. Highly visible, the sultan constantly appeared before the Istanbul populace, who, 'addicts of spectacle and pageantry',[9] were continually involved in one way or another in imperial pomp and display. Indeed, according to the sixteenth-century Ottoman writer Latifi, the people of Istanbul were so used to seeing high and exalted personages that for them mere common men had less value than a dog.[10] Public criers constantly called their attention to the imperial nature of the city, announcing sultans' orders, or issuing instructions, informing them of wars or the death or accession of a sultan,[11] as they did for example, for Selim II in 1566, shouting out that now the period of Sultan Selim Han had begun.[12]

The sultan appeared every Friday, with rare exceptions such as Murad III, who stopped doing this towards the end of his reign, a decision for which he was severely censored by the contemporary chronicler Selaniki.[13] During the procession to and from the mosque, the sultans were greeted by the people whom they saluted in turn and whose petitions they received. They visited the tombs of their ancestors, went to Eyüp at the time of their accessions, visited their ministers or the female members of their family at Eski Saray, the old palace where the women of previous sultans lived, and took pleasure trips on the Bosphorus or to the numerous gardens and pavilions within and outside the city. They moved house; the royal household of Selim III (1789–1807) moved each year in late April or early May from Topkapı palace to Beşiktaş palace for the summer, and back again for the winter at the end of September or beginning of October. They went hunting, they inspected the imperial fleet or visited the troops. On all these occasions they were on display, seen and often accessible.

Such display served to ensure legitimacy; to emphasise, at some times more than others, the religious role of the sultans, who were to use the title

[8] Luigi Bassano, *I costumi et i modi particolari de la vita de Turchi, descritti da M. Luigi Bassano da Zara* ([Roma], 1545), f. 13v.

[9] Selaniki, *Tarih*, I, p. 8.

[10] Latifi, *Evsâf-ı İstanbul*, ed. Nermin Suner (Pekin) (Istanbul, 1977), pp. 66–7.

[11] Abdi, *1730 Patrona İhtilâli Hakkında Bir Eser Abdi Tarihi*, ed. Faik Reşit Unat (Ankara, 1943), p. 50; Destari, *Destârî Sâlih Tarihi. Patrona Halil Ayaklanması Hakkında Bir Kaynak*, ed. Bekir Sıtkı Baykal (Ankara, 1962), p. 32; Selaniki, *Tarih*, II, p. 714; Gerlach, *Günlüğü*, I, pp. 116, 159; Ahmed Cavid, *Hadîka-ı Vekāyi'*, ed. Adnan Baycar (Ankara, 1998), p. 69.

[12] Selaniki, *Tarih*, I, p. 42.

[13] Selaniki, *Tarih*, II, pp. 444–5.

of caliph at various times from the mid sixteenth century until the abolition of the caliphate in 1924; to demonstrate military might and victory; and to present luxury and wealth, an impression that was not lost on visiting ambassadors and others, often overawed by the magnificent richness of this seat of Ottoman power. Even in the dying days of the empire, when the population had become heartily fed up with it,[14] pageantry was maintained, clearly considered important in legitimising sultanic rule to the last.

Far from gaining legitimacy from any aura of invisibility, the sultan's legitimacy was thus inextricably bound up with his being seen. Even Murad III, a sultan more reluctant than most to appear in public, did come out of the palace, even if, on rare occasions, according to Domenico, his physician, 'so that the people may see him and not have thoughts of rebellion against him'.[15] This need for visibility was as true for the post-1453 empire as it had been during the early days of the state when, partly due to the lack of a law of succession, an invisible sultan spelt unrest and instability. It was for this reason that the ministers went to such lengths to conceal the death of Mehmed I in 1421, when the sultan, on his deathbed and aware that he would expire before his son Murad II arrived, warned them not to reveal his death but to prepare for trouble. Despite the ministers' attempts to run affairs as if nothing untoward had happened, the soldiers became uneasy, asking, in the words of the early Ottoman chronicler Aşıkpaşazade, 'what has happened to our leader? He does not appear'. The ministers' reply that the doctors would not allow the sultan to come out did not prove satisfactory. Instead, the sultan made an appearance, with a young man placed behind the corpse to move its arms. Seeing the sultan apparently stroking his beard, the *ağa*s (leaders) of the janissaries (infantry troops originally recruited through the *devşirme*, the compulsory levy on Christians, particularly in the Balkans) returned to their affairs and the corpse was quickly hoisted up and whisked back into the palace.[16]

It was not merely a matter of being seen that was important, but being seen in the capital. Just before the grand vezir İshak Paşa retired to Thessalonike, he advised Bayezid II (1481–1512) that if he wished to remain sultan for a long time, the most important thing to do was to stay in Istanbul and not to leave except for a very good reason.[17] The impact on

[14] Halid Ziya Uşaklıgil, *Saray ve Ötesi* (Istanbul, 2003), p. 149.

[15] Domenico, *Domenico's Istanbul*, trans. M. J. L. Austin and ed. Geoffrey Lewis (Wiltshire, 2001), p. 28; 'Relazione di Giovani Moro, Bailo a Costantinopoli, 1590', in Luigi Firpo (ed.), *Relazioni di ambasciatori Veneti al senato*, vol. XIII *Costantinopoli (1590–1793)* (Turin, 1984), p. 332.

[16] Aşıkpaşazade, *Chronik*, *bab* 81, pp. 84–5.

[17] Richard F. Kreutel (ed.), *Haniwaldanus Anonimi'ne Göre Sultan Bayezid-i Veli (1481–1512)*, trans. Necdet Öztürk (Istanbul, 1997), p. 15.

the city of a prolonged sultanic absence became clear when the sultans began to reside in Edirne during the latter part of the seventeenth century. Without the sultan, the city suffered. 'Half burnt and half in ruins', due to the lack of attention from officials, the world of the capital was taken over by fools and rogues, while Ahmed II's (1691–95) grand vezir dedicated himself to hunting rather than to government.[18] Mustafa II (1695–1703) did not attend to or show concern for either the order of Istanbul or the condition of its population. Istanbul was left alone, abandoned and disordered, neglected and forgotten.[19] Although ambassadors negotiating peace were received in Istanbul, the sultan Mustafa II returned again to Edirne as soon as an agreement had been concluded, abandoning the capital once more. It was evident, as Defterdar Sarı Mehmed Paşa wrote, that Istanbul would remain far from the eyes of the men of state.[20]

In contrast, Edirne thrived. New quarters sprang up, caravansarays and houses were built. From Mehmed IV's reign (1648–87) onwards, Edirne slid more and more into becoming not the second city but the capital, replacing the primacy of Istanbul. It was in Edirne now that the major royal events took place. Mehmed IV had his sons Mustafa II and Ahmed III (1703–30) circumcised there, for which fifteen days of celebrations were laid on. Three thousand poor boys were also circumcised at the state's expense and food given to both rich and poor.[21] Shortly afterwards, his daughter Hatice Sultan was married, to the accompaniment of another fifteen-day period of festivities.[22]

By the time Mustafa II came to the throne the change was even more pronounced. He had his sons circumcised there and even removed his mother from Istanbul to Edirne on his accession in 1695.[23] His three, very young daughters, aged four or five, were married there, and the construction of new palaces ordered for them. The grand vezir Hüseyin Paşa presented the sultan with a mansion he had bought on the banks of the Tunca river, to which a new pavilion and pool were added, an event which agitated the population in Istanbul, for they perceived this as

[18] Abdülkadir Özcan (ed.), *Anonim Osmanlı Tarihi (1099–1116/1688–1704)* (Ankara, 2000), p. 52.
[19] Özcan, *Anonim*, p. 225.
[20] Defterdar Sarı Mehmed Paşa, *Zübde-i Vekayiât, Tahlil ve Metin (1066–1116/1656–1704)*, ed. Abdülkadir Özcan (Ankara, 1995), p. 783.
[21] İsazade, *'Îsâ-zâde Târîhi (Metin ve Tahlîl)*, ed. Ziya Yılmazer (Istanbul, 1996), pp. 137–43.
[22] Nabi, *Nabi'nin Surnâmesi. Vakaayi'-i Hıtân-ı Şehzadegân-ı Hazret-i Sultan Muhammed-i Gaazi Li Nabi Efendi*, ed. Agâh Sırrı Levend (Istanbul, 1944), pp. 22–71.
[23] Özcan, *Anonim*, p. 108.

the beginning of *yalı*s (the great summer houses in Istanbul on the Bosphorus) in Edirne, signifying the weakening of Istanbul's position.[24]

All this led to mutterings and discontent in the capital. There was gossip about the expenses for the weddings of the sultan's daughters, and rumour had it that every household in Istanbul would be taxed to pay for them.[25] Important religious officials and other high-up people complained that such expenses were a waste of the money of the state treasury. It was also, in effect, turning Edirne into the empire's capital.[26] While spending the winter there was permissible,[27] or even prolonged periods hunting there as Mehmed IV did, total sultanic absence from the capital, stripping it of its prestige and its pageantry, was unacceptable. For the contemporary Ottoman historian Naima, Mehmed IV, despite his long absences from the capital, had never abandoned Istanbul; returning from time to time, he had 'not left its people in despair'. Mustafa II, in contrast, had 'completely wiped the city from his mind', making it known that Edirne would be his city of residence. Hearing this, the people of Istanbul 'lost all hope and desire, and fell into despair'.[28] The era ended in 1703 with what became known as the Edirne incident, when the people of Istanbul, united, according to Naima, by their despair at their city's loss of centrality,[29] revolted, in part, against the failure of the sultan to reside in his capital.

It is perhaps significant that Ahmed III, the first sultan to come to the throne in Istanbul after the interval in Edirne, whose entry through the Edirne Kapı after his accession ceremony at Eyüp greatly pleased all, rich and poor alike,[30] went every Friday to a different mosque,[31] so ensuring a high level of visibility in different parts of the city. Perhaps for the same reasons, Mahmud I (1730–54), who succeeded in the aftermath of the Patrona Halil revolt and the overthrow of Ahmed III, also went to a different mosque each Friday in the period immediately after his accession, at first to the Fatih mosque and then to the new Valide Sultan mosque and the Bayezid mosque.[32] Mahmud II (1808–39), succeeding to the throne in a similar period of upheaval, went to different mosques for the last prayer at night during Ramazan of 1808.[33] It should be noted, however, that other sultans, too, adopted this policy, Mehmed III going first after his accession to Ayasofya for Friday prayer,[34]

[24] Özcan, *Anonim*, p. 225. [25] Özcan, *Anonim*, p. 225.
[26] Defterdar Sarı Mehmed Paşa, *Zübde*, p. 783. [27] Selaniki, *Tarih*, I, p. 66.
[28] Naima, *Târih-i Na'îmâ*, 4 vols., ed. Mehmet İpşirli (Ankara, 2007), IV, pp. 1886–7.
[29] Naima, *Târih*, IV, p. 1887. [30] Defterdar Sarı Mehmed Paşa, *Zübde*, p. 822.
[31] Özcan, *Anonim*, p. 262. [32] Destari, *Tarihi*, pp. 22–4.
[33] Cabi Ömer Efendi, *Câbî Târihi*, 2 vols., ed. Mehmet Ali Beyhan (Ankara, 2003), I, p. 264.
[34] Selaniki, *Tarih*, II, p. 440.

and subsequently on following Fridays to the Süleymaniye and Bayezid mosques.[35] It may therefore have been a practice designed to achieve high profile for a new sultan in general, not merely when the sultan had succeeded in a period of difficulty.

Whether this was the case or not, what remained significant was the presence of the ruler in the capital. The absence of the sultan reduced the city, for without him, or at least without Murad IV in the words of the contemporary historian Peçevi, 'the world was powerless and weak and the people were like soulless shells', their souls returning to them and their faces lighting up only on his return from the Yerevan campaign in 1635.[36] 'The world experienced new life and endless joy' when Süleyman I returned from fighting in Iran in 1554,[37] the population having several years earlier responded with similar delight at his return from campaign when the streets and markets overflowed with festivities to celebrate his triumphant entry.[38]

While the sultans' absences were usually related to campaigns, and their returns thus bound up in expressions of victorious triumph, the sultan was not merely a military figure. From the mid sixteenth century, sultans began to employ the title of caliph, although it was not one they made a great deal of use of until times of trouble encouraged them to clutch more firmly at religious legitimacy. The presence of the sultan as religious leader was thus also significant, and it was to see 'the face of the caliph of Islam' that the rich pilgrims from the European territory of the empire stopped in Istanbul on their way to Mecca. They watched him as he processed to or from the Friday prayer, and if they did not manage to obtain a good sighting of him they would stay in the city for another week, or even longer, until they did.[39]

While it was undoubtedly the case that the position of sultan carried with it an inherent aspect of spiritual sanctification, this was not necessarily linked to the title of caliph. Bayezid II, who died in 1512, was referred to as 'Veli', a saint, a holy man. According to Hoca Sadeddin, a *şeyhülislam* (head of the religious establishment) under Mehmed III who gave the information as proven fact not rumour, soil from Bayezid's grave cured many diseases and any prayers made over his tomb would be accepted.[40] This spiritual power can also be observed in a much earlier period, when

35 Selaniki, *Tarih*, II, pp. 449, 454. 36 Peçevi, *Tarihi*, II, p. 494.
37 Peçevi, *Tarihi*, I, p. 182. 38 Peçevi, *Tarihi*, I, pp. 103–4.
39 Ahmet Cevdet Paşa, *Ma'rûzât*, ed. Yusuf Halaçoğlu (Istanbul, 1980), p. 58; Taylesanizade, *Taylesanizâde Hafız Abdullah Efendi Tarihi: İstanbul'un Uzun Dört Yılı (1785–1789)*, ed. Feridun M. Emecen (Istanbul, 2003), p. 332.
40 Hoca Sadettin Efendi, *Tacü't-Tevarih*, 5 vols., ed. İsmet Parmaksızoğlu (Ankara, 1999), IV, p. 105.

the grave of the nephew of Osman (d.*c.*1324), Aydoğdu, was believed to have the power to cure sick horses if they were walked around it three times.[41] This spirituality was also attached to sultans at a much later period. Cabi, writing at the beginning of the nineteenth century, ascribed it to Mahmud II, recounting two stories of two separate women who went blind after cursing the sultan because of the bad quality and scarcity of bread. As a result of these events, 'this saintliness and power of sanctity of the sultan was thus seen by all and was a well-known truth'.[42] It was also generally believed that if the sultan prayed at the funeral of someone who had died of plague, the plague would leave the city. Rumours were rife that Mahmud attended prayers for funerals in Ayasofya in Ramazan 1812, and one might argue that his appearance at such funerals in a time of great plague was calculated with this popular belief in mind.[43] Sultans themselves could deliver effective curses, that of Ahmed III after his removal from the throne having the power, according to the contemporary Abdi, to bring disaster or death to those cursed.[44]

At the end of the empire, even if mocked, such belief in the divine power of the sultan continued. When a major fire broke out in September 1918, Mehmed VI (Vahdeddin) (1918–22), following the tradition whereby sultans oversaw firefighting personally, prepared to attend the blaze. His chief secretary Lütfi Simavi suggested that he should do so dressed in military uniform, as this would have a good effect on the people. The grand vezir and the chief of police were informed of the sultan's imminent arrival. The sultan retired to have a bath and prepare, deciding to dress in civilian clothing as donning a military uniform would take too long. By the time he was ready, Lütfi Simavi informed him that the fire was now under control and about to be put out.

> The sultan smiled knowingly and replied, 'we'll get there just at the right time'. There is a conviction among the people that if the sultan goes to a fire, the fire will immediately be extinguished. With the sultan present, officials and fire-fighters redouble their efforts and as a result the fire is put out as fast as possible, and this is attributed to the sultan's spiritual power![45]

In part bound up with religious duty, if not with being caliph per se, was a role which all sultans were expected to fulfil and one which was noted and commented on by the people. This was the role of dispenser of justice, as essential to the persona of the good sultan in the post-1453 world as it had

[41] Aşıkpaşazade, *Chronik*, *bab* 17, p. 22. [42] Cabi, *Târihi*, I, pp. 603, 604–5.
[43] Cabi, *Târihi*, II, p. 891. [44] Abdi, *Tarihi*, p. 50.
[45] Lütfü Simavi, *Son Osmanlı Sarayında Gördüklerim. Sultan Mehmed Reşad Hanın ve Halifenin Sarayında Gördüklerim*, ed. Sami Kara and Nurer Uğurlu (Istanbul, 2004), facsimile pp. 150–1, quotation p. 151.

been for the early rulers of the Ottoman state. Well before the conquest of Constantinople, Bayezid I (1389–1402) had conducted justice, sitting in the early morning in an open space raised above the people. Those who had grievances could present them to him.[46]

The concept of immediate justice from an accessible ruler was part of the style of Ottoman rule in Istanbul where the sultan received petitions in the *divan* (the council of state), on the streets as he moved round the city or went to and from Friday prayer, or as he relaxed in one of his many pavilions. Just as Bayezid had observed the populace from his broad eminence, so too did the sharp eyes of Murad III shoot into every corner of every street, watching the people as they approached with their petitions.[47] Such people could be Muslims, Christians or Jews, like those who waited in the streets to present their petitions to Murad III as he rode by,[48] or the people of Galata who rode across the water to accost him as he relaxed in the Sultan Bayezid Han Kasrı, a pavilion on the shore below Topkapı, and to complain about their *kadı* (judge and important official), Abdülkerim-zade Kadı Abdullah, whose dismissal they thus secured.[49] Just as the inhabitants of Galata protested about their *kadı*, so did the Greek Orthodox community turn to the sultan to intervene over their patriarch, this time in an attempt to keep him rather than have him removed.[50] They appealed to him also to judge in matters of extortion, such as that which extracted sixteen thousand ducats from Metrophanes at a rate of two thousand ducats per annum in the eight years of his patriarchate.[51]

It was for justice that many people came to the city, going to the *divan*, where they waited many days to present their grievances,[52] or approaching to hand in their petitions during the sultan's procession to and from Friday prayer. Such complaints concerned the ill treatment and oppression meted out by the *timar* holders (those who held land grants in return for military service), depredations by bandits, unjust tax collectors, suffering due to famine and poverty, or attack from across the frontiers of the empire, which could lead to enslavement of women and seizure of goods, as it did for the people of Babadağı on the Danube in 1595, who warned Mehmed III that the honour of the Muslims was being trampled.[53]

[46] İsmail Hakkı Uzunçarşılı, *Osmanlı Devletinin Merkez ve Bahriye Teşkilâtı* (Ankara, 1988), p. 1.
[47] Gerlach, *Günlüğü*, II, p. 602. [48] Gerlach, *Günlüğü*, II, p. 524.
[49] Selaniki, *Tarih*, I, p. 237.
[50] Ahmet Refik, *Hicri On Birinci Asırda İstanbul Hayatı (1000–1100)* (Istanbul, 1931), p. 44, *hüküm* 84.
[51] Gerlach, *Günlüğü*, I, p. 407. [52] Gerlach, *Günlüğü*, I, pp. 249–50.
[53] Selaniki, *Tarih*, II, p. 481.

The enormous volume of petitions which bombarded Mehmed III and threatened to engulf Murad III, who was assailed by thousands of them every time he left his palace,[54] indicates that there was a belief in their effectiveness and in the power of the sultan to find solutions. It also shows to what extent power was personal: all could access it, and all could, at least in theory, expect satisfaction. If there was corruption in the system, which there most conspicuously was, this, in the popular imagination, related to the ministers, not to the sultan. Evil counsel perverted justice, not the sultan, who remained above criticism – at least in most cases.

Petitions clearly did have an impact, as in the case of Kara Hızır, the apparently very corrupt *subaşı* (the official in charge of order in the city) of Istanbul, against whom Süleyman I received a deluge of complaints in 1545 and who was in consequence removed from his post.[55] This effectiveness, while pleasing to the petitioners, was less so for the sultan's ministers. The level of trust that existed between them and their master was often slim, if not non-existent. Ahmed III, when removed from the throne in 1730, advised his successor Mahmud I not to trust anyone except himself and to change his vezirs often,[56] a policy adopted also in the following century by Abdülhamid II (1876–1909), a very untrusting sultan. Selim III (1789–1807) clearly had little faith in his own officials and issued frequent instructions for the removal of those he had reason to believe were not doing their jobs properly. He had good reason for his suspicions, for they were instrumental in his removal and failed to inform him of the initial revolt that led to his downfall.[57] After his deposition, he advised his successor, Mustafa IV (1807–08), never to trust his ministers.

As sultan Mustafa was coming from the *kafes* [the secluded quarters of the palace where the princes lived] and as sultan Selim was leaving the throne room, they met each other and embraced and wept. Sultan Selim said 'my son, go and sit on the throne, may it bring you good luck because this is the fate it brought me' and kissed him on his forehead. Mustafa kissed his feet. Selim continued his words 'I will give you some advice. Never indulge your servants and do not believe their words. They destroyed me and this is the result. Take a lesson from this'.[58]

[54] Halil İnalcık, 'Adâletnâmeler', *Türk Tarih Kurumu Belgeler*, II/3–4 (1965), p. 105; Peçevi, *Tarihi*, II, p. 277.

[55] Halil Sahillioğlu (ed.), *Topkapı Sarayı Arşivi H.951–952 ve E-12321 Numaralı Mühimme Defteri* (Istanbul, 2002), pp. 215–16, *hüküm* 281.

[56] Abdi, *Tarihi*, p. 41.

[57] Oğulukyan, *Georg Oğulukyan'ın Ruznamesi. 1806–1810 İsyanları. III. Selim, IV. Mustafa, II. Mahmud ve Alemdar Mustafa Paşa*, trans. and ed. Hrand D. Andreasyan (Istanbul, 1972), p. 4.

[58] Oğulukyan, *Ruznamesi*, p. 11.

In this climate of mutual distrust, ministers regarded petitions with suspicion and disliked the practice of handing petitions to the sultan during his procession to Friday prayer. Petitions had the potential to reveal ministers' own wrongdoings and, in consequence, they 'feared paying for their bad deeds with their lives', in the words of the the early seventeenth-century Venetian ambassador Ottaviano Bon.[59] Indeed, in 1693, both the grand vezir and the *defterdar* (chancellor of the exchequer) fell victim to the hundreds of petitions that were handed to the sultan at every *divan* and on every Friday as he went to Friday prayer.[60] Officials therefore tried, where possible, to block such petitions, not always successfully and sometimes with disastrous results. The janissary *ağa* was removed from his post by Mehmed III at the beginning of his reign, after he had seen the janissaries preventing the people of Ruse and Silistria from approaching him after Friday prayer.[61] This perhaps also accounts for the remark by the anonymous author of an eighteenth-century chronicle that one of the duties of the grand vezir was to analyse petitions with caution, not accepting their claims at face value but bearing in mind motivation such as revenge or desire for favour or reward. Petitions, the writer cautioned, should always be carefully investigated.[62] Writing two centuries earlier, the ex-grand vezir Lütfi Paşa also advised that petitions should be thoroughly investigated, and that punishments of important officials for small offences should be proportionate to the crime, for if they were excessive this would encourage people to misuse petitions for their own personal motives.[63] This would certainly have been a point of view agreeable to ministers, for whom very careful checking, if not total destruction, would often have been desirable.

The high-profile presence of the sultan in the city was manifest also by the reverse practice: the presence of the disguised sultan – a practice which both kept the sultan informed about the true state of affairs in the capital (a further source of worry and irritation to the ministers), and gave an omnipresent aura to his person, for the sultan could be present even if not seen. This strengthened the popular belief in the sultan as an all-seeing being, who was informed about and cared for the condition of his people in the city. It also carried a more threatening message, making sedition or anti-government gossiping inadvisable.

Disguised variously as a *sipahi* (cavalry soldier), *softa* (religious student), bombardier, sailor, guide or man responsible for the upkeep of

[59] Ottaviano Bon, *A Description of the Grand Signor's Seraglio or the Turkish Emperours Court* (London, 1650), p. 94.

[60] Özcan, *Anonim*, p. 47. [61] Selaniki, *Tarih*, II, p. 463. [62] Özcan, *Anonim*, p. 39.

[63] Mübahat S. Kütükoğlu, 'Lütfi Paşa Âsafnâmesi (Yeni Bir Metin Tesisi Denemesi)', in *Prof. Dr. Bekir Kütükoğlu'na Armağan* (Istanbul, 1991), pp. 68–9.

water conduits,[64] sultans toured their city accompanied by a special bodyguard, checking military establishments, social conditions, the implementation of fiscal measures or praying among the people in the mosques. While Mahmud II prayed[65] or, together with the grand admiral, inspected equipment at the dockyards,[66] and Ahmed I (1603–17) observed the army in Üsküdar,[67] Ahmed III checked the janissary barracks[68] or went to see if fiscal measures introduced in 1704 after currency changes and the punishment of counterfeiters were being carried out.[69] Selim III, constantly out and about, was usually much displeased by what he saw. The city was overcrowded and people were rioting over bread; there were too many lepers and beggars on the streets; sailors behaved disgracefully, and the brawling of the *softa*s was unacceptable.[70] Mahmud II was himself witness to the pressures caused by bread shortages during his tours of the city in disguise at the beginning of the following century.[71]

That the sultan, and indeed other officials such as the grand vezir,[72] wandered the city in disguise was known to the foreign diplomats and other westerners in the city, who found it most peculiar. 'It appears strange', wrote Charles Pertusier in the early nineteenth century, 'that the prime-minister of an empire, so vast, should demean himself by putting on a disguise, and going about with a view to finding out what is going on. Our astonishment will be more increased, when we learn that even the Sultan himself does this'.[73] Western curiosity amused Mehmed VI (Vahdeddin), who heartily enjoyed the account given by Lütfi Simavi of the interest of one foreign ambassador.

Every day there was a new rumour that the sultan was going around in disguise and inspecting the government officers incognito, and talking to the people in the markets and the coffee houses. On one occasion an ambassador during a conversation with me had even brought up the subject and wanted to know the truth about this. I did not give a direct answer but contented myself with saying that the sultan was very active. I learned afterwards that this ambassador took my words to

[64] Enver Ziya Karal, *Selim III'ün Hat-tı Hümayunları – Nizam-ı Cedit – 1789–1807* (Ankara, 1988), p. 95; Mehmet Ali Beyhan (ed.), *Saray Günlüğü (1802–1809)* (Istanbul, 2007), p. 23.

[65] Cabi, *Târihi*, I, p. 259. [66] Cabi, *Târihi*, I, p. 213.

[67] Safi, *Mustafa Sâfî'nin Zübdetü't-Tevârîh'i*, 2 vols., ed. İbrahim Hakkı Çuhadar (Ankara, 2003), I, pp. 162–3.

[68] Özcan, *Anonim*, p. 265. [69] Özcan, *Anonim*, pp. 283–4.

[70] Karal, *Hümayunları*, pp. 96–7, 105. [71] Cabi, *Târihi*, I, pp. 597–8, 604–5.

[72] Cabi, *Târihi*, I, p. 260.

[73] Charles Pertusier, *Picturesque Promenades in and Near Constantinople, and on the Waters of the Bosphorus* (London, 1820), pp. 128–9.

mean that it was true and told this to many other foreigners. I reported this to the sultan and we both laughed.[74]

The impact of the populace

Often presented as distant and shadowy figures immured in Topkapı palace, men whose individual significance paled as the centuries progressed, the sultans were also credited by western observers with possessing absolute and arbitrary power, a popular view still encountered in some depictions of the Ottoman ruler. For observers from the West in the fifteenth century, it was this characteristic that marked the Ottomans out as something different and 'oriental', as Niccolò Tignosi put it in his *Expugnatio costantinopolitana.*[75] For Machiavelli in *The Prince*, the arbitrary power of the Ottoman sultan contrasted with the negotiatory power of the French king, and formed a dividing line between the system of governance in the West and that in the East.[76]

Arbitrary power, and its corollary of cruelty and barbarity, coloured many of the western accounts of the Ottoman empire. For some, such depictions were applied to an individual sultan, such as Mehmed II, who was perceived by many as being especially cruel – perhaps a reaction to his particular success in shattering the world vision of Christendom and seizing Constantinople. The Genoese merchant Jacopo de Promontorio, who commented on the sultan's ability arbitrarily to put to death any of his officials or subjects,[77] related a story, repeated with some additions by the sixteenth-century historian Spandounes, demonstrating the true character of the ruler. In the story, Mehmed forbade anyone to touch a juicy young melon growing in the palace gardens. 'But one of the boys who followed him as personal servants, provoked by childish gluttony, picked it and ate it. The Emperor turned round and, not finding the melon or the culprit, was determined to find him by any means; so he had the stomachs of fourteen of the boys opened. It was the fourteenth who proved to have eaten the melon'.[78] Spandounes also related the fate of a *kadı* from Bursa, who, having been found to have taken bribes, was brought to Istanbul and skinned alive. His son replaced him, but was warned that should he commit any offence, he would suffer the same fate. 'The carpet on

[74] Simavi, *Gördüklerim*, facsimile p. 152.
[75] Tignosi, 'Expugnatio', p. 106.
[76] Niccolò Machiavelli, *Il Principe e Discorsi sopra la prima deca di Tito Livio, con introduzione di Giuliano Procacci*, ed. Sergio Bertelli (Milan, 1960), pp. 26–7.
[77] Jacopo de Promontorio, *Aufzeichnungen*, pp. 91–2.
[78] Spandounes, *Origin*, p. 53; Jacopo de Promontorio, *Aufzeichnungen*, p. 92.

which he sat in the court at Bursa was the pelt of his late father'.[79] These stories highlight the level of credulity about Mehmed in the West, and perhaps also the terror that he inspired.

Not surprisingly, reality was different and the Ottoman sultans were not able simply to steamroll over opposition any more than their counterparts in the West, nor to act with total disregard for ministers, military men or the population in general. Even Mehmed II was forced to backtrack on his taxation plans after his conquest of Istanbul, when the population revolted against them by leaving the city.[80] His son and successor, Bayezid II, a less forceful figure than his father, had to reverse many of Mehmed's fiscal policies, faced with implacable opposition from those elements of society which had suffered under them, in particular the *ulema* (the religious establishment). No sultan could rule in disregard of the population of Istanbul, and the reactions of the people in the streets had an impact on the ruler and his ministers even to the point of influencing the choice of ruler. When Mustafa I (1617–18, 1622–23) was brought to the throne in 1617, his mental incapacity gave cause for concern, and it was for this reason that his accession was opposed by the chief black eunuch, Mustafa Ağa, a figure of great influence during the reign of Mustafa's predecessor Ahmed I. His objection was overruled by the *şeyhülislam* Esad Efendi and *sadaret kaymakamı* (the official who represented the grand vezir in Istanbul when he was on campaign) Sofu Mehmed Paşa, who argued that the only alternative to Mustafa was the very young boy Osman, son of Ahmed I, whose accession at such a young age would provoke a reaction from the populace. If they did not place Mustafa on the throne it would be impossible, they said, to protect themselves from 'the tongue of the people'. Mustafa had been secluded in the palace, and it was hoped that once he had begun to have social contact his mental condition would improve and he would function normally.[81] The promised beneficial effects of social contact did not materialise. Instead, Mustafa's appearance in Eyüp for the accession ceremony made it clear that he was not normal. The people 'did not look favourably on him and understood that he was not in his right mind'.[82] His mental incapacity could not escape the notice of his vezirs, whose turbans he pulled off and whose beards he tugged when they came to consult him on matters of state, or of those who observed him throwing money to the birds and the fish as he took pleasure

[79] Spandounes, *Origin*, p. 54.

[80] Aşıkpaşazade, *Chronik*, *bab* 124, pp. 133–4; Neşri, *Čihannüma*, p. 181; Neşri, *Kitab-ı Cihan-nüma*, II, pp. 708–10; Tursun Bey, *History*, f. 53a–55b; Kate Fleet, 'Power and economy: early Ottoman economic practice', *Eurasian Studies*, 3/1 (2004), pp. 119–27.

[81] Peçevi, *Tarihi*, II, p. 452.

[82] Peçevi, *Tarihi*, II, p. 452; Naima, *Târih*, II, p. 438.

trips in his boat. 'This situation was seen by all the men of state and the people, and they understood that he was psychologically disturbed'. He was removed from the throne and replaced in 1618 by the boy Osman.[83] Despite his decided drawbacks as ruler, Mustafa was brought back onto the throne again in 1622, after the overthrow and murder of Osman II. People compared the two unfavourably,[84] 'the present emperor being a foole' in the estimation of the English ambassador Sir Thomas Roe.[85]

Popular reaction was also evident when it came to the Ottoman practice of fratricide, which appears to have begun in the reign of Murad I (1362–89) and which was justified as necessary for the stability of the state. As a result of the killing of Selim II's five 'innocent' sons on their father's death in 1574, 'God made the angels listen to the lamentations of the people of Istanbul and made the living people witness the meaning and heed the warning' of such slaughter.[86] Similar lamentation was heard twenty-one years later, after the strangling by Mehmed III of his nineteen brothers, 'innocent and sinless boys seized from their mothers' knees'.[87] John Sanderson, who saw the bodies pass by for burial, accompanied by seven vezirs 'in blacke, ould, bacest vestures', wrote in a letter that they were to be pitied 'beinge inosents [i.e. infants], though Turks'.[88] The strangling of these innocent victims[89] was a 'terrible deed [which] left no one without pain' or feeling compassion.[90]

Although the impact of public lamentation may not in the case of fratricide actually have caused the abandonment of the practice, this being more related to the policy of keeping the male heirs in the palace and to the decline in the number of males available, public lamentation could have an effect. When, in 1614, Cossacks sacked the castle of Sinop, it was the grief of those who had fled to Istanbul and whose 'weeping and lamenting reached the heavens' which alerted Ahmed I, not his grand vezir and son-in-law Nasuh Paşa, who denied that any such disaster had occurred. The *şeyhülislam*, however, confirmed it. To have lied to the sultan was not a wise move, and executioners were duly dispatched to Nasuh Paşa's palace. They arrived when Ahmed was there talking to the *paşa*. The sultan withdrew to the window, the minister was killed and his

[83] Peçevi, *Tarihi*, II, pp. 452–3. [84] Naima, *Târih*, II, p. 496.
[85] Sir Thomas Roe, *The Negotiations of Sir Thomas Roe in his Embassy to the Ottoman Porte from the Year 1621 to 1628 Inclusive (Containing …)* (London, 1740), p. 150.
[86] Selaniki, *Tarih*, I, p. 102. [87] Peçevi, *Tarihi*, II, p. 361.
[88] John Sanderson, *The Travels of John Sanderson in the Levant 1584–1602*, ed. Sir William Foster (London, 1931), p. 141.
[89] Naima, *Târih*, I, p. 79. [90] Selaniki, *Tarih*, II, p. 436.

body buried on the order of the sultan next to İbrahim Paşa, the grand vezir of Süleyman I, who had suffered a similar fate.[91]

Influenced by public lamentation, the sultans were also forced to take into account the corrosive current of rumour which flowed through the city like blood through veins. The power of rumour could affect the markets, as plans for a campaign sent speculators hurrying to stockpile in anticipation of price rises.[92] It frightened the sultans and the grand vezirs alike, with one grand vezir, Alemdar Mustafa Paşa, acknowledging at the beginning of the nineteenth century the anxiety caused him by the report of a janissary plot against him. The provider of this rumour was imprisoned and, once the rumour had proved unfounded, killed, Alemdar Mustafa Paşa commenting, 'just think what kind of seditious words he might produce for the people of Istanbul'.[93] Alemdar Mustafa Paşa responded firmly to scurrilous coffee house conversation,[94] and it led Mahmud II to ban people coming together to gossip in the mosques as if they were coffee houses.[95]

Mosques – not merely places for prayers but also for seditious rumour[96]– coffee houses, barbers' shops and wine houses were hives of gossip and rumour about state affairs and the performance of officials.[97] While Selaniki might regard the gossipers in the coffee houses in the late sixteenth century as idle and worthless people whose lies and calumnies knew no end and no limits, the impact of rumour could not be underestimated, and he himself acknowledged that on occasion some of what was said was true.[98]

For Selaniki, the prevalence of rumour was the responsibility of the ministers who failed to prevent it, something which he remarked would never have happened in an earlier age.[99] This was the case, for example, with those rumours which began to circulate in January 1595 about Murad III's health. According to Selaniki's account, those who were 'clear-headed and intelligent among the population' advised that in the current climate of difficulty and instability, and in order to protect the honour of religion and the state, people should not gossip in this way. The sultan was in fact seriously ill, but this was not revealed by the officials. The doctors announced that the sultan's bladder condition had worsened due to the coldness of the weather, but that the medicine they were giving him was having an effect, which it was not. The mother of

[91] Peçevi, *Tarihi*, II, p. 443.
[92] Selaniki, *Tarih*, II, p. 670. [93] Cabi, *Târihi*, I, pp. 186–7, quotation p. 187.
[94] Cabi, *Târihi*, I, pp. 223–4. [95] Cabi, *Târihi*, I, p. 252. [96] Cabi, *Târihi*, I, p. 257.
[97] Cabi, *Târihi*, I, pp. 174, 178–9, 214, 220, 221, 223–4, 224–5, 229.
[98] Selaniki, *Tarih*, II, pp. 707–8. [99] Selaniki, *Tarih*, I, p. 421.

Mehmed, who was very soon to become Mehmed III, summoned her son from Manisa and the pretence that the sultan was not seriously ill was continued, his death being concealed even from the vezirs.[100]

Rumour could either simmer or explode into a mass reaction. It could force the *şeyhülislam* into upholding the complaints of mosque-goers, fired up by members of the *ulema*, that the sultan was not going on campaign and so allowing Muslim women to be enslaved by infidels, and backing the popular reaction demanding that soldiers be sent to support the fighters of Islam on the frontiers, to whom money, food and munitions should be sent.[101] It could compel the sultan to respond, justifying his military decisions and his diplomacy. Mehmed III was forced to reply to complaints circulating among the janissaries and the coffee house-goers about his failure to attack Pec, a campaign they argued that all supported and were willing to participate in. Mehmed countered this criticism, announcing that he was intending to launch an offensive against Pec, but recalled the unworthy behaviour of his troops in the last campaign when they had fled. Expressing his hopes that God would help him as he had before, his message contained a veiled concern about a repetition of such behaviour.[102] Even Süleyman I was not immune from public rebuke, when he came in for angry criticism about the amount of money he had lavished on hosting Alkas Mirza, the brother of the Safavid ruler of Iran, Shah Tahmasp. The populace, annoyed that Alkas Mirza, a non-Sunni who was there simply to save his own head, having fled after intriguing against the shah, was distinctly unhappy to have the Persians, blasphemous deniers of the true belief, among them. The sultan's response was to claim that he had done what was necessary for the honour of the state, concluding that 'If he [Alkas Mirza] betrays us, then it will be in the hands of God'.[103]

Even at a much more personal level, sultans were the object of gossip to which they needed to be seen to respond. Persistent rumours that Rüstem Paşa, who was to marry Mihrimah Sultan, the daughter of Süleyman I, had leprosy resulted in a doctor being summoned to check him for lice, it being believed that lice were not found on lepers. Declared to have lice, Rüstem Paşa was permitted to marry.[104]

While the population gossiped incessantly and about everything, 'saying whatever fell onto their tongues, lies and calumnies for their own benefit', in the words of an eighteenth-century anonymous historian,[105] the palace collected reports on what the people were chattering about. The

[100] Selaniki, *Tarih*, I, pp. 425–6, quotation p. 425.
[101] Selaniki, *Tarih*, II, p. 525. [102] Selaniki, *Tarih*, II, pp. 707–8.
[103] Peçevi, *Tarihi*, I, p. 146. [104] Peçevi, *Tarihi*, I, p. 20. [105] Özcan, *Anonim*, p. 111.

sultans themselves were in a position to pick up information on their trips round the city in disguise. High-up officials, too, used disguise to collect information, though not always successfully, the *kaymakam* Rüştü Paşa being recognised when busy collecting information in disguise in a coffee house in 1813 and his questions being answered accordingly.[106] Spies were employed to pass on information on conversations in popular venues such as coffee shops, *hamams* and barbers' shops. In 1808, a barber's shop in Beyazıt was closed as a result of the report made by a state official in disguise on its clientele's discussions of state affairs.[107] The report of a female spy in the Sultan Bayezid *hamam* on the conversation of women there who were talking about state affairs led to the arrest and imprisonment of the women involved.[108] In the reign of Abdülhamid II, spying produced an enormous quantity of information, all collected and recorded in the voluminous spy reports kept in the Yıldız palace, as people reported on their neighbours and fed pernicious rumours to the palace.[109] Mischief makers could whisper into the ears of high officials of state and so destroy the object of their gossip. One feeble-minded old man was seized and imprisoned at the end of the sixteenth century after he had fallen into the company of scoundrels and heretics with bad beliefs and bad characters, denizens of the coffee house, and about whom such mischief makers reported. Accused of claiming to be a mahdi, he was eventually hanged, his fate sealed in the coffee houses of Istanbul where 'he fell onto the tongue of strangers… tongues wagged and the story circulated'.[110]

It is possible that the palace itself indulged in reverse or counter-rumour. In a letter dated July 1622 to Mr Secretary Calvert, Sir Thomas Roe wrote, 'Wee have now bene 14 daies in a calme… I know not to whatt to impute the late quietness, whether to their ramazan or lent now beeing; or to the policy of some, who have spread abroad prophecies, that the 15th of this moneth, if any motion, the streets should runne with bloud'.[111] Silence was not always a good sign. In September 1623 Roe reported that all seemed calm and quiet, but continued, 'the most disordered assume a face of obedience, (which I once thought banished this citty) and choose rather submission to lawers, then threatened destruction; the calme is as violent as the storme: the first actions showe peace; butt so, as to prepare for necessity of warre'.[112] Roe was not apparently the only ambassador to be aware of the significance of silence:

[106] Cabi, *Târihi*, II, p. 947. [107] Cabi, *Târihi*, I, p. 224. [108] Cabi, *Târihi*, I, p. 392.
[109] Asaf Tugay, *İbret. Abdülhamid'e Verilen Jurnaller ve Jurnalciler. Jurnalcilerin Tam Listesi* (Istanbul, n.d.).
[110] Selaniki, *Tarih*, II, pp. 703–4. [111] Roe, *Negotiations*, p. 64.
[112] Roe, *Negotiations*, p. 179.

It is told that in the time of the janissaries when the ambassadors wrote their reports for their own states on events in Istanbul, the report of the Swedish ambassador was always correct. When the other ambassadors pressured him asking 'where do you get the correct information from?', he said 'my information is not based on rumour but is perhaps the result of thought and perception. The key to this is to think of the position in the Ottoman empire as if it were in Europe and then reverse it. For example, if you see the janissaries muttering and grumbling in the coffee houses, you report to your countries "in comparison to the European situation, Istanbul is on the point of revolution". But I, turning things upside down, write "there is security and order in Istanbul" and this turns out to be true, because by grumbling, the janissaries get things off their chests and they do not attempt to revolt. And when you see the janissaries reticent and silent you report that "now there are signs of ease and order in Istanbul" but I, however, on the contrary, come to the conclusion that this silence is the sign of revolution, and that the janissaries will continue in such silence for a while until they reach exploding point and then will suddenly attempt revolt and revolution'.[113]

By no means all-powerful, or the absolute ruler of Machiavelli, the Ottoman sultan was constrained to shape policy with the reaction of the people of the city in mind. Popular reaction had consequences – even to the extent of open revolt in the case of the Edirne incident, or again in 1730 when the lack of interest displayed by the sultan and his ministers[114] was reflected in the behaviour of the *kaymakam*, who, unconcerned about the conditions in the city, spent his time planting tulips, according to popular perception.[115] Sultans had thus to consider, respond to, appease or, on occasion, according to Selim III, frighten the people[116] in order to ensure an equilibrium of power in Istanbul. One way in which they maintained this balance was through pageantry.

Pageantry

That feasting and festivity were essential to maintain order in the city and that the population had to be allowed enjoyment was realised by Selim II, who regarded making the people of the city joyful an essential element of successful rule and one that his ancestors had also followed. In this he was supported by his secretary Feridun Bey, who is credited by Selaniki with having pointed out to the grand vezir that 'by nature people cannot bear constant repression, they sometimes want release'.[117]

[113] Ahmed Cevdet Paşa, *Ma'rûzât*, p. 57. [114] Abdi, *Tarihi*, p. 26; Destari, *Tarihi*, pp. 7–8.
[115] Abdi, *Tarihi*, p. 29. [116] Karal, *Hümayunları*, p. 97. [117] Selaniki, *Tarih*, I, pp. 61–2.

As Feridun Bey had realised, people's lives and levels of enjoyment were greatly enhanced by festivities and celebrations. Imperial pageantry coloured the city, whether for the birth of royal children, such as the twin sons of Ahmed II in 1692/93,[118] İbrahim's (1640–48) son Mehmed IV, whose birth was particularly well received in 1642 and was followed by three days and nights of celebration,[119] or Osman II (1618–22), for whom there were seven;[120] the marriages of the sultans' daughters or the circumcisions of their sons; military departures and arrivals; or religious festivities at the end of the holy month of Ramazan, the birth of the Prophet or the holy nights of Regaip and Berat, when the city was illuminated by lanterns and lamps strung out between the minarets.[121]

The city rang to a constant barrage of noise. Cannon were constantly going off, either for a royal birth, a circumcision or an accession. Ships saluted as they passed Topkapı palace, and cannon were fired for victories of one sort or another, or for Ramazan. Ahmed III ordered that they be fired three times a day for the birth of his first child, Fatma Sultan in 1704,[122] and three days of cannon firing followed the birth of Abdülhamid I's son, Mahmud II.[123] The birth of Prince Mehmed, son of Sultan Mustafa III, was similarly greeted with cannon, which were fired all over the empire on the sultan's orders.[124] Abdülmecid (1839–61) ordered cannon to be fired for his accession in 1839,[125] and cannon roared from the imperial arsenal for the accession of Selim II in 1566.[126] When Murad III went to Eyüp for his accession, cannon were fired on all sides.[127] The imperial fleet contributed to this endless stream of explosions, saluting as they sailed past Topkapı palace or performing for the sultan. Sultans such as Mustafa III watched the departure of the imperial navy for the Black Sea, cannon blazing, from Yalı Köşkü,[128] or enjoyed a cannon display, as Mahmud II did when the navy performed for him off Beşiktaş.[129] The dramatic booming of cannon and crash of guns, designed to terrify the enemy as Kılıç Ali Paşa's fleet left Beşiktaş in 1572, was such that 'the eyes and ears of the heavens became blind and deaf'.[130]

118 Özcan, *Anonim*, p. 44. 119 Naima, *Târih*, III, p. 953.
120 Naima, *Târih*, I, p. 289. 121 Selaniki, *Tarih*, I, pp. 197–8.
122 Özcan, *Anonim*, p. 289. 123 Taylesanizade, *Tarihi*, p. 82.
124 Çeşmizade Mustafa Reşîd, *Çeşmî-zâde Tarihi*, ed. Bekir Kütükoğlu (Istanbul, 1959), pp. 11–12.
125 Ahmet Refik, *Hicri On Üçüncü Asırda İstanbul Hayatı (1200–1255)* (Istanbul, 1932), p. 33, *hüküm* 23.
126 Selaniki, *Tarih*, I, p. 42. 127 Gerlach, *Günlüğü*, I, p. 165.
128 Çeşmizade, *Tarihi*, p. 82. 129 Cabi, *Târihi*, I, pp. 202–3.
130 Selaniki, *Tarih*, I, p. 86.

Such displays were not always for mere amusement, or attempts at terrorising, for some had a more practical aspect related to naval training: to fire cannon was one thing, to hit the desired target was another. Selim III watched one such exercise as, the area having been cleared of any boats and the imperial ships dispatched to the safety of Beşiktaş, two corvets set out from the imperial dockyards and fired on a ship anchored for that purpose in the waters before the palace. Simultaneously cannon were fired from Tophane and the ship satisfactorily sunk.[131]

Not all the results of cannon salvos were as pleasing. When two galleys returning from Egypt in 1595 fired their cannon, the windows of the pavilion where Murad III was sitting broke, showering glass over the *divan* and the sultan. Such a thing had never happened before, according to the historian Naima, even though the huge galleys had regularly fired their cannon, causing the ground to vibrate as if in an earthquake. Agitated, the sultan interpreted this as a bad omen, foretelling that this would be the last time he would come to the pavilion.[132] Aware of the possible negative effects of cannon fire, Mustafa III ordered there to be none until his heavily pregnant concubine had given birth, fearing that violent explosions might produce a miscarriage. No ship, merchant or naval, coming from the Black Sea on its way to the Mediterranean was to salute before Topkapı.[133] Mahmud II showed similar concern for his pregnant concubine in 1812, when he forbade a ship on its way to Tunisia from firing its cannon in front of Beşiktaş palace.[134]

Apart from a constant booming of cannon, the city resounded to the banging and whooshing of fireworks, which frequently lit up the skies and which were set off for births, circumcisions, marriages or just general celebrations.[135] The sound of the fireworks let off in 1530 for the circumcision celebrations of Mehmed, Mustafa and Selim, the sons of Süleyman I, were heard everywhere.[136] Fireworks shot into the air from rafts in the sea off Topkapı on which firework castles had been made, and from many other nearby parts of the city for the circumcision of the sons of Mehmed III in 1597.[137] Ahmed III watched from Aynalı Kavak Kasrı the fireworks set off from rafts for his three sons, part of the fifteen days of celebrations organised for their circumcision, the fourteenth day of which included a

[131] Cabi, *Târihi*, I, p. 99.

[132] Naima, *Târih*, I, p. 78; Peçevi, *Tarihi*, II, pp. 359–60; Gelibolulu Mustafa Ali, *Gelibolulu Mustafa Âlî ve Künhü'l-Ahbâr'ında II. Selim, III. Murat ve III. Mehmet Devirleri*, 3 vols., ed. Faris Çerçi (Kayseri, 2000), III, p. 626.

[133] Ahmet Refik, *Hicri On İkinci Asırda İstanbul Hayatı (1100–1200)* (Istanbul, 1930), p. 193, *hüküm* 233.

[134] Cabi, *Târihi*, II, p. 844.

[135] Selaniki, *Tarih*, II, p. 702.

[136] Peçevi, *Tarihi*, I, pp. 84–5.

[137] Selaniki, *Tarih*, II, p. 692.

magnificent firework display both from sea and land in Ok Meydanı.[138] Weddings were also marked with fireworks, those for the eldest daughter of Ahmed I in June 1615 lasting many days before and after the marriage, both day and night, in Topkapı and in the house of the groom. For three nights, firework castles were set alight on boats anchored in the sea off Topkapı and an infinity of rockets was fired into the air.[139] Both the night before the wedding of the princess to the governor of Rumeli in July 1575 and the night after were illuminated by fireworks.[140]

Fireworks had to please. The official in charge of firework displays was sacked in 1784/85 because the people of the palace were not satisfied with those on the rafts off Beşiktaş palace to mark the birth of Mahmud II. The following week, rafts were brought to Tophane and a new display laid on. This one was very much liked and the person in charge was promoted.[141]

It was not just fireworks that enlivened the everyday lives of the city's inhabitants, for the city was a carnival of spectacle for their entertainment. They went to see the elephant which the Persian ambassador had given to Selim III – a great success also in Edirne, where the animal was sent next.[142] They could also amuse themselves observing the experiment with a balloon made by the English convert Selim Ağa at the beginning of the nineteenth century.[143] They looked on in amazement at the more than 360 *nahıl* (a decoration, made in particular for imperial weddings and circumcisions, in the shape of a tree), decorated with flowers, candles and tulle, used in the circumcision ceremony of Murad III's son Mehmed, the 100 lions 100 lion cubs made out of sugar, the 100 tigers and tiger cubs, 100 large elephants and 100 baby elephants, 100 horses, 100 mules and 100 camels, all swimming in sugar. After them came 100 each of peregrine falcons, vultures, royal falcons, partridges, peacocks, cockerels, ducks and geese. People watched them as they passed, gazing at the colours, and it was as if beautiful flowers had opened.[144]

The state put a great deal of time and money into choreographing spectacle and into providing the populace of the city with dramatic entertainment. That for the birth of İbrahim's son Ahmed involved three nights of continuous festivity, during which the shores of the

[138] Seyid Vehbi, *Sûrnâme (Üçüncü Ahmed'in Oğullarının Sünnet Düğünü)*, ed. Reşad Ekrem Koçu (Istanbul, 1939), pp. 21, 23–4, 36. See also Levni's miniatures on the event, Esin Atıl (ed.), *Levni ve Surname: Bir Osmanlı Şenliğinin Öyküsü* (Istanbul, 1999).

[139] Crescenzio Dei Crescenzi, 'Letter di Costantinopoli del 1615. A un amico', in Michele Giustiniani, *Lettere memorabilia dell'Abbate Michele Giustiniani, Patrizio Genovese de' Sig.ri di Scio. Parte II* (Rome, 1699), no. XVII, p. 72.

[140] Gerlach, *Günlüğü*, I, p. 201. [141] Taylesanizade, *Tarihi*, p. 90.

[142] Cabi, *Târihi*, I, p. 52. [143] Cabi, *Târihi*, I, p. 59.

[144] Gelibolulu Mustafa Ali, *Câmi'u'l-Buhûr Der Mecâlis-i Sûr*, ed. Ali Öztekin (Ankara, 1996), p. 105.

Bosphorus were illuminated and the boats at the jetties lit up with candles and lanterns. People packed into boats, stretching from Tersane to Üsküdar, watched pyrotechnic displays and looked on, dazzled by the illuminations.[145] Conjurers performed on rafts at sea during the four days of celebrations for the birth of Hatice Sultan, daughter of Mustafa III in 1768, each day's raft being the responsibility of one particular official – the head of the dockyards, the commander of the artillery, the commander of the armoury regiment and the head of the customs.[146] The twenty days of festivities for the circumcision of Mehmed, Mustafa and Selim, sons of Süleyman I, involved many entertainments in different parts of the city, ending on the last day with great entertainments in Kağıthane, horse races, archery competitions, acrobats, wrestlers and firework displays.[147] Those laid on for the celebrations for the circumcision of the three sons of Ahmed III included wrestling, gypsies dancing and wrestling with bears, acrobats, conjurers, tightrope walkers, competitions such as climbing up a pole at the top of which was a silver jug, puppeteers, dancers and, at night, shadow plays (*Karagöz* and *Hacivad*), all watched by hundreds of thousands of people in Ok Meydanı. Musicians and dancers performed on rafts illuminated with lanterns, floating in front of the Tersane Kasrı. On the fourteenth day of the celebrations there was a major display staged on the water and watched by Ahmed III from Aynalı Kavak Kasrı. The boats of those who came to see it were so numerous that they covered the water and their oars could not move, according to the contemporary description of the event given by Seyid Vehbi, for whom the boats were so full that it was like judgement day. The foreign ambassadors were invited to these celebrations on different days – the French and Russian on one day, the Dutch and Austrian, the Venetian, and the ambassador from Dubrovnik on others. They brought gifts and were given feasts presented on silver and golden plates and set out in a European style.[148]

The very costly[149] celebrations in 1582 for the circumcision of Mehmed, the eldest son of Murad III who was to become Mehmed III, went on for a staggering sixty days, during which time the city was lit up every night with hundreds of torches and thousands of lanterns.[150] Before his circumcision, Mehmed processed on horseback through the streets, accompanied by a retinue and musicians playing drums and

[145] Topçular Katibi, *Tarihi*, II, p. 1169.
[146] Çeşmizade, *Tarihi*, pp. 93–4. [147] Peçevi, *Tarihi*, I, pp. 84–5.
[148] Seyid Vehbi, *Sûrnâme*, pp. 17, 19, 21, 23–4, 29, 32, 34–6.
[149] Selaniki, *Tarih*, I, p. 133. [150] Gelibolulu Mustafa Ali, *Sûr*, p. 225.

horns and making a great deal of noise.[151] He was dressed very magnificently. Over a garment of white silk he wore a red-coloured satin garment ornamented with rubies and diamonds. He was girded with a dagger and a sword.[152] This display was designed to incorporate the populace:

> With this music and noisy crowds, this shah of the world
> Made an excursion in Istanbul like the sun
> He showed his beautiful countenance to all the people of
> Istanbul
> He took their blessing and greeted them.[153]

This enormous event was not without problems, and the crowds were so great that it was impossible to control them. A special unit of five hundred men, all dressed in kaftans of Moroccan leather and carrying oil-filled skin bags, whose job was to control the crowds and clear the routes, was used to drench them with linseed oil to keep order.[154] One of the attractions was two male elephants, one little and one big, and one giraffe, which were displayed at At Meydanı. At one point the large elephant suddenly broke loose. In a state of excitement, with his eyes ablaze, he expelled water from his trunk over those watching, who fled as if from a great, noisy shower of rain.[155] Fear of potential trouble led Ahmed III to restrict the celebrations for the birth of his first child, his daughter Fatma Sultan, in 1704, to the daytime only.[156] Those for the daughter of Mahmud II, Ayşe Sultan, in 1809, were also cut short, after the sultan, during a tour in disguise, observed women watching the fireworks from boats on the Bosphorus, from the shores and even from in front of Maçka Sarayı above Beşiktaş. Although the celebrations were planned to continue for several days more, Mahmud cancelled them, fearing that there might be trouble if so many women continued to go out and about at night.[157]

The city was awash with pageantry. Parades and processions wound through the streets, impressing and overawing with their displays of wealth and power. The sultans not only appeared regularly, but did so in style. Selim II, on his way to the Friday mosque at the beginning of January 1574, wore a sword of solid gold, ornamented lavishly with jewels. His feet, encased in jewel-studded shoes, sat in gold, bejewelled stirrups

[151] Gelibolulu Mustafa Ali, *Sûr*, pp. 121–4. [152] Gelibolulu Mustafa Ali, *Sûr*, pp. 118–21.
[153] Gelibolulu Mustafa Ali, *Sûr*, p. 124.
[154] Gelibolulu Mustafa Ali, *Sûr*, pp. 194–6; Gelibolulu Mustafa Ali, *Künhü'l-Ahbâr*, III, p. 395.
[155] Gelibolulu Mustafa Ali, *Sûr*, pp. 211–12. [156] Özcan, *Anonim*, p. 289.
[157] Cabi, *Târihi*, I, pp. 515–16.

and his knee guards were gilded with gold. Wearing a garment embroidered with gold thread and a white turban, he rode a horse whose harnesses and trappings, too, were decorated with gold and precious stones. In front of him were the janissaries with their tall, plumed headgear, the janissary *ağa* on a very beautiful horse, and behind them officials of the palace. Directly behind the sultan came two boys on horseback, both with long plaited hair hanging down below their ears, carrying bows and decorated quivers full of arrows, and behind them were the chief secretary and the chief eunuch, and other officials on donkeys who distributed money to the people. One person walking in front of the procession carried a bag made of red velvet, inside which was the Qu'ran.[158]

The procession to Friday prayer resembled that for the accession of a new sultan, except that for that occasion there were many more horsemen accompanying him and everything was more spectacular, according to Gerlach.[159] For the accession, sultans went to Eyüp, where they visited the tomb of Eyüb el Ensari, the companion of the Prophet who was martyred at the Arab siege of Constantinople in 674. Some sultans went there by boat up the Golden Horn (Haliç) and then returned on horseback, passing back into the city through the Edirne Kapı accompanied by a large retinue, as Süleyman II did in 1687.[160] Both Murad III[161] and Mehmed III went by sea and came back by land, while their retinues went by land.[162] Some, like Osman II, went by land and returned by sea, and others, like Mahmud I, went there and back by land.[163] Accompanied by great retinues, the sultans were watched by enormous crowds. When Murad III passed through the streets of the city on his way back from Eyüp, he was accompanied by two thousand people. A man of medium height, brown-bearded and with a nose that resembled the beak of a falcon, according to Gerlach, he wore a garment made of silk worked with gold thread. The Habsburg ambassador decorated the door of the embassy building with carpets and sat in front of it in a beautiful chair, his servants standing by him dressed in clothes of Damascus cloth. When the sultan passed the door they presented their respects to him.[164]

While sultans had for centuries ridden to or from Eyüp, Mahmud I returning mounted on a horse 'as swift as the wind',[165] Sultan Mehmed V

158 Gerlach, *Günlüğü*, I, p. 115. 159 Gerlach, *Günlüğü*, I, p. 165.
160 Defterdar Sarı Mehmed Paşa, *Zübde*, p. 822; İsazade, *Târîhi*, p. 207.
161 Selaniki, *Tarih*, I, pp. 105–6. 162 Selaniki, *Tarih*, II, p. 455.
163 Abdi, *Tarihi*, p. 45; Peçevi, *Tarihi*, II, p. 452; Destari, *Tarihi*, p. 22.
164 Gerlach, *Günlüğü*, I, p. 165.
165 Abdi, *Tarihi*, p. 45. Interestingly, although Abdi refers to the sword, Destari Salih, who gives an account of the same event, refers to Mahmud I being girded with 'tir ve tirkeş', arrows and quiver; Destari, *Tarihi*, pp. 22–4.

(Reşad) (1909–18) did not adopt this custom, but, being old and fat, went there by ferry, the Söğütlü ferry, and came back by carriage. The return by land was unfortunate, according to Simavi. A sea return, he argued, would have been better, for it would have avoided the narrow streets between ugly crumbling wooden houses through which the carriage passed.[166] This said, however, the use of carriages instead of horses for public ceremonies was in general a good thing, for 'it was indeed very ridiculous to see the odd behaviour of the grand vezirs and the *şeyhülislams* who had never mounted a horse and who had never held reins in their hands' and to be treated to an unwanted glimpse of their white undergarments as they struggled unskilfully with their mounts.[167] The last girding of an Ottoman sultan was on 13 September 1918, when Mehmed VI (Vahdeddin) travelled to Eyüp in the imperial boat for the ceremony.[168]

Sometimes the sultans appeared for more prosaic reasons, such as rabbit hunting. The prospect of catching a glimpse of the sultan even on these occasions greatly excited westerners, and the convert and high Ottoman official Adam Neuser's offer to take Heberer, an ex-Ottoman galley slave, and his companions to watch Murad III on a hunting expedition in 1588 was snapped up with great pleasure. He took them to Has Bahçe, an imperial garden by the sea, from where, shortly afterwards, they saw the sultan on a magnificent imperial boat, which was red and decorated with gold leaf. The oarsmen were wearing snow-white clothes and red conical hats. Passing through Has Bahçe, the sultan and his retinue rode off into the mountains, Heberer and his companions in hot pursuit. They were rewarded with a clear view of the royal personage. The sultan was preceded by the janissary *ağa*, dressed in garments embroidered with silver and gold thread and made up of flowery cloth, and wearing a beautiful, large white plume. He was mounted on a very magnificent horse, whose saddle was gilded with gold and decorated with precious stones. Behind him came about a hundred janissaries, who were in turn followed by three high officials, looking very magnificent in their turbans and garments with silver thread. Their horses had covers of beautiful cloths and their saddles and harnesses were gilded with gold and decorated with precious stones. Behind came the sultan, wearing a garment made of golden thread and riding an incredibly beautiful horse. The saddle and harness of the horse were so precious that their value was incalculable. The plume on his turban resembled the feathers of a black swallow and was surrounded with precious stones, among which was a

[166] Simavi, *Gördüklerim*, facsimile pp. 19–20.
[167] Simavi, *Gördüklerim*, facsimile p. 20, fn.1.
[168] Simavi, *Gördüklerim*, facsimile pp. 153–4.

diamond that had been bought for sixty thousand ducats. At fifty paces from the sultan there were forty servants guarding him. These servants opened the way for him, shouting, 'Make way, make way', and prevented the people from approaching nearer than fifty or sixty paces to him. Behind the sultan there were about sixty archers, who acted as bodyguards. In one hand they held a bow and in the other an arrow, and on their backs they had quivers with very swift arrows. They were followed by other riders, some of whom carried cushions on the back of their saddles, on which sat animals which resembled tigers, or they had hawks, falcons or other wild birds. Dogs walked beside them, their colours very beautiful, but whose height, Heberer noted, was shorter than the hunting dogs in his own country. As the sultan passed Heberer and his companions, they took off their hats as a mark of respect. Realising they were foreigners, the sultan sent someone to ask who they were. Replying that they were German aristocrats, they sent a message to the sultan that they were happy to see him in good health. In response, the sultan greeted them graciously, and went on.[169]

Of somewhat more significance in the political sphere was the sultan's part in military pageantry (although hunting expeditions, particularly those of Ahmed I, were presented almost as departures on campaign[170]), when the might of the Ottoman realm and the awesome power of its military resources were displayed. Any departure on campaign or triumphant return from victorious battle was heralded with great pomp, or, as John Sanderson put it in a letter of 1597, 'triumphant pompe unspeakable'.[171] For Bartolomeus Georgievitz, captured at the battle of Mohács in 1526, there was nothing to compare to the splendours of victory celebrations:

> I verily believe, and do confess, for those dayes he celebrates for Victory, no Mortal Eye, (nay, not the Moon or Sun) did ere behold a spectacle more glorious and resplendent, for order, number, silence, richness, state, and magnificence in all kindes. It is impossible for onely man to be exalted to a loftier degree of sublimation, then this Pagan when trimphful.[172]

The entry of Mustafa II into the city from Edirne in 1695 occasioned many festivities. He was met at Davut Paşa by a great retinue and escorted from there to Topkapı palace. On his way, young and old received him and the craftsmen and traders spread out cloth before him. The praying for God to bless him and the greetings of the people were of such

169 Michael Heberer, *Osmanlıda Bir Köle. Brettenli Michael Heberer'in Anıları 1585–1588*, trans. Türkis Noyan (Istanbul, 2003), pp. 283–5.

170 See, for example, Safi, *Tevârîh.*

171 Sanderson, *Travels*, p. 166.

172 Bartholomeus Georgievitz, *The Rarities of Turkey Gathered by One that was Sold Seven Times as Slave in the Turkish Empire…* (London, 1661), p. 46.

4. Victory procession, in Schweigger, *Ein newe Reyssbeschreibung*, between pp. 176 and 177.

magnitude that the sultan was almost reduced to tears. The shops were crowded with people watching. When the procession reached the gate of Topkapı, animals were slaughtered and cannon were fired off simultaneously from the dockyards, arsenal, Saray Burnu and galleys. The noise was so great that the sky and the earth trembled.[173]

The magnificence of the preparations for Murad IV's departure for Baghdad was so great that it was, in Peçevi's words, difficult to relate.[174] This departure involved the entire city's population, either as part of the enormous processions involved in sending off the army or as spectators, watching, cheering and praying for success. Teachers and pupils prayed, merchants rolled out their best cloths under the hooves of the sultan's horse, and crowds of women watched. The crush was such that many fell under the feet of the crowds and were trampled to death, their bodies reduced to dust by the mass of spectators.[175] Similar scenes greeted the army's return.

Sanderson's account, although perhaps displaying a certain English idiosyncrasy, shows the enormous pageantry of the departure of the Ottoman ruler on campaign at the end of the sixteenth century.

[173] Özcan, *Anonim*, p. 117. [174] Peçevi, *Tarihi*, II, p. 494.
[175] Topçular Katibi, *Tarihi*, II, pp. 1071–2.

> When the Great Turke went out of the citie towards the warrs it was with wounderfull great solemnitie and noteable order, to[o] longe to describe particu[l]erlie. But I remember a great number of dogs ledd after him, well manned and in thier best aparrell; his haukes by horsmen carried in great number; tame lions and olifants, with other beasts of many sorts; but espetially the jarraff before spoken of, beinge prince of all the beasts, was ledd by three chaines of three sundry men stalkinge before him. For it is the custome that, the Great Turke in person goinge one warefare, most or all in generall the cheefe men and beasts attend him out of the cities. And at his retorne it is laweful for all thier women, both smaule and great, to mete him without the waules; at other tim[e]s the women of any accompt or credit never come in multitudes emongest the men.[176]

Any military departure, not merely that led by the sultan, required pomp and pageantry, both on land and at sea. Sultans appeared to send their armies and navies off to war, as Ahmed III did when he crossed to Üsküdar to watch the army leave for Iran. There the soldiers lined up in great order, and behind them the people who had come to see the sultan, lined up in their turn.[177] The armies were, of course, magnificent. The commander-in-chief İbrahim Paşa left for Hungary in 1599, with an army composed of soldiers magnificently dressed, equipped with shields ornamented with gold, golden-coloured spears and elegant quivers, and with the strongest of horses ornamented with plumes. The soldiers were hardy, valiant and as brave as lions, able to break through the enemy ranks and so strong as to be capable of wrestling lions to the ground. The imperial army was embellished and adorned in every way, its soldiers were the bravest and most valiant, and its grandeur and majesty was so great that it made the enemy jealous. All prayed so hard for this wondrous army that the prayers 'reached the court of heaven'.[178]

People came not just to see, and pray for, the lion-hearted troops, but also to watch the departure of the fleet and the launching of new ships. Many people, including the Italian traveller Giovanni Francesco Gemelli Careri, in Istanbul at the end of the seventeenth century, went to look at the fleet about to set out via the Black Sea to the Danube. Careri's curiosity aroused suspicions that he was a spy, but 'finding I was no Venetian, but went out of meer curiosity to see the galliots, and hulls of galleasses, with a great number of people', the authorities released him.[179]

176 Sanderson, *Travels*, pp. 59–60. Peçevi referred to Mehmed III setting off from Istanbul on campaign in 1595 in the same way as his predecessors had; Peçevi, *Tarihi*, II, p. 373.

177 Destari, *Tarihi*, pp. 5–6.

178 Selaniki, *Tarih*, II, pp. 806–7.

179 Giovanni Francesco Careri, 'A voyage round the world by Dr John Francis Gemelle Careri in six parts. Part I containing the most remarkable things he saw in Turkey', in John Churchill (ed.), *A Collection of Voyages and Travels Some now First Printed from Original Manuscripts Others now First Published in English in Six Volumes* (London, 1732), IV, p. 86.

5. Wedding procession, in Schweigger, *Ein newe Reyssbeschreibung*, between pp. 206 and 207.

When, in 1596, the magnificent and beautifully decorated flagship built for the vezir Halil Paşa was launched, the *divan* did not take place; instead, all the high officials, as well as the high *ulema* and *şeyh*s (leaders of religious orders), came to the imperial dockyard. Prayers were held for victory over the enemies of Islam, animals were sacrificed and alms were distributed to the poor. Cannon were fired 'joyfully' and all the people came out to watch.[180] So many people went, both by land and by sea, to watch the launching of the grand admiral Sinan Paşa's new and magnificent galley, that Heberer regarded the number as impossible to calculate. The French ambassador was forced to hire a boat in order to obtain a good view of the ceremony.[181]

The arrival as well as the departure of ships drew large crowds. When, in 1791, corsair ships from Algeria and Tunisia arrived, led by Seydi Ali in the galleon *Hıfz-ı Huda* (Protected by God), a vessel so large that it could not dock until the following day due to lack of wind, the people lined up on the jetty to watch and pray, recalling for the contemporary Ahmed Cavid the poem, 'Hey brave hero have you come with God's blessing?/ Hey bloody sword, have you come from a bloody holy war?'[182] Captured vessels also drew crowds, that seized from the Christians by Kılıç Ali in 1573 also attracting the attention of Gerlach, who went to see it with his companions.[183]

Military pageantry served not just to impress the populace of the city, but also to send a message to foreign envoys and ambassadors. That sultanic procession had a distinct message of power was not lost on Domenico, the doctor of Murad III who noted the sultan's use of it when preparing for war against the Persians, when he rode across the city accompanied by a huge retinue of cavalry.

> He did it to terrify the Ambassador of the Persians, who was there at the time… The Grand Turk Murat had one of his pashas tell this ambassador that all this cavalry which he had seen were only the chickens in the coop and that he should consider how infinite a number remained outside in so many fields.[184]

No doubt such processions and sultans, 'being accompanied by 3000 Ianisaries, besides Bashawes, Chawses and Hagars' on the way to Ayasofya for Friday prayer, reinforced the impression of a very well-stocked coop indeed.[185]

It was also a very, very rich coop. Much of what was on display in the city was magnificent, and wealth and luxury were evident in all the pageantry

[180] Selaniki, *Tarih*, II, p. 585. [181] Heberer, *Köle*, pp. 316–17.
[182] Ahmed Cavid, *Hadîka*, p. 153. [183] Gerlach, *Günlüğü*, I, p. 109.
[184] Domenico, *Istanbul*, p. 30.
[185] William Lithgow, *The Totall Discourse of the Rare Adventures, and Painefull Peregrinations of Long Nineteene Yeares Travayles, from Scotland, to….* (London, 1623), p. 138.

and spectacle for which Istanbul was famous. The clothes of the sultan, the outfits of his retinue and his ministers, down to the trappings of his horse – all spelt money and power. Perhaps it was the weddings of the daughters of the sultans which displayed wealth most blatantly. Not only did the brides pass through the streets surrounded by enormous entourages on their way to the houses of their new husbands, but the presents given to the bride or to various members of her family, including the sultan, were also on display, carried along to Topkapı or to the bride's new home. In 1768, El Hac Mehmed Emin Paşa, who was to be married to Şah Sultan, daughter of Mustafa III, presented the sultan with 3 sugar gardens, 18 porcelain bowls of candied fruits on 6 trays, 20 English crystal shallow bowls filled with candied fruits, 24 crystal bowls of candied fruit, 2 crystal glass covers decorated with flower blossom and honeycombs on 24 trays, 120 baskets of fruit, 40 trays of blossom and 4 baskets of Frankish blossom, along with a decorated horse. He also presented gifts to Selim and Mehmed, the sultan's sons, to his daughters Mihrişah and Beyhan, and to the mother of Şah Sultan. Each of them received a sugar garden and 15 coffers of candied fruits, 15 coffers of dried fruits, 40 baskets each of juicy fruit and 10 trays each of blossom. To the bride he gave a large diamond ring in a golden coffer decorated with diamonds on a gold tray, a plume with diamonds, a diamond crown, a pair of large diamond and emerald earrings, a veil decorated with diamonds, emeralds and pearls, a pair of metal clasps with diamonds and with buttons of emerald and pearls, a pair of diamond bracelets, a diamond belt set with jewels, a mirror decorated with diamonds, a pair of lightweight slippers ornamented with diamonds, emeralds, delicate pearls and the most brilliant rubies, a pair of shoes decorated with diamonds, emeralds, pearls and rubies, a pair of clogs decorated with diamonds and other jewels, three rolls of Istanbul brocade, five silver trays for carrying the aforementioned jewels, a silver *nahıl*, thirty-eight small and large *nahıl*, two silver coffers of candies, two sugar gardens, thirty coffers of candied fruits, thirty gold-leaf coffers of dried fruits, forty baskets of succulent fruit and a *nahıl* of blossom.[186] Those who escorted this impressive array of presents from the house of the grand vezir to Topkapı were no less spectacular than the gifts.[187]

The wedding in June 1615 of the eldest daughter of Ahmed I, a girl of sixteen, to the considerably older grand admiral, a man of around fifty (as Crescenzio dei Crescenzi commented in a letter in which he described the event), involved equally spectacular pageantry. First, the presents, all of a quantity and quality worthy of the daughter of a major

[186] Çeşmizade, *Tarihi*, pp. 71–3. [187] Çeşmizade, *Tarihi*, pp. 71–3.

world prince, wound their way from the Eski Saray to the house of the groom, accompanied by around six hundred high state officials, foreign dignitaries and other important personages, behind whom followed around a thousand janissaries, the *kadı*s, *paşa*s, vezirs and the *şeyhülislam* on horseback, and around forty men on horseback playing various trumpets, pipes and drums and other 'barbarous' instruments.[188] Next came the presents, all revealed and on display: a great mass of jewels, a closed casket of rock crystal of such translucence that the extremely large pearl earrings, other pendants, rings and very rich jewels could all be clearly seen within it; more bowls loaded with jewels followed. After the jewels came the clothes: great quantities of handkerchiefs, shirts worked with gold and richly ornamented, and jackets with the richest of gems, all so precious, dei Crescenzi gushed, that nothing richer could ever have been seen. Then came bed furnishings, richly decorated with jewels and tapestries of crimson velvet. Fourteen closed carriages, each with four horses and accompanied by two black eunuchs on horseback, followed, together with the female slaves and the old women. Behind these were other female slaves with their hands and faces covered, all dressed in gold brocade, accompanied by male slaves of the palace, with thirty eunuchs following behind. Next followed more room furnishings, sofas and chests, eighteen mules loaded with carpets and twelve with copper utensils for the kitchen.[189]

The next day, the sultan's daughter herself went in procession to the house of the groom. Much larger than that of the preceding day, dei Crescenzi felt unable to describe in detail all the officials who took part, for that alone, he wrote, would take a whole day. Apart from the janissaries, who now numbered one thousand five hundred, the *kadı*s, *paşa*s and the *şeyhülislam*, and men on horseback playing trumpets, pipes and drums, there were also ten gypsies jumping and dancing in a buffooning manner and around thirty other gypsies, playing harps and lutes and singing in a gypsy manner so barbarous 'as to shame an innkeeper'.[190] There was also a madman, described in some detail by dei Crescenzi, who explained that madmen were held to be saints by the Turks. This sight was, he noted, 'the most bizarre thing I have ever seen'.[191] Behind, on foot, two by two, came the men of the arsenal and next twenty other men, with hammers, axes and other things for breaking, cutting and sawing. A great multitude of slaves and people from the arsenal carried two very large *nahıl*s, with fruits, birds and other animals of wax of many colours. These were followed by another bejewelled and gold *nahıl*. Fifty mounted black eunuchs preceded the

[188] Dei Crescenzi, 'Letter', p. 66.
[189] Dei Crescenzi, 'Letter', p. 68.
[190] Dei Crescenzi, 'Letter', p. 69.
[191] Dei Crescenzi, 'Letter', p. 70.

bride, who was on horseback but under an awning of crimson velvet. This reached to the ground and covered her completely. Her horse was led by black eunuchs. There followed a most beautiful horse with rich jewelled trappings, led by a black eunuch; then a carriage of red velvet, with its wood decorated in gold, accompanied by two black eunuchs on horseback and one on foot who carried a little ladder of silver on his shoulders for ease of entering the carriage. He, in turn, was followed by two eunuchs preceding twenty-five female slaves on horseback with their hands and faces covered and dressed in gold brocade, who brought up the end of the procession. The impact of this display was dramatic, for Greeks and Armenians, dei Crescenzi recorded, were so moved by the sumptuous gifts that they converted to Islam.[192]

Two large *nahıl*s for the wedding were made by the wife and mother-in-law of Topçular Katibi Abdülkadir Efendi, who wrote an extensive account of the period. They were made in Aksaray and Odun Kapısı and taken from there to Eski Saray. One hundred people carried each *nahıl*, preceded through the streets by carpenters, who destroyed shops or any obstructions along the route to make way for them. Such *nahıl*s could take two years to make.[193]

The gifts for the wedding of the daughter of Mehmed III in 1598 to Mehmed Paşa contained other, perhaps even more exotic, presents. Jewels and *nahıl*s as tall as minarets were taken from the house of Mehmed Paşa in At Pazarı near Aksaray, through Divan Yolu (the road leading from the Edirne Kapı to Topkapı), to the Eski Saray. Elephants, giraffes, horses, camels, lions and tigers made of sugar and twelve castles and twelve horses made of fireworks were sent as presents to the sultan.[194]

Wealth and opulence also played a part in another important pageant in the city, this time clearly establishing spiritual credentials for the sultan and linking Istanbul firmly with the holy cities of Mecca and Medina. This was the departure of the *sürre*, the cover for the Qaba together with lavish presents and gifts of money that were sent annually from Istanbul. This involved much celebration, which, in 1786, lasted night and day for a week.[195] The *sürre* was sent from the palace across the water to Üsküdar, from where it began its journey southwards. In 1766, the *sürre*, ornamented with freshly minted gold, was carried from the palace by the *bostancıbaşı* (commander of the imperial guards) and other high officials, all dressed in great finery, to the Bahçe Kapı, where it was loaded onto a boat and transported to Üsküdar.[196] The return of the old Qaba cover

[192] Dei Crescenzi, 'Letter', pp. 65–72. [193] Topçular Katibi, *Tarihi*, I, pp. 596–8.
[194] Selaniki, *Tarih*, II, pp. 777–9. [195] Taylesanizade, *Tarihi*, pp. 148–9.
[196] Çeşmizade, *Tarihi*, p. 10; same thing two years later, p. 69.

6. Departure of the *sürre* for Mecca, in Amicis, *Constantinople*, p. 421.

could also be an occasion for display. In Ramazan of 1597 it was sent by the Sharif of Mecca and Medina to Istanbul to celebrate the accession of the sultan Mehmed III. It arrived in Üsküdar, where it was received by the *bostancıbaşı* and his men and put on a galley. It was taken first to the tomb of Eyüb El-Ensari, where it was placed on his coffin. After the night in Eyüp, it was loaded onto a special camel and in a crowded procession, accompanied by the *ulema* (religious establishment) and high officials, entered the city through Edirne Kapı. From there it processed to the *Bab-ı Hümayun*, surrounded by emotional crowds who prayed and wept.[197] The power of this procession so moved the people that many Jews and Christians became Muslim as a result, perhaps driven by motives somewhat more spiritual than those of the Greeks and the Armenians, who converted as a result of the sumptuous wedding of Ahmed I's daughter in 1615.[198]

Pageantry was not merely a matter of the raw display of power, wealth and legitimation of the ruler. It was also pure celebration and an important release valve on the pressure cooker of the city, a way of allowing the

[197] Selaniki, *Tarih*, II, pp. 682–3. [198] Selaniki, *Tarih*, II, pp. 682–3.

masses to let off steam harmlessly and be happily entertained. In addition, it was a way of providing welfare. Celebrations for circumcisions, weddings, accessions and military victories involved feeding, alms and distribution of money. The poor were filled with both abundant food and joy at the circumcision festivities for the sons of Bayezid II in 1490.[199] The *ulema* were fed and the janissaries and other guilds provided with a rich variety of food at the wedding of İbrahim Paşa in 1522.[200] The poor received quantities of food daily during the sixty-day celebrations for the circumcision of Murad III's eldest son Mehmed in 1582, when a great kitchen was set up in At Meydanı and five hundred cooks prepared food each day for the poor, the hungry and destitute. Great bowls of food were spread out from the walls of Ahmed Paşa Sarayı to Dikilitaş, upon which the crowds fell like pillaging hordes.[201] On the thirteenth day of the celebrations for the circumcision of the three sons of Ahmed III at Ok Meydanı, an enormous banquet was laid out which went on from morning to night. Food was given to everyone who came, men, children, and women, who sat separately, protected by the soldiers of the grand vezir. For the banquet alone, ten thousand trays of rice coloured with saffron were prepared.[202]

Food was distributed on the departure of the *sürre* for Mecca four hundred to five hundred copper dishes of food being prepared for the poor in November 1702, for example,[203] and at Eyüp, on the occasion of accession ceremonies. Eyüp in general was always extremely crowded, because people went there to make sacrifices for religious reasons. According to Latifi, writing in the sixteenth century, one thousand rams per day were sacrificed, drawing people who came there to receive the meat as alms.[204] Unflatteringly described in the anonymous eighteenth-century *Risale-i Garibe* (The Treatise of Strange Things) as 'the ravens of Eyüp who tore each other to pieces in the plundering of sacrificial meat',[205] they were not all perhaps the deserving poor. Even the opening of a new pavilion could occasion a sacrifice and distribution of food to the poor and destitute,

[199] İbn Kemal, *İbn Kemâl Tevârîḫ-i Âl-i Osmân, VIII. Defter*, ed. Ahmet Uğur (Ankara, 1997), p. 119.

[200] Peçevi, *Tarihi*, I, p. 50.

[201] Gelibolulu Mustafa Ali, *Sûr*, pp. 215–17; Selaniki, *Tarih*, I, p. 133; Peçevi, *Tarihi*, I, pp. 311–13; Hasan Beyzade Ahmed Paşa, *Hasan Bey-zâde Târîhi*, 3 vols., ed. Şevki Nezihi Aykut (Ankara, 2004), II, p. 292.

[202] Seyid Vehbi, *Sûrnâme*, pp. 10, 36.

[203] Özcan, *Anonim*, p. 186.

[204] Latifi, *İstanbul*, p. 63.

[205] Hayati Develi (ed.), *XVIII. Yüzyıl İstanbul Hayatına Dair Risale-i Garibe* (Istanbul, 1998), p. 22.

as happened for the inauguration of the new pavilion which replaced the Sultan Bayezid Han Kasrı in 1593.[206]

Other acts of charity were performed and alms were distributed to mark numerous celebrations, such as the victory at Egri in 1596, after which the *valide sultan* (the title given to the mother of the sultan) ordered bountiful alms to be given to the poor and destitute, and to widows and orphans.[207] Sultans such as Mehmed III,[208] Mahmud I[209] and Ahmed III[210] made distributions to the poor on their accession ceremonies at Eyüp. Sultans ordered and paid for the circumcision of poor boys at the time of the circumcisions of their own sons, five thousand being carried out on the poor at the time of the circumcision celebrations for the three sons of Ahmed III.[211] At the 1870 celebrations for the circumcisions of the sons of Abdülaziz (1861–76), more than two thousand seven hundred boys of the people of the city were circumcised. The barracks in Gümüşsuyu were prepared for these circumcisions, with one thousand circumcision beds and the dormitories highly decorated.[212]

On special occasions coins were scattered to the crowds. Süleyman I and his three sons, Mustafa, Mehmed and Selim, showered the crowds with silver and gold coins;[213] Mustafa I threw them about all over the place for no apparent reason;[214] Selim III had them scattered during his procession to Eyüp;[215] and the crowds caught them during the wedding of Halil Paşa in 1593.[216] During the wedding of İbrahim Paşa to the daughter of the sultan in 1586, shiny new *akçe*s (silver coins) cascaded through the air and into the hands of the waiting populace, not all of them the needy poor, but 'plunderers', who scooped them up into the skirts of their robes and took them away in hoards.[217] Every two or three days during the circumcision celebration for Mehmed, son of Murad III, trays of silver and gold coins were thrown into the crowds of people, who, waiting with their hands out below the place from which the sultan distributed them, fought and trampled each other in their efforts to seize them. Somewhat disgusted by their unprepossessing display of greed, the contemporary Gelibolulu Mustafa Ali commented that 'for coins many penniless people lost their lives'.[218]

206 Selaniki, *Tarih*, I, p. 320. 207 Selaniki, *Tarih*, II, p. 638.
208 Selaniki, *Tarih*, II, pp. 455, 607. 209 Abdi, *Tarihi*, p. 45.
210. Defterdar Sarı Mehmed Paşa, *Zübde*, p. 822. 211 Seyid Vehbi, *Sûrnâme*, pp. 7–8.
212 Ahmed Lütfi Efendi, *Vak'a-nüvis Ahmed Lûtfi Efendi Tarihi, C. XII*, ed. M. Münir Aktepe (Ankara, 1989), p. 96.
213 Gelibolulu Mustafa Ali, *Sûr*, p. 280. 214 Peçevi, *Tarihi*, II, pp. 452–3.
215 Taylesanizade, *Tarihi*, p. 367. 216 Selaniki, *Tarih*, I, p. 343.
217 Selaniki, *Tarih*, I, p. 170.
218 Gelibolulu Mustafa Ali, *Sûr*, pp. 254–6, quotation p. 256.

Involvement of the populace

Pageantry drew the Istanbul population into participation in the successes and triumphs of the empire and the celebrations and festivities of its ruling family. Popular participation became a factor in the empire's achievements, which were, in turn, the successes of the people of the empire's capital. The people wept and prayed incessantly for God's assistance, sometimes spontaneously, at other times encouraged or ordered to do so by the sultans. They prayed on the birth of Mehmed, son of Mustafa III, for his health and success,[219] and their prayers for God's protection of Mehmed IV on his accession rose to the heavens in 1648.[220] They prayed for rain in Ok Meydanı in 1596, and then, rain having failed to fall, they prayed again in great crowds in the Fatih mosque.[221] In April 1575 a great procession was organised, attended by the most important *paşa*s, which visited many mosques, praying for rain to end the long drought.[222] In May they were praying together for rain again;[223] and again a year later, in April 1576, when the sultan set off for Eyüp to conduct prayers there for this purpose. Shops were to remain closed until the prayer was over, and the entire city prayed – Muslims in the mosques, Jews in the synagogues.[224] In 1595 prayers were ordered for rain and snow, and the *şeyhülislam* and the *ulema* appeared in Ok Meydanı to pray with the great crowds assembled there.[225] When there was a drought at the beginning of Ahmed I's reign, the grand vezir, Mehmed Paşa, requested, and was granted, the sultan's permission to hold prayers in Ok Meydanı and to cancel the *divan* for the occasion. On the day of the prayer, the grand vezir again requested that the prayers should continue for a further two days, as had been the case in the past, that the criers should be sent to announce this in Istanbul, Galata, Üsküdar and Eyüp, and that the *divan* should be cancelled. This request, too, was acceded to.[226]

They also prayed for salvation against plague, which struck frequently and with devastating results. When plague ravaged the city in 1592, Murad III ordered communal prayers at dawn in Ok Meydanı, as well as prayer in Alemdağı, regarded as a holy site, on the Anatolian side of the city, to be attended by all, the poor and the *ulema*. Boats were laid on to transport the *ulema* and the *şeyh*s, and a crowd assembled, so enormous

[219] Çeşmizade, *Tarihi*, pp. 11–12. [220] Naima, *Târih*, III, p. 1171.
[221] Selaniki, *Tarih*, II, pp. 595–6, 600. [222] Gerlach, *Günlüğü*, I, p. 186.
[223] Gerlach, *Günlüğü*, I, p. 189. [224] Gerlach, *Günlüğü*, I, p. 309.
[225] Selaniki, *Tarih*, II, p. 626.
[226] Cengiz Orhonlu (ed.), *Osmanlı Tarihine Âid Belgeler. Telhîsler (1597–1607)* (Istanbul, 1970), p. 108, *hüküm* 129, p. 111, *hüküm* 137.

that it was 'without limit and without comparison'. Shops remained closed while the people waited overnight at Alemdağı before praying together at dawn for God's intervention. These prayers were apparently successful, at least according to Selaniki, who reported that the next day the daily death toll dropped from 325 to 100 and the ill rose from their beds cured.[227] Six years later, in 1598, the people were once more at Ok Meydanı praying against plague, ordered to do so by the sultan, who had himself been urged to take this action by the *ulema*.[228] Not all such prayers were so orchestrated. In 1812, during Friday prayer in the Beylerbeyi mosque, Mahmud II sent a note down to the imam (prayer leader) sitting in front of the mimbar, instructing him to pray for the plague to be lifted from the people of Islam.[229]

The military successes of the state were very much the successes of the population, and military pageantry and display, so common in the city, involved more than the mere exhibition of force and triumphant victory over enemy armies. The Ottoman soldiers were a source of pride for the inhabitants, who identified with them and were given a sense of security and superiority by this identification, as well as a sense of divine blessing. All those who, in December 1596, saw the fully armed regiments of the sailors and leaders of the *gazi*s, the soldiers of the *mucahidin* regiment, the four thousand marines, the corsairs and the brave musketeers of Algiers, cried out, 'God is great'. The regiment of Algiers fired off their guns and the great noise rose to the heavens, terrifying all who heard it.[230]

This popular involvement in military performance was also reflected in communal prayer for military victories, either asking divine support for them or giving thanks to God for assistance in achieving them. Here, too, prayer served to weld all the inhabitants of the city together into a unit, identified with, an integral part of and made vicariously successful by the might of the Ottoman empire. Crowds at the departure on campaign of Süleyman I prayed for the success of the Muslim army.[231] They prayed for the victory of the army departing for Hungary under the commander-in-chief İbrahim Paşa in 1599 with such gusto that their prayers rose up to the court of heaven.[232] The entire population of the city prayed, on Murad III's instructions, for the victory of the grand vezir Ferhad Paşa away on campaign,[233] while 'the angels in the Heavens added their amen, amen to the prayers that were said' for the Ottoman navy as it set sail from Istanbul

[227] Selaniki, *Tarih*, I, pp. 285–7, quotation p. 287. [228] Selaniki, *Tarih*, II, p. 759.
[229] Cabi, *Târihi*, II, p. 908. [230] Selaniki, *Tarih*, II, pp. 652–4.
[231] Selaniki, *Tarih*, I, pp. 14–15. [232] Selaniki, *Tarih*, II, pp. 806–7.
[233] Hikmet Ülker (ed.), *Sultanın Emir Defteri (51 Nolu Mühimme)* (Istanbul, 2003), pp. 60–1, *hüküm* 115, and facsimile p. 36.

with its cannon blazing in 1594.[234] They also offered prayers of thanks for victory, Mehmed III ordering the news of the glorious conquest and just holy war to be announced throughout the city to the assembled crowds, who were to pray and thank God for this victory.[235]

Such communal prayers, for which even the *divan* could be cancelled,[236] were very large affairs, as Sanderson reported in a letter from Pera in August 1596 to Sir Robert Cecil.

> Eighteen dayes past came newes to the Great Sultana and Vizier that the Grand Signor with his hoast was passed the Danubium and enteringe the enemies land; whearfore presentlie proclamation was made that prayer should be in the fields; which was performed the 12th present, two mile without the waules of Constantinople. By credible report ther was to the number of 6 or 700 thowsand Turks at the least. (Also the Sultana freed all the prisoners of Constantinople and Galata which weare for debt, satisfienge their creditors; and many others, except for notoriouse crimes, also sett at libertie.) This was begine at the breake of day, and continued some three or four howers. For the space also of six dayes after they used continually great devotion in all their churches of Constantinople.[237]

People were often required to do more than pray and a less spiritual response to military victory was also necessary. The city had physically to reflect the splendour of such triumph. Tradesmen and craftsmen were ordered by Mehmed III to decorate their shops, and the cloth merchants to display their sumptuous cloth in celebration of the victory at Egri in Hungary.[238] They celebrated vigorously and actively for his return from campaign in December 1596, when 'the whole world, mankind, rich and poor, young and old, all creation, with heart and soul longed to see the face of sultan, the great monarch, the *gazi* sultan and there was such a crowd of people that no description can do justice to it'.[239] All the merchants of the cloth market displayed their best brocades, satins, velvets and silks, spread out for many yards before the sultan, and held up for him to see; the Jews, Christians and Armenians unfurled their highly valuable cloth even further, exceeding even the yards covered by their fellow Muslim merchants. The display of more than two thousand weavers was so good that Selaniki regarded it as having been among the best. There was much sacrificing. Each of the *mütevelli*s (officials in charge of *vakıf*s, charitable foundations) of the imperial *vakıf*s sacrificed three cattle and ten sheep; each from the mosque complexes established by vezirs

234 Selaniki, *Tarih*, I, pp. 376–7, quotation p. 377.
235 Selaniki, *Tarih*, II, p. 648.
236 Selaniki, *Tarih*, II, pp. 509–10.
237 Sanderson, *Travels*, pp. 156–7.
238 Selaniki, *Tarih*, II, p. 655. Similar scenes for his departure on this campaign; Selaniki, *Tarih*, II, pp. 609–14.
239 Selaniki, *Tarih*, II, p. 652.

sacrificed one cattle and five sheep; and the butchers of the city and the other shop owners sacrificed many hundreds of sheep. The crowds were greatly moved by the occasion and all 'wiped the ground with their faces as they humbled themselves before him [the sultan] and gave thanks to him'. The *mütevelli*s of the imperial *vakıf*s, religious figures, students and teachers stood on either side of the road, each *mütevelli* with a censer in his hand, full of amber and musk-smelling incense.

> When they and all the assembled crowds opened their hands and prayed and thanked God for this illustrious and glorious conquest, all the children on all sides cried and wept, calling out amen, amen, and their sound reached the court of heaven. There was nobody who did not cry or remained unaffected by this. The eyes of the illustrious sultan, the protector of religion… too filled with tears and the soldiers were very touched by this.[240]

Shops were decorated for other occasions too, and tradesmen and craftsmen laid on displays of their arts for processions which wound their way through the streets of the city. Such a procession was staged for the birth of Ahmed III's daughter Fatma in 1704.[241] Illuminations were also used, such as the *mahya* (display in lights) erected by the population to celebrate Abdülaziz's return from Europe in 1867, which read 'long live the sultan' and was positioned where it could be seen from the sultan's residence.[242] Rich and poor hung lanterns and candles on the doors of their houses to celebrate the return of the sultan from the Yerevan campaign in 1635.[243]

Active and enthusiastic participation could bring satisfactory results. On his way back to Istanbul from Egypt, where he had been very well received, with much public display and noise, Abdülaziz visited İzmir. Here, all the different nations received him with great applause, and even 'madams and mademoiselles fell to their knees in the street and cried out "vive le sultan"'. Delighted at such a reception, the sultan remarked that he had not seen from the people of Istanbul such signs of affection as he had seen in Egypt and İzmir, thus precipitating a quick shift in the capital away from what the statesman and historian Ahmed Cevdet Paşa referred to as the old tradition of remaining silent before the sultan as a mark of reverence and respect, to this new style of rapturous and noisy reception, which, from now on, seeped into Istanbul. There was, however, one crucial difference – at least for Ahmed Cevdet – for although the people of Istanbul began to clap, they did so in a very well-mannered and

[240] Selaniki, *Tarih*, II, pp. 652–3. [241] Özcan, *Anonim*, p. 289.
[242] A. Süheyl Ünver, *Risale 3. Mahya ve Mahyacılık* (Istanbul, 1932), reprinted in A. Süheyl Ünver, *İstanbul Risaleleri 1*, ed. İsmail Kara (Istanbul, 1995), p. 50.
[243] Topçular Katibi, *Tarihi*, II, p. 1040.

courteous way. The Istanbul people were, for him, thus many times better in city celebrations than those of Egypt and İzmir.

The three days of festivities put on for Abdülaziz's return were certainly magnificent. Craftsmen positively vied with each other to lay on the most striking display. Little gardens of flowers and lemon trees were made up in pots, branches of daphne ornamented the shop fronts and were draped at the entrances to the *hans* (complexes used by merchants and traders as inns to stay in, places to store goods and as markets for sales), shops were festooned with lanterns, everywhere so illuminated in this feverish desire to display that lamps simply sold out and it became impossible to procure one anywhere in the city. The streets were turned into magnificent *yalı* gardens, shops into bridal chambers. The Grand Bazaar, usually closed at night but given special permission to remain open for this occasion by the grand vezir Fuad Paşa, glowed with splendour, so crowded that it was almost impossible to walk round it. The city resounded to the sound of music, as musicians played and military bands moved through the city. Despite all the crowding – so great that it was impossible to get from the Grand Bazaar to Asmaaltı – women were apparently unmolested and there was no impropriety, as everyone wandered happily, enjoying themselves in the no doubt slightly rosy estimation of Ahmed Cevdet, who remarked that 'in brief all the people of Istanbul, looking at each other, organised such a city celebration that its like had never been seen before', and found its wonders impossible to describe in words. The sultan, perhaps unsurprisingly, was delighted.

These celebrations, according to Ahmed Cevdet, were the brainchild of Fuad Paşa. A very inventive man who 'worshipped the sultan', Fuad Paşa orchestrated these unequalled celebrations, which had the useful effect of making the sultan loved by the people. Such love was rewarding. Ministers, who had decided to annul certain tax concessions and the exemption of the Istanbul population from military conscription, now changed their minds. After this display of love and emotion expressed by the capital's populace for its ruler, the implementation was postponed.[244]

Pageantry served many purposes: it could, as in the case of Abdülaziz's return, bring immediate benefit to the population. In more general terms, it also brought them both entertainment and relief from everyday pressures. It provided welfare – material in the form of food and financial handouts, and spiritual in the form of communal prayer. The population was made a collective unit by it and was incorporated through it into the successful enterprise of the empire. A city of pageantry, Istanbul was also

[244] Ahmet Cevdet Paşa, *Ma'rûzât*, pp. 58–60.

the capital, the focus of power and the seat of the sultan. The sultan, far from a remote figure or a ruler possessed of absolute authority, negotiated his power, surviving the dangerous intricacies of the Ottoman political world, in which he often had very little trust in many of his ministers, who came into and out of office at a rapid rate, and was acutely aware of the populace of the city, who needed to be accommodated, incorporated into the affairs of the state and its ruling family with which they were to identify, and whose welfare the sultan needed to ensure. Above all, the sultan was visible and accessible to the population, the source of justice and, perhaps more by implication than open expression, a spiritual figure.

3 Fear and death

Istanbul was a violent city where life was precarious and death lurked just around the corner. Danger could strike at any moment in the form of mob violence, seditious revolt, riot, street violence or straightforward crime. The state could inflict sudden and fatal punishment, or the city could fall victim to earthquakes or floods. Plague was rampant and pernicious fires broke out constantly, rolling at horrifying speed through the city, consuming everything in their wake, caught in a sea of flame and reduced to smouldering ashes.

In a city where fear and death were normal attributes of everyday life, people coped by praying and by turning to magic. They resorted to doctors and medicines, and purchased amulets to protect themselves from evil. They pulled down the shutters of their shops and hid away in their houses. They resorted to bribes. They did not, however, succumb to the supine fatalism that western observers were so fond of ascribing to them, or the 'vehement fatalism' the Austrian-turned-Ottoman ambassador Franz von Werner (Murad Efendi) attributed to the Istanbul 'proletariat' in the 1870s which allowed them to find satisfaction with their situation.[1]

The violence of nature

Part of what made the city dangerous was its geographical position in the centre of an active earthquake zone. Earthquakes struck often and were frequently devastating, such as that in 1658/59.[2] One of the most destructive occurred in 1509, destroying a huge number of buildings and killing many thousands, crushed under falling masonry, 'all smothered and dead, and lid up in heapes unburied'.[3] Minarets were destroyed, mosque domes split, crashing to the ground, and house chimneys were demolished. Even the palace buildings were damaged.[4] The quake struck in the middle of the

[1] Murad Efendi, *Türkiye Manzaraları*, trans. Alev Sunata Kırım (Istanbul, 2007), p. 59.
[2] İsazade, *Târîhi*, p. 53. [3] Lithgow, *Discourse*, p. 138.
[4] İbn Kemal, *VIII. Defter*, pp. 279–80.

night and the earth shook until morning, men and women weeping and praying; no one slept.[5] Tremors continued for forty days, night and day, according to one contemporary anonymous chronicle,[6] and forty-five days in the later account written by Solakzade.[7] People abandoned their homes and lived out in the open, in gardens or courtyards.[8] This earthquake, which came to be known as Little Judgement Day, was of a ferocity and size not seen before, and the damage it caused was so devastating that Bayezid II ordered the transfer of eighty thousand soldiers from all over the empire to Istanbul to repair the city walls. Having placed the janissary *ağa* Yunus Ağa in charge, Bayezid himself left for the safer environment of Edirne.[9]

Set astride a major waterway linking the Black Sea and the Mediterranean, the city was often hit by massive storms and floods. Great floods swept the market stalls in Üsküdar into the sea together with all their produce in 1785/86.[10] The great rain storm of 1745 affected the entire city, destroying nearly two hundred houses in Kasımpaşa, and bringing rain which tasted salty like the sea, a phenomenon which caused 'the people with discernment to ask for God's forgiveness'.[11] The huge flood of 1790 was accompanied by rain that, unlike the great flood forty-five years earlier, only tasted slightly salty. This flood, however, was so huge that for the contemporary Ahmed Cavid it could fairly be described as the second flood after that of Noah, devastating the city and the surrounding area and leaving many drowned.[12] One great storm, that of 1563, was accompanied by seventy-four lightning strikes, and rain which poured down without ceasing for an entire day and night. It provoked a huge and devastating flood in which many people and animals perished. It destroyed the bays of the arches of a newly built aqueduct and houses along the Haliç, ripped up a huge plane tree in Kağıthane, and even entered the tomb of Eyüb El-Ensari.[13]

One flood that clearly had legendary proportions was that which struck in the summer of 1490, when a black cloud suddenly appeared, and Istanbul, a city of such great proportions, disappeared into the blackness. The rain was torrential and the lightning such that had one seen it, Solakzade wrote, one would have thought that the end of the world was approaching. One streak of lightning hit the church of Güngörmez near At Meydanı, then used as a gunpowder store. The power of the lightning

[5] Öztürk, *Anonim*, p. 139, facsimile p. 128. [6] Öztürk, *Anonim*, p. 139, facsimile p. 128.
[7] Solakzade, *Solak-zâde Tarihi*, 2 vols., ed. Vahid Çabuk (Ankara, 1989), I, pp. 345–8.
[8] Öztürk, *Anonim*, p. 139, facsimile p. 128; Solakzade, *Tarihi*, I, pp. 345–8.
[9] Öztürk, *Anonim*, p. 139, facsimile pp. 128–9. [10] Taylesanizade, *Tarihi*, p. 162.
[11] Ahmed Cavid, *Hadîka*, p. 36. [12] Ahmed Cavid, *Hadîka*, p. 36.
[13] Selaniki, *Tarih*, I, pp. 1–2.

strike was such that the dome, 'a black mountain', flew into the sky, landing in the sea, and the building exploded in a detonation so massive that not even its foundations were left. The four *mahalle*s (districts, neighbourhoods) around it, which together formed a small town, were totally obliterated and all the inhabitants buried in an instant. Great stones from this explosion were shot across the Bosphorus, some even reaching as far as Galata and Üsküdar according to one, perhaps exaggerated, account.[14]

The contemporary Kemalpaşazade described the disaster:

> Any man who was hit was instantly killed, his life's blood was spilt on the ground, the vessel of his body smashed to smithereens. The *mahalle*s around were reduced to rubble, many hundreds of houses were destroyed and turned into dust ... People's heads and feet were crushed and they were buried under the stones and soil. Ceilings crashed into walls, masonry and timber collided and hundreds of people were buried alive. Much later, some were dug out and pulled from the earth and masonry. They were still alive but the colour had drained from their faces, and they had lost their minds from shock and were as people lying in their graves. The hand of death had closed the mouths of many before they had even opened their eyes from sleep. Neither had their graves been dug, nor their winding sheets sown, nor their bodies washed, nor buried. People awoke as the roofs of their houses were collapsing in this overwhelming calamity. They thought that the end of the world had suddenly come and that the skies had fallen in on them.[15]

In the winter the city could be hit by devastating blizzards, preventing ships from sailing, and freezing streams, rivers and even springs, as happened in the winter of 1595. That winter, mills were unable to turn because of the cold, and, in consequence, bread prices shot up. A loaf which before had cost two *akçe*s (silver coins) became hard to find for three. Even the sultan could not venture out for Friday prayer, for the road was closed because of the snow and the horses were unable to keep their footing on the ice.[16] Several centuries later, blizzards could still paralyse the city, that in December 1910 causing the cancellation of the sultan's attendance at Friday prayer.[17] Istanbul was also victim to massive hailstones. 'Lumps of ice as large as a man's foot' fell on the city on 5 February 1832 and were reported on by the English publication the *Children's Friend*.[18]

Great winds, in particular the north-east[19] and south-west winds, appeared frequently and cyclones could suddenly emerge, completely

[14] Solakzade, *Tarihi*, I, p. 410; İbn Kemal, *VIII. Defter*, pp. 121–2.
[15] İbn Kemal, *VIII. Defter*, p. 121. [16] Selaniki, *Tarih*, II, p. 444.
[17] Simavi, *Gördüklerim*, facsimile [birinci kısım], p. 135.
[18] *Children's Friend*, 1 March 1832, pp. 68–71, quotation p. 69.
[19] Selaniki, *Tarih*, I, p. 109.

unexpectedly, from clear blue skies. When this happened, as in 1785 for example, the sea was whipped into a frenzy. On this particular occasion, tiles were torn from roofs and wooden boarding from houses. Boats collided and sank, taking many thousands to their deaths; 169 fishing boats went down with all hands. After the storm more than three thousand bodies washed up on the shore at Yedikule.[20]

Subject to the violence of the elements, the inhabitants of Istanbul were prey to another natural killer. In a city the size of Istanbul, where people were crowded together in close proximity with little or no sanitation, plague was inevitably both frequent and severe. In the summer of 1467, a terrible plague swept through Istanbul, causing 'incredible suffering... utterly unheard-of and unbearable'. The death rate was such that bodies were left unburied for there was no one to dig the graves.[21] Death was often swift and unpleasant, those infected, according to Lithgow, in Istanbul in the early seventeenth century, having 'the halfe of their one side rot, and fall away in so that you may easily discerne the whole intrailes of their bowels'.[22]

Many died in such outbreaks: six hundred each day in the 1467 outbreak; one thousand falling victim in the first five days of the plague in 1492, twenty-five thousand in the following ten days and thirty thousand in the subsequent seventeen days.[23] That of 1586 left nobody untouched,[24] and many thousands were killed in 1812, when death rates rose as high as 2,004 per day, excluding those who were buried within the city walls.[25] In that outbreak there were so many people to be buried and so few to do it that men were unable to open their shops, being called on instead to bury the dead.[26] Plague hit the resident embassies, Sanderson noting that sixteen people at the English embassy caught it, eight of whom died, when he was there in the 1590s. One of the victims fell ill in Sanderson's own room and died a few days later.[27] It also claimed the wife of the English ambassador, Sir Thomas Glover, in November 1608.[28] In the great plague of 1573 several people in the household of Aurelio Santa Croce died, as did many in the house of the Venetian *bailo* Marcantonio Barbaro.[29] By the time the Persian ambassador left the city in 1584, after his stay of two and a half years, none of those who had come

20 Taylesanizade, *Tarihi*, pp. 62–3. 21 Kritoboulos, *History*, p. 220, quotation p. 221.
22 Lithgow, *Discourse*, p. 138. 23 Solakzade, *Tarihi*, I, p. 412.
24 Selaniki, *Tarih*, I, pp. 173–4.
25 Cabi, *Târihi*, II, pp. 898, 902; Pertusier, *Promenades*, pp. 116–17.
26 Cabi, *Târihi*, II, p. 913. 27 Sanderson, *Travels*, pp. 12–13.
28 Sanderson, *Travels*, p. 259.
29 'Aurelio Santa Croce al séguito del bailo Marcantonio Barbaro, notizie da Costantinopoli', in Maria Pia Pedani-Fabris (ed.), *Relazioni di ambasciatori veneti al senato*, vol. XIV, *Costantinopoli Relazioni inedite (1512–1789)* (Turin, 1996), p. 218.

with him was still alive, all of them having died of plague.[30] The plague in the year of his departure was so great that 'the sighs and groans reached the All-hearing God in the heavens and there was no one whose heart was not burnt and who did not weep from the pain and separation of death'.[31] Members of the Ottoman ruling family were no more immune than anyone else. The plague of 1598 swept through Topkapı and Eski Saray, killing many, including nineteen of Murad III's daughters. More than one hundred and twenty-eight people died in Eski Saray alone.[32] Apart from plague, many fell victim to other diseases. Abdülhamid I's son Mehmed died in the outbreak of smallpox which struck in 1785,[33] and which killed many other royal babies in the palace.[34] A major cholera outbreak struck in 1870 and the death rate was so dramatic that 'of eight to ten people taking one body for burial, five to six would collapse and die on the way and be buried together with it at the same funeral'.[35]

The royal family may have been affected, but this was not the result of any fatalistic resignation. Although Pertusier regarded the Turks as totally fatalistic in the face of plague, for 'they in general gave themselves up, despairing of even being able to counteract the irrevocable destiny which hovered over them',[36] this certainly did not apply to the sultans, or presumably anyone else with the means to escape, nor in fact to those in the 1812 plague which Pertusier was describing, when *yalı* owners fled the plague to the malaria-ridden Asian coast, which they found preferable.[37] In 1492, Bayezid II remained in Edirne for four months, waiting for the devastating plague in Istanbul to die down, not returning until the city had been rescued from this 'bitter punishment'.[38] Mehmed III did not return to Topkapı Palace until the plague which ravaged Topkapı and Eski Saray had died down in 1598.[39] That people fled the plague whenever possible is supported by the *fetva* (religious legal opinion) issued by the sixteenth-century *şeyhülislam* Ebussuud Efendi, in response to a question as to whether it was canonically permissible to escape from the plague. The answer was that fleeing the wrath of God and seeking his favour was lawful.[40]

30 Selaniki, *Tarih*, I, pp. 146–7. 31 Selaniki, *Tarih*, I, p. 148.
32 Selaniki, *Tarih*, II, pp. 759, 760, 762, 763, 768.
33 Taylesanizade, *Tarihi*, pp. 116–17, 106.
34 Ahmed Vâsıf Efendi, *Mehâsinü'l-Âsâr ve Hakāikü'l-Ahbâr*, ed. Mücteba İlgürel (Ankara, 1994), pp. 292, 298, 300, 312.
35 Sadri Sema, *Eski İstanbul Hatıraları*, ed. Ali Şükrü Çoruk (Istanbul, 2002), p. 31.
36 Pertusier, *Promenades*, pp. 116–17. 37 Cabi, *Târihi*, II, p. 912.
38 Solakzade, *Tarihi*, I, p. 412. 39 Selaniki, *Tarih*, II, pp. 759, 760, 762, 763, 768.
40 M. Ertuğrul Düzdağ, *Şeyhülislâm Ebussuûd Efendi Fetvaları Işığında 16. Asır Türk Hayatı* (Istanbul, 1972), p. 182, *hüküm* 913.

There was a further menace that was even harder to escape than plague, and this was fire, perhaps the greatest killer of all. An unchanging feature of Istanbul, from its first days as Ottoman capital city to its end in 1923, fire was an ever-present destructive presence in the lives of the city dwellers of which they lived in constant fear.[41] As Basmajean, the Armenian priest who left the Ottoman empire for the United States in the 1880s, reported, 'if there is anything the people fear at Constantinople more than another it is fire'.[42] Nothing could equal its devastation,[43] and the speed at which fires spread was terrifying, as 'the torrents of flames roll[ed] like waves of the sea when it is agitated by a furious tempest'.[44] Once started, fire could spread quickly through whole quarters, resulting in massive destruction and reducing thousands of houses to ashes in a matter of hours, particularly when there was wind.[45] On one occasion, fifty thousand to seventy thousand went up in smoke in three days.[46] The great fire in 1693/94, which started at Odun Kapı, was split into several wings by the wind and spread rapidly to other parts of the city. It blazed uncontrolled for twenty-four hours and resulted in enormous damage. A few days later, a further massive conflagration erupted again at Odun Kapı and created even greater damage.[47] The frequency of such blazes ensured that many lost their houses more than once; Lady Mary Wortley Montagu noted in the early eighteenth century that most families had had their houses burnt down once or twice.[48] The grandmother of Yorgo Zarifi, a member of one of the famous nineteenth-century Istanbul banking families, lost hers five times during her lifetime.[49]

Fires took out whole areas of the city; they prevented the sultan from going to Friday prayer[50] and the *divan* from meeting;[51] they burnt down the palace kitchens,[52] flared up in the munitions factory[53] and broke out

[41] Ahmet Cemaleddin Saraçoğlu, *Eski İstanbul'dan Hatıralar*, ed. İsmail Dervişoğlu (Istanbul, 2005), p. 138.

[42] G. Y. Basmajean, *Social and Religious Life in the Orient* (New York, 1890), p. 142.

[43] Albert Smith, *A Month at Constantinople* (London, 1851), p. 107.

[44] Paul Lucas, *Voyage du Sieur Paul Lucas, fait en MDCCXIV...*, 2 vols. (Amsterdam, 1720), II, pp. 75–6.

[45] Jean de Thévenot, *Voyages de Mr de Thevenot tant en Europe qu'en Asie et en Afrique*, 3 vols. (Paris, 1689), I, p. 80; Lucas, *Voyage*, II, p. 75; Bassano, *Costumi*, f. 15v–16r.

[46] P. Ğ. İnciciyan, *XVIII. Asırda İstanbul*, trans. and ed. Hrand D. Andreasyan (Istanbul, 1956), p. 70. İnciciyan lists nineteen major fires between 1618 and 1795.

[47] Özcan, *Anonim*, p. 51.

[48] Lady Mary Wortley Montagu, *The Turkish Embassy Letters*, ed. Malcolm Jack (London, 2001), p. 108.

[49] Yorgo L. Zarifi, *Hatıralarım. Kaybolan Bir Dünya İstanbul 1800–1920*, trans. Karin Skotiniyadis (Istanbul, 2005), p. 122.

[50] Beyhan, *Saray Günlüğü*, p. 105. [51] Selaniki, *Tarih*, II, pp. 739–40.

[52] Selaniki, *Tarih*, I, p. 90. [53] Selaniki, *Tarih*, II, pp. 614–15.

on board ships. When they met gunpowder, the result was explosive. In 1596 an accident occurred in an imperial workshop, where naphtha oil and sulphur were being mixed for use on campaign. Fire broke out and spread to the nearby gunmakers, who were working with gunpowder. A massive fire 'like the fires of hell' exploded and spread to the blacksmith's inside Odun Kapı and from there to the surrounding districts. Many artisans' shops were destroyed.[54] Even fires that did not begin on land could be lethal, and those which broke out on ships were also capable of inflicting heavy damage on areas along the shore, as the vessels drifted like lighted torches, ready to ignite anything they touched. In 1766, a galley anchored between Bahçe Kapı and Galata caught fire during the night, and floating ablaze into other ships burnt them too. It then floated slowly on towards the shore, where it set fire to the Jewish houses between Cibali and Tüfekhane, as well as the Cibali market. Several of the ships set ablaze by the galley floated off to different parts of the Haliç, blown by the south-west wind, to Azap Kapı, Divanhane and Ayvansaray. One appeared before the imperial dockyards and burnt the Tersane Sarayı Kasrı to ashes. All this destruction was achieved in the space of a mere five or six hours.[55]

One hundred years later, in 1870, a fire in Pera took only six hours to destroy two-thirds of the quarter, killing thousands and destroying countless buildings.[56] Homes, nightclubs, hotels, theatres and embassies all went up in flames, including the British embassy, which had already burnt down once before in the devastating fire of 1831[57] and whose loss so annoyed the English.[58] The fire spread very rapidly, with 'sheets of flame extending sometimes a mile in length, and being carried along by a strong wind with inconceivable rapidity'.[59] Splinters of burning wood were showered in all directions by the wind. After thirteen hours it had been put out, leaving the streets devastated, houses in smouldering ruins and the ground hot and still burning.[60] Sections from damaged buildings

54 Selaniki, *Tarih*, II, p. 604. 55 Çeşmizade, *Tarihi*, pp. 10–11.

56 Ahmed Lütfi Efendi, *Tarihi, C. XII*, pp. 94–5; Basmajean, *Life*, p. 142; Reşad Ekrem Koçu, *İstanbul Tulumbacıları* (Istanbul, 2005), p. 479; Anna Brassey, *Sunshine and Storm in the East* (London, 1880), pp. 65–6; 'A Lady's account of the great fire at Pera', *Glasgow Daily Herald*, Thursday 30 June 1870, p. 2; *Belfast Newsletter*, Saturday 25 June 1870, Monday 27 June 1870; *Glasgow Daily Herald*, Thursday June 9 1870, p. 2, Monday June 20 1870, p. 5.

57 Smith, *Constantinople*, p. 254; *Glasgow Daily Herald*, Thursday June 9 1870; *Children's Friend*, 1 March 1832, p. 69; *Bell's Life in London and Sporting Chronicle*, Sunday April 20 1823, p. 480.

58 *Glasgow Daily Herald*, Thursday 9 June 1870, p. 2; *Manchester Weekly Times*, Saturday 2 June 1870, p. 2.

59 *Manchester Weekly Times*, Saturday 2 June 1870, p. 2.

60 'A Lady's account of the great fire at Pera', p. 2.

continued to crash to the ground, killing yet more people who had survived the fire itself. Cannon were used to bring down buildings that were beyond saving and were dangerous.[61] This fire was of such magnitude that, in the words of the *Belfast Newsletter*, 'there are few greater calamities on record'.[62] The state and private individuals contributed considerable sums of money, food and tents to help those affected by the blaze, ten thousand lira coming from the sultan's private purse alone. The khedive of Egypt sent aid, and the five thousand lira set aside in the budget for the illuminations for the annual celebrations for the accession of the sultan were diverted to relief aid.[63] The British, somewhat unusually for that period, were impressed.

> The arrangements made by the Government for the immediate relief of those rendered homeless and penniless in supplying them with food, and tents to cover them, leave nothing to be desired… The commission which has been named by the Government to apply the funds collected is of such well-known standing, that, what may sound strange to ears not accustomed to Turkish doings, the public have confidence that the money entrusted to them for distribution will in this instance reach the objects for which it was intended. It is gratifying to be able to notice the immense amount of private relief that is being daily distributed. In the large camps formed immediately outside, our English ladies are leading the van in showing a noble example in the cause of charity.[64]

Five years earlier, a two-day fire in Hocapaşa *mahalle* had burnt down hundreds of houses in Cağaloğlu, Kadırga, Kumkapı, Nişancı and Sultanahmet, and left the area devastated.

> Sheep and goats grazed in the ruins and open spaces. There, geese, turkeys, ducks and chickens scratched around for food, cockerels crowed, donkeys rolled over and laid down, crows [perched] in the burnt branches of the trees. The fire burnt the whole of Istanbul, and left all the people of the city in a state of utter helplessness.[65]

It took many years for these places to recover.[66] In the last quarter of the nineteenth century, there were said to have been eight fires a month in Istanbul.[67]

Fire resulted in a constantly changing city landscape, as whole areas were wiped out by the flames, leaving nothing but 'dismal memorials' of fire that could run for several miles.[68] In the early nineteenth century,

[61] *Glasgow Daily Herald*, Monday 20 June 1870, p. 5.
[62] *Belfast Newsletter*, Saturday 25 June 1870.
[63] Ahmed Lütfi Efendi, *Tarihi, C. XII*, p. 95; *Belfast Newsletter*, Saturday 25 June 1870; *Glasgow Daily Herald*, Monday 20 June, 1870, p. 5.
[64] *Belfast Newsletter*, Monday 27 June 1870. [65] Sadri Sema, *Hatıraları*, p. 138.
[66] Sadri Sema, *Hatıraları*, pp. 137–8. [67] Koçu, *Tulumbacıları*, p. 481.
[68] Careri, 'Voyage', p. 74.

Pertusier referred to 'a quarter called Batala, now a heap of ruins, from the effects of a conflagration, but very populous a few months before'.[69] Not all this devastation was due solely to the fires themselves; nearby buildings were destroyed in an attempt to prevent the flames spreading, as was done by the janissaries in the fire near Tahtakale in 1589.[70] In the seventeenth century, *baltacı*s (firemen equipped with axes), paid by the sultan, were used to put out fires and prevent them spreading. When a fire had taken hold, they destroyed the neighbouring houses with their axes, demolishing as many as twenty to thirty buildings in the immediate path of the flames. However, the fires spread so quickly that their progress was often faster than that of the *baltacı*s.[71] According to Tournefort, in Istanbul at the beginning of the eighteenth century, the only way to prevent fire spreading and eating up the whole city was to knock down all buildings in its way.[72] Rashid Rida, the Arab journalist and writer who was in Istanbul in 1910, recorded that the method selected in Istanbul for struggling with fire was the destruction of the houses adjacent to the seat of the conflagration. The destruction teams acquired extremely good skills in demolition, he said, because they had constant practice and were well trained.[73]

The percentage of houses destroyed by firefighters rather than by fire itself could be high. In the fire that broke out on the night of 3 September 1804, two hundred of the seven hundred houses destroyed were demolished to prevent the spread of the blaze. This fire – which began in a pipe shop in Çivici Limanı in Tophane and spread rapidly, first to the gunner barracks and then to the surrounding area, despite attempts to put it out led by Selim III, who arrived by boat from Çırağan palace and sought to spur the firefighters on to greater efforts by financial inducements – destroyed the barracks, the Ketenci *hamam*, the Tophane mosque and the Defterdar mosque.[74]

Fire had a massive economic cost, wiping out markets, factories and ateliers, and paralysing the economic activity of the city. In 1593 fire took out half of Saraçhane, together with all the shops of the cheap shoemakers and the saddlemakers, the bookbinders' and feltmakers' ateliers, as well as the Büyük Karaman Pazarı and At Pazarı, leading Selaniki to remark wryly, 'I have never seen a customer as greedy as fire'.[75] Many *han*s and markets went up in flames. In 1594, the Yeni Han, part of the *vakıf* of Sinan Paşa near Tavuk Pazarı, went up in smoke;[76] a few months later, a

69 Pertusier, *Promenades*, p. 47. 70 Selaniki, *Tarih*, I, p. 213.
71 Thévenot, *Voyages*, I, pp. 80–1.
72 Joseph Pitton de Tournefort, *Relation d'un voyage du Levant*, 3 vols. (Paris, 1717), I, p. 470.
73 Rashid Rida (Reşid Rıza), *İttihad-ı Osmani'den Arap İsyanına*, trans. and ed. Özgür Kavak (Istanbul, 2007), p. 179.
74 Beyhan, *Saray Günlüğü*, pp. 75–6. 75 Selaniki, *Tarih*, I, p. 316.

major fire in the market next to Ayasofya destroyed many shops and houses, deeply upsetting the sultan, who regarded a fire in this area, so close to his palace, as a warning from God.[77] *Han*s were rebuilt and then promptly burnt down again. A fire that broke out at night in an oven in the İplikçiler Hanı in Irgat Pazarı on 2 February 1803 destroyed both the *han* and five to ten shops.[78] Rebuilt, the İplikçiler Hanı was once more reduced to smouldering ruins only six months later, by a blaze which also demolished four *han*s, Makasçılar Çarşısı and many shops.[79]

Many foreign merchants were affected by fire. 'The Turkey merchants [were] thrown into the greatest excitement' by the massive 1831 fire in Galata, where their warehouses were situated.[80] One fire, which started in a warehouse in Galata in 1682/83, burnt undetected for fifteen days. When the warehouse was opened and air rushed in, the fire exploded and the warehouse and all the goods inside were reduced to ashes. The goods belonged to Ottoman Greeks and Europeans, and were of such value that they were the equivalent of 'an Egyptian treasure'.[81] Tournefort noted that the constant fires in Galata spelt ruin for many families because of the loss of merchandise. 'Foreign merchants', he wrote, 'learnt to build their stores at Galata of stone, set apart from each other, the only windows being those which were absolutely necessary and whose shutters and doors were furnished with sacks'.[82]

In contrast to the view expressed in 1870 in the *Belfast Newsletter*, when the inhabitants of Istanbul, followers of 'the fatal habit of ignoring the mischances of the future', were compared unfavourably with 'the more prudent Westerners',[83] the Ottomans took all possible precautions against fire. Watchtowers were scattered throughout the city and night patrols watched for fires and sought to take precautions against them.[84] People were to be prepared for fires and to attempt to put them out themselves as soon as they began. In 1572 an order sent to the *kadı* of Istanbul forbade the people of a district in which a fire had broken out from fleeing without trying first to extinguish it. Every house was to have a barrel full of water

77 Selaniki, *Tarih*, I, p. 416. 78 Beyhan, *Saray Günlüğü*, p. 74.
79 Beyhan, *Saray Günlüğü*, p. 74.
80 *The Satirist; or The Censor of the Times*, Sunday 2 October 1831, p. 207.
81 İsazade, *Târîhi*, pp. 178–9. 82 Tournefort, *Relations*, I, pp. 469–70.
83 *Belfast Newsletter*, Saturday 25 June 1870. Reporting on the fire in Pera in 1856 the *Belfast Newsletter* (Friday 25 July 1856) adopted a different approach, noting that the Istanbul firemen 'were rendering good and untiring service and proving that the calm fatalism and *laissez aller* principle, so often ascribed to them, has not, in 1856, too sound a foundation in fact. They were doing their duty, and doing it well'.
84 Bassano, *Costumi*, f. 15v – 16r; Murad Efendi, *Manzaraları*, p. 43; Pertusier, *Promenades*, p. 93; Cemil (Paşa) Topuzlu, *İstibdat-Meşrutiyet-Cumhuriyet Devirlerinde 80 Yıllık Hatıralarım* (Istanbul, 2002), p. 116.

ready and a ladder reaching to the roof. Those who did not ensure that their houses were thus equipped were to be punished. Places (such as *hamams* and bakeries) that were particularly liable to fires were to be checked every two to three months.[85] In 1696 Mustafa II ordered the governor of Istanbul, Osman Paşa, not to give permission for the construction of buildings from thin board, which tended to catch fire easily. Buildings were instead to be made using stone, lime and mud, as they were in Aleppo, Damascus and Anatolia.[86] Several years later, in 1702, he instructed the authorities to ensure that there was no shortage of bricks, lime or roof tiles for the people of Istanbul, to enable them to implement his order that buildings and shops in certain areas, including in the vicinity of the Istanbul cloth market, should be constructed of stone or brick.[87]

As we have seen, the sultans personally directed firefighting efforts – Selim III, for example, appearing frequently at the site of blazes.[88] The level of western interest in and credulity about the figure of the Ottoman sultan is evident in this titillating nineteenth-century account of his role in fire control:

> The Sultan must personally inspect the efforts employed by the civil and military authorities to extinguish the fires which break out either in the city or the suburbs, or the villages on the shores of the Bosphorus. If a fire breaks out in the night, the *Silih-dar* [guard] is informed of it, and he instantly acquaints the *Aukuslar-Aya*, who enters the harem, goes straight to the bed-chamber of the Sultan, and announces the event to the five maids who keep watch alternately during the night. One of these maids then puts on a red turban (the sign of fire), enters the Sultan's bed-chamber, and if he be asleep, approaches the bed, and begins to chafe his feet very gently. The Sultan awaking, perceives the red turban, and immediately demands in what quarter is the fire, on learning which he rises, dresses himself, goes to the *selamlik* [public quarters], and with his whole retinue proceeds to the place where the fire has broken out.[89]

Apart from the sultan, grand vezirs and other ministers personally oversaw firefighting, a practice that continued to the very end of the empire; Talat Paşa, for example, one of the triumvirate in charge of the empire at the outbreak of the First World War, oversaw the extinguishing of a fire in Vefa and Zeyrek in mid September 1918.[90] Several years before, Mahmud

[85] Ahmet Refik, *Onuncu Asr-ı Hicrî de İstanbul Hayatı (1495–1591)* (Istanbul, 1988) pp. 60–1, *hüküm* 5; Koçu, *Tulumbacıları*, pp. 15–16.

[86] Ahmet Refik, *Hicri On İkinci Asırda*, p. 21, *hüküm* 32.

[87] Ahmet Refik, *Hicri On İkinci Asırda*, pp. 35–6, *hüküm* 53. For an earlier order dated 1560, see Ahmet Refik, *Onuncu Asr-ı Hicrî*, p. 59, *hüküm* 2.

[88] Beyhan, *Saray Günlüğü*, p. 73.

[89] 'A peep at Constantinople. The Seraglio', *Ladies' Cabinet of Fashion, Music and Romance*, Friday 1 July 1836, pp. 40–1.

[90] Simavi, *Gördüklerim*, facsimile [üçüncü kısım], p. 150.

Şevket Paşa, the war minister, was injured, struck on the head by falling timber in 1911 when overseeing the extinguishing of a major fire in Mercan and Laleli which destroyed the war ministry.[91] Sometimes injuries sustained in firefighting could be far greater. In 1500/01 the grand vezir Mesih Paşa crossed the Haliç with the janissaries to put out a major fire in Galata which had broken out near a gunpowder depot. When the fire reached the depot, there was a sudden explosion and a huge stone struck both Mesih Paşa and the *kadı* of Galata, who was also in attendance, fatally injuring them both; they died five days later.[92] In the early nineteenth century, the janissary *ağa* was also killed fighting a fire in Çarşamba Pazarı, when a wall collapsed on him.[93] On occasion it was a combination of fire and greed which brought disaster. When the grand vezir attended a fire in Galata in 1786, he put great effort into encouraging those who were putting out the fire. Settled on the upper floor of a nearby house, he distributed money lavishly as an inducement to stimulate greater activity. This act encouraged such crowds that the house, unable to bear the weight, collapsed, crushing those on the floor below. The grand vezir was also injured and his body covered in scratches.[94]

Apart from losing their lives, officials could lose their jobs for actual or perceived incompetence over firefighting. At the end of the seventeenth century, it was the accusation of inattention that brought down Hüseyin Paşa, who lost his job as governor of Istanbul. Ever since coming to office, Istanbul had never once been free of fire and this was perceived, perhaps somewhat unfairly given the prevalence of fires, as being due to Hüseyin Paşa's negligence.[95] When illness impeded the janissary *ağa* Cafer Ağa from attending a blaze in 1568/69, the janissaries had apparently not bothered to fight the fire as they should and, in consequence, it raged out of control for an entire day and night. Cafer Ağa was sacked.[96] The janissaries were not always keen to act, unless prompted to do so by the presence of authority. It was only the arrival of the *bostancıbaşı* Ferhad Ağa at the fire in 1596, for example, which forced them to begin to work.[97]

Before the early eighteenth century, it was the janissaries who were used as firefighters, and it was they who 'ran to the fires' when they broke out, as the sixteenth-century Venetian ambassador Bernardo Navagero put it.[98] At the beginning of the eighteenth century, a French engineer who

[91] Simavi, *Gördüklerim*, facsimile [üçüncü kısım], p. 20. [92] Solakzade, *Tarihi*, I, p. 424.
[93] Cabi, *Târihi*, I, p. 94. [94] Ahmed Vâsıf Efendi, *Ahbâr*, p. 338.
[95] Özcan, *Anonim*, p. 51. [96] Selaniki, *Tarih*, I, pp. 76–7. [97] Selaniki, *Tarih*, II, p. 604.
[98] Bernardo Navagero, 'Relazione dell'impero ottomano del clarissimo Bernardo Navagero stato Bailo a Costantinopoli fatta in pregadi nel mese di febbraio de 1553', in Eugenio Albèri, *Relazioni degli ambasciatori veneti al Senato*, series III (Florence, 1842–55), I, p. 55; Selaniki, *Tarih*, I, p. 246–7, who refers to this old custom.

7. *Tulumbacıs*, in Hermann Barth, *Konstantinopel* (Leipzig and Berlin, 1901), p. 10.

converted to Islam, taking the name Gerçek Davud, invented a machine called a *tulumba* (a fire engine), which was found to be very useful in putting out fires. In consequence, the then grand vezir Nevşehirli Damad İbrahim Paşa set up a *tulumba ocağı* (a firefighting unit), made up of janissaries, and placed Gerçek Davud, now with the title *ağa*, at its head.[99] After the dissolving of the *tulumba ocağı* in 1826 with the destruction of the janissaries, each *mahalle* provided its own *tulumba* and created its own *tulumbacı* unit.[100]

In the nineteenth century, the *mahalle tulumbacı*s were a well-established group, with their own style of dress, special coded language and place in society. Every quarter had its own *tulumbacı* unit, made up of thirty or sometimes as many as sixty or seventy men, paid by the owners of the houses which had burnt or had been threatened by fire. It was their job to run from one fire to another and extinguish them. The *tulumbacı* was not merely to fight fires; he was also required to have other attributes. He

[99] İnciciyan, *İstanbul*, p. 70; Koçu, *Tulumbacıları*, pp. 21–4. According to Ahmed Lütfi Efendi, the inventor of the fire engine was a certain Hüsameddin, *Tarihi, C. XII*, p. 95.

[100] Koçu, *Tulumbacıları*, pp. 21–2.

was to be brave, manly, serious, loyal, not to talk too much, not to lie and not to steal. He was to have a frowning countenance, do everything for his friends, protect his neighbours, throw stones at prostitutes and drive them from the *mahalle*, lead raids on houses where prostitution was suspected of taking place, and always show respect.[101] Despite this all-encompassing list of virtues, Basmajean was very scathing about the *tulumbacıs*, whom he described as being mostly porters and boatmen, not trained firefighters. Although 'stout and strong... their instruments are small and inefficient to quench the flames... The slow work seems better adapted to nourish the flames than to quench them'.[102]

It was one thing to set up firefighting forces, it was another to ensure that they worked effectively. Firefighting in the city was certainly not easy. The winds made it very hard to contain or control the flames; the prevalence of wooden houses, despite government attempts to insist on construction in stone, turned much of the city into a tinder box; and the narrow streets made it impossible to fight the fires effectively. Firemen attempted to quench the massive blaze in 1833 with hand pumps, as the streets were too narrow to allow the entry of fire engines.[103] Fires could also behave in very unpredictable ways, at least according to one report in a British paper of a fire in 1823, when the Turks beheld

> With astonishment and consternation ... the conflagration confine its devastating fury to the Turkish houses alone, and when it approached the Christian dwellings, as if checked by a supernatural power turn back on the quarters of the Musselmen; nay, many houses not belonging to Mahometans remained uninjured in the midst of the flames.[104]

Added to these problems was arson, Thévenot claiming in the seventeenth century that fires were sometimes started by those who then seized the opportunity to pillage the houses, in the confusion of people rushing to deal with the blaze.[105] Arson was suspected in the fires that broke out in the imperial musket factory in September 1833,[106] in the imperial arsenal in 1831,[107] and in the great 1870 fire.[108] Arsonists used the opportunity of

[101] Sermet Muhtar Alus, *30 Sene Evvel İstanbul. 1900'lu Yılların Başında Şehir Hayatı*, ed. Faruk Ilıkan (Istanbul, 2005), pp. 112–13; Sadri Sema, *Hatıraları*, p. 162; Balıkhane Nazırı Ali Rıza Bey, *Eski Zamanlarda İstanbul Hayatı*, ed. Ali Şükrü Çoruk (Istanbul, 2001), pp. 45–7.

[102] Basmajean, *Life*, pp. 142–3. [103] *John Bull*, Monday 30 September 1833, p. 312.

[104] *Bell's Life in London and Sporting Chronicle*, Sunday 20 April 1823, p. 480.

[105] Thévenot, *Voyages*, I, pp. 80–1. Count Forbin states that fires were used as a means of protest; Count Forbin, *Travels in Greece, Turkey and the Holy Land in 1817–18* (London, 1819), p. 15.

[106] *John Bull*, Monday 30 September 1833, p. 312.

[107] *The Satirist; or The Censor of the Times*, Sunday 2 October 1831, p. 207.

[108] *Belfast Newsletter*, Monday 27 June 1870.

other blazes to profit from the absence of firefighters engaged elsewhere. Their fires could then go unattended, creating further chaos and giving freer rein to pillaging and looting in the subsequent confusion.[109] On occasion, the sultan would intervene to demand an investigation of suspected arson, as Süleyman I did in December 1544, when he sent an order from Edirne for an immediate investigation into the fire that had destroyed the house of Hacı Hamza in the Eminsinan *mahalle*, near the Gedik Ahmed Paşa *hamam*. Although the fire did not harm the other houses, the sultan wanted to know without delay who had burnt the house down, whether it was the house owner, one of the servants or someone from outside. If anyone was found to have done this he was to be imprisoned.[110]

On at least one occasion, fire was used as a cover for an attempted assassination. The grand vezir Alemdar Mustafa Paşa was a figure much hated by the janissaries, who feared the innovations in army structure he might bring in. They therefore decided to kill him by starting a fire that, as grand vezir, he would attend, at which point the plotters would shoot him. In Ramazan 1808, they started a fire in a saddle shop near Saraçhane in the evening, and positioned shooters in a bakery opposite, and in a pastry bakery on the corner. Fifteen more people took up position in a room over a greengrocer's. Gradually, the smell of burning spread and flames began to appear behind the shutters. As it was Ramazan, many people were out on the streets and noticed the fire. They reported it to the janissary security unit that was based near the fire, but these janissaries, knowing about the assassination plan, did not wish to intervene. The people, however, insisted, demanding to know why they were not responding. The janissaries therefore broke into the shop and the people of the *mahalle* put the fire out.[111]

The firefighters themselves were not always the firemen they might have been. When, in 1589, a particularly large fire destroyed markets, Jewish *mahalle*s, a flea market, mosques and *mahalle*s in the space of twenty-four hours, the janissaries busied themselves plundering, as if in a foreign country, their negligence and indifference resulting in the devastation of the city and the destruction of *vakıf*s.[112] This particular fire was not an unmitigated disaster for all, for Selaniki reported that as a result of it 'important people gained land'.[113] On occasion, people were thankful if the fire went out before the arrival of the janissaries, not so

[109] Taylesanizade, *Tarihi*, pp. 118 and 160–1.
[110] Sahillioğlu, *Mühimme Defteri*, pp. 5–6, *hüküm* 4.
[111] Cabi, *Târihi*, I, pp. 269–70. [112] Selaniki, *Tarih*, I, p. 213.
[113] Selaniki, *Tarih*, I, p. 213.

much because of the extinguishing itself, but because 'Muslims were delivered from the plundering of the tyrannical janissaries and other rabble'.[114] They also had reason to be grateful if the fire broke out in the daytime, for this curbed janissary looting.[115] In 1598, when fire erupted among the packsaddle makers near the Büyük Karaman Pazarı, and a row of shops, bookbinders, and many other shops and *mahalle*s were burnt down, the 'plundering' janissaries were once more at work, pillaging goods rather than putting out the fire. 'In these… days', Selaniki wrote, 'the eyes of the widows were full of tears and their sighs coloured the heavens'.[116] It was not just the janissaries who took advantage of fire to plunder. In 1766, when the *defterdar* İbrahim Şarım Efendi's house caught fire, everything in the house was either burnt or plundered, various gardeners and stewards benefiting from the confusion to steal. As Çeşmizade Mustafa Reşid dryly noted, when thieves came into the house from outside at night, the situation could be dealt with, but when the thieves were already inside, it was quite a different matter.[117]

The nineteenth century was no different and firefighting still left much to be desired. Firefighters sometimes had to be offered financial incentives before they would do anything. In the 1833 fire, certain rich house owners paid large sums to save their mansions, which was done by throwing carpets over them and constantly keeping them wet with water from the pumps.[118] The *Glasgow Daily Herald* reported that the firefighters in the 1870 Pera fire plundered wherever they went, and when people protested they threatened them with knives. The owners of property had to 'bribe them to do the work it was their duty to do for nothing. People were actually killed for protecting their own property'.[119] The *Belfast Newsletter* noted that there had been a great deal of robbery during this fire, the extent of which was 'something without parallel… It may almost be affirmed that there has been more property stolen than fell in the flames'.[120] Such plundering might have been without parallel, but it was not rare. In the 1856 fire in Pera, 'many ruffians and robbers (Crimean scum mostly) were abroad… They reaped a rich harvest; and, as an instance, I may record that Major Brett, commanding the depot of the Turkish Contingent, was plundered not only of his plate, but even of his decorations. Such is Pera'.[121]

[114] Selaniki, *Tarih*, II, p. 601. [115] Selaniki, *Tarih*, II, p. 604.
[116] Selaniki, *Tarih*, II, pp. 739–40. [117] Çeşmizade, *Tarihi*, p. 29.
[118] *John Bull*, Monday 30 September 1833, p. 312.
[119] *Glasgow Daily Herald*, Monday 20 June 1870, p. 5.
[120] *Belfast Newsletter*, Monday 27 June 1870. [121] *Belfast Newsletter*, Friday 25 July 1856.

Comments about the effectiveness of the firefighters in the dying days of the empire were often scathing. According to Yorgo Zarifi, the *tulumbacıs* were more interested in pillaging from burning buildings than putting out fires. His grandfather even hired a Bulgarian doorman, whom he armed to stop any *tulumbacı* from entering his house.[122] Even the mayor of Istanbul in 1912, Cemil Paşa (Topuzlu), mocked *mahalle* firefighting. While the *mahalle* watchmen, recent immigrants from Anatolia with barely comprehensible accents, beat the pavements with large sticks and bellowed out the names (usually incorrectly) of the affected areas, 'dogs howled ominously, the *mahalle tulumbacıs* yelled at the top of their voices, and cannon were fired…, and because of the burning of a shack or a house in some distant part of the city or on the outskirts at midnight, the whole of Istanbul remained sleepless and disturbed'.[123]

Rashid Rida commented that nothing surprised him more during his stay in the city than the incompetence of the government firemen.[124] He could see no point in the activity of the firefighters, young men who rushed forward in a rowdy and undisciplined manner to the fire.[125] For Rida, the destruction of Çırağan palace, reduced to ashes in 1909 as a result of the failure to take the necessary precautions against fire, should have been a lesson for the government. The incompetence of government firefighting was even more evident for him in the fire that swept through government offices.

> The first thing that comes to the mind of someone thinking about these events is that administrators who are unable to prevent the devastation of fires which happened everyday in their capital, will be unable to demonstrate any competent administration as long as this inability continues, since the people who remain passively looking at their own houses in ruins will certainly be incapable of making distant houses prosperous.[126]

Rashid Rida was not the only one to criticise the destruction. For Lütfi Simavi, too, the destruction of Çırağan palace, right on the waterfront, was unfortunate. Not knowing how to use the seawater to extinguish the flames, the firemen had not done so.[127] This was not the only unfortunate example of incompetent firefighting. A major fire in Bab-ı Ali in December 1910 destroyed offices of the Council of State, a very large part of the ministry of the interior and part of the office of the grand vezir, leading Simavi to write:

[122] Zarifi, *Hatıralarım*, p. 125. [123] Topuzlu, *Hatıralarım*, pp. 115–16.
[124] Rashid Rida, *İttihad*, p. 179. [125] Rashid Rida, *İttihad*, p. 179.
[126] Rashid Rida, *İttihad*, pp. 180–1, quotation p. 181.
[127] Simavi, *Gördüklerim*, facsimile [birinci kısım], pp. 88–9.

As long as there were highly inflammable wooden houses in Istanbul, such narrow streets, fire hydrants whose keys were not findable, fire brigades whose equipment was insufficient, it would be impossible to prevent such disasters.[128]

Fires were dangerous for another reason: they attracted crowds, who would turn out to watch the progress of the flames. This was perceived as a potential threat by the government of Abdülhamid II, which did not encourage any sort of gathering whatsoever. On such occasions, state officials would immediately appear to ensure that no unpleasant political events were going on.[129] No demonstration was welcome to Abdülhamid, who spent much of his time behind the walls of his palace at Yıldız, fearing attack of one sort or another from his many enemies.

Natural disasters, with their sudden and often devastating descent on the city, created a fundamental level of uncertainty among Istanbul's inhabitants. People's lives hung in a balance over which they had no control. This led them to pray, often communally, for God to lift the terror from them; to flee, having ascertained first if this was canonically appropriate; or to turn to the doctors. The medical profession was not always a safe one for those who practised it. When the six-year-old son of Selim II died in August 1572, three of the most famous doctors were given three hundred bastinadoes each for having allowed him to die.[130] In this harsh environment, where sudden natural destruction was always possible, people believed strongly in signs and portents, and in the power of amulets, *şeyh*s and shrines. Fear and the attempt to protect oneself from the arbitrary hand of fate were part of everyday life. But what made existence in the city so precarious was not just the natural world (if on occasion assisted by the hand of man), but also the inherent violence of the population itself, either in terms of mob violence, political revolution, violent crime and general thuggery, or the violence of the state, either in response to sedition or as a method of control through inspiring terror.

The violence of man

Istanbul owed its violence in part to its position as capital, which ensured that political revolutions were inevitably played out on its streets. In addition, in those times when the government was weakened by military defeat, economic crises or some insufficiency of the sultan, the level of

128 Simavi, *Gördüklerim*, facsimile [birinci kısım], pp. 133–4, quotation p. 134.
129 Alus, *İstanbul*, p. 115.
130 'Anonimo al séguito del bailo Marcantonio Barbaro, diario di prigionia', in Pedani-Fabris, *Relazioni*, p. 172.

8. Janissary and *sipahi*, in Schweigger, *Ein newe Reyssbeschreibung*, p. 164.

violence increased and the inability of the state to control the streets was heightened. Certain factors in particular contributed to the level of violence: military presence within the city and immigration into it.

The janissaries, and the *sipahi*s were major players in political upheaval, bringing down sultans, beheading grand vezirs and hanging officials of state. No sultan could run the city without taking the janissaries into account, and power in Istanbul swung like a pendulum between these two power centres, sometimes sultans managing to stand against them and sometimes completely unable to do so, Osman II even being deposed and murdered by them in 1622. It could be argued that what transformed the empire in the nineteenth century was not the beginning of the famous period of reform, the *Tanzimat*, in 1839, but the destruction of the janissaries in 1826 by Mahmud II, who, after much careful planning, had them massacred in what came to be known as 'the auspicious event'.

Unruly janissary behaviour marked the city from the very beginnings of its life as the Ottoman capital. After the death of Mehmed II, they plundered it;[131] they terrorised his son Bayezid II, ultimately pressuring him into abdicating in favour of his son Selim I;[132] they forced Selim II to pay them money shortly after his accession.[133] Bayezid II found himself having to backtrack swiftly due to janissary opposition when he arrested Gedik Ahmed Paşa, intending to have him killed. Upon discovering the arrest late at night, Gedik Ahmed's son sped to the janissary barracks to give the news. 'How', he shouted out, 'could you brave soldiers allow such a vile crime? Did you not share the same bread and salt with my father?' In great commotion, the janissaries set out for the palace, where they bellowed for the gates to be opened. Appearing behind a barred window above the gate, a fearful Bayezid asked what the janissaries wanted. Insulting him, calling his morals into question and asking if such behaviour became him, the janissaries demanded that he immediately produce Gedik Ahmed. 'If you do not bring him, think what we will do to you', they roared by way of encouragement. Requesting them to be calm, Bayezid promised to do as they wished. Gedik Ahmed was produced, showing obvious signs of having been extensively tortured. The janissary response was such that 'a great fear seized the sultan's heart and his colour drained away'.[134]

Dissatisfaction with pay was often a spark for revolt, either because it was regarded as insufficient, because it was paid in debased coinage or, in the case of the armourers in 1703, who threatened not to go on campaign in Georgia over it, because it was in arrears.[135] Such pay-related revolts could be violent, Sanderson reporting on one such incident involving *sipahi*s and Murad III towards the end of the sixteenth century:

> Onse for thier pay the Spahies demaunded, in the time of Sultan Moratt; who, not beinge answeared as they desiered, made an uprore in the court, that the viseroyes weare glad to hide themselves in the Turks lodgings for feare of thier lives, and most of the household servants of the meaner sort came out with spits, tonges, and other kitchen tooles to end the fray; who cleared the Seraglio of the Spahies. At that broyle was slaine of all sorts some 200 or more.[136]

Selaniki noted that the bodies of those who were killed in this incident were thrown into the sea and their clothes sold in the flea market.[137]

Paying in debased coinage could have dire consequences. In 1589 it cost the *beylerbeyi* (provincial governor) Mehmed Paşa his head. Holding him responsible, the *sipahi*s petitioned Murad III to hand him over, but the sultan, willing to give in to any other demands, refused to sacrifice the

[131] Öztürk, *Anonim*, p. 130. [132] Öztürk, *Anonim*, p. 142.
[133] Selaniki, *Tarih*, I, pp. 54–6. [134] Kreutel, *Haniwaldanus*, pp. 9–11.
[135] Özcan, *Anonim*, p. 212. [136] Sanderson, *Travels*, p. 57.
[137] Selaniki, *Tarih*, I, pp. 302–3.

paşa, of whom he was very fond. Annoyed, the janissaries turned to threats: 'if the *beylerbeyi*'s head does not come into our hands today, we shall not leave the *divan* ... Let [the sultan] see that we shall find a sultan [to replace him]'.[138] Unable to stand against them, Murad III was in the end forced, very unwillingly, to hand him over. The *sipahi*s took him to the place of execution, where they cut off his head. Kicking it as if it were a football, they rolled the head along until they arrived at At Meydanı. No one was able to extract it from them until, finally, a steward paid four hundred gold coins to buy it and buried it with the body. Murad, 'weeping and cursing the janissaries', was extremely distressed by the event and concerned for the honour of the sultanate in an environment where the sultan was so blatantly unable to protect even his own top officials.[139] Sanderson also reported on this incident, noting that 'they had the Beglerbeyes head (whome the Great Turke espetially loved) given them, which they spurned about the court'.[140]

This might have been an event the like of which had never before been seen, at least for Murad III,[141] but it was certainly to be seen many times afterwards. In 1655, the janissaries and *sipahi*s demanded, and got, the head of the grand vezir İbşir Paşa, through a carefully orchestrated manipulation of rumour about him, which reached such heights that even women and children were gossiping and the city was at bursting point.[142] The death toll was higher over payment in debased coinage in March 1656, when the janissaries united with the *sipahi*s in a serious revolt, partly due to payment of salaries in debased copper coinage and partly because the janissaries returning from the campaign in Crete had not been paid their salary, and, to make matters worse, felt that they had been treated insultingly. As a result of this revolt, known as the 'plane-tree incident', thirty government officials ended up swinging from the plane tree in front of the Sultan Ahmed mosque. During this revolt, the *sipahi*s even went as far as to hack to pieces the envoy of the *şeyhülislam* and to hang his body parts on the railings of the military band house. The *şeyhülislam* resigned and a new one was appointed. But the *sipahi*s did not like him, maintaining that he was a 'drunk' and totally unsuitable. A janissary cook would have made a better *şeyhülislam*. He too was removed and a new one put in his place.[143]

Sultans like Murad III were perfectly aware of the danger of giving way to the janissaries and *sipahi*s, even if they were not always able to

138 Selaniki, *Tarih*, I, p. 211. 139 Peçevi, *Tarihi*, II, pp. 286–7; Selaniki, *Tarih*, I, p. 211.
140 Sanderson, *Travels*, p. 57. 141 Peçevi, *Tarihi*, II, p. 286.
142 İsazade, *Târîhi*, pp. 18–19; Naima, *Târih*, IV, pp. 1607–12.
143 Naima, *Târih*, IV, pp. 1648–55; İsazade, *Târîhi*, pp. 24–6.

avoid it. Some were more successful than others. In 1595, Mehmed III refused to hand over the grand vezir Ferhad Paşa, whom the *sipahi*s wanted, fearing that this would only be the beginning of their demands.[144] Selaniki, who approved of the sultan's decision, commented that had the sultan given way the position would have been much worse.[145] While sultans in the earlier centuries were, in general, more able to stand firm against the janissaries and *sipahi*s, partly aided by the many campaigns which kept the troops busy and financially satisfied, the sultans' ability to oppose them successfully declined as the centuries rolled on. When the janissaries demanded Nevşehirli Damad İbrahim Paşa's head in 1730, the *ulema* told Ahmed III, 'my lord, if the slaves [i.e. the janissaries] want the *paşa*, it is impossible not to hand him over'.[146]

Many times the state proved quite incapable of opposing janissary violence and, as Selaniki noted, the janissaries 'got what they demanded and what they wanted they got'.[147] At such times it was the janissaries, rather than the sultan, who dictated policy and dominated the political landscape of the city. Periods of particular ferocity involved dramatic overthrows of the established order, with sultans falling and the city descending into chaos, notably in 1622, 1703, 1730 and 1807. In 1618, Mustafa I, who proved to be mentally unstable, was removed from the throne after only one year and was replaced by the very young son of Ahmed III, Osman II, known as Genç Osman (Young Osman). His reign was not to last long either, and in 1622 a janissary revolt brought him down, despite his execution of his grand vezir Dilaver Paşa, designed to appease them and save his throne, and his gift to them of the chief eunuch, whom they promptly tore apart. In the immediate aftermath of Osman's deposition, Sir Thomas Roe commented in a letter to the Lord Admiral, 'here is noe government, no justice; but the soulderers are kings, judges and executioners'.[148] The following month he noted, 'Eaven now, at the finishing of this letter, the Janysaries are in new combustion, and will have more heads to satisfy their revenge, Ab insano populo libera nos, Domine'.[149] In this situation, as Roe had noted in May, 'there is no care of the publicque'.[150]

Chaos continued into the following year, when, one year after the deposition, Roe was again commenting on the dominance of the janissaries and the failure of government. 'The insolencyes of the souldiers continew and this day, within the Seraglio, the bustengies [*bostancı*s]

[144] Peçevi, *Tarihi*, II, p. 362. [145] Selaniki, *Tarih*, II, pp. 468–72.
[146] Destari, *Tarihi*, p. 14. [147] Selaniki, *Tarih*, I, p. 60. [148] Roe, *Negotiations*, p. 54.
[149] Roe, *Negotiations*, p. 55. [150] Roe, *Negotiations*, p. 150.

9. At Meydanı, in Pertusier, *Promenades*, frontispiece.

have risen against their Cape, and deposed him'.[151] This was a situation in which 'the vizier mayateynes his authoritye by continuall donatiues to the Janizaries, and hath compounded twice with them in 14 dayes; which he gathers up agayne by confiscations and oppressions intolerable'.[152]

The beginning of the following century saw a further period of political collapse, this time occasioned in part by the absence of the sultans from the capital city. In 1703, the Edirne incident erupted, leading to the abdication of Mustafa II and the return of the royal family to Istanbul. In the early summer of that year there was much unrest in the city, and in July the janissaries went into open revolt. Prisoners were released from prisons by the rebels and joined the revolt. The governor, Abdullah Paşa, fled and the city descended into chaos. Control, such as it was, was now in the hands of the rebels, who used Orta Cami, the mosque near their barracks, as their headquarters. They demanded the return of the sultan from Edirne, saying, 'let our ruler come back to Istanbul which is the ancient capital and let him stay here';[153] and the handing over of the *şeyhülislam* Feyzullah Efendi, his sons and his men, with whom they were not satisfied. Meanwhile, a tense calm settled over the city as its population awaited developments.

> All the soldiers and the *esnaf* [craftsmen and tradesmen], armed to the teeth, sat day and night in At Meydanı, every day their numbers increased and with God's decree there was manifest among them a justice that cannot be described. While five thousand to ten thousand scoundrels and like men gathered together in one place criers would call out if a man lost his money, shouting for 'a Muslim who has lost an *akçe* in a black purse'. If a toothbrush or an ablution towel was lost it would be brought and placed under the commanders' standard. And there was no transgression against anyone. Although there was absolutely no fear of the authorities, there was no drunk to be found. Unbelievers did not go out. Although there were so many foreigners in Galata, they all shut up their houses and went to their *yalı*s and farms. There was no attack or molestation on women or boys. The population was amazed at this for at other times when attention was paid to the authorities there was no lack of shedding of blood, drunkenness and fire. Naive people, thinking that these deeds of janissaries were according to the sharia and that it was thus that they had taken control, deceived themselves and they were filled with joy. But then the janissaries plotted such mischief as had never been seen in history.[154]

In 1703 the janissaries demonstrated that they could completely overthrow the control of the sultan and, perhaps more interestingly, that they could, at least for a period, establish calm. This made them an even more dangerous force for the sultans, for it showed them to be not merely a force

[151] Roe, *Negotiations*, p. 150. [152] Roe, *Negotiations*, p. 150.
[153] Özcan, *Anonim*, p. 229. [154] Özcan, *Anonim*, p. 230.

of disruption and even terror, but also a serious contender for power in the capital. As Hasan Ağa, the leader of the janissaries in an earlier revolt, the plane-tree incident, had put it in an audience with Mehmed IV, 'the peasants create the treasury, the treasury creates the soldiers and the soldiers create the sultan'.[155]

Less than thirty years later, however, the janissaries revolted again, this time with none of the apparent control that they had exhibited in 1703. In an orgy of violence under their leader Patrona Halil, the grand admiral Mustafa Paşa, the *kethüda* (title of a high Ottoman official) Mehmed Paşa and the grand vezir Nevşehirli Damad İbrahim Paşa were killed, the latter strangled on the order of the sultan in a vain attempt to keep his throne. The body of Mustafa Paşa was strung up in front of Horhor Çeşmesi, and that of Mehmed Paşa hung up by the gate of Et Meydanı. According to rumours, the body of Mehmed Paşa was then either thrown into a well full of rubbish, thrown into the sea or buried in the garden of his mansion near the Süleymaniye. The body of Mustafa Paşa was collected and buried in the garden of the tomb and *medrese* (theological college) of Merzifonlu Kara Mustafa Paşa, who was an ancestor of the grand admiral's. The janissaries refused to accept that the body of the grand vezir was in fact his and demanded that it be sent back to the palace. The motive behind this was apparently to create another crisis in order to bring down the sultan. They tied the corpse to the tail of a donkey and dragged it through the streets to the Bab-ı Hümayun, the entrance gate of Topkapı palace, announcing that they would not accept it. Ahmed III, stalling for time, promised that if they returned the next morning he would give them the real one. Meanwhile the body lay unclaimed and was torn apart by dogs. Later, the poet and historian Şakir Bey paid money to some of the rebels to collect findable pieces of the body of his patron and secretly buried them at night in the garden by the library and fountain built by İbrahim Paşa.[156] Once again, janissary violence had removed a sultan from his throne and shown quite clearly how delicate the balance of power was and how fine the line between control and anarchy.

After the accession of Mahmud I, the rebels continued to create trouble in the city. According to the contemporary Abdi, they had made themselves rich from the revolt, but that was not enough to satisfy them.

> Wherever there was a rich man in the city, they sent men there and took money from him, and the people of Istanbul were amazed by the tyranny and oppression.

155 Naima, *Târih*, IV, p. 1653.

156 Abdi, *Tarihi*, pp. 38–40; Destari, *Tarihi*, pp. 16–17, M. Münir Aktepe, *Patrona İsyanı (1730)* (Istanbul, 1958), pp. 152–4.

> Bandits raided houses and stripped the people like highwaymen. Day and night there was no peace and the world was wretched.[157]

In a reversal of the events a little earlier, Patrona Halil was now killed by the sultan, and his corpse and that of another of the rebel leaders, Muslı, were thrown from the Bab-ı Hümayun.

Just as the eighteenth century had been ushered in amid violence and rebellion, so the nineteenth century followed a similar pattern, when Selim III, a very reforming and therefore no doubt truly irritating sultan, had driven the janissaries (who had proved themselves so useless by losing Egypt to Napoleon in 1798 and were due for replacement by Selim's New Order army) to a frenzy of fury. In 1807 they struck under the leadership of Kabakçı Mustafa. Selim was removed from the throne and replaced by his cousin Mustafa IV, whose occupation of it was of very short duration. Mustafa's reign was largely taken up by political intrigue, as Alemdar Mustafa Paşa manoeuvred to return Selim to the throne, having Kabakçı Mustafa murdered, exiling those who had been behind the sultan's deposition and suppressing the rebels. Mustafa, at first pleased to use Alemdar to restore order, then became aware of the danger and of Alemdar's true intention. Speedily he dispatched men to murder Selim and Prince Mahmud, also confined within the palace. Selim was killed, but Mahmud managed to escape over the palace roofs and was promptly put on the throne by Alemdar, who became his grand vezir. Alemdar's heavy-handed approach, however, quickly alienated the janissaries and precipitated a further revolt. The janissaries demanded Alemdar's head, which they did not get, Alemdar choosing instead to blow himself up in an ammunition store, taking a large number of janissaries with him. They also demanded, but did not get, (at least, not at first) those of Kadı Paşa and the grand admiral Ramiz Paşa; after a failed attempt to defeat the janissaries in Istanbul, they both fled. Kadı Paşa was later caught and his head cut off at the beginning of 1809. Ramiz Paşa fled to Russia but was also caught, and his head, too, was removed in 1813.[158]

The tradition of dramatic political change continued at the beginning of the twentieth century, with the Young Turk Revolution in 1908. This time the janissaries were not involved, for they had been destroyed eighty-two years earlier by Mahmud II. The revolution was political and largely unbloody, as Abdülhamid II was forced to bring back the parliament and constitution he had established briefly in 1876 and abrogated two years later. The movement behind this political pressure was the Committee of Union and Progress, which, after a shaky patch with the religiously driven

[157] Abdi, *Tarihi*, p. 51. [158] Cabi, *Târihi*, II, pp. 967–8.

counter-coup of 1909, crushed by the Ottoman army under Mahmud Şevket Paşa (later to be hit by falling timber while fighting a fire at the war ministry), came to dominate the political scene, taking over dictatorial power under the triumvirate of Enver, Talat and Cemal Paşas in 1913 in the Bab-ı Ali coup.

One of the aspects of janissary violence, and the one most threatening from the sultan's point of view, was its role in the politics of the state. Seditious actions by the janissaries could have dire consequences for any sultan or his ministers. But there was a further aspect to the problem of the janissary presence within the city, this time one which had a more direct impact on the everyday lives of its inhabitants, although they too could be caught up in the revolts of rebelling troops. This aspect was inter-janissary violence, which became a common feature of Istanbul life in the eighteenth and particularly the early nineteenth centuries. While such clashes had always occurred, their impact on the city had been kept to a minimum in the earlier centuries as they were restricted to areas outside Istanbul. When they began to break out within the confines of the city, their effect was felt by all the inhabitants. Inter-janissary fighting could be very violent and was always disruptive of public order.

In 1811, an inter-janissary quarrel erupted in Beyazıt involving a great deal of shooting. Security officers went hotfoot to the *sekbanbaşı* (deputy of the janissary *ağa*), Çelebi Ağazade, who had only come into the job a few days before, to tell him that a major fight had broken out and that something must be done about it. Unruffled, Çelebi Ağazade replied, 'sit down, have a coffee, you're tired after rushing over here'. Coffee was ordered and Çelebi Ağazade asked them whether, given the size of the fight and the amount of gunfire, there were any deaths. The police officers replied, 'no, no we haven't seen any deaths'. 'Ah', Çelebi Ağazade replied, 'then let's not be hasty, let's go when there are a couple of hundred deaths'. He then set off for the security unit in Beyazıt, where the officers urged him to go to the scene of the fight for the situation was out of hand. Çelebi Ağazade asked if there had been any deaths and proposed, if so, that they remove the bodies, but the officers replied that no, there had been no deaths. Çelebi Ağazade expressed surprise: 'what, there aren't even a hundred deaths in a fight with all these guns? What kind of a fight is this?' and he ordered himself a coffee. He then moved on to Ağa Kapısı (janissary headquarters), where he gathered together various janissary leaders and security officers and told them:

'I don't need this kind of soldier and I will not go to the place where the fight is. If you do not disperse these men who are behaving in this way, take their weapons and send them back to the barracks, I will not send you to your garrisons. I shall immediately have you executed in the stables and have your bodies put in Kum Meydanı in front of the Tekkeli Köşk and let's see if these base soldiers whom you helped, passing by on their way to their barracks or their garrisons or the prisons, can help you then'. Within less than two hours the officers he had assembled had gathered all the weapons and sent the men to their barracks.[159]

Fighting between janissaries and *sipahi*s was also a problem. During the circumcision celebrations for Mehmed, son of Murad III, some of the *sipahi*s organised various secret entertainments and took prostitutes into their barracks. When the *subaşı* raided the barracks and attempted to extract the prostitutes, the *sipahi*s resisted, tied up the *subaşı* and took him off to At Meydanı. This action greatly annoyed the janissaries there and a fight broke out between them and the *sipahi*s, prompting the intervention of Ferhad Paşa, then janissary *ağa*. It was at this point that two *sipahi*s were killed. The entire affray was being watched by the sultan from the bay window of a nearby building. Wishing the fighting to be stopped, he lowered a cloth from the window as a signal that the brawling should cease. The grand vezir, Sinan Paşa, very put out about the deaths of the two *sipahi*s, instructed Ferhad Paşa to leave, taking his janissaries with him, at which point the incident came to an end.[160]

It was not just a matter of inter-janissary or janissary-*sipahi* fighting, but, on a lower level, the janissaries represented a violent mob, disruptive, aggressive and often out of control. At periods when the state was weak such violence went unchecked, but whenever it was able, the government punished janissary violence severely. Instances of common criminality, such as the knifing of two white concubines by two janissaries in 1812, resulted in the hanging of the culprits, who had followed the women as they walked down Divan Yolu with a female slave trader and had shouted comments at them. The slave dealer had reprimanded them, telling them either to pay up and buy the women if they liked them, or to leave them alone. Insulted, the men had waylaid the concubines and stabbed them.[161]

In the period of chaos between 1807 and 1809, the janissaries were often no more than a lawless mob, forcibly buying goods at below their market price, fighting over prostitutes and trying to change debased coinage, for full-weight coinage, in what amounted to 'a type of plundering', in the words of the janissary *ağa* in 1809.[162] In 1811 they even sent a letter to one of the moneychangers, a Jew called Uzun (Tall) Yako, saying that if he

159 Cabi, *Târihi*, II, pp. 728–9.
160 Peçevi, *Tarihi*, II, p. 312; Naima, *Târih*, IV, pp. 1914–15; Hasan Beyzade, *Târîhi*, II, pp. 294–6.
161 Cabi, *Târihi*, II, p. 913. 162 Cabi, *Târihi*, I, p. 461.

did not leave them five hundred *kuruş* (small denomination coin) with a certain grocer, they would kill him. Yako wrote a note on the letter and sent it back to them. The note read, 'whenever they kill me, they will find around five hundred *akçe*s on me, so they won't go empty handed. But as long as I am alive I will not give money to anyone'.[163]

Janissaries at any period were capable of reacting violently if their economic interests were affected, or in revenge for an injury to one of their own. The janissary attack in 1596 on the house of the *subaşı*, Rıdvan Çavuş, near Tahtakale, when Rıdvan Çavuş and the people in the house barely escaped with their lives, was motivated by fury over his policy during Ramazan, when he had ordered that anyone found drunk should be killed, wine houses were to be kept closed and no public swings erected for the celebrations at the end of the month. These swings, of which Selaniki heartily disapproved for they drew the good people of Islam into sinful activity, provided the janissaries who ran them with a very lucrative income.[164] The attack on the house of Deli İbrahim Paşa five years earlier was also for revenge. Janissaries set fire to his stables and broke down the door of his house. Offering them money, Deli İbrahim threw purses on the ground before them and, seizing the moment when the soldiers were occupied collecting the coins from the floor, escaped over the rooftops. The janissaries stripped the house clean, even plundering the presents the *paşa* had prepared for the sultan, before torching it. In the inquiry that followed, the sultan demanded to know what had led the janissaries to this abominable act. They replied that Deli İbrahim was unjust and that while he was the governor of Erzurum he had killed a janissary.[165] Others also were to complain about his oppression of the people and he was later jailed in the prison of Yeni Hisar and then Yedikule in 1594 – an imprisonment which apparently delighted the populace – and his wealth seized. The following year he was strangled and his corpse thrown into the Bosphorus at Narlı Kapı. According to rumour, his body was retrieved from the sea by his servants, who buried it in Çizmecibaşı Tekkesi in Tophane.[166]

What made the janissaries even more dangerous and hard to control was their embedded position within the society. The janissaries had started life as the elite fighting force of the empire, the massed infantry that was the powerhouse of the mighty Ottoman military machine, which propelled it forward in a seemingly endless wave of conquest. Units of these fighting forces had been stationed in the city since its conquest in 1453. However, by as early as the end of the next century their elite military role had begun to break down, as the campaigns began to slow

[163] Cabi, *Târihi*, II, pp. 741–2. [164] Selaniki, *Tarih*, II, p. 601.
[165] Selaniki, *Tarih*, I, pp. 247–8. [166] Selaniki, *Tarih*, I, pp. 355–6, 362, 367; II, p. 439.

and they spent more time in the city than fighting out on the frontiers. From now on, the janissaries transformed from professional, full-time soldiers into inhabitants of the city with a military identity but also another profession or trade. For Selaniki, it was the reign of Murad III that marked the beginnings of the janissary problem for the state. The standard of those entering the ranks of the janissaries had declined, discipline had broken down and no loyalty or respect for the state remained, as noted also by Koçi Bey in 1631.[167] Murad III himself was concerned that military men had begun to buy and sell and become traders. They had shops, and were selling in the streets, in the markets and on the jetties. They were even profiteering, buying commodities from ships and preventing others from doing so, and then, ignoring the *narh* (the fixed price), selling them at higher prices. They paid no attention to the market authorities, to the *kadı* or to the market inspector. Murad ordered that such practices should stop; soldiers should not be involved in trade but should occupy themselves with warfare.[168] One of the reasons, according to Gelibolulu Mustafa Ali, for the dire state of affairs in the 1590s was that the janissaries and the *sipahi*s had become market traders and begun to buy and sell as they wanted.[169]

This submerging of the janissary presence into the mass of the population of the city resulted in the janissaries becoming artisans, owning shops and following professions. By 1792, janissaries owned around 40 per cent of the shops and work places in the Haliç area of the city.[170] This has led to an interpretation of the janissaries which sees them as guildsmen, protectors of their guilds and even stout defenders of protectionism. However, although a janissary might be a tanner or a coffee shop owner, he was also a janissary, with a strong communal loyalty to his regiment and with the backing of this organisation. From the state's point of view, a janissary remained a janissary and was, following the dress codes imposed on all members of Ottoman society, to dress as one – Selim III, for example, insisting that the janissaries should wear clothes that distinguished them from the rest of the population.[171] The interests the janissary/guildsman thus sought to protect tended to be his own rather than those of the guild, and his position as janissary, however tenuous the

[167] Selaniki, *Tarih*, II, p. 471; Koçi Bey, *Koçi Bey Risaleleri*, ed. Zuhuri Danışman and Seda Çakmakçıoğlu (Istanbul, 2008), p. 58.
[168] Ahmet Refik, *Onuncu Asr-ı Hicrî*, pp. 130–1, *hüküm* 50.
[169] Gelibolulu Mustafa Ali, *Künhü'l-Ahbâr*, III, p. 677.
[170] Betül Başaran, 'III. Selim ve İstanbul Şehir Siyaseti (1789–1792)', in Noémi Lévy and Alexandre Toumarkine (eds.), *Osmanlı'da Asayiş, Suç ve Ceza 18.–20. Yüzyıllar* (Istanbul, n.d.), p. 123.
[171] Karal, *Hümayunları*, p. 101.

military link might be, was what gave him the muscle to abuse his role as trader or craftsman.

It was military backing that allowed the janissaries to trample the interests of other traders or other members of society, and raised them to a position above the law. The untouchability of a janissary, even when declared to be acting illegally by the *kadı* of Istanbul, is evident in the case of a young *serdengeçti ağası* (commander of commando-like troops), who, despite his title, had never been on campaign, itself another telling sign of the level to which the janissary had become a soldier in name only. In 1811, this young man appeared before one of the coffee shops near Yeni Cami, accompanied by several 'similarly lawless friends' from the same janissary regiment. This coffee house was one of a number of highly successful and popular coffee shops in that area. Twenty-five to thirty years earlier they had been butchers' shops, but had been closed by imperial order, after which the shops had been left empty, and then gradually reoccupied. The *serdengeçti ağası* claimed that as the premises had originally belonged to his father, who, after the shops had been closed, had left the area, the shop was now his. Proceeding with his friends to the Istanbul *kadı*, he staked his claim to the premises. Not receiving the outcome he wanted there, for the Istanbul *kadı* backed the status quo, he set off with his supporters to Ağa Kapısı, to appear before the *sekbanbaşı*. The *sekbanbaşı* removed them politely, saying he would look into the matter. The next day the *serdengeçti ağası* took some sheep, went to the coffee house, slaughtered them and hung them in front of the shop. Some of his friends did the same. The coffee shop owner protested as this was totally illegal, and, taking the decision of the Istanbul *kadı* together with his own petition, went to the *kadı*, the sultan and the *sekbanbaşı*. Although his case was upheld, the *sekbanbaşı* even assuring him that the janissary would be imprisoned and punished, nothing happened and the janissary was left to hang his sheep in front of the shop and strut up and down outside it with his friends, showing off and flashing his weapons.[172]

Dual identity as a guildsman and a janissary could also serve one well in other illegal activities, for until the nineteenth century the police or security forces of the city were run by the janissaries. Thus, when a tanner named Keleş, who was also a janissary, kidnapped a perfectly respectable woman from the courtyard of the Üsküdar İskelesi mosque in 1809 and took her off to the tannery, the Üsküdar security unit, janissaries from the same regiment as the tanner, refused to do anything, merely exclaiming, 'what can we do in these times of chaos?' It was a group of local men who

[172] Cabi, *Târihi*, II, p. 727.

went to the tannery and rescued her, before putting her on a boat and sending her over the water to the European side.[173]

Although the janissaries were without doubt a major contributor to the lawlessness and violence of the Istanbul streets, they were by no means alone, for the city was also home to a large number of sailors. As well as being the capital, Istanbul was a huge seaport. Many foreign sailors docked there, and many were drawn there from other parts of the empire to work in the navy and the imperial dockyards, where they joined the large sailor population already resident in the city. The grand admiral, responsible for the behaviour of the seamen, spent much of his time dealing with brawls which broke out frequently in Galata, where the presence of sailors was at its highest. Such fighting could be very violent, leaving the grand admiral to wade in under gunfire to bring the brawling sailors under control, remove the dead bodies and seal the locations of the fight – a coffee house in the case of a major fight put down by Abdülhamid I's grand admiral Hasan Paşa.[174] A serious conflict among the sailors which broke out in 1788 in Galata and left many dead prompted Abdülhamid I to send an order to the governor of the city, in which he expressed his anger about the constant trouble caused by the sailors and instructed the governor to warn the grand admiral, Hasan Paşa, that this situation had to be brought under control. On the very same day, yet another major fight broke out among the sailors in Galata and several men were killed. Taking several hundred musketeers, Hasan Paşa himself went to the scene of the fighting, stormed the coffee houses and dispersed all those present. Seizing all weapons, he placed guards on the gates of the city. This very firm response by the grand admiral had the effect of reassuring the city's population, at least to some extent, for the constant violent brawling of the sailors was a major source of concern to them.[175]

The high level of alcohol consumption that was the reason for much of the brawling could also kill the sailors for other reasons. When, in 1788, very bad weather conditions forced the imperial fleet to anchor at Büyükdere and some of the crew barely escaped with their lives, the sailors rushed to Galata to give thanks for their survival. They drank and a fight broke out in which several were injured. Rounding up some prostitutes they set off to their barracks for a night of fun. That night, a fire broke out in Tahtahan, the location of the barracks, destroying three *han*s, two mills, one bakery, a compass maker's, a fur cap maker's, pistol shops and other premises. Several sailors, oblivious in a drunken stupor, were killed,

173 Cabi, *Târihi*, I, p. 481. 174 Taylesanizade, *Tarihi*, p. 125.
175 Taylesanizade, *Tarihi*, pp. 282–3.

together with thirty-five prostitutes. Fifty prostitutes were rescued stark naked.[176]

Reports that sailors in the market in Üsküdar were plotting to seize respectable women had Selim III hurrying off there in disguise. When he arrived, however, they had gone. In an angry missive to the governor, he made it known that had he been there he would have punished them. 'What is this?' he asked, 'I do not want such disobedient, worthless sailors. They are not what I need. And you, open your eyes to this as well, otherwise it will not be good for you'.[177]

As with the janissaries whose violence could go unpunished in times of political weakness due to their military backing, so, too, did the sailors benefit from the chaos of the times to indulge in general thuggery, from which the population at large could do very little to protect itself. This was particularly true in the period of chaos after the overthrow of Selim III, when sailors such as Üsküdari Deli (Mad) Mehmed profited from the disorder of the times to indulge in mafia-like activity. When he hired the Dere *hamam* in Kasımpaşa and proceeded to cut down trees in the neighbouring gardens, timber prices being very high at that time, the locals were too frightened to protest.[178] He adopted a similar approach when looking for a wife.

Having become a captain, Deli Mehmed announced his intention to marry. His friend, the son of Bursavi Haracızade el-Hac Esad Ağa, told him that he had a sister. He also informed his father about his friend, and proposed that his father agree to the match as Deli Mehmed was much respected by the grand admiral. The father agreed and accepted a six hundred and fifty *kuruş ağırlık* (the present given by a prospective groom). While Esad Ağa was happy with the arrangement, his brother Hacı Said Efendi, was not, pointing out that there had never been a sailor, or captain, in their family and that Deli Mehmed was a notorious drunk. He advised that although there had been a promise, no betrothal had taken place and that they should get out of the arrangement by giving back the *ağırlık*. Deli Mehmed, informed of this plan by the girl's brother, gathered eight or so ruffians and, drunk, proceeded at night to the house of Esad Ağa in Üsküdar. Dragging his prospective father-in-law outside, he beat him up, injuring him in several places, and demanded, 'why have you not given me my wife yet?' The wedding was fixed, he had invited men of the grand admiral to it, and now he wanted the bride handed over.

Conveniently, the house of Esad Ağa was just next door to the Şeyh mosque. Deli Mehmed summoned the *şeyh* of the mosque to perform the

[176] Taylesanizade, *Tarihi*, p. 293. [177] Karal, *Hümayunları*, p. 97.
[178] Cabi, *Târihi*, I, p. 189.

marriage at once. The *şeyh* was not keen. 'My son I am not the imam of the *mahalle*. Call the imam tomorrow and let him perform the ceremony'. Undeterred, and asking simply, 'Aren't you a Muslim', Deli Mehmed forced him to perform the ceremony. The girl's obliging brother led Deli Mehmed into the harem, where he seized the girl and dragged her off to his house in Kasımpaşa, where the wedding celebrations were performed the following day, to the accompaniment of many dancers. Esad Ağa appealed to the grand vezir, who passed the matter on to the grand admiral Hüseyin Paşa. Hüseyin Paşa summoned Deli Mehmed and Esad Ağa and questioned them. Deli Mehmed defended himself well, explaining that he was engaged to the girl, that his father-in-law, who had accepted the *ağırlık*, had kept dragging his feet over giving her to him, and that even if he had entered the harem he had done so with the man's son to take his own wife. His defence was accepted.[179]

The capital and an enormous seaport, Istanbul was also a rich metropolis which acted as a magnet for the populations of the provinces. While in the fifteenth and early sixteenth centuries the sultans wished to increase the city's population, bringing people into it from various parts of the empire, by the second half of the sixteenth century the problem had become a reverse one, with the beginnings of the migration problem that was to hit Istanbul very badly by the eighteenth century. At the end of the sixteenth and in the first half of the seventeenth centuries, the Celali revolts resulted in a movement of peasants, abandoning their lands and fleeing the violence in Anatolia for the safety of the capital. By the mid seventeenth century, even the area around the city itself had been occupied by migrants.[180] The problem of immigration into Istanbul became a major source of concern for the sultans in the following century, when masses streamed in from the provinces, driven from their homes by economic problems, wars and the general corruption in provincial administration. These migrants from the European territories and from Anatolia began to represent a threat to the order and provisioning of the city, in particular the single men who were housed in barracks which, according to Evliya Çelebi, the seventeenth-century Ottoman traveller, housed up to two thousand men each,[181] or lived in *hamam*s and *han*s, and who, despite the efforts of the state, proved impossible to control. As early as the 1730s, these migrants were active participants in

[179] Cabi, *Târihi*, I, p. 188.

[180] Topçular Katibi, *Tarihi*, I, p. 458; Orhan Şaik Gökyay, *Kâtip Çelebi. Hayatı, Kişiliği ve Eserlerinden Seçmeler* (İstanbul, n.d.), pp. 240–1.

[181] Evliya Çelebi b. Derviş Muhammed Zilli, *Evliya Çelebi Seyahatnamesi. Topkapı Sarayı Bağdat 304 Yazmasının Transkripsiyonu-Dizinie I Kitap*, ed. Orhan Şaik Gökyay (Istanbul, 1995), p. 134.

the political upheavals of the capital.[182] Such levels of migration also represented an economic problem, destabilising the city's markets and causing price increases and unemployment. Migrants gravitated to certain unskilled jobs, in particular as porters and boatmen, groups which, by the beginning of the nineteenth century, were as out of control and disruptive as the janissaries. This migrant population added a further pool of young, single men, who could easily become swept up in the general violence of the capital, whether it be political or more common, everyday criminality.

The state response

Faced with these levels of violence, the state responded in various ways. From the point of view of the ordinary inhabitants of the city, such responses added yet another strand to the texture of violence which made up their lives and which served to make survival uncertain and arbitrary violence a normal occurrence.

As in any other state, the Ottomans sought to control movement, at times imposing curfews, as Ahmed I did as soon as he came to the throne in 1603,[183] and strictly controlling any movement at night, when anyone moving around the city was required to carry a lantern. Failure to do so led to immediate imprisonment, or even sometimes instant execution.[184] Murad IV, when out in disguise at night, would have anyone he found without a lantern put to death on the spot. One night in the Hocapaşa *mahalle*, he met the son of the imam of the mosque of Hocapaşa returning to his house just by the mosque after the night prayer. Murad asked the young man if he had not heard about his order to carry a lantern at night, and before he had time to answer, he was killed.[185] The movement of women in particular was controlled, for their presence on the streets was seen as a potential provocation to unrest, especially at times of overexcited celebrations, such as Ramazan. In Ramazan 1810, the women of Üsküdar were too much in evidence for the authorities; having begun merely by visiting friends, they then began to go to the mosques, and then to wander round the markets until late and go promenading. At this point the authorities reacted and imposed a curfew, announced by public criers, banning women from going out at night.[186]

182 M. Münir Aktepe, 'XVIII. Asrın İlk Yarısında İstanbul'un Nüfus Mes'elesine Dâir Bâzı Vesikalar', *İstanbul Üniversitesi Edebiyat Fakültesi Tarih Dergisi*, 9/13 (1958), p. 9.
183 Naima, *Târih*, I, p. 265.
184 Ahmet Rasim, *Ramazan Sohbetleri* (Ankara, 2007), pp. 15–19.
185 Naima, *Târih*, II, p. 756. 186 Cabi, *Târihi*, I, p. 690.

Nightwatchmen patrolled the *mahalle*s, and janissary security forces or (after their establishment in the nineteenth century) the police maintained order in the various divisions of the city. Potential hotspots such as brothels were kept under surveillance, and information on potential troublemakers collected through various information networks. According to the Venetian ambassador Pietro Foscarini, in Istanbul in 1637, Murad IV was extremely well informed about what went on in his capital and, according to Foscarini's successor Alvise Contarini, had spies everywhere.[187] Government officials could also collect information from the inhabitants of the *mahalle*s, as was the case in 1811, when the *bostancıbaşı* Abdullah Ağa laid on a reception for various respectable inhabitants of Üsküdar at Yalı Köşkü. After talking to them about the great lack of order everywhere, he asked them to inform him if they knew of anyone, however important, involved in unacceptable activities, assuring them that the authorities would do everything possible about the situation.[188]

The state tried various ways to tackle the problem of the military and the immigrants within the city. In a move designed specifically to control the sailors, who had up to that point lived in the barracks for the migrant workers in Galata and Kasımpaşa, the government built special barracks for them in the late eighteenth century, without any marked success, for sailors continued to elude control just as they had before.[189] In an attempt to control immigration and to protect the order and stability of the city by using the concept of collective responsibility, the state imposed a guarantor system. Under this system, all immigrants were required to have a guarantor who was a settled inhabitant of the city and an upright and honest member of society. From the middle of the sixteenth century, sultans strove more and more to impose the use of the guarantor, as the problems of migration within the city increased. In 1567 Selim II gave the responsibility of controlling all migrants from the European territories or from Anatolia to the *mahalle* authorities. Under an order from 1580, any migrant without a guarantor, and without a job, was forbidden from staying in the *mahalle*s, the barracks, caravansarays or shops. If anyone permitted this, having accepted a bribe, or assisted such migrants, they would be sent to the galleys.[190] Despite such efforts to impose control, it was clear that not only did these attempts fail, but the situation even deteriorated. By the

187 'Relazione di Pietro Foscarini bailo', in Luigi Firpo (ed.), *Relazioni di ambasciatori veneti al senato*, vol. XIII, *Costantinopoli (1590–1793)* (Turin, 1984), p. 97; 'Relazione di Costantinopoli del bailo Alvise Contarini', in Luigi, *Relazioni*, p. 368.

188 Cabi, *Târihi*, II, p. 757.

189 Ahmed Vâsıf Efendi, *Ahbâr*, pp. 134–5; Cabi, *Târihi*, I, p. 207.

190 Ahmet Refik, *Onuncu Asr-ı Hicrî*, pp. 139–40, *hüküm* 5, 145–6, *hüküm* 13.

time of Mahmud I, the response to such migration was to turn the migrants back without even attempting to put the guarantor system in place. Selim III sought to approach the matter in a more systematic manner, introducing six-monthly checks of buildings where illegal migrants might be found, and registering migrants and their guarantors.[191] By the reign of Mahmud II, a more drastic solution to the problem was found, when the barracks for migrant workers were gradually demolished. This was a popular move, for the violence that issued from the barracks had reached such proportions that the entire population of the city was heartily fed up with these hives of prostitution, aggression and even, according to some, disease. The guarantor system had by this stage completely collapsed, no one willing to undertake that kind of responsibility. The barracks in Galata and Bahçe Kapı were demolished in 1812 during a major outbreak of plague, which itself gave a pretext for the demolition.[192] The janissary problem was finally disposed of in an even more drastic manner by the same sultan when he had them massacred in the 'auspicious event' of 1826.

There were two specific aspects to the state's approach to violence and crime which had a particular impact on the lives of the people of the city: collectiveness and display. Ottoman society functioned as a collection of blocks in which people were grouped together according to shared characteristics and in which individuality was irrelevant. Thus the inhabitants of Istanbul belonged to groups – religious ones, for example, in the case of the Orthodox under the patriarch and the Jews under the chief rabbi. From an administrative point of view, this made them easier to handle, much in the same way that tax collection was made administratively simpler by the imposition on occasion of a block tax collected annually, which absolved the government of the more complex requirements of collection from individuals. Similarly, craftsmen and traders in Istanbul were grouped into *esnaf*, trading collectives or guilds, such as that of the porters, the boatmen or the copper workers. It was these guilds that took part in the processions for special occasions, such as the circumcisions of the sultans' sons, when their members displayed their own particular craft. Guild officials were responsible for the behaviour of their members, the payment of dues, the maintenance of professional standards and activities in the market. Here, too, the state benefited from minimising state intervention while maximising control, the responsibility for provision falling on someone else.

[191] Karal, *Hümayunları*, p. 96; Aktepe, 'İstanbul'un Nüfus Mes'elesi', p. 29; Başaran, 'III. Selim', p. 120.
[192] Cabi, *Târihi*, I, p. 209; II, pp. 761–2, 914.

Sultans attempted to use collectiveness as a form of violence prevention, playing one group off against another, as Süleyman I did when he threatened the janissaries that he would use the migrant men housed in the barracks against them.[193] They also applied it in their methods of investigation of crime, for torture, a very common means of extracting information, could be all-encompassing, and used on those who happened to be in the vicinity of a crime rather than involved specifically in it. Merchants in the market where a theft had occurred, for example, could be seized and tortured.[194]

This collective approach thus applied equally to the application of justice and to the investigation of crime, where a group could be punished for the actions, or suspected actions, of one of its members. Just as guild leaders were held responsible for the wrongdoings of guild members, so too could the Greek Orthodox patriarch or the chief rabbi be held responsible for the behaviour of their congregations. Mere suspicion could be sufficient for random punishment of group members, regardless of any proof of group involvement, let alone individual guilt. When, in 1528, a house was broken into, its inhabitants murdered and everything stolen, suspicion fell on various unmarried Albanians who worked as day labourers. In consequence, eight hundred single male bakers, candlemakers, criers, cooks and woodcutters were seized in the markets and on the streets, and killed on the spot. The reason for the severity and arbitrariness of this punishment was to put fear into ruffians and robbers in order to prevent any such incident occurring again, an aim that was successful according to Peçevi.[195] However, its very excessiveness seems to have been regarded as going too far, at least for Müneccimbaşı Ahmed Dede, for whom Süleyman I's arbitrary execution of street vendors rounded up on the streets, as a response to the robbery and murder, was not in accordance with the sharia.[196]

It would appear that punishment had to be within the bounds of what was socially tolerable. Excessive cruelty could lead to the downfall of the officials responsible, John Sanderson commenting on the violence of government under Hasan Paşa during the absence of the sultan on campaign, and on his great cruelty, for which 'the Queene Mother gott his head at hir sonns retorne'.[197] When, in the same period, the grand vezir Ferhad Paşa informed the sultan that those behind an attempted janissary

193 Evliya Çelebi, *Seyahatnamesi. I Kitap*, p. 134.

194 Selaniki, *Tarih*, I, p. 231–2.

195 Peçevi, *Tarihi*, I, p. 72.

196 Müneccimbaşı Ahmed Dede, *Müneccimbaşı Tarihi*, trans. İsmail Erünsal, 2 vols. (Istanbul, n.d.), II, pp. 529–30.

197 Sanderson, *Travels*, p. 87.

revolt (one of the demands of which had been Ferhad Paşa's head) were ex-*serdar* (military commander) Sinan Paşa and Cığalazade Sinan Paşa, the sultan ordered ex-*serdar* Sinan Paşa blinded and Cığalazade Sinan Paşa exiled. Ferhad Paşa, however, did not carry out the blinding, persuaded not to do so by some of his men, who regarded the punishment as tyrannous and argued that blinding had not been used before in the Ottoman state, and that if the grand vezir were to impose it he would gain a bad reputation among the people, while there was also the risk that blinding might become an established practice, thus causing the suffering of many innocent people, for which Ferhad Paşa would be responsible. The grand vezir did not therefore blind ex-*serdar* Sinan Paşa, merely exiling him to Malkara, and Cığalazade to Şebinkarahisar, or Akşehir according to Selaniki.[198] Whether blinding had or had not been used before by the Ottomans – and it apparently had been by Murad I, who was said to have blinded his son Savcı after he revolted against his father jointly with Andronikos, the son of the Byzantine John V in 1373[199] – the important aspect of the story is the perception of the limits of punishment and the importance of popular reaction. As with everything in the Ottoman state, excessiveness was to be avoided unless it was clearly advantageous.

Even at a much more minor level, over-zealous policing and unjustified punishment were not to be tolerated, Selim III's grand admiral warning the chief janissary security officer in Üsküdar, whose arrest of two innocent sailors simply to impress and appear efficient had infuriated him, that there would have to be very strong reasons for bringing accusations against the people and frightening them half to death, and assuring him that if he behaved like that again he would personally go to Üsküdar and hang him on a tree.[200]

While such collectiveness had distinct advantages in establishing order, creating, in effect, a pyramid of command with the sultan balanced, however precariously, on the top, it also had a negative side. With such unity came strength, and solidarity in violence could be very dangerous. Just as the janissaries could react violently to protect their own members, so other groups could react in the same way. The *kadı*s, for example, incensed, according to Roe, by the grand vezir 'rashly' having a *kadı* beaten on the feet, were stirred to join the *sipahi*s in revolt.[201] When, in 1590, *kadı*s were arrested for abusing their positions, other *kadı*s hurried off to the coffee houses where they could find *danişmend*s (assistants to the

[198] Peçevi, *Tarihi*, II, p. 362; Selaniki, *Tarih*, II, p. 473.
[199] Doukas, *Historia*, p. 44; Doukas, *Decline*, p. 79.
[200] Cabi, *Târihi*, I, pp. 192–3. [201] Roe, *Negotiations*, p. 159.

10. Punishment, in Schweigger, *Ein newe Reyssbeschreibung*, p. 173.

*kadı*s) and theological students, firing them up with talk of the *kadı*s' arrest as a betrayal of the *ulema*, and dwelling on the implications of these arrests for them all. People gathered in Fatih mosque, but some among them informed the grand vezir and, in consequence, seven *kadı*s were seized and put in prison in Yedikule.[202]

Apart from their attempts to curb crime and violence by treating the inhabitants of the city as blocks of group interests, the sultans also used the city as a canvas for the graphic illustration of the application of punishment, where visuality and violence were intended to terrify and deter. The decapitated heads of rebels were displayed on the *ibret taşı*, the 'example stone', situated in front of Orta Kapı, the middle gate within Topkapı palace. Traitors, such as the seventeen non-Muslim Ottomans who had helped the enemy on a campaign in 1790, were hanged from various city gates 'as an example to the others'.[203] The bodies of prostitutes, protected from male gaze by being put first into sacks, were also hanged. Selim III, for example, selected six infamous prostitutes, after a round-up he had ordered in the city, whom he had hanged from six different gates, warning

[202] Selaniki, *Tarih*, I, p. 225. [203] Ahmed Cavid, *Hadîka*, p. 41.

that any caught in future would be 'fed to the fish'.[204] Many prostitutes were drowned or their bodies thrown into the sea after strangulation.[205] Not all prostitutes, however, drowned, for some were rescued from the sea by boatmen who cruised around Zindan Kapısı between Yemiş İskelesi and Eminönü, ready to pull them out.[206] People could be put to death instantly for violation of the law, such as the various dress codes when those caught on the streets wearing garments to which they were not entitled could be killed on the spot. Shopkeepers who infringed market practices could end their lives swinging in front of their shops, a clear warning to others.

Punishment could also be extremely violent, a graphic reminder of the rule of law. When, in 1596, a janissary known for his shameful behaviour seized the beautiful virgin son of an imam of good family and openly wandered around with him, retribution was dramatic and terrible. The two were captured in Üsküdar and the boy made to say what had happened to him. The janissary was then wrapped in rags in Tophane and put into the mouth of a cannon, which was then fired. This horrific form of punishment terrified the populace.[207] Executions such as this were both brutal and public, a sharp and effective warning to the population and a demonstration of state power. This applied particularly in the case of rebels such as Hüseyin Paşa, whose end in 1600 was particularly unpleasant. Stripped of his clothes, his hands and legs were broken with an axe and he was placed naked backwards on a packhorse. Straps were wound around his neck and burning candles put in them. He was then killed publicly and his body impaled on a hook before the Odun Kapı.[208]

Brutality was also used in cases of immorality, which Heberer was at pains to explain that the Turks punished, contrary to the western belief that every kind of immorality was permissible in Ottoman society. To support this, he related the case of an Ottoman Greek man and a Muslim widow, who, having been imprisoned for having an affair, were paraded through the streets of the city tied together on a donkey, the woman in front and the man behind, facing backwards. The halter was given to the woman and the tail to the man. When they reached Balık Pazarı, the man was stripped, his hands and feet tied and he was impaled alive, the hook passing through his ribs and out the other side. The woman, who was placed in a sack, was drowned in the sea in front of his very eyes, her body

204 Ahmed Cavid, *Hadîka*, pp. 203–4; Selaniki, *Tarih*, II, p. 715.
205 Selaniki, *Tarih*, II, p. 597; Cabi, *Târihi*, I, p. 195.
206 Develi, *Risale-i Garibe*, p. 23.
207 Selaniki, *Tarih*, II, p. 622.
208 Selaniki, *Tarih*, II, p. 847.

11. Punishment of a harlot, in Jean Dumont (Sieur du Mont), *A New Voyage to the Levant* (London, 1705), between pp. 266 and 267.

given afterwards to her relatives. The man stayed alive for three days until someone gave him poison to save him from the pain.[209]

The state could also humiliate, shaming rather than shocking with brutality. This was certainly the case in 1577, when two foreigners, a Venetian shipowner and a seaman working with him, were caught at Galata with two women, one Turk and one Ottoman Greek. The shipowner, having neither a hat on his head nor shoes on his feet and dressed only in cotton underwear, was paraded humiliatingly past the Losa, where

[209] Heberer, *Köle*, pp. 212–13.

all the merchants and his friends were assembled, and taken to the *subaşı*. The shipowner was beaten ninety-seven times, but the other sailor, having been led astray by the shipowner, was only beaten a few times on the soles of his feet. The women were beaten on their buttocks, without their clothes being removed, and were then sent to prison. Initially the men were to be circumcised, a punishment then reduced to a fine of 1,000 *thaler*s to be paid to the *subaşı*, a figure brought down to 400 to 500 *thaler*s because of the imploring of the merchants. A further sum of 1,000 *thaler*s was paid to the sultan. The men were released a month later, the shipowner having to pay the seaman's fine as well as his own, since the seaman had no money. The whole experience had proved an expensive one, for as Gerlach noted, the sailors' entertainment had cost them nearly 2,000 *thaler*s.[210]

Not all state responses to crime were violent, and punishments also included imprisonment, exile or the galleys. The more important members of society were incarcerated in the infamous Yedikule, where their stay was perhaps not that uncomfortable, Lithgow noting rather unexpectedly that 'the air [there] is wholesome, and good to dispel melancholy'.[211] Whatever the punishment was, there was always an element of arbitrariness and a fluidity which meant that there was, in practice, no strict set of rules equating certain types of violence with certain forms of punishment. Application fluctuated period to period and individual to individual. The level of punishment for the same crime could vary according to the social rank of the accused; and the individual predilections of the sultans affected the punishments meted out. Just as some grand vezirs could survive certain transgressions and others could not – Nasuh Paşa paying with his head for his failure to inform his father-in-law Ahmed I of the Cossack capture of Sinop, while Ferhad Paşa kept his under Murad III, despite his deceit over the true position in Moldavia[212] – so, too, individuals could find themselves treated differently for the same crime. Servants were killed, more socially important people were not; prostitutes could be killed for prostitution, their clients not. People could be killed immediately for acts of insanity, as was the man who threw a stone at Selim III at Friday prayer,[213] or dispatched to a mental hospital,[214] or exiled. The man who seized the flag from the mimbar during the Friday prayer at Ayasofya, calling on the 'community of Muhammad' to follow him in 1703, was exiled to Lemnos as a prisoner after investigation revealed that he was clearly mad.[215] Those condemned could be tortured

210 Gerlach, *Günlüğü*, II, pp. 603, 614. 211 Careri, 'Voyage', p. 75.
212 Gelibolulu Mustafa Ali, *Künhü'l-Ahbâr*, III, p. 621. 213 Cabi, *Târihi*, I, pp. 89–90.
214 Cabi, *Târihi*, I, pp. 89–90. 215 Özcan, *Anonim*, p. 226.

horribly before being executed for theft, or they could, on appeal to the sultan, simply be hanged.[216]

The level of punishment could be very much related to the personality of the authority in charge in the city. The janissary *ağa* Köse Mehmed Ağa, active in the 1630s, was known for his very harsh treatment of the janissaries and his tough justice. Whenever he caught a prostitute he hanged her. His reputation for brutality was such that when summoned before him, people would immediately do their ritual ablutions and arrange their wills.[217] Certain sultans were more given to firm punishment than others, Selim III being particularly determined in his drive against prostitution, ordering the authorities to comb the city day and night, hunting down brothels and imprisoning their owners, male and female.[218] Murad IV's instant rendering of justice during his tours of the city in disguise at night, killing any he found contravening his many commands, was such that the discovery of the corpses on the streets in the mornings left the populace quite terrified. People became paralysed with fear to the extent that they stopped talking altogether, convinced that the very walls had ears.[219]

Arbitrariness and fluidity made the exact nature of punishment uncertain. It was always open to alteration and negotiation, due to the corruption of the system. Even if the situation in the seventeenth century was not quite as dismal as portrayed by an anonymous contemporary historian, who regarded it as one of total corruption in which an illiterate boor could be appointed a steward and the only thing that counted was money,[220] corruption was often rampant. Ahmed III saw it for himself during his tours of the city in disguise.[221] In 1623, the English ambassador Sir Thomas Roe clearly had no high regard for the grand vezir, for he wrote to Sir Dudley Carleton in May, 'wee live vnder a vizier, whose conscience and quiltiness keepes him awake, so that hee hath a squint-eye vpon all wayes'.[222] Much later, Abdülhamid II was to regard his navy minister in much the same way.

Bribery was an effective way of perverting justice and buying protection against the law. Thieves and murderers were able to buy their freedom, even though sentenced to be hanged, by paying hefty bribes to the *subaşı* of Istanbul, Kara Hızır, in the 1540s.[223] Kara Hızır was able to extort money not only from those who were guilty, but even those who were not. On one occasion he accused a perfectly respectable woman of taking men into her

[216] Selaniki, *Tarih*, I, pp. 231–2. [217] Naima, *Târih*, II, p. 740.
[218] Ahmed Cavid, *Hadîka*, pp. 194–5. [219] Naima, *Târih*, II, pp. 756–7.
[220] Özcan, *Anonim*, pp. 266–7. [221] Özcan, *Anonim*, pp. 266–7.
[222] Roe, *Negotiations*, p. 157. [223] Sahillioğlu, *Mühimme Defteri*, pp. 215–16, *hüküm* 281.

house for prostitution and informed her that the sultan had ordered her to be tortured. Terrified, the woman, whose honour and upright behaviour the entire *mahalle* vouched for, paid him one hundred gold coins and was released.[224] The Rasputin-like figure at the court of İbrahim I, Cinci Hüseyin Efendi, known as Cinci Hoca, functioned solely on the production of bribes, and as head judge bestowed no position, even the most minor, without payment of a suitable sum.[225] More minor officials considerably augmented their income through bribes, a *subaşı* taking weekly bribes in 1594 to turn a blind eye to illegal *boza* houses (shops selling *boza*, a drink made of fermented millet).[226] In the reign of Murad III, the city security men used to patrol along the seashore, searching the areas frequented by prostitutes and extracting six or seven or even eight ducats from any they found by threatening to hand them over to the *subaşı*. Those who were caught were willing to pay, for they knew that if they appeared before the *subaşı* they would have to pay considerably more, and, if thrown into prison, even if they were innocent, they would not get out without paying a huge sum of money.[227]

The impact of the state's attempts to control violence in the city, with its use of violence to deter, barbarity to terrify and display both to stun and to prevent violence, combined with the corruption and the abrupt and arbitrary nature of much punishment, including instant killing, served in many ways to further the cheapness of life for the people of the city, who could thus fall victim not just to the violence of rebels or the brutality of general criminality, but also to that of the state.

The role of the population

While the sultans thus attempted to control violence and curb crime, the people responded to violence in the city, whether carried out by the janissaries, the state or the common criminal, in a variety of ways: they participated, willingly or unwillingly, they watched, terrified or entertained, and they banded together to protect themselves. In short, they both contributed to the violent nature of the Ottoman capital and were victims of it.

The major political upheavals in the capital inevitably affected the people of the city in one way or another. In 1703, 'all the people of Istanbul, willingly or not, joined in the revolt',[228] as the anonymous author of a contemporary Ottoman history put it. The opinion expressed

[224] Sahillioğlu, *Mühimme Defteri*, p. 216, *hüküm* 281. [225] Naima, *Târih*, III, p. 1173.
[226] Ahmet Refik, *Hicri On Birinci Asırda*, p. 18, *hüküm* 35.
[227] Gerlach, *Günlüğü*, II, p. 522. [228] Özcan, *Anonim*, p. 228.

by this anonymous historian that the people were forced to join the rebellion would indicate that the population was inevitably involved in revolt, compelled into participation whether they liked it or not. But the population appears to have had much more independence of choice than this view would lead one to believe. The people were by no means always dragged willy-nilly into rebellion and could instead choose to remain out of it. In the 1730 rebellion under Patrona Halil which overthrew Ahmed III, they did just that, and 'not knowing where the situation would lead and without taking sides locked themselves in fear in their houses'.[229]

The highly volatile and fast-changing political scene from 1807 to 1809 left the population often unwilling victims of violence. The bombarding by the grand admiral Ramiz Paşa of Ağa Kapısı, the area where the janissaries were gathered – an act of revenge according to the contemporary Cabi – not only failed to disperse them, but had quite the reverse effect from that desired. The bombardments presented the janissaries with an anti-government propaganda weapon and also turned the population, terrified under a hail of cannon fire, into janissary supporters. Much of the cannon fire did not hit its target, but instead rained down on other areas, such as Kumkapı, Beyazıt, Vefa and Süleymaniye. Even the Süleymaniye mosque itself was hit, a cannonball entering one of the windows. One also struck the mansion of a high official, Osman Ağa, in Hocapaşa, killing a man there. The Valide mosque in Bahçe Kapı was also hit. As all those in Ağa Kapısı sat tense and terrified under this attack, men were dispatched on horseback to announce around the district, 'oh people of Muhammad, these people will destroy the mosques with cannon fire and will surrender Istanbul to the infidels',[230] a statement to which considerable weight was added by the hit on the Süleymaniye. At the same time, a crowd of people had gathered at Çöplük and Eminönü to watch the cannon firing. Mistaken for the janissaries, they were fired on too, and killed.[231]

Not all violence required participation. Some of it was pure spectacle, in much the same way as massive conflagrations were. It appealed to the crowd, even if not, according to Evliya Çelebi, to the good-natured, gentle, refined and gentlemanly members of the population, when, in July 1649, many 'opium addicts, gossipers and busybodies' hurried from the city to Üsküdar to watch the battle between the janissaries and the Celali rebels under their 'bandit' leaders Gürcü Nebi, Katırcıoğlu Mehmed and Kazzaz Ahmed. While the grand vezir settled in Çamlıca and the number of janissaries and *sipahi*s in Üsküdar rose to ten thousand,

[229] Abdi, *Tarihi*, p. 28. [230] Cabi, *Târihi*, I, pp. 279–80, quotation p. 279.
[231] Cabi, *Târihi*, I, pp. 279–80; Oğulukyan, *Ruznamesi*, p. 41.

necessitating a daily delivery of five thousand loaves of bread and shipments of water from Kırk Çeşme, for the weather was hot,[232] thousands streamed to Üsküdar, dressed in their finest garments, to seek out suitable spots there and in Bağlar, and by Karacaahmet Sultan Tekkesi and Miskinler Tekkesi, from where they could comfortably watch the battle that was soon to break out. People agitated about which vineyard or hill would be best to watch from. Some settled for picnics on the way, stopping on the main road to eat pastrami, *sucuk* (savoury sausage), *kaşkaval* cheese, roasted chickpeas, nuts and hazelnuts. As if on a promenade to Kağıthane or enjoying themselves at Ok Meydanı, they sat squashed together in heaps, hoisting up their garments around them as they plonked themselves down on gravestones or among the vines, some letting off fireworks, some playing ball games, reciting poetry or singing, all horsing around. Some even wandered around among the soldiers, smoking pipes and fanning themselves against the heat, or, once the battle had started, asked those hurrying off to fight for water or fire for their pipes. Some had even brought their bows and quivers of arrows. Despite the antiquated condition of these arms, with their moth-eaten feathers, their owners were keen to talk big, promising to break these perfidious Celalis. Others forecast disaster if the Celalis prevailed, predicting that all the people of Üsküdar would throw themselves into the sea at Kız Kulesi, and that not one of those poor, wretched people would be able to find a boat even for one thousand gold pieces. Once battle was joined, it lasted throughout the day, those watching with binoculars reporting on its progress, until finally the Celali forces withdrew.

Evliya Çelebi was indignant about the behaviour of this crowd, who watched as if at an amusing entertainment, while for those fighting it was a matter of life and death. His description was not flattering:

> A multitude of weak, puny and wretched, locust-legged, hairless-limbed addicts and hordes of the ill-omened with their noses running with mucus, bent double as if in prayer, necks and mouths twisted, with huge lips and saliva running onto their chests, with their tongues lolling out, gathered together and in that stifling heat, dressed in thin outer garments or white Indian cloth of Ahmedebad, sat side by side, some of them with fans, some with back-scratchers, and watched the battle.[233]

Apart from watching the spectacle of fighting, crowds also gathered to look at the bodies of the fallen. Despite keeping out of the 1730 Patrona Halil rebellion, choosing instead to lock themselves away in their houses

[232] Naima, *Târih*, III, pp. 1222–32.

[233] Evliya Çelebi, *Seyahatname (Gördüklerim) Evliya Çelebi*, ed. Mustafa Nihat Özön and Nijat Özön (Istanbul, 2005), pp. 208–11.

to await the outcome, they emerged to look with hatred at the bodies of the grand admiral Mustafa Paşa and the steward Mehmed Paşa, almost as if taking revenge on them,[234] and to gaze with loathing at the body of the grand vezir Nevşehirli Damad İbrahim Paşa, satisfactorily removed thanks to Patrona Halil. But very shortly afterwards, when Patrona Halil himself fell, killed by the new sultan Mahmud I, the people, now pleased with this event, came to look this time at his body, cast before the Bab-ı Hümayun, and to give thanks for his death.[235] Public criers were dispatched around the city to announce the good news of the death of the rebel leaders, and the people, delighted by this event and in a sharp turnaround from their earlier position, when they had heartily supported Patrona Halil, prayed to God for the prosperity of the sultan.[236] While pleased with Patrona Halil's removal of İbrahim Paşa, they were not pleased with the turmoil that followed. Having gazed with hatred at the body of the fallen grand vezir, they now looked with pleasure on that of Patrona Halil, a clear display of just how fickle popular support could be.

In 1807 the public were again looking at corpses, this time at that of the steward of the former *valide sultan* Yusuf Paşa, whose head was brought from Bursa, where he had been exiled and then killed, and placed on the *ibret taşı*.[237] The head attracted large crowds and 'for three days many people came to look at the head as if going to a show, and no one left without saying something insulting'.[238] This activity apparently had a calming influence, for the inflamed passions of the people were cooled and the level of popular agitation fell.[239] In 1809 they were even more active in their reaction to the head of Kadı Paşa on the *ibret taşı*. The city was shaken to its foundations by the news of his fall, at least according to the contemporary Oğulukyan. 'All the people rushed there. They swore at the head, many of them pulled at its beard, and they spat on it so much that the head was completely smothered in spittle. Not even a hair of the beard remained'.[240] Many came to kick the head, angry that Kadı Paşa had tried to destroy the janissaries and replace them with a new army, and that, had this plan succeeded, no janissary would have been left alive in Istanbul.[241]

The violence in the city was by no means all political and the population was prey also to common criminality, to thuggery, theft, abduction and murder. People were murdered, kidnapped, raped and robbed, as in any

[234] Aktepe, *Patrona İsyanı*, p. 152. [235] Abdi, *Tarihi*, p. 58.
[236] Destari, *Tarihi*, p. 32. [237] Cabi, *Târihi*, I, pp. 153–4.
[238] Oğulukyan, *Ruznamesi*, pp. 14–15.
[239] Ubeydullah Kuşmani and Ebubekir Efendi, *Asiler ve Gaziler. Kabakçı Mustafa Risalesi*, ed. Aysel Danacı Yıldız (Istanbul, 2007), p. 129.
[240] Oğulukyan, *Ruznamesi*, p. 46. [241] Cabi, *Târihi*, I, p. 393.

other metropolis, and men, even religious ones, coveted other men's goods. When a man's arm was found in the Hocapaşa public lavatories in 1807, the governor of the city, Musa Paşa, ordered an investigation. It was discovered that two mullahs in a *medrese* had killed the man for his possessions and had also thrown one hip and two feet into the lavatories of the Sultan Ahmed mosque, a crime for which they were hanged.[242] One Istanbul murder hit the the *Glasgow Herald*, which ran a story in February 1876 about a double murder 'of a mysterious and startling nature', which had taken place in Pera and involved two Armenian sisters, whose bodies were found six months after their disappearance. Oddly, as the paper noted, the landlord of one of the sisters had not reacted when the rent fell overdue, and had not attempted to get another tenant, 'a circumstance which, coupled with the fact that the blood of the murdered woman oozed through the ceiling of a room inhabited by him, tends to criminate him as at least privy to the deed'. A Galata stockbroker was also implicated.[243]

The motivation for some murders was opaque and, despite high-level investigation, eluded a solution. Even such a powerful *bostancıbaşı* as Zernişanizade İsmail Ağa was unable to bring the case of a body in a trunk to a successful conclusion. In 1805/6, a boat offloaded a wooden chest on the jetty outside Ahır Kapı. It was given to a porter to take to customs, where he was told he would find the owner. The porter took the chest but the owner was not there, so he left the chest and went away. After a few days a disgusting smell began to rise from the chest and, when it was opened, a man's body was found inside. No one knew who the man was. The government was informed because the body had come from outside (and because the body came from the sea), and the grand vezir and the sultan questioned the *bostancıbaşı* İsmail Ağa, pointing out that if this had been a straightforward murder, the body would have been thrown from the boat into the sea. It was very hard to think of any explanation for why it had been intentionally brought to the customs. Despite all his efforts, the *bostancıbaşı* İsmail Ağa was unable to obtain any information and the case remained unsolved.[244]

Even when the victim was a very important member of society, and the investigator the grand vezir himself, results sometimes eluded the authorities. When the vezir Yusuf Paşa was discovered very early one morning, stabbed to death in his house in Kuru Çeşme in 1590, the grand vezir Sinan Paşa himself appeared at dawn to conduct the investigation. Rounding up his steward, *ağa*s and other servants, he imprisoned and tortured them, without success. The investigation was extremely

[242] Cabi, *Târihi*, I, p. 124. [243] *Glasgow Daily Herald*, Tuesday 29 February 1876, p. 2.
[244] Cabi, *Târihi*, I, pp. 91–2.

thorough, even spreading to the foreign embassies. Despite this, the culprits were not found. Much later, the bodies of two of his servants who had murdered him (Yusuf Paşa apparently treated his servants very badly) were found. The discovery of their bodies so long after the event caused much amazement and the suspicion that important people had in some way had a hand in the *paşa*'s murder.[245]

One way in which the population responded to criminality was by using group identities. Just as the state used collectivity as a method of dealing with and controlling violence, so too did the population itself, often responding to criminal activity as a group. Such groups could be professional, as in the case of those who united in the face of the continuous despotic behaviour of the porters in 1810,[246] or the tradesmen who, in 1811, beat and severely injured soldiers with the poles they used to close the shutters of their shops, after the men had begun fighting in the courtyard of Yeni Cami (Valide Sultan mosque) over a woman.[247] Or the group could be made up of men of the same religion, who banded together to protect themselves against persecution. Jews in Balat in 1810 attacked the janissary security unit there, determined to defend themselves against the oppression they were suffering at its hands, regardless of the consequences. After the attack, some of them were caught and some hanged.[248]

One of the strongest identifiers for the Istanbul population, and indeed for any Ottoman, wherever he found himself in the empire, was the *mahalle*.

Mahalle

One unit central to the city, a physical manifestation of collectiveness of which the urban fabric was constituted, was the *mahalle*, the districts or neighbourhoods into which the city was divided. State authority and control was orchestrated not so much by direct presence, but through the officials of the *mahalle*, the imam and, in the later nineteenth century, the *muhtar* (the secular headman of the *mahalle*) and the *kadı*. It was the imam and the *kadı* who ran the affairs of the *mahalle*, delivering justice, administering punishment, controlling immoral activity such as prostitution and protecting the honour of the neighbourhood. The state made the *mahalle* responsible for controlling the movements of foreigners and troublemakers within it and could, in times of an increase in disturbances in the city or a crime wave, order the *mahalle* to watch the movements of its

245 Selaniki, *Tarih*, I, p. 226. 246 Cabi, *Târihi*, I, pp. 630–1.
247 Cabi, *Târihi*, II, p. 732. 248 Cabi, *Târihi*, I, pp. 602–3.

inhabitants, reporting anything suspicious to the authorities.[249] The imams, *kadı*s and muezzins were to report on any immoral women, and were not to allow the presence of any such women in their *mahalle*s.[250]

The *mahalle* itself had a strong sense of identity, people living in it identifying strongly with it and being collectively concerned for behaviour within it. Popular pressure in a *mahalle*, known as *mahalle baskını* (*mahalle* raiding) regulated behaviour, and activities disapproved of by the population could come under collective attack. Any movements by people who came into the *mahalle* from outside were keenly observed and reported on by the inhabitants, neighbours carefully watching neighbours and checking that their behaviour was upright and as it should be. If an unknown man was seen to enter the house of a woman under suspicion, or if this was heard about, the whole *mahalle* went into action and a *mahalle* raid was set in motion.

Such raiding was noisy, public and most effective. As soon as the presence of an unrelated man in a woman's house was sighted, everyone was informed and men assembled in the coffee house to organise a raid. The raiding party consisted of the police, the imam, the *muhtar*, some of the leading men of the *mahalle*, the nightwatchmen with their sticks and the young men of the *mahalle*, carrying sticks and even guns. Led by the watchmen carrying their lanterns the party set off and, reaching the target, surrounded the house to prevent the man escaping. They made a great deal of noise, shouting that they would not tolerate this immoral behaviour, and demanding that the door be opened. If the door was not opened immediately, the imam ordered that it be broken down and the men all rushed in and began searching the house from top to bottom. If they did not find the man, they dispersed, possibly apologising to the woman, although there was in any case nothing she could do. If they did find the man, they dragged him out into the street and insulting him, spitting in his face and humiliating him in front of the entire *mahalle*, they took him to the police station. Returning then to the house, they informed the woman that she was to leave the *mahalle* the next day, and she was thus expelled.[251]

The *mahalle* had considerable freedom of action, expelling not just women, but also any men who indulged in drinking and other activities with women whom they invited into their houses.[252] This freedom meant

249 Ahmet Refik, *Onuncu Asr-ı Hicrî*, p. 138, *hüküm* 3.

250 Ahmet Refik, *Onuncu Asr-ı Hicrî*, pp. 38–9, *hüküm* 2.

251 Abdülaziz Bey, *Osmanlı Âdet, Merasim ve Tabirleri*, ed. Kazım Arısan and Duygu Arısan Günay (Istanbul, 2002), pp. 339–41.

252 Düzdağ, *Ebussuûd Efendi*, p. 57, *hüküm* 172.

12. A street in Pera, in Amicis, *Constantinople*, p. 21.

that the *mahalle* could, in practice, act in a way that made it tantamount to autonomous. This could lead, in turn, to considerable flexibility in the application of the law, whose course could be altered by the presentation of money, a commodity which Gerlach noted in the 1570s 'sorts out many problems'.[253] Gerlach described how the *kadı* of his own *mahalle* was instructed to provide information on any immoral women in the district, being threatened with punishment if he did not comply.

> Today those charged with investigating prostitutes came to the street in front of our house. A *kadı* and an *emir* appeared in front of the mosque, that is they sat a green-turbaned official there and called the imam and other religious men from the mosque and said that they had to inform them if there were any women leading an unsuitable life in their district and if they did not the sultan would punish them. Those who had information about the existence of such women wrote the name on a piece of paper and placed it in front of the *kadı*... women who were as yet unmarried and women without husbands bribed the men of religion and ensured that they were not denounced.[254]

Investigations at this time had produced a list of two hundred and fifty women, some of whom, however, protested that they had been falsely accused and that such calumny was the result of the jealousy of the imams and their assistants in the *mahalle* mosque, who had wanted to punish those who had not sent them rice and other foods and clothes in Ramazan *bayramı* (the religious festival at the end of the month of fasting) and *kurban bayramı* (the religious festival of sacrifice), as was the custom. Unmarried women who had given money to the imams had not been denounced.

Since the state relied on the *kadı*s and imams of the *mahalle* to provide the information concerning illegal activities in their areas, these men had the power either to provide false information or no information at all. However, the state was not always convinced of the reliability of the information it received – no doubt well aware of the power of bribery, which was, after all, rife at all levels of the bureaucracy. As a result of the complaints of the women accused here of prostitution, apparently due to their failure to provide the requisite presents to the local religious officials, the sultan ordered the investigation to be conducted again to ensure that no injustice had been committed.[255]

The state's suspicions were also aroused in the case of the arrest of a young Muslim sailor in a non-Muslim *mahalle* in 1808. A well-known troublemaker, who spent much of his time sitting in the local wine houses being abusive to the non-Muslims and not paying for his drink, he was caught one night by the *mahalle* guards, who, having planted a piece of

[253] Gerlach, *Günlüğü*, II, p. 624. [254] Gerlach, *Günlüğü*, II, p. 624.
[255] Gerlach, *Günlüğü*, II, pp. 640–1.

cloth filled with gunpowder on him, accused him of being an arsonist. Suspicious of the *mahalle*'s motive and in view of the sailor's youth, the grand vezir merely sent him to the galleys.[256]

The case of the sailor gives an idea of the degree to which the *mahalle* could operate its own justice, using it against those from outside whom it did not like, or putting pressure on the behaviour, in particular the morality, of its inhabitants. Independent of the officials, the members of the *mahalle* also formed what amounted to a neighbourhood watch, which ensured that everybody's movements were constantly scrutinised by the inhabitants whose sharp eyes missed nothing.

Much crime came to light or was punished as a result of the amateur detective work of *mahalle* inhabitants, and local knowledge could cost dearly those involved in nefarious activities. Halil Ağa, known as Forsa Halil, one of the high palace officials and the former head of the armourers, who owned a garden in the Yeni Kapı, was known as a lustful and abominable scoundrel. It was common knowledge that his slaves and servants ran a prostitution business and used to bring in prostitutes, strip them of their clothes, kill them and dump them in the wells and water closets. Even his own slave girls worked as prostitutes, with men from outside as clients. All the people of the *mahalle* followed these developments. When Halil Ağa was away, the *mahalle* leaders raided the house and caught the slaves at work with men from outside. They registered what was going on, searched the wells and the places where the bodies were buried and found the corpses of more than ten men and women. The servants were made to talk, confessing that 'this has always been our master's habit and custom'. Three of Halil Ağa's servants were tortured to death and he himself imprisoned.[257]

It was local observation that brought to light other equally unattractive scams, such as that involving a certain Mehmed Ağa, the local muezzin and the muezzin's wife in Silivri Kapı, executed for murder in 1786/87. Every month Mehmed Ağa would marry one or two women, found for him by the muezzin's wife. Shortly afterwards he would announce that his wife had fallen sick and died and the muezzin's wife would then prepare and wash the body for burial. In this way many women were killed and their property appropriated.[258]

It was the persistence of an observant neighbour that also brought the *şeyh* Manevi Efendi to justice at the beginning of the eighteenth century. After the death of her husband, the Yedikule warden from whom she inherited money, Meryem married Şeyh Manevi Efendi. Three or four

[256] Cabi, *Târihi*, I, p. 335. [257] Selaniki, *Tarih*, II, p. 546.
[258] Taylesanizade, *Tarihi*, p. 184.

months later, Meryem died and her body was taken out for burial. Seeing the coffin emerging, a female neighbour asked who had died and was told that it was Manevi Efendi's wife, who had died the night before. The neighbour was most surprised, for she had seen her only the evening before when she was perfectly healthy but frightened, begging the neighbour not to leave her alone. With her suspicions aroused, the neighbour went to Topkapı and spoke to the head of the security unit, telling him not to put the body into the grave. She then went to the governor. The next development was a letter written by the *kadı* of Istanbul to the grand vezir in which he stated that the wife of Şeyh Manevi Efendi had died of strangulation in the *mahalle* of Kasap İlyas. The governor issued an order instructing that the matter be investigated. An official was appointed and the coffin opened. When the women looked in (no men being allowed to do so), they found that there were rope injuries round the woman's throat, marks of several blows to her head, black bruises on her hands and that her nose was ripped. Further, her hair had not been unplaited (as done after death and before burial) and the body had not been put in a winding sheet, as was customary, but placed in a bad-quality cloth sheet. The *şeyh* was now questioned and replied that he had no idea who was responsible, claiming that he too would open a case to find the culprit. Investigations in the *mahalle* revealed that the *şeyh* had a bad reputation. The woman had no heirs. The case went to the *kadı*, but during the hearing the *şeyh* became ill and died.[259]

Mahalle inhabitants were particularly sharp observers when it came to matters of morality. In this they were quite effective, as Ahmet Rasim recalled at the beginning of the twentieth century:

> Upon looking round, and noting carefully, I understood that it was not just the police who were keeping an eye on prostitution, but also the young bucks of the *mahalle*, and the important men of the *mahalle* and the women of the *mahalle* who all set up their own watch groups.

'Among so many watching eyes', as he put it, it was very difficult to slip in and out of houses at night or in the early morning unobserved.[260]

One aspect of punishment connected with morality, and one that was most effective in the *mahalle*, was public shaming, a particularly effective humiliation in a small, tight community. Initially a *mahalle* punishment, it became in the reign of Selim III a state punishment, an example of grass roots turning into state procedure, when those caught with prostitutes were made to marry them. Such a marriage was a source of great shame, and had been so in earlier centuries, as the cursing of such men by the

[259] Özcan, *Anonim*, p. 182. [260] Ahmet Rasim, *Fuhş-i Atik* (Istanbul, 2005), p. 177.

author of the *Risale-i Garibe* makes clear.[261] According to Ahmed Cavid, such public humiliation was successful, and fear of such a humiliating marriage persuaded many men to avoid prostitutes.[262]

Men could pay large bribes to avoid the public shame involved in being caught with a prostitute and ran considerable risks to avoid exposure, as Mahmud, a master tanner and son of a *hacı* (a man who had been on pilgrimage), did when caught with a woman by the janissary head of security of Üsküdar in Ramazan 1810. In order to avoid the shame, Mahmud, a man both well-off and usually of moral and upstanding character, paid a five hundred *kuruş* bribe to the janissary security head.

The further ramifications of the case illustrate both the importance of shame and the power of bribery within the bureaucracy of the time. The raid in which Mahmud had been caught had been conducted illegally, for such raids required the presence of a representative of the *kadı*, and no such man had been present. But the imam of the *mahalle* had been there. He, too, required a bribe, both from the tanner and from the janissary security head, to ensure his silence. Money having changed hands, all were now content and everything seemed satisfactorily settled. Unfortunately for those concerned, the Üsküdar *kadı* Hamzazade Efendi got to hear of the matter and demanded half of the bribe. All – the janissary security head, the imam and the tanner, arrested on the *kadı*'s orders and interrogated by an *ağa* from the local Üsküdar security unit – denied that any such thing had occurred, the tanner maintaining that any such allegation was mere malicious gossip put around by his enemies, and pointing out that if he had wanted to indulge in this way he had only to go to the slave market and buy a concubine with whom sex would be his legal right. A bribe was now paid also to the *ağa*, who returned to the *kadı* explaining that they had held the tanner in prison for two days but that it was still not clear why he was there. No case had been opened against him, nobody had come forward accusing him of sexual assault on their daughter, wife or sister, or of any immoral behaviour in the vicinity of their home. The master tanner was a member of a strong guild and any mishandling of the situation would lead to the intervention of the guild to protect him. Although they could send the tanner to Ağa Kapısı, the janissary headquarters, this might cause unnecessary complications. Convinced, the *kadı* gave up his pursuit of the tanner, the janissary security head, the imam and the bribe, and died a few days later.[263]

The *mahalle* represented both security and tight social control, a mechanism for order in an often violent world. For many of the inhabitants of

[261] Develi, *Risale-i Garibe*, p. 31. [262] Ahmed Cavid, *Hadîka*, p. 204.
[263] Cabi, *Târihi*, I, pp. 709–10.

Istanbul, from the poorest *mahalle* to the confines of the palace itself, the magnificent and enormous metropolis was a death trap where they could fall foul of janissary violence, state retribution or the whims of nature at any moment. Life was both cheap and uncertain. But there was an institution which eased existence for many in the capital: the *vakıf*.

4 Welfare

One of the central institutions of Istanbul was the *vakıf*. Usually translated as 'pious foundation', this gives a somewhat misleading impression, for it conveys only one aspect of the organisation. Undoubtedly religious, it was also a quintessential system of welfare, used both to develop the economy of the city and to guarantee the material conditions and well-being of many of the city's inhabitants. It contained elements of prestige and display, and of protection of family wealth.

For many of the inhabitants of the city, it was a cradle-to-grave institution, for a man could be born in a *vakıf* house, sleep in a *vakıf* cradle, eat and drink from *vakıf* provisions, read in *vakıf* libraries, teach in a *vakıf* school, take his wage from the *vakıf* administration and, when he died, be put in a *vakıf* coffin and be buried in a *vakıf* graveyard.[1] It was the *vakıf* institution that fed, educated, housed, washed and gave medical treatment to the population. It provided the people with a livelihood and rescued them in times of natural disaster. They went shopping in *vakıf* shops, they prayed in *vakıf* mosques; and the physical features of their city were to a very great extent shaped by the *vakıf*. In short, life in Istanbul without the *vakıf* institution was unthinkable.

A *vakıf* was an endowment, the income from which was allocated to charitable purposes. *Vakıf*s ranged from the great, imperial complexes to very small endowments, and could consist of property, shops, *hamam*s, caravansarays or agricultural land, or they could be cash *vakıf*s, the interest from which was used for charitable purposes. Income from the *vakıf*s paid for the upkeep and running of mosques, schools, hospitals and commercial *han*s. Such income also paid for an enormous range of other social welfare services: water and food distribution to the poor, clothing, schooling, feeding and even outings for orphan children, water jugs and

[1] Bahaeddin Yediyıldız, *XVIII. Yüzyılda Türkiye'de Vakıf Müessesesi. Bir Sosyal Tarih İncelemesi* (Ankara, 2003), p. vii.

13. Charity to animals, in Jean-Antoine Guer, *Moeurs et usages des Turcs*, 2 vols. (Paris, 1747), I, between pp. 220 and 221.

wood for schools, oil for lamps and lead for the roofs of *mescit*s (small mosques), and for recitations from the Qu'ran or prayers for the souls of the dead.[2] Money from *vakıf*s was used to pay for bread to be distributed

[2] Ömer Lütfi Barkan and Ekrem Hakkı Ayverdi (eds.), *İstanbul Vakıfları Tahrîr Defteri 953 (1546) Târîhli* (Istanbul, 1970), no. 214, p. 33; no. 297, p. 49; no. 316, p. 53; no. 328, p. 53; no. 358, p. 60; no. 363, pp. 61–2; no. 847, p. 150; no. 1323, p. 236; no. 1511, p. 256;

to street dogs and rice for feeding birds;[3] it could even go to paying for a public lavatory.[4] Special acts of charity came out of *vakıf* coffers, Bayezid II 'because of compassion' ordering the *mütevelli* of Cami-i Cedid to pay an extra *akçe* to a former janissary who had lost his sight and appealed to the sultan for help.[5]

Some *vakıf*s were extremely large, consisting of enormous mosque complexes, such as those established by the sultans and the vezirs. Such complexes, centred round a mosque, provided schools (according to Evliya Çelebi, all imperial and vezir mosques had primary schools),[6] hospitals, soup kitchens, *hamam*s and caravansarays. The imperial complexes fed many people from their soup kitchens, that of Bayezid II, for example, feeding a thousand people per day, providing them with both quantity and much variety.[7] They could also offer other, more seasonal services. In one particularly cold winter, in 1813, when there was a scarcity of coal and timber in the city due to plague, the patients from the Sultan Ahmed hospital were transferred to the Süleymaniye, and poor immigrants and their families were moved in to prevent them from dying from cold, and were given other charitable assistance.[8]

Apart from the free welfare offered by these institutions, such major *vakıf*s also provided employment to those who ran them, and included shops, markets and other commercial activities to provide the income to sustain them. Many major *vakıf*s were set up by women, such as Hürrem Sultan, the wife of Süleyman I, known in Europe as Roxelana,[9] or the mother of Mehmed IV, whose mosque was supported by a large complex of shops.[10] The wives of the vezirs, too, endowed charitable institutions, the wife of Vezir Mahmud Paşa, for example, requesting before her death in 1598 that her husband ensure that one-third of her property be used for charity.[11] Many others, of a much lower social position, also endowed small *vakıf*s, for, according to Spandounes, all Turks, 'large and small, are constantly

no. 1788, p. 304; no. 1832, p. 314; no. 2107, pp. 356–7; Halim Baki Kunter, 'Türk Vakıfları ve Vakfiyeleri Üzerine Mücmel Bir Etüd', *Vakıflar Dergisi*, no. 1 (1938), pp. 118–19, 125; Özcan, *Anonim*, p. 101.

3 Kunter, 'Türk Vakıfları', pp. 105, 111.

4 Kunter, 'Türk Vakıfları', p. 111.

5 İlhan Şahin and Feridun Emecen (eds.), *Osmanlılarda Divân-Bürokrasi-Ahkâm. II. Bâyezid Dönemine Ait 906/1501 Tarihli Ahkâm Defteri* (Istanbul, 1994), p. 65, *hüküm* 228. See also Ömer Lütfi Barkan, 'Fatih Câmi ve İmareti Tesîslerinin 1489–1490 Yıllarına Âit Muhasebe Bilânçoları', *İstanbul Üniversitesi İktisat Fakültesi Mecmuası*, 23/1–2 (1962–63), pp. 239–341; Barkan, 'Ayasofya Camii ve Eyüp Türbesinin 1489–1491 Yıllarına Âit Muhasebe Bilânçoları', *İstanbul Üniversitesi İktisat Fakültesi Mecmuası*, 23/1–2 (1962–63), pp. 342–98.

6 Evliya Çelebi, *Seyahatnamesi, I Kitap*, p. 131.

7 Hoca Sadettin Efendi, *Tacü't-Tevarih*, IV, p. 108.

8 Cabi, *Târihi*, II, pp. 944–5.

9 Peçevi, *Tarihi*, I, pp. 226–8.

10 Careri, 'Voyage', p. 72.

11 Selaniki, *Tarih*, II, p. 767.

engaged on such pious and charitable works – far more so than we Christians'.[12]

'Very vain in building mosques and hospitals',[13] the Ottomans erected many *vakıfs* and mosque complexes, Evliya Çelebi regarding the capital as the city with more such complexes than any other city he had seen in his fifty-one years of travel.[14] Such *vakıf* buildings impressed Salomon Schweigger, a German Protestant priest attached to the Habsburg embassy in the mid sixteenth century, who noted that the Turks gave 'great importance to the imposing appearance of *vakıf* buildings such as mosques and schools and for this they do not spare any expense'.[15]

One of the most famous of the imperial *vakıfs* was that of Mehmed II, the Fatih mosque complex, centred round the magnificent Fatih mosque, completed in 1470, and described in an Italian source from the late sixteenth century:

> Mervailous is the greatnes and magnificence of it, beinge made in the similitude of the Sofia, and hath about it 100 howses covered with lead, of a round cube fation, ordeyned to receive straingers and travailers of what nation or religion soever they be; where they may rest (as alike at other churches) with thier horses and servants three days together, yf they please, and have thier charges borne, not paying anything for thier owne and servants diet. Besides ther are without the circuett of the church over 150 lodginges for the poore of the citie, unto whome they geve to eate and to every one of them in money an asper a day. It hath also a place where they geve siropp and medisens of free cost to all that demand, and another for government of the madd people. The said Sultan Mahemett left for the maintenance hearof sixty thowsand ducketts yearelie rent in that time, which nowe doth import above 200,000; for they have of the rest of Sofia, to which also, besides other revenewe, belongeth the besistans and in a manner all the principall shopps in the citie, even until you come to the Seralio of the Great Turke, which paieth rent therto 1001 aspers per day.[16]

Among its main functions was that of feeding the populace, including poor women who went there to eat.[17] In 1490 food was distributed daily, morning and evening, to 1,117 people;[18] by 1530, a thousand people were being fed there twice a day.[19] Every day, 3, 300 *fodlas* (a type of bread) were baked.[20] According to Ünver's calculations for 1545, the soup

[12] Spandounes, *Origin*, p. 134.
[13] Careri, 'Voyage', p. 88. [14] Evliya Çelebi, *Seyahatnamesi, I Kitap*, p. 132.
[15] Salomon Schweigger, *Sultanlar Kentine Yolculuk 1578–1581*, trans. S. Türkis Noyan and ed. Heidi Stein (Istanbul, 2004), p. 122.
[16] Sanderson, *Travels*, p. 70.
[17] A. Süheyl Ünver, *Risale 7. İstanbul Üniversitesi Tarihine Başlangıç. Fatih Külliyesi ve Zamanı İlim Hayatı* (Istanbul, 1946), reprinted in Ünver, *İstanbul Risaleleri 1*, p. 246.
[18] Barkan and Ayverdi, *Tahrîr Defteri*, p. xi. [19] Ünver, *Fatih Külliyesi*, p. 246.
[20] Ünver, *Fatih Külliyesi*, p. 287.

kitchen was feeding around two thousand five hundred to three thousand people per day.[21] The ingredients bought for its soup kitchen in the late fifteenth/early sixteenth century, depending on the season, included mutton, salt, wheat, flour, parsley, onion, cumin, pepper, chickpeas, courgettes, sour grapes, yoghurt, chard, rice, oil, honey, grapes, plums, almonds, figs, starch, saffron, trotters, cinnamon and cloves. Food served consisted of rice soup, wheat soup, *dane* (a kind of rice cooked with butter), saffron rice, *zirva* (a kind of sweet meal cooked with starch, sugar/honey, dry sultanas and dry figs), *fodla*, *yahni* (meat stew with onions), *ekşi aş* (meat stew with plums), meat, pickled grapes, pickled aubergine and pickled onions.[22]

Apart from feeding, the complex also had a hospital, which included a *hamam* for patients, where both the patients and their clothes were washed.[23] Guests were accommodated free, and could stay for three days.[24] The hospital attracted the admiration of western observers, impressed both by the services offered and by the fact that such services were free. Spandounes noted that

> the hospital is open to all, Christians, Jews and Turks; and its doctors give free treatment and food three times a day. I have seen men of the upper class and other grand persons lodging here, their horses being cared for. It has fourteen medical students and they attend lectures from their masters, who are well paid.[25]

The Süleymaniye, the greatest of all the imperial complexes according to Spandounes,[26] consisted of a mosque, tombs, schools, a medical school, a soup kitchen, a mental hospital, a caravansaray and stables, a hospital, a *hamam* for men and commercial buildings.[27] Süleyman I also built several other mosque complexes in the city: that named after his father Selim I, the mosque complex of Şehzade Sultan Mehmed, and two caravansarays, a mosque, schools and a soup kitchen for his daughter Mihrimah in Üsküdar.[28]

The all-encompassing nature of these *vakıf*s is indicated by the comments of Hoca Sadeddin Efendi in his *Tacü't-Tevarih* (The Crown of Histories), written in the sixteenth century, in which he describes the students, 'those lucky people', who passed their time in the school and filled their stomachs with the appetising food which emerged in great quantities every morning and every evening from the soup kitchen.

[21] A. Süheyl Ünver (ed.), *Fâtih Aşhânesi Tevzînâmesi* (Istanbul, 1953), p. 11, fn. 9.
[22] Ünver, *Fatih Külliyesi*, p. 288.
[23] Ünver, *Fatih Külliyesi*, pp. 244–5.
[24] Ünver, *Fatih Külliyesi*, p. 246.
[25] Spandounes, *Origin*, p. 134.
[26] Spandounes, *Origin*, p. 134.
[27] Doğan Kuban, *Kent ve Mimarlık Üzerine İstanbul Yazıları* (Istanbul, 1998), p. 112.
[28] Peçevi, *Tarihi*, I, pp. 224–8.

With light hearts they would pray for the giver of this blessing and return to their lessons. The poor, both men and women, whoever they were, returned to their houses with vessels full [of food] and thus they escaped the anxieties of hunger. Beautiful guest houses and inns were erected for travellers and for those who came from different countries, and a variety of foods was ordered to be prepared for them. According to the conditions inscribed in their dignified foundation deeds, rich tables were laid out every day in these guest houses and appetising foods were arranged, the variety of food being increased according to the rank of the travellers, and so it became the custom to offer lavish hospitality. In order to gobble from the tables laiden with this wealth of food, those who were not travellers dressed in travelling garments and came there and filled their stomachs. The numbers of those who came to the guest houses was such that it was not possible to distinguish the false from the genuine travellers among those who sat there. Apart from this, a great caravansaray was built in which the travellers could tie up their horses and place their goods and where their servants could stay. Here the animals were given barley from the *vakıf* storehouses. This reed pen whose mouth is separated into two does not has the strength to describe the hospital which was built for the sick who needed medicine. If able doctors do not understand this, they should pretend to be ill and stay there like the great numbers of those who are sick in order to experience the care and kindness shown there. A separate *hamam* was built for the sick and the benevolence was made complete by the appointment of people employed to wash the patients' clothes and clean the patients and smooth away their suffering. A school building was also built for the education of the children. A considerable amount of money was specially set aside from the well-kept *vakıf*s for poor and orphaned children.[29]

Imperial *vakıf*s were thus the main plank of social welfare by which the sultans, and high-up vezirs, provided for the people of the city. Schweigger, who himself benefited on several occasions from the soup kitchens while travelling to Istanbul in the later sixteenth century, wrote: 'If you ask me, this kind of *vakıf* [here referring to soup kitchens] is more valuable than the monuments of the ancient Romans such as the columns, the tapering columns and the statues, and the Egyptian pyramids, because all these ancient works are of no more use than for demonstrating great art. They are of no use to God or man'.[30]

Apart from building such large mosque complexes, sultans also undertook other constructions designed to improve the living conditions of Istanbul's inhabitants, some – such as the waterway built by Süleyman I to bring the waters of Kırk Çeşme to the city – costing as much as the mosque complexes themselves. According to the seventeenth-century historian Peçevi, the people had until that point been in need of every drop of water, and he expressed the hope that Süleyman would receive

[29] Hoca Sadettin Efendi, *Tacü't-Tevarih*, III, pp. 180–1.

[30] Schweigger, *Yolculuk*, p. 128.

great blessings from God for this admirable act of charity.[31] Süleyman also built a bridge at Büyükçekmece which considerably improved travelling conditions, for the area was the site of many accidents, especially in winter, with loaded carts and caravans sinking hopelessly into the mud or snow.[32] Certain sultans were particularly renowned for their charity. Bayezid II was apparently so given to acts of philanthropy that he emptied his treasury, making 'the poor of Istanbul rich with his continuous charity'.[33] It was calculated that his alms in 1504 came to eighty-six thousand *yük* (one *yük* being the equivalent of one hundred thousand *akçe*s). He was even credited with employing spies to seek out those in need, who, preferring to conceal their poverty, withdrew quietly (but in this case uselessly) out of sight.[34] It was not only sultans who were so generous. Others too were known for their alms giving. By the time the vezir Hüseyin Paşa died in 1702, leaving *vakıf*s in Istanbul consisting of schools and a mosque, he had given thousands of *akçe*s each year as *sadaka* (voluntary charitable gifts to the poor) to the *şeyh*s and the poor of the city.[35]

Such welfare was a fundamental religious duty, and one, at least for the author of a nineteenth-century book on morality, which brought that real and permanent pleasure to be found in human life from helping the poor and the destitute.[36] The best companions a man could have were friends, wealth and good works. But a man could only trust the last of these, for on his death his wealth would not even leave the door of his house, and his friends could only go with him as far as his burial and not beyond. His good works, on the other hand, would follow him into his grave. Never deserting him, they would ensure that those he left behind would remember him.[37] The performance of charity is a central tenet of Islam. The giving of *zekat*, alms, is one of the five pillars of the religion, the five commandments which every Muslim must perform, and the faithful are also encouraged to give *sadaka*. It was (and is) believed that performing an act which continued to bring benefit to the community after your death, such as building a mosque, a fountain, a school or a hospital, would bring you added blessings from God even after death. The importance of surviving children is related to this, for such children will pray for you after your death, or will perform good deeds after you are gone, and these, too, will bring you benefit. Prayers said for your soul, the act of being remembered in the community, whose members would pray for you, all

[31] Peçevi, *Tarihi*, I, p. 225; Evliya Çelebi, *Seyahatnamesi, I Kitap*, p. 66.
[32] Peçevi, *Tarihi*, I, p. 225. [33] Hoca Sadettin Efendi, *Tacü't-Tevarih*, IV, p. 106.
[34] Hoca Sadettin Efendi, *Tacü't-Tevarih*, IV, pp. 106–7. [35] Özcan, *Anonim*, pp. 163–5.
[36] Ahmet Rıfat, *Tasvir-i Ahlak. Ahlak Sözlüğü*, ed. Hüseyin Algül (Istanbul, n.d.), p. 372.
[37] Ahmet Rıfat, *Ahlak*, pp. 136–7.

these acts ensured further blessings in the other world. It is for this reason that fountains, for example, often carry inscriptions asking those using the waters to pray for the soul of the person who built it.

The motivation for these charitable acts was thus related to the desire to receive God's blessings, for as a Turkish proverb says, 'Do good and throw it into the sea, even if the fish don't understand, God will know'. Such charity was also designed to create and instil an idea of community and develop a bond among the *ümmet*, the body of Muslim believers. One of the *hadith*s, the sayings of the Prophet, states that 'the one who sleeps well-fed while his neighbour goes hungry is not one of us'.

Charity applied to all, regardless of religion, something noted and commented on by many western travellers, who were surprised at both the lack of religious division and at the open-handed approach which provided for rich as well as poor, Spandounes drawing attention to the fact that in the hospitals 'even those who are not sick can stay and eat free for three days whether they are poor, rich, Christians, Hebrew or Turk'.[38] While the Ottoman empire was a Muslim empire and the different strata of society were segmented in part along religious lines – a different dress code applying to Christians and Jews from that used by the Muslims, for example – the concept of a rigidly divided society, made up of a dominant Muslim mass and small, implicitly downtrodden, non-Muslim minorities, confuses the reality of how Ottoman society worked. As the *vakıf* institution makes clear, at least when it came to charity, religious denomination was not necessarily significant. The Orthodox patriarch certainly concerned himself with his Christian flock, handing an *akçe* after Saturday mass to each of the poor who came, and to those who kissed his hand on Sundays and other holy days.[39] But Christians and Jews could equally receive charity from the mosques, and non-Muslims set up *vakıf*s.[40]

While the giving of charity might be a noble deed, the receiving of it was not always conducted in the same spirit, and not all the recipients were deserving. This, for the anonymous author of the eighteenth-century *Risale-i Garibe*, was clearly the case with the many beggars who roamed the city streets and represented not just an irritation, but a threat to security for many of the sultans. Among those whom this author complained about were the 'professional', newly converted Muslims, both men and women, who, shoving out their hands in the direction of passing Muslims at the mosques, announced, 'I have just become a Muslim'.[41]

[38] Spandounes, *Origin*, p. 134. [39] Gerlach, *Günlüğü*, II, p. 524.
[40] Kunter, 'Türk Vakıfları', pp. 120–1. [41] Develi, *Risale-i Garibe*, p. 42.

Stephan Gerlach, a Protestant priest attached to the Habsburg embassy, witnessed such a scene in 1577:

On 4 June I saw an Armenian who had recently become a Muslim pass before our door with his wife and child. On his head he wore a white turban of the type they wear and in his hand there was an arrow. He was carrying the child in his arms. His wife, covered like Turkish women, was walking behind him. An old Turk was walking in front of them, carrying a wooden bowl in his hand and asking those who passed for alms for this new convert. He had apparently gathered a great deal of money. Those following behind paraded them through the streets of the city playing a shawm and drum.[42]

Other irritating beggars were those slaves who collected money claiming that they had been slaves for twenty years and needed help to buy their freedom;[43] or those 'cursed individuals' who collected money from Christians and Jews by shouting 'Allah' at them; and those who begged by singing religious hymns with their wives in the courtyard of the Sultan Bayezid mosque. There were also those 'thieves' who begged, though perfectly healthy, and those 'dogs' who pretended to be blind and crippled;[44] those persistent and talented beggars who could extract 'dough from a house without flour', and those lying on pavements like corpses and pretending that they had not eaten anything for two days.[45] There were even what amounted to begging rings, run by the unscrupulous as lucrative business ventures. They bought blind male and female slaves and set them to beg on the streets. Others put chains around people's necks and led them about, pretending they were debtors and collecting money to rescue them from their penury. Still others took the sick to beg, some of whom had contagious diseases which then spread unchecked among the populace. These practices, together with religious students begging aggressively in groups, were banned by Selim II in 1568, no doubt with limited effect.[46] In the nineteenth century, the begging of men and women 'who were capable of wringing water from a stone' had become a major social problem with which the state needed to grapple.[47]

Beggars who were perceived as a threat to order in the city were sometimes exiled from the capital. In 1759/60, the sultan ordered the removal to İznik of forty-three beggars who were perfectly capable of work but had chosen to be professional beggars, hassling innocent people on the street. The order presented the exile as being motivated by a desire to rescue these people from abominable beggary by sending them elsewhere, where

[42] Gerlach, *Günlüğü*, II, p. 596. [43] Develi, *Risale-i Garibe*, p. 42.
[44] Develi, *Risale-i Garibe*, p. 42. [45] Develi, *Risale-i Garibe*, p. 42.
[46] Ahmet Refik, *Onuncu Asr-ı Hicrî*, p. 139, *hüküm* 4.
[47] Basiretçi Ali Efendi, *İstanbul Mektupları*, ed. Nuri Sağlam (Istanbul, 2001), p. 173.

14. The Galata bridge, in Amicis, *Constantinople*, p. 25.

they would be found suitable employment, rather than the simple ejection of undesirable elements from the city's streets.[48] Certainly not all those who begged in the streets of the capital were there entirely due to destitution. Many came from the provinces, escaping various difficulties, not all devastating, and in search of an alternative income source. The seventeenth-century historian Selaniki was particularly scathing about

[48] Ahmet Refik, *Hicri On İkinci Asırda*, pp. 194–5, *hüküm* 235.

those who arrived from the province of Hungary, whom he described as escaping their duty of fighting in the holy war against the infidel. Having lived comfortably, indulging in profiteering in times of peace, they now begged in Istanbul, busily spreading anti-Ottoman propaganda by claiming that the infidel enemies were (unexpectedly) both upright and strong, and were not in fact killing the Muslims or enslaving Muslim women.[49] During Selim III's reign, inspectors were sent to shops, schools and *zaviye*s (dervish lodges) to register those who had come in from the provinces. Only those who had work and had someone who could stand guarantor for them were allowed to stay. Lepers who were begging were to be removed.[50]

Some begging was seasonal, or directly related to dire conditions in the provinces. Begging increased in Ramazan, the month of fasting when, traditionally, a high level of alms-giving took place. In 1874, the prominent journalist Basiretçi Ali Efendi drew the attention of the authorities to the numbers of children from Anatolia who flooded into the city every year in Ramazan and begged from Christians as well as Muslims, in coffee houses, casinos and similar establishments. He linked this to the famine and poverty in Anatolia and urged the government to do something about the situation there.[51]

Both rich and the capital city, Istanbul was a magnet for migration. The movement of population from the provinces became acute in the eighteenth century, when immigration became a particular problem,[52] Selim III, for example, being much concerned about overcrowding towards the end of the century. Many of those who flooded into the city ended up as beggars on the city streets or the Karaköy (Galata) bridge, an infamous haunt for begging in late Ottoman Istanbul. There

> the most crippled and poverty-stricken addicts that ever existed were lined up side by side, guests of the pavements. It was like something from a living public health exhibition: lepers, syphilitics, the scabious, the blind, those with ringworm, the paralysed, the lame, hunchbacks, cripples, all wrapped winter and summer in rags, half naked, with babes in arms, with moans, cries for help, prayers, calls to God, beseechings on their lips, all came together here, and stayed immovably in their places until nightfall.[53]

Many of the often overwhelming social problems of the city were handled by the *vakıf*s, one of whose central roles was that of provider of welfare.

[49] Selaniki, *Tarih*, I, pp. 364–5.
[50] Karal, *Hümayunları*, pp. 95–6. [51] Basiretçi Ali Efendi, *Mektupları*, pp. 341–2, 350.
[52] Aktepe, 'İstanbul'un Nüfus Mes'elesi', pp. 1–30.
[53] Alus, *İstanbul*, pp. 268–7. For an earlier description, see Basiretçi Ali Efendi, *Mektupları*, p. 650.

Not all, however, could be thus accommodated and many fell through the net of charitable provision.

While religious motivation was a major factor in the founding of *vakıf*s, the *vakıf* was not only a matter of religious duty and the attaining of God's blessings. To build a magnificent mosque, and especially to do so in the capital, was also a matter of prestige, an act aimed at displaying and legitimising power. As Gelibolulu Mustafa Ali commented so scathingly in the late sixteenth century:

> To build *mescit*s and mosques in the prosperous seat of the sultan and to construct *tekke*s [dervish lodges] and *medrese*s [schools] in a famous capital are not pious deeds to acquire heavenly reward. Every thinking and intelligent person knows that such deeds are only for political power and fame. There are thousands of towns and villages whose inhabitants are in need of *mescit*s and *tekke*s. And there are many villages on well-frequented routes whose people and visitors are hungry and seek food from the *imaret* [soup kitchen]. Therefore it is appropriate for those eager to build for charitable purposes to find such a deserving location and construct *imaret*s and *mescit*s there. But those who undertake charitable acts hypocritically and for fame of course will seek to acquire renown in the cities which are capitals.[54]

One of the first acts of Mehmed II after his conquest of Constantinople was to select the best site in the middle of the city and to build a mosque, the Fatih mosque, on it.[55] Over the next 150 years, several major imperial mosques were erected in Istanbul, those of Bayezid II, Süleyman I and then, after a pause, that of Ahmed I, the last of the great sultanic mosques. Apart from any pious intention, these mosques were designed to impress the magnificence and power of the ruler on the inhabitants of the empire, linking the sultan to God as well as to temporal power. They were the site of legitimation of rule, for political power was marked for a ruler by having the *hutbe* (the Friday sermon) read in his name. Thus Mehmed II did just this in Ayasofya on the first Friday after his conquest of Constantinople.[56]

These great imperial structures were sources of great pride, and much play is made in Ottoman chronicles of their stunning beauty and elegance. Everything about the mosques was magnificent, even the candles inside that of Mehmed II being so numerous that 'it looked like the dome of the sky ornamented with stars'.[57] For Hoca Sadeddin Efendi, the mosque of Bayezid II 'was so ornamented with coloured porphyry that even the most able architects were suspicious as to whether it could have been made by

[54] Gelibolulu Mustafa Ali, *Mevâıdün-Nefāis fi-Kavâıdil-Mecâlis*, ed. Mehmet Şeker (Ankara, 1997), p. 357.

[55] Kritoboulos, *History*, p. 140.

[56] Aşıkpaşazade, *Chronik*, *bab* 123, p. 132.

[57] Solakzade, *Tarihi*, I, p. 361.

man ... The marble of its high walls had been so polished that the reflections of those praying were reflected exactly as they were. Those who saw this thought that they were the images of holy souls'.[58] He was so overcome at describing the fountain in the mosque courtyard that 'water flow[ed] from the sweet mouth of my pen'.[59]

Not only for internal consumption, the mosques were also designed to dazzle those from beyond the frontiers, who were to be left in no doubt about the enormity of the wealth and strength of the Ottoman state. In 1567, the Persian ambassador, on his way to see the sultan, then in Edirne, was extremely well received in Istanbul and given a tour of the city, which included *hamam*s and the imperial mosques. He prayed at both the Süleymaniye and the mosque of Selim I.[60] Some European travellers were quite stunned by the Süleymaniye. On one occasion, according to Evliya Çelebi, ten Europeans, experts in geometry and architecture, entered the mosque and began to look in wonder at the beauty of the interior. Overcome by amazement, each stuck a finger in his mouth. Their gaze shifted to the doors inlaid with mother-of-pearl, at which point they slowly shook their heads from side to side in disbelief, and put two fingers in their mouths. They then turned their eyes to all aspects of the building; they inspected the outside, the arches, the domes and the minarets. Totally dumbstruck by the magnificence and perfection of the building, they not only took off their hats, but, in a gesture of total bewilderment, put all ten fingers in their mouths at the same time, so amazed were they by the sight before them.

Evliya Çelebi, anxious to learn more about the impressions of these European visitors to the Süleymaniye, requested their translator to ask them, 'How did you find this building?' One of them immediately replied, 'Every living creature and every great building is beautiful either in its interior or its exterior, but never both. But the inside and the outside of this mosque have been built in such an elegant manner that we have never seen such a perfect and complete example of the science of geometry in all Firengistan [Europe]'.[61]

Lavish and magnificent, stunning feats of architectural engineering, these mosques vied with each other to be the biggest and the best. Mehmed II issued instructions that his mosque in the newly conquered capital was to vie in 'height, beauty, and size ... with the largest and finest of the temples already existing there. He bade them select and prepare materials for this, the very best marbles and other costly polished stones,

[58] Hoca Sadettin Efendi, *Tacü't-Tevarih*, IV, pp. 107–8.
[59] Hoca Sadettin Efendi, *Tacü't-Tevarih*, IV, p. 108.
[60] Selaniki, *Tarih*, I, pp. 69. [61] Evliya Çelebi, *Seyahatnamesi, I Kitap*, pp. 65–6.

as well as an abundance of columns of suitable size and beauty plus iron, copper and lead in large quantities, and every other needed material'.[62]

The building to beat for Mehmed II, and his successors, was Ayasofya, an edifice rather unflatteringly described by Tursun Bey, a chancery official during Mehmed's reign, as the work of an apprentice. Others were more complimentary. For Nicolas de Nicolay, who accompanied the French ambassador to the court of Süleyman I in the mid sixteenth century, it was 'a work of grandeur, a structure of beauty and richness beyond compare';[63] for Domenico, doctor to Murad III, an attempt to describe it would be 'to embark upon too vast an ocean'.[64] While acknowledging the influence of Ayasofya, Tursun Bey, however, was convinced that Mehmed's mosque surpassed it, for it 'brought together all the arts of Ayasofya, but was enriched by the most recent developments of a new, fresh style unequalled in beauty, in which was evident the luminosity and the miracle of the white hand of Moses'.[65]

Although Mehmed's mosque may, in the eyes of Tursun Bey, have surpassed Ayasofya, the pre-eminence of the building as an object of emulation remained intact for many. Ahmed I was apparently similarly affected by the desire to make his mosque exceed Ayasofya in form and beauty, apparently successfully.[66] The result, according to Cafer Efendi, author of a treatise on architecture written in the early seventeenth century, was the most beautiful of all the sultanic mosques in Istanbul, the 'commander of the army of mosques'.[67] Several centuries later, its beauty still appealed. For the well-known poet, writer and literary historian of the early Turkish Republic, Ahmet Hamdi Tanpınar, the interior of the Sultan Ahmed mosque was comparable to 'the garden of heaven', 'a blue spring dream'.[68]

Süleyman I, too, was determined to build the best, and his architect, the famous Mimar Sinan, architect of the Şehzade, Süleymaniye and Selimiye mosques, as well as many other mosques and buildings throughout the Ottoman empire, was determined to top the mosque with a dome of greater proportions than that of Ayasofya.[69] What he created was 'a

[62] Kritoboulos, *History*, 71, p. 140.
[63] Nicolas de Nicolay, *Dans l'empire de Soliman le Magnifique*, ed. Marie-Christine Gomez-Géraud and Stéphane Yérasimos (Paris, 1989), p. 134.
[64] Domenico, *Istanbul*, p. 4. [65] Tursun Bey, *Tarih*, p. 70.
[66] Careri, 'Voyage', p. 71; Dimitri Kantemir, *Osmanlı İmparatorluğu'nun Yükşeliş ve Çöküş Tarihi*, 2 vols., trans. Özdemir Çobanoğlu (Istanbul, 2005), I, pp. 283, 541.
[67] Cafer Efendi, *Risāle-i Mi'māriyye. An Early-Seventeenth Century Ottoman Treatise on Architecture*, ed. Howard Crane (Leiden, 1987), p. 74.
[68] Ahmet Hamdi Tanpınar, *Beş Şehir* (Istanbul, 2001), pp. 173, 172.
[69] 'Mimar Sinan'ın Hatıraları: 2, Kırkçeşme Sularını Nasıl Getirdim', *Hayat Tarih Mecmuası*, no. 6 (July 1966), p. 46.

wourke which meriteth to be matched with the seven wounders of the wourld',[70] a verdict with which the traveller Giovanni Francesco Gemelli Careri was later to agree, for he described it as 'the finest without dispute of all I had seen yet'.[71] For Domenico, it was the most beautiful mosque, apart from Ayasofya. 'It is', he wrote, 'adorned with the most beautiful columns of different marbles, and around this mosque are the buildings of hospitals, colleges, baths and other habitations, all in use'.[72]

The sultans spent lavishly on their great mosques, which represented great feats of organisation. Domenico credited Süleyman with having spent two and a half million gold pieces on the construction of the Süleymaniye.[73] Pillars were brought for its construction, one from Alexandria and one from Baalbek; white marble from the island of Marmara; porphyry marble from other parts; green marble from Arabia. Its doors were made from ebony and inlaid with pearl by the most able craftsmen. The glass was coloured and engraved by the most famous glassworker, Sarhoş İbrahim. The inside of the dome was inscribed with calligraphy written by the most famous calligrapher, Karahisari. Each door had different inscriptions, carved by the most famous carvers. Thousands of *acemi oğlan*s (conscripted boys later to become janissaries) were used to erect the pillars.[74]

Ahmed I, even before laying the foundations of his mosque, had already paid out great sums buying buildings, including palaces of vezirs which he destroyed to make way for it.[75] His mosque, for which he spared no cost, and whose beauty, for Careri, exceeded that of Ayasofya,[76] was a project in which he took a deep personal interest, even taking part in its construction, filling the skirt of his robe with earth alongside the ordinary workmen, and exclaiming, 'Oh God, this is the service of your slave Ahmed, let it be acceptable to you in your sight'.[77] It was said that he went to the building every day and paid the workers personally.[78] Despite his exertions, Ahmed was not to live to see the completion of his mosque, for he died in 1617, shortly before it was finished.

Ahmed I's was to be the last great imperial mosque, though other imperial mosques were built, in particular that of the *valide sultan* Turhan Sultan, a mosque of such beauty that, 'in a word, the eye can behold nothing more beautiful, either for symmetry or costliness'.[79] The vezirs also built mosques – for example, the Köprülüs, the famous family

[70] Sanderson, *Travels*, p. 71. [71] Careri, 'Voyage', p. 73.
[72] Domenico, *Istanbul*, p. 4. [73] Domenico, *Istanbul*, p. 4.
[74] 'Kırkçeşme', pp. 45–6.
[75] Evliya Çelebi, *Seyahatnamesi, I Kitap*, p. 87; Topçular Katibi, *Tarihi*, I, p. 561.
[76] Careri, 'Voyage', p. 71. [77] Evliya Çelebi, *Seyahatnamesi, I Kitap*, p. 87.
[78] Kantemir, *Tarihi*, I, p. 283. [79] Careri, 'Voyage', p. 72.

of grand vezirs active in the second half of the seventeenth century, or, just after the conquest, the grand vezir Mahmud Paşa.

It is generally argued that financial constraints put an end to great imperial mosque-building enterprises. It is perhaps worth remembering that the great enemies of the Ottoman empire in the fifteenth to the early seventeenth centuries were either Mamluk Egypt or Safavid Iran, both Muslim powers. The threat of Egypt was ended by the Ottoman conquest of 1517, and the danger from Iran had decreased considerably by the end of Ahmed's reign. When it came to the nineteenth century, in contrast to the first one hundred and fifty years of the empire's existence, the great building efforts of the sultans were not directed towards mosques but to the great palaces, such as Dolmabahçe, Çırağan, Beşiktaş and Beylerbeyi, highly visible on the shores of the Bosphorus. Emulation and competition were now related to Europe and these palaces were built very much with the European image in mind.

Apart from the presentation of power and legitimising of rule performed by the great imperial mosques, *vakıf*s, large and small, made a further, and essential, contribution to the functioning of Ottoman society. They were fundamental to the economic well-being of the city. They provided employment, commercial premises and stimulated economic activity, and much of the everyday commercial life of the city was inextricably bound up with them. The *vakıf*s also contributed to the maintenance of the city's infrastructure, paying, for example, for the upkeep of roads in their vicinity. The *vakıf* of the Armenian Church in Balat regularly paid for the repair and renewal of roads in the area, and the Süleymaniye *vakıf* contributed to the repair of the roads from Yedi Kule to Eğri Kapı outside the walls of the city.[80]

The building of a mosque complex required an enormous labour force, from ordinary labourers to specialist craftsmen; it involved vast quantities of material and its construction could take many years, that of Ahmed I, for example, taking eight years, from 1609 to 1617. The mere fact of its construction thus represented a major economic stimulus. Once built, the complexes directly employed large numbers of people to run them; 700 worked for the Süleymaniye complex,[81] and in 1490, 496 were working in that of Mehmed II.[82] The income required for the enterprise was generated by a whole range of commercial ventures owned by the complex, thus indirectly giving employment to many thousands more and further

[80] Cengiz Orhonlu, 'Mesleki Bir Kuruluş Olarak Kaldırımcılık ve Osmanlı Şehir Yolları Hakkında Bazı Düşünceler', in Cengiz Orhonlu, *Osmanlı İmparatorluğunda Şehircilik ve Ulaşım Üzerine Araştırmalar*, ed. Salih Özbaran (İzmir, 1984), p. 43.

[81] Kuban, *İstanbul*, p. 112.

[82] Barkan and Ayverdi, *Tahrîr Defteri*, p. xi.

stimulating economic activity. Apart from the major mosque complexes, there were other, much smaller *vakıf*s, all drawing their income from commercial enterprises which they owned. Thus caravansarays, *hamam*s, accommodation and houses rented out, shops, coffee shops, *bozahane*s (shops selling *boza*, a drink made from fermented millet), markets, mills, bakeries, workshops, public weighing machines, storehouses for sheep heads and trotters, slaughterhouses, presses, dye-houses and tanners, could all be *vakıf* property. In 1478, the income from 2,360 shops, 1,300 houses, 4 caravansarays, 30 *bozahane*s and 23 storehouses for sheep heads and trotters was assigned to the upkeep and the labour force of the Ayasofya mosque alone.[83] The Süleymaniye complex received income from 221 villages, 30 arable fields, 2 *mahalle*s, 7 mills, 2 fisheries, 2 wharves, 1 pasture, 2 farms, the production of 5 villages and 2 islands.[84] Mustafa III's *vakıf*, endowed in 1773/74, included glassworks, dairies, a tile factory, a candle factory, a sulphur factory, workshops for silk brocade cushions, a buckshot factory and presses, established both on imperial lands and on lands bought specifically for the purpose from the *vakıf* of Mahmud Paşa.[85]

The daily life of the population of Istanbul was thus dominated by the *vakıf*s. Craftsmen worked in ateliers owned by *vakıf*s and sold their goods in *vakıf*-owned shops and markets; merchants used the caravansarays of the *vakıf*s; people ate and drank in the coffee houses and *bozahane*s owned by *vakıf*s, lived in rooms they rented from the *vakıf*, went to *vakıf*-owned *hamam*s, and shopped in grocers and bakeries all owned by *vakıf*s. In short, the economic life of the city rotated to a very high degree around the *vakıf*, dependent on and stimulated by it. Not only was the *vakıf* central to the welfare provision of Istanbul, it was also pivotal to its economy.

This was true from the very beginning of the city's life as Ottoman capital. Mehmed II made great use of the *vakıf* institution after his conquest of Constantinople, and had numerous caravansarays, markets, shops and other economic activities built to sustain it. This resulted in a major boost to economic activity and to revitalising the city. His complex, the Fatih complex, had thirty-five villages in the area around the city assigned to it,[86] and owned hundreds of shops in the city as well as the Saraçlar (saddlers') market, with its one hundred and ten shops.[87] Four *han*s were built for the travellers and merchants, and the income from these and from the shops

[83] Barkan and Ayverdi, *Tahrîr Defteri*, p. xv, n. 26. [84] Kuban, *İstanbul*, p. 112.
[85] Kunter, 'Türk Vakıfları', pp. 127–8.
[86] *Fatih Mehmet II Vakfiyeleri* (Ankara, 1938), pp. 207–8, facsimile pp. 65–72.
[87] *Fatih*, pp. 209–12, facsimile pp. 73–93.

attached to them was assigned to the *vakıf*;[88] houses were constructed for people of the city and the income from these houses also went to cover the expenses of the *vakıf*.[89] Mehmed had fourteen *hamams* built, eleven in the old city and three in Galata, for 'the necessities of the people', and fifty-four flour mills. The income from the *hamams* and the mills went to his *vakıf*.[90]

Although the conditions of a *vakıf* were established in its foundation deed, such conditions were not immutable, and, as with everything Ottoman, the *vakıf* displayed both flexibility and pragmatism. This contributed to the institution's ability to function effectively over considerable time spans. It also meant that the *vakıf* could respond quickly to changing economic conditions – an important asset for the economy of the city. When Istanbul was hit, for example, by a devastating earthquake or major fire – events that were not uncommon – the fact that the *vakıf* could alter the conditions of its foundation deed, sell property and reassign income meant that it could often adapt fast and deal with the devastation effectively, rebuilding commercial premises and continuing its welfare activity. Changing needs could lead to a change in structure, departing from the stipulations set out in the original foundation deed; and *vakıf* property could be sold, shops in Galata belonging to the *vakıf* of Ayasofya, for example, being sold off in 1565.[91] It was as a result of the new requirements of the time that Bayezid II prepared a new deed and increased the number of people working in the Fatih *vakıf* established by his father Mehmed II.[92] While a *vakıf* was set up for the upkeep of the tomb of Selim II at his death, a similar arrangement was not made when Murad III died. Instead, income from the *vakıf* of Selim II, being greater than the sum required for the upkeep of Selim's tomb, was assigned to Murad III's tomb, which was to be administered by the *mütevelli* of Selim II's *vakıf*.[93]

Fires and earthquakes had a further impact on the *vakıfs*, for they contributed to a constantly changing cityscape. In an environment where boundary markers such as houses could easily, and often, be destroyed, the boundaries of *vakıf* property also tended to be fluid. Further, boundaries were inclined to creep over time, either unintentionally or as a result of corruption, and to absorb land that was not originally part of the *vakıf*. This could result in disputes between *vakıfs* over property rights. The Ayasofya *vakıf* was involved in such a dispute in 1583,

88 *Fatih*, pp. 212–13, facsimile pp. 65–72.
89 *Fatih*, pp. 213–39, facsimile pp. 95–228.
90 *Fatih*, p. 213, facsimile pp. 93–5, pp. 239–42, facsimile pp. 228–41.
91 *5 Numaralı Mühimme Defteri (973/1565–1566)*, 2 vols. (Ankara, 1994), I, p. 60, *hüküm* 319, II, facsimile pp. 126–7.
92 Ünver, *Fatih Külliyesi*, p. 265, fn. 17.
93 Selaniki, *Tarih*, II, pp. 485–6.

when it was discovered that income from much of its property in Galata was not coming to the *vakıf*, but had instead been appropriated by other people, a situation which the sultan wanted stopped. Some other properties elsewhere became a bone of contention between the Ayasofya *vakıf* and the Rüstem Paşa *vakıf*. These properties, which belonged to the Ayasofya *vakıf*, were being used by the Rüstem Paşa *vakıf*, and only nine thousand *akçe*s out of the income of three hundred thousand *akçe*s was actually going to the Ayasofya *vakıf*. The situation was such that the Rüstem Paşa *vakıf* was even selling some of the shops which formed part of these properties.[94]

While *vakıfs* contributed so effectively to the economic well-being of the city, they also undoubtedly had the same effect for the families of those who founded them. It has often been argued that for vezirs and *paşa*s, the founding of a *vakıf* was a way of preserving family wealth. In an environment where the rise in politics was in inverse ratio to the likelihood of a natural death, the creation of a *vakıf* could protect wealth and property and ensure that it remained in the hands of the family rather than the state. Ottoman politics was particularly robust, and turnover fast, as Sir Thomas Roe, English ambassador between 1621 and 1628, indicated in a letter to Calvert in 1622. 'There is no likelihood', he wrote, 'that the vizier can stand long; I think now they choose them as wee doe mellons, tast and throw away, until we find one good'.[95] Certainly officials were fearful for the survival of their property, even of their *vakıf* properties, after death. In 1598, when the *bostancıbaşı* Ferhad Ağa came to execute Hasan Paşa at Yedikule, Hasan Paşa requested that as an act of grace his *vakıf*s not be dismantled and his body be buried by the public fountain which he had built.[96]

Although there is an element of truth in the idea that the foundation of a *vakıf* was seen as a protective measure against the rapacious hands of the sultan, it is also conceivable that what protected such *vakıf*s from a sultan, whose powers could no doubt stretch to seizure of inherited wealth, whether inside a *vakıf* or not, was the fact that they provided essential welfare to the population of the city. Under these circumstances, it was not necessarily in the interests of any sultan to seize what was performing a most useful social function and contributing to the stability of his capital. As the centuries went by, however, the charitable element of the *vakıf* began to decline, and by the eighteenth century, many *vakıf*s had corrupted into mere vehicles of tax evasion. *Vakıf* wealth, devoted, at least in theory, and very much in practice in the earlier period, to charitable purposes, was non-taxable by the state, which by this period was losing a

[94] Ülker, *Emir Defteri*, pp. 157–8, facsimile p. 97, *hüküm* 328. [95] Roe, *Negotiations*, p. 64.
[96] Selaniki, *Tarih*, II, p. 736.

considerable amount of income due to the disappearance of economic assets into *vakıf* endowments.

In any case, whether used for this purpose in the earlier period or not, protection of wealth was more a matter of concern for the vezirs and high-ranking officials, not for those of lesser rank or for women, for whom seizure of wealth was not an issue. What motivated many people, apart from the desire for *sevab* (God's reward for a pious act performed on earth), was the ability to set up the inheritance of their wealth and property as they wished. The founding of a *vakıf* allowed them to sidestep the provisions of Islamic inheritance law, naming the heirs they wanted and excluding those they did not, and preserving their wealth intact, and not subdivided as required under religious law. Control remained permanently with the family, the *mütevelli* always being chosen from among them. The protecting here was thus not from the state but from the inheritance laws.

This system also allowed for circumventing these laws in order to allow freed slaves to be beneficiaries of the legacies of their former masters. The stricture that former slaves could not benefit from the inheritance of their former masters did not fit well with the psychology or order of social relations in Istanbul, as pointed out by the eminent Ottoman historians Barkan and Ayverdi, who argued that in a system where slaves had no hope for the future, it would have been difficult to motivate them and thus ensure the greatest possible return from their labour.[97] Many slaves – apart from those manumitted without condition as an act of charity – were freed on the death of their master. Concubines who were mothers of their master's children automatically became free on his death. Other slaves attained freedom after the fulfilment of certain conditions stipulated in contractual agreements with their masters. Under such agreements they were able to buy their freedom after a number of years, or after having carried out the conditions laid down in the contract. Under these contracts, slaves could earn a fixed income from trade or from some other economic activity, such as cloth weaving, building up the sum necessary for their ultimate payment for freedom. But freedom required the economic means to be able to survive, capital, equipment and a place to live. This was particularly true for old women, old retainers and mothers of children, and it was in this context that many different types of *vakıf*s were set up to support freed slaves in one way or another. *Vakıf*s could be established in which the *mütevelli* was a freed slave or where this post was

[97] Barkan and Ayverdi, *Tahrîr Defteri*, p. xxv.

given to members of his or her family. Income from the *vakıf* could also be left to freed slaves or a house assigned for them to live in.[98]

Setting up a *vakıf* was one thing, protecting it from embezzlement was another. The great centrality of *vakıf*s made running them extremely important and resulted in strict controls over their administration, heavy punishment for corruption or mismanagement of their affairs, and crushing censure at times of the incompetence of their officials. Apparent irregularities in the accounts of the Süleymaniye *vakıf* in 1703 led to an investigation headed by the grand vezir,[99] and Bayezid II ordered an investigation of finances of the *vakıf* of Mehmed II in 1501. As part of this investigation, the *kadı* of Kütahya was ordered to examine the *mütevelli*s of the property belonging to Mehmed II's *vakıf*, as well as all the others working there, including those who collected taxes for the *vakıf*, the scribes and all other officials involved. People were to be sent to check production village by village, investigating income both in cash, grain or any other produce, and everything, large or small, was to be counted and entered into a register. The detailed registers of the *vakıf* officials were to be examined, and if there was no discrepancy between them and the register drawn up by the investigators, then a detailed register was to be prepared. But if any discrepancy of whatever sort was discovered, the sultan was to be informed of it and of who was responsible. Anybody with a just complaint against the *mütevelli* or any other official of the *vakıf* was to come forward, and have the complaint registered and sent to the sultan.[100]

Selaniki, who was himself in charge of imperial *vakıf* finances from 1596 to 1598, provided many examples of embezzlement and sternly criticised the standards of many of the *mütevelli*s of his day. The 'pimp' Işık Ali Çelebi, as Selaniki described him, *mütevelli* of the *vakıf* of Mehmed II, was investigated in 1596 for embezzlement, a 'betrayal' of his position, which he denied. Found guilty, however, he was removed from his post.[101] Two years later, in 1598, there appears to have been a major problem in the imperial *vakıf*s, for the *mütevelli*s were removed and replaced by those whom Selaniki described as known and trusted people. Mustafa Çelebi, the former *mütevelli* of the Muradiye *vakıf* in Edirne, became the *mütevelli* of Süleymaniye; Kalender Çavuş became the *mütevelli* of Sultan Selim I; and Edirneli Kemalzade was appointed *mütevelli* of Sultan Mehmed II.[102] This wholesale replacement of

98 Barkan and Ayverdi, *Tahrîr Defteri*, no. 395, pp. 67–71; no. 1148, pp. 201–2; no. 1727, p. 294.
99 Özcan, *Anonim*, p. 204.
100 Şahin and Emecen, *Ahkâm Defteri*, p. 86, *hüküm* 309.
101 Selaniki, *Tarih*, II, p. 569.
102 Selaniki, *Tarih*, II, pp. 741–2.

15. A public scribe, in Amicis, *Constantinople*, p. 427.

personnel was not apparently totally effective, for only two years later, in 1600, the *mütevelli* of the Bayezid II *vakıf*, Kaba-bulak, unflatteringly referred to by Selaniki as a wandering opium seller engaged in all kinds of illicit activities, was also removed from his position.[103] It was in this year too that the *şeyhülislam* Sunullah Efendi expressed his unhappiness with the situation in the imperial *vakıf*s. During the prayers for the birth of the Prophet in the imperial mosques, *mütevelli*s attended only to the important people, offering them sherbet and food in front of the poor and other attendees, whom they ignored, behaviour which was totally unacceptable. 'This is an ugly injustice', the *şeyhülislam* noted, adding that if they were to feed others than those required by the *vakıf* conditions – that is, the patients in the hospitals and the students in the schools – these should be the poor and the lepers, not the rich. 'If the injustices increase and if

[103] Selaniki, *Tarih*, II, p. 851.

inappropriate expenses are entered into the *vakıf* accounts, this is evil and illegal'.[104]

This was a period in which, according to Selaniki, the great imperial *vakıf*s were moving towards destruction, due to the giving of bribes and presents from *vakıf* budgets.[105] Certainly, some distributions in a later period seem to have been rather less charitable than others, money from the *vakıf* of Mustafa III being distributed in 1790 by his son Selim III to various officials in the palace as gifts at festival time.[106] Selaniki was also greatly concerned about the standard of the appointments made, arguing that because people who should not have been *mütevelli*s were occupying these positions, *vakıf* expenses exceeded income to such an extent that food was not being cooked in the soup kitchens, and each *vakıf* was excessively in debt.[107] Noting that *mütevelli*s should be good and upright Muslims, experienced and knowledgeable about divine and mundane affairs, he complained that people who did not know even the simplest of prayers and were bereft of basic hygiene were made *mütevelli*s. In consequence, such men occupied a rank higher than that of many important officials of state, a situation which Selaniki saw as intolerable.[108]

Selaniki was by no means the only person upset by ill-management of *vakıf* affairs, nor was this the only period in which it occurred. Well aware of the possibility of embezzlement and fraud, donors themselves inserted prayers into their deeds for the managers and *kadı*s who acted in accordance with the clauses and conditions of the *vakıf*. 'May you find God's mercy', they wrote, 'and may you obtain your desires in the two worlds'. Not perhaps entirely hopeful of the efficacy of such prayers, many included other prayers for those officials who did not implement the conditions of the *vakıf* and who diverted the money of the endowment for illicit purposes. For those the prayers read, 'May they be cursed by God, the angels and the people', 'May they be among the sinners in the sight of God, who is the assistance and the sovereign of man'.[109]

Social space

Just as the *vakıf* was a powerhouse of Istanbul's economy, however fraudulent the practices of its officials might be on occasion, *vakıf* properties, the mosques and mosque courtyards, the markets, coffee houses and

[104] Selaniki, *Tarih*, II, p. 826. [105] Ahmed Cavid, *Hadîka*, p. 16.
[106] Ahmed Cavid, *Hadîka*, p. 16. [107] Selaniki, *Tarih*, II, pp. 741–2.
[108] Selaniki, *Tarih*, II, pp. 851–2.
[109] Hasan Yüksel, *Osmanlı Sosyal ve Ekonomik Hayatında Vakıfların Rolü (1585–1683)* (Sivas, 1998), p. 67.

hamams, the schools, libraries, soup kitchens and hospitals, were the forum for much social exchange and where many of the inhabitants of the city spent much of their leisure time. The mosque gardens, especially those of Mehmed II, Eyüp, Beyazid II and Ayasofya, turned into markets in Ramazan, with pedlars selling their wares and beggars working their way through the crowds. Petition writers set up stalls, finding ready customers who needed documents written for them. Market stalls were erected and, according to nineteenth-century sources, sold many different types of prayer beads, books (in particular, Qu'rans) and even manuscripts, which were displayed in glass cabinets. There were stalls selling cloth, shawls, porcelain (in particular from the famous porcelain workshop in Yıldız palace), prayer mats, Hacı Cemali soap from Crete, many varieties of spices, many kinds of food, *pastırma* (pastrami) from Kayseri, *sucuk* from Tekirdağ, chickpeas from Kara Biga, butter from Aleppo, Trabzon and Derne, olives from Tirilye, beans from Sekinik, and rice from Feyyum and Reşit. The Tobacco Régie (the European-run monopoly set up to handle tobacco production and sales in 1883) had a stall selling special tobacco for Ramazan. Such markets in Ramazan – a month of particularly high spending, as people bought presents and special foods for *iftar* (the meal at the end of the day breaking the fast) – and for the festival at the month's end, were extremely crowded and buzzed with commercial activity.[110] More such activity occurred in areas just outside the mosques, around graveyards and *mescit*s. Here there were little shops belonging to *üfürükçü*s (people who claimed to cure the sick by breathing on them), or those writing amulets to ward off evil, or to curse, or those who cast spells. These shops were made very atmospheric by their owners, who sat in their green robes and Moroccan slippers waiting for their customers, their aura increased by their location. Some who set themselves up in the graveyards even used the graves as stalls.[111]

Mosque courtyards could also be meeting places for particular groups. The Yeni Cami (Valide Sultan mosque) in Eminönü, for example, was a meeting point for those who came from the provinces, where they would gather to talk and share their troubles. It was so well known that people would go there to look for their relatives or for people from the same region, to receive news about events back home, or to find those with whom they could send greetings to their relations and friends back in their villages, using the services of the many petition writers to be found there in cases when they needed something written. In the immediate vicinity of

[110] Abdülaziz Bey, *Osmanlı*, pp. 251–2; Ercümend Ekrem Talu, *Geçmiş Zaman Olur Ki. Anılar* (Ankara, 2005), pp. 63–4.

[111] Sadri Sema, *Hatıraları*, pp. 257–8.

16. Cover of Hüseyin Rahmi (Gürpinar)'s novel *Muhabbet Tılsımı* (Istanbul, 1928), showing a young boy with a magician in a graveyard (from the private collection of Ebru Boyar).

the mosque there were shops of all types, selling clothes, shoes and fezes, as well as itinerant barbers, bird sellers, and purveyors of all types of food – kebab sellers, those selling *ayran* (a drink made of yoghurt) and lemonade sellers.[112]

[112] Sadri Sema, *Hatıraları*, pp. 239–43.

17. Feeding pigeons at the Valide Sultan mosque, in Brassey, *Sunshine*, p. 344.

Apart from being social and commercial gathering points, mosques were also ideal locations for spreading information and gossip, for general muttering and complaining about the current political state of affairs, and, more dangerously, for inciting sedition and revolt. Abdülhamid II was so concerned about this possibility that he dispatched his own spies into the crowded mosques, who, looking around furtively during the prayer, checked to see if there were any secret exchanges going on. These men were presumably rather conspicuous, for, according to Ahmed Rasim, some of them had never before entered a mosque, but now became most devout, attending prayers five times a day.[113] As Ahmet Hamdi Tanpınar wrote about the Sultan Ahmed mosque:

What a pity that this mosque which is calmness, repose and contemplation within its walls and presents time to us as musical harmony was from the time of its

[113] Ahmet Rasim, *Ramazan*, p. 26.

completion in the period of Mustafa I to 1826 the witness to revolutions following one after the other. The masses, infected with hatred and greed, beat on its doors like the seven-headed dragons, they fought bloody battles under the arches of its courtyard. The most bloody *fetva*s were read from its mimbars. Until the suppressing of revolt in 1826, all the wickedness of Ottoman history flowed round it.[114]

Indeed the mosque was an eyewitness of many major political events, from the fall of sultans to bloody military revolts. Shortly after its completion, members of the *ulema*, state officials and janissaries met there to plot the downfall of Osman II. Early in the next century, the mosque was witness to another revolt and deposition, this time of Mustafa II. The plane tree in the square in front of it was the gallows for around thirty officials, strung up there during the plane-tree incident in 1656. Shortly before this, in 1648, the marble of its interior had turned red with the blood of revolting *sipahi*s, mown down by the janissaries[115] after the *sipahi*s had rebelled over their assignment to the Crete campaign and the insufficiency of their pay.[116] Other less dramatic, but certainly shameful, events occurred within the mosque; in 1786 a fight broke out over sherbet and sweets, after the *mevlüt* (religious ceremony) for the birth of the Prophet. Windows were broken and the carpets besmirched with sugar and sherbet.[117]

The Sultan Ahmed mosque did not have a monopoly of political violence or unbecoming brawling. The janissaries often used Orta Cami (mosque) as their headquarters for revolts, and it was in the mosque of Ayasofya where men gathered to take the decision to remove Mehmed IV and to replace him with Süleyman II.[118] Religious students were not immune from violent confrontations, indulging in a serious clash in 1786/87 in the courtyards of the Sultan Selim I mosque and the Sultan Mehmed II mosque (the Fatih mosque), where two groups armed with pistols and knives fought each other before escaping into the Müftü *hamam*. Many men, including the police, were injured, and the *şeyhülislam* ordered the raiding of the schools. Of those students who were caught, some were exiled and some hanged.[119]

It was not only that the mosques could be settings of violence or meeting places for rebels which concerned the sultan and his ministers. It was also the influence of the preachers within them that had worrying implications. One such was the prayer leader of the Süleymaniye mosque during the reign of Ahmed I who was very popular among the people.

[114] Tanpınar, *Beş Şehir*, p. 174.
[115] Evliya Çelebi, *(Gördüklerim)*, p. 181. [116] Naima, *Târih*, III, pp. 1184–5.
[117] Taylesanizade, *Tarihi*, p. 122. [118] İsazade, *Târîhi*, p. 205.
[119] Taylesanizade, *Tarihi*, p. 184.

Not only did great crowds come to hear him, but they also deferred to him in matters of justice, for they regarded him as a man of great learning. He in turn dealt with them in clear language that they could understand, in contrast to the often convoluted language of the court. He was described as preaching very bravely and fearlessly, willing to attack statesmen if he saw fit and even, on occasion, to insult them. Such behaviour inevitably brought him into conflict with the authorities and he was exiled several times, but was each time brought back due to the great respect in which he was held.[120]

A source of religious piety and God's blessings, an insurance for assistance in the next world, *vakıf*s were a fundamental component of the lives of the people, providing them with food, shelter, medical care, education and work. In turn, they guaranteed social stability for the state, while the sultans used the institution to impress their power and wealth on their subjects, as well as on those from beyond the frontiers. It was an engine of the economy, an essential piston in the economic machinery of state, and it was this aspect of the *vakıf* institution which helped turn Istanbul into a consuming city.

[120] Peçevi, *Tarihi*, II, p. 451.

5 The consuming city

Apart from the splendours of sultanic pomp and the magnificence of the imperial mosques, Istanbul was also characterised by its markets, for it was, above all things, a city of commerce, an opulent international emporium where, in the words of Latifi, 'the buyers and the sellers of the market of the world all come together'.[1] It attracted foreign merchants from well beyond the empire, from China and India in the east to England, and later America, in the west, from Russia to the north and sub-Saharan Africa to the south. It was the central nexus of the empire from which all networks of commercial power radiated outwards, connecting Ottoman merchants and traders to the capital. A supremely important port, Istanbul's prosperity and wealth was dependent on the sea and the arrival of ships in its harbours.[2]

The markets of the Ottoman capital displayed goods from all over the globe, its shops 'stuffed with all rare and exquisite merchandice, as [is] of inestimable valewe, pretiouse stones and pearles, zebulini [sables] and other ritch furs of all sorts, silkes and cloth of gould, bowes, arrowes, buckelers, and swourds'.[3] Its markets glittered with 'Satins, Silks, Velvets, Cloth of Silver and Gold, and the most exquisitely wrought Handkerchiefs, that can be found in the world; with infinite other commodities, the relation of which would be tedious'.[4] These rich and graceful markets, whose greatness reflected that of the city itself, afforded every luxury, from spices and slaves and the richest, most bejewelled cloth imaginable, to armour and horse trappings, in short, 'all things a man can desire'.[5] For Heberer, Istanbul displayed before his eyes magnificent goods the like of which he had never seen in Christian lands.[6] This might be what Pertusier rather primly referred to as 'sordid commerce which calculates the value

[1] Latifi, *Evsâf*, p. 42. [2] Kütükoğlu, 'Lütfi Paşa Âsafnâmesi', pp. 88–9.
[3] Sanderson, *Travels*, pp. 78–9. [4] Lithgow, *Discourse*, p. 136.
[5] Careri, 'Voyage', pp. 68, 72. [6] Heberer, *Köle*, p. 312.

of every breeze, and the quarter it blows from',[7] but it was what made the city rich and its people devotees of consumption.

Controlling the market

From the very inception of the Ottoman state, economic factors had moulded its development, influencing routes of conquest and driving internal policies and external relations. It was the commercial potential of the city that had been a factor in Mehmed II's desire to capture Constantinople, and he invested heavily in stimulating and developing the market once he had the city in his possession. He brought in traders and craftsmen, built *han*s and caravansarays, shops and bazaars, and used *vakıf* foundations to stimulate economic activities.

This thriving trading entrepôt was also a huge, sprawling metropolis, whose population at all times of its history as the Ottoman capital far exceeded that of many European cities, such as Rome or Paris. It was, in Latifi's graphic phrase, so crowded that 'even if Jesus were to return and descend from heaven and wished to come to the city, he would not find space to leave even a needle'.[8] One of the sultan's main duties – for reasons of order and stability apart from any less pragmatic considerations – was to ensure this population against starvation, for a starving population represented a great danger to the delicate balance in the city's internal existence.[9] The sultans were often uncomfortably aware of the power of the population of the city, and their survival as rulers was a question of careful calculation of the many factors involved in maintaining political equilibrium. One of these was the ability to feed the population and to provide a market in which prices were fixed equitably, the quality of goods was guaranteed and market practices were effectively policed. From an Ottoman state perspective, one of the prerequisites for the population to live in security and calm was order in the market.[10]

A fundamental element in ensuring a contented population was to guarantee supplies of wheat to the city. Bread was an essential staple in people's diet and scarcity of bread led to immediate unrest, with crowds struggling to seize loaves or rioting in queues outside the bakeries. In 1573 the city was hit by great scarcities, and many people went for eight or ten

[7] Pertusier, *Promenades*, p. 3. [8] Latifi, *Evsâf*, p. 13.
[9] For provisioning of the city, see Salih Aynural, *İstanbul Değirmenleri ve Fırınları. Zahire Ticareti (1740–1840)* (Istanbul, 2001); Rhoads Murphey, 'Provisioning Istanbul: the state and subsistence in the early modern Middle East', in Rhoads Murphey, *Studies on Ottoman Society and Culture, 16th–18th Centuries* (Aldershot, 2007), no. V.
[10] Mübahat S. Kütükoğlu (ed.), *Osmanlılarda Narh Müessesesi ve 1640 Tarihli Narh Defteri* (Istanbul, 1983), p. 7.

days without seeing or tasting bread, and even that which they had to fight to get was 'black, full of soil, stinking and made you nauseous just to look at it'.[11] In 1789, those who did manage to grab loaves ended up with bread of such indescribable quality that it was like mud, and everyone, men, women and children, Muslims and non-Muslims alike, all lamented and complained.[12] Dearth in food supplies or high prices could force the market traders into revolt,[13] or even drive the women onto the streets in open and public protest. At the beginning of May 1808, women carrying sticks advanced on the house of the Istanbul *kadı*, the official responsible for the provisioning of the city, and, bursting in, surprised him at his midday meal. Lifting up the lids on the various dishes arrayed before him, they exclaimed, 'infidel scoundrel, while you are eating this abundance of food, we are dying of hunger and paying twenty-five *para* [small denomination coin] for liver'. So saying, they advanced menacingly towards him. Thoroughly frightened, the *kadı* fled from his meal and into the harem. The women continued their protest, presenting a petition to the sultan on his way to Friday prayer in the Bayezid mosque, as they marched along the street carrying poles topped with liver and guts. As they handed over their petition they shook their poles and shouted, 'oh our sultan, wake up and think of us. We cannot stand the prices. We are starving'. The action, however, was pointless, according to Oğulukyan, for Mustafa IV was powerless to do anything about the situation.[14] His failure to provision the city properly and to control the prices of foodstuffs contributed to his downfall less than a year later.

The sultans responded to this need to feed the populace in a number of ways. Food was distributed on every public occasion – at circumcisions, at accessions, at wedding ceremonies. It was handed out to thousands, from the *vakıf* and dervish soup kitchens. The sultans also put much effort into ensuring the provisioning of the city and, as the Byzantines had before them, paid great attention to bringing in the necessary supplies of basic foodstuffs to the capital. Wheat was imported from different parts of the empire, mostly from western Anatolia, Thrace, Egypt, Bulgaria, Wallachia and Moldavia. Meat supplies came mostly from the European territories – Murad III, for example, sending instructions there in 1583 for sheep to be provided to the butchers of the city.[15] Meat could also come from Anatolia, even from as far away as Diyarbakır in times of shortage in

[11] Aurelio Santa Croce, 'Aurelio Santa Croce al séguito del bailo Marcantonio Barbaro, notizie da Costantinopoli', in Pedani-Fabris, *Relazioni*, XIV, pp. 230–1.
[12] Taylesanizade, *Tarihi*, p. 408.
[13] Aktepe, 'İstanbul'un Nüfus Mes'elesi', p. 17. [14] Oğulukyan, *Ruznamesi*, p. 22.
[15] Ülker, *Emir Defteri*, pp. 44–5, facsimile p. 26, *hüküm* 88.

the city.[16] Dairy products were produced in the surrounding regions, as was much of the fruit consumed there. Some foodstuffs came from further afield: figs and raisins from western Anatolia, nuts from the Black Sea, chestnuts from Bursa, olives and olive oil from Greece, or from the area to the south and from the islands, which also supplied cheeses, as did Wallachia and Bulgaria.

The government tried to ensure supplies of basic foodstuffs by issuing instructions to officials in different parts of the empire to provide the capital's requirements, in particular grain and meat, but also other products, such as dried fruits, almonds, sesame and black-eyed beans, as requested from the *kadı*s of Aydın and Saruhan, for example, by Murad III in 1583.[17] Mahmud II ordered grain to be sent to the city from the Mediterranean region and from Anatolia.[18] Apart from issuing instructions over supplies, in times of shortage, the government could also resort to forced purchases or impose fixed prices – not always a successful policy, for it could act as a disincentive to peasants who had no reason to produce for sale if prices were too low.

Controlling the provisioning of the capital was by no means easy. It was difficult to organise effective shipping, particularly for the Black Sea, where the shipping season was short. It was necessary to put in place a complex system of grain storage. Provisioning was also prey to poor harvests and famines, which hit the empire regularly and had an immediate impact on the food supplies of the city, as well as, on occasion, driving starving peasants towards the city in a desperate attempt to find work, and so further adding to the problem of dearth within Istanbul itself. Giovanni Moro, the Venetian ambassador, reported in 1590 that much agricultural land had been abandoned and was no longer productive.[19] Weather conditions in the winter could also hit the supply lines of meat; sixteen thousand sheep with their shepherds, donkeys and dogs on their way to Istanbul all froze to death near Silivri in 1786/87.[20] Animals could also die in great numbers if brought to the city in the wrong season and held outside the city with insufficient fodder, as was done in the winter of 1783, when as many as eighty thousand sheep brought from Wallachia died.[21] Another major problem, which became particularly pronounced at the end of the sixteenth and beginning of the seventeenth and again in the eighteenth centuries, was warfare and rebellions, which both prevented agricultural

[16] Ahmet Refik, *Onuncu Asr-ı Hicrî*, pp. 79–80, *hüküm* 4.
[17] Ülker, *Emir Defteri*, p. 139, facsimile p. 87, *hüküm* 268.
[18] Cabi, *Târihi*, I, p. 584.
[19] Giovanni Moro, 'Relazione di Giovanni Moro Bailo a Costantinopoli, 1590', in Firpo, *Relazioni*, XIII, p. 333.
[20] Taylesanizade, *Tarihi*, p. 184.
[21] Ahmed Vasıf Efendi, *Ahbâr*, pp. 71–2.

activity, ravaged the land and led to great dislocations of population, with many fleeing into the already overcrowded capital city.

A further problem was related to competition, for grain was needed also by the great city-states of Italy, in particular Venice. Both Genoa and Venice had traditionally imported grain from Anatolia, Thrace and the Black Sea to supply the mother cities and to feed their colonies in the Levant. In times of shortage, they still looked to these regions as suppliers. They thus competed with Istanbul in times when other sources of supply were insufficient and offered merchants an alternative and at times more lucrative market for Ottoman grain or other commodities. In 1583, Murad III was faced with the loss of shipments of grain, black-eyed beans and other foodstuffs which were destined for Istanbul, but which ended up instead sold to 'base infidels' by the captains of various non-Muslim ships, ships from the islands and from Foça, who claimed to be loading the commodities for Istanbul.[22]

The sultans tried to deal with this competition by imposing strict controls over the shipping of foodstuffs. Murad III responded to his loss of grain by issuing a stern warning to the *kadı* of İzmir. Only those who had an imperial document were to be allowed to load foodstuffs, and anyone claiming to be loading provisions for Istanbul but not in possession of such a permit was not under any circumstances to be allowed to do so. The quantity of grain loaded and the date of the shipment were to be registered and the register dispatched with a trustworthy man to the sultan.[23] Süleyman I also struggled to enforce supplies in 1545, when the suppliers of sheep for the city showed a distinct disinclination to co-operate with imperial policy over the provisioning of the capital.[24]

Another form of competition for supplies was caused by military campaigns, when supply of grain could be siphoned off to the armies, so leaving Istanbul short or even without provisions. The consequence of this was dearth and rising prices. When, after the crushing defeat inflicted on them by the Persians in 1585, the Ottomans launched a new campaign, the capital was hit by high prices and low food supplies as available provisions were dispatched with the massed battalions into Anatolia. Bread became difficult to get and only small quantities could be distributed to the people massed outside the bakeries, when crowds of two hundred received only twenty loaves. The bread they did receive was so hot that it

[22] Ülker, *Emir Defteri*, p. 115, facsimile p. 70, *hüküm* 218.
[23] Ülker, *Emir Defteri*, p. 115, facsimile p. 70, *hüküm* 218.
[24] Sahillioğlu, *H.951–952 ve E-12321 Numaralı Mühimme*, pp. 125–6, *hüküm* 158; pp. 126–7, *hüküm* 159.

'sat in the stomachs' of those who ate it.[25] In 1596, during Ramazan, traditionally a month of high spending, the preparations for a campaign against Hungary resulted in exceptionally high prices and great scarcities. Never before, according to Selaniki, had Istanbul suffered such a dearth, with one hundred *dirhem* (approximately three grams) of bread selling for one *akçe* (silver coin) or more, an *okka* (around 1.2 kilograms) of meat at twelve or more and a *kile* (around two hundred and forty-two kilograms) of barley fetching forty *akçe*s or above. These dire conditions continued for a year.[26]

The government also struggled with speculators and profiteers within the city who tried to hoard grain and capitalise on and manipulate rising markets. Profiteering could be both lucrative and dangerous for those who indulged in it. When the wars with Persia at the end of the sixteenth century caused prices to increase, speculators cornered grain and other foodstuffs coming into the city and hoarded them in their warehouses in order to force prices up still further. A government investigation resulted in the discovery of both the individuals and the location of their warehouses, which were immediately destroyed. Wheat and barley prices promptly fell by half, to the delight of the poor and destitute, who offered thanks to God for their deliverance.[27] The great famine of 1573 caused the population to mutter and the vezirs to be afraid, according to Aurelio Santa Croce, in Istanbul at the time with the Venetian ambassador Marcantonio Barbaro. Santa Croce reported that voices had begun to be heard on all sides, complaining that the proper provisioning had not been carried out, and that the *paşa*s had warehouses full of grain which they were hoarding for speculative purposes. In order to free themselves from this accusation, the *paşa*s opened their warehouses and dispensed the grain, which they maintained was there for the sustenance of their own households and not for any speculating.[28]

Speculators also cornered the markets by preventing grain from reaching the city, buying it in ports before it was shipped to the city and hoarding it there, sending it to Istanbul only in times of shortage, and then only in small quantities. In the same year as Santa Croce reported on the discontent of the population over hoarding in the city, the sultan sent an order to the *kadı* of Tekirdağ, forbidding the selling of grain there to anyone without a permit from Istanbul. Istanbul bakers had complained to the court that while before, grain had arrived regularly from Tekirdağ and there had in consequence been no shortage, over the past two or three years, profiteers had prevented grain ships from reaching the city, buying

[25] Heberer, *Köle*, pp. 159–60. [26] Selaniki, *Tarih*, II, pp. 592–3.
[27] Selaniki, *Tarih*, I, p. 276.
[28] Santa Croce, 'Séguito del bailo Marcantonio Barbaro', p. 231.

the grain from them and then hoarding it, releasing it in small quantities when there was a shortage.[29]

Officials could also forcibly buy grain cheap and sell it in the city at high prices. In 1810, the head of intelligence, Kara Hasan Ağa, forced a merchant bringing wheat to Istanbul to sell him the grain, which had cost the merchant eighteen *para* per *okka*, for thirteen *para* per *okka*. Kara Hasan sold it on the market for a considerable mark-up, the market price being twenty-two *para* per *okka*. Other traders therefore ceased bringing in wheat, taking it instead to other locations, including İzmir. This was a time at which there was already a great scarcity of supplies which was threatening to undermine order in the city. The merchant sent a petition to the government protesting about his treatment and the Istanbul governor asked Kara Hasan for an explanation. Kara Hasan replied that he had bought the wheat in order to satisfy the needs of the foreign Christian embassies in Galata. This response was relayed back to the merchant, who, in consequence, complained directly to the sultan. Kara Hasan was forced to pay the full price to the merchant, so making up his loss on the original sale, and was exiled to Lemnos.[30]

Despite the complexity of provisioning such a massive capital, bread riots and famine were the exception rather than the rule, and for much of the time the city was effectively provisioned. For Careri, Istanbul in the late seventeenth century was clearly not a city deprived of food. 'It abounds', he wrote, 'in good fruit all the year; as also in fish, flesh, excellent bread, and all an Epicure can desire, at very reasonable rates'.[31]

Regulating supplies of foodstuffs to the city was only one aspect of the economic policy of the sultans within the city as they strove to keep a contented population, for they had also to control the city markets. The often volatile economic climate, buffeted by rampant inflation or crippled by financial crises related to costly campaigns undertaken to defend or advance the empire's frontiers, made ensuring a stable market very difficult indeed. Throughout its existence, the empire underwent various periods of considerable economic hardship, and was often faced with the almost impossible task of maintaining the value of its currency. The first major fall in the value of the *akçe* occurred in the later part of the reign of Mehmed II, between 1460 and 1480, to be followed a century later by a drastic and rapid devaluation from 1565. Government attempts to deal with the situation proved ineffective and the beginning of the following century also saw a continuing debasement of the coinage which continued into the 1640s. The seventeenth century was one in which the monetary

[29] Ahmet Refik, *Onuncu Asr-ı Hicrî*, pp. 91–2, *hüküm* 27.
[30] Cabi, *Târihi*, I, p. 610. [31] Careri, 'Voyage', p. 68.

18. Market place of Tophane, in Robert Walsh, *Constantinople and the Scenery of the Seven Churches of Asia Minor* (London and Paris, [1839?]), frontispiece.

system disintegrated, as the empire came under the effect of the appearance on its markets of foreign coinage and the continued impact of intercontinental specie movement, compounded by the internal fiscal and economic problems of the state. In 1691, that resulted in a greater use of the small copper coins, the *mangır*, whose circulation so increased that there was no copper left in the treasury.[32] While the currency remained relatively stable over the first half of the eighteenth century, it devalued rapidly again over the period 1760 to 1812. In 1790 the financial difficulties were such that the government announced that everyone was to hand over their gold and silver, with the exception of seals and weapons, to the mint. The markets were raided and silver was seized from anyone who had attempted to conceal it.[33] From the mid nineteenth century, the government became increasingly enmeshed in a series of loans, which ultimately led to the state's bankruptcy in 1875, and the foundation of the European-controlled Public Debt Administration in 1881, which was ultimately to control a considerable portion of the empire's economy.

Government responses to economic crises often served merely to exacerbate the problems, and debasement of the coinage resorted to by a series of sultans over the centuries precipitated further economic collapse. According to Peçevi, the policy adopted by Murad III of debasing the *akçe* and using this debased coinage to pay salaries resulted in open revolt. Prices rocketed up to such an extent that people were unable to buy anything and a price revolution began.[34] Any loss in the value of the *akçe* had a negative effect on prices and thus on the population, which became crushed under the weight of the high cost of living. Debased coinage and inefficient currency policy by the government drove the market traders to distraction and, in 1651, to vociferous protesting to the grand vezir, the *şeyhülislam* and the sultan.[35]

Whatever the problems and however difficult the task, it was essential that the government maintain control over the market and ensure the economic well-being of the people. Without this, the sultan lost credibility as a ruler able to guarantee the security of his subjects. If the state could not control the market, according to Gelibolulu Mustafa Ali, then unworthy people would start to increase their capital by illegal means; those going on campaign for the empire would be forced to sell their property and goods to cover their expenses; and purchases made at black market prices would result in ill-provisioned and starving soldiers. This would serve the enemies of the empire by pushing its armies into defeat.[36]

[32] Özcan, *Anonim*, p. 21. [33] Ahmed Cavid, *Hadîka*, p. 69.
[34] Peçevi, *Tarihi*, II, p. 284.
[35] Naima, *Târih*, pp. 1319–21; Gökyay, *Kâtip Çelebi*, pp. 88–9. [36] Kütükoğlu, *Narh*, p. 6.

At times of political instability, controlling the market became increasingly difficult, and the economic conditions of the inhabitants of the city slumped further, only serving to compound the sultan's difficulties. A very tangible sign of such instability was the closing of shops, either on the order of rebels or as a protest by the shopkeepers themselves over insecurity and violence in the city. In 1648, during the unrest in the period of İbrahim's deposal, shops were closed.[37] In 1703, during the Edirne incident, the rebels ordered the closure of the markets and shops, the only shops permitted to stay open being bakeries, butchers and grocers.[38] In the Patrona Halil revolt in 1730, the traders in the markets and the shopkeepers all responded to the demand by those in revolt that they close their premises and cease trading. Pulling down their shutters in great crowds, according to Abdi, they streamed to their homes, where they shut themselves up, refusing to be reassured by the janissary *ağa*'s protestations that all was under control and that they had no need to fear. Despite his attempts to calm the people, they remained firmly at home and the shops stayed closed.[39] This position continued even after the accession of Mahmud I.[40] In the 1807 rebellion against Selim III, the demand was for the shops to remain open, the janissaries instructing shopowners not to close, but banning wine houses from selling wine.[41]

It was not always as a result of revolt that the shops shut. Shopkeepers also pulled down their shutters at other times when the violence reached unacceptable levels. In the period following Selim III's downfall, sailors in Üsküdar extracted money, cheese and other foodstuffs by force from grocers' shops, even killing one grocer and injuring two others. As a reaction to this, the grocers locked up their premises for several days, to the considerable discomfort of the poor of the *mahalle*, who were, according to Cabi, reduced to a miserable condition. These closures due to excessive violence against shopkeepers were a common problem in other areas of Istanbul in this period, as janissary extortion of foods, spices and money, together with their demands to change debased coinage for true coins, reached such a peak that shopkeepers closed their shops in protest.[42] To prevent them forcing tradesmen to sell at below market prices, or simply taking goods from the shopkeepers, soldiers were not allowed to go shopping in the markets without an escort, one man to groups of five or six janissaries.[43]

[37] Naima, *Târih*, III, p. 1153. [38] Özcan, *Anonim*, p. 228. [39] Abdi, *Tarihi*, pp. 29–30.
[40] Abdi, *Tarihi*, p. 44.
[41] Ubeydullah Kuşmani and Ebubekir Efendi, *Asiler ve Gaziler*, p. 54.
[42] Cabi, *Târihi*, I, pp. 387, 482, II, pp. 741–2. [43] Cabi, *Târihi*, II, p. 729.

Whatever reason led to such closure, the result was the same: a highlighting of and increase in instability, and a crippling of economic activity. This inability of the market to function effectively was a clear and dangerous sign of the failure of political authority within the city, and thus served further to undermine the position of the sultan in a period in which he was already weakened politically. Any government inability to secure the satisfactory working of the market thus threatened the sultan's political strength. This was also evident when the janissaries, not the state, were able to control prices, forcing the guilds to sell their goods cheaply.[44] The action of the janissaries struck at the heart of the government's competence and posed a very real threat to order, not just physically but in the undermining impact it had on the government's perceived ability to guarantee stability, for setting prices and controlling price levels was the prerogative of the sultan.

The mechanism by which the sultans controlled market prices and the standards of commodities was known in Ottoman as *narh*.[45] For the ex-grand vezir of Süleyman I, Lütfi Paşa, the writer of the *Asafname*, one of the earliest Ottoman works of advice for a sultan on how to rule, the *narh* was one of the most important duties of the state and one which the vezirs should take seriously. He also argued that men of state should not be personally involved in trade, for if they were their interests would then lie with their own profits and not with those of the state.[46] Under the system of *narh*, fixed prices were established for commodities including basic foodstuffs, as well as other, more luxurious items, such as coffee, wine and even opium, or for non-food commodities, such as soap, pens, ink and paper, cloth, furs, footwear, carpets and storage chests. It also established prices for services such as those of gravediggers and porters, prices in the *hamam*, and passenger charges on boats.[47] Apart from fixing the prices for commodities and services, the system also involved controls over the weight and the quality of goods, in particular, bread, which was checked to ensure it was properly baked. Animals were not to be overloaded, food was to be cooked properly and in clean pots and washed in clean water.

The establishment and regulation of *narh* in the city was the job of the *kadı* of Istanbul. This he did in consultation with a wide range of officials. The process of setting *narh* involved much intense negotiation, for sellers clearly wanted to make as great a profit as possible, while the state wished to set prices at the lowest level it could. Once the prices had been

[44] Cabi, *Târihi*, I, pp. 485, 488, II, pp. 741, 837.
[45] For a very useful explanation of *narh*, see Kütükoğlu, *Narh*, pp. 4–38.
[46] Kütükoğlu, 'Lütfi Paşa Âsafnâmesi', pp. 79–80.
[47] Kütükoğlu, *Narh*, pp. 91–338.

established, they were registered in the state accounts and then sent out to the officials of the city. These new prices were announced by public criers to the guilds and the population. If the guilds felt that the *narh* level was too low, they could appeal for an increase to the *kadı*, who would order an investigation. If the *kadı* wished to change the prices, he would present a case to the grand vezir who would, in turn, take the matter to the sultan. If the change was accepted, instructions would then be issued to the *kadı* to implement the new *narh*. While, under normal conditions, the establishment of prices was relatively straightforward, every new debasement of the currency required a new *narh* pricing, and periods of dearth, bad harvests and natural disasters, or times of major campaigns, necessitated an alteration in the *narh*.

Natural disasters could also be used by those who wished to force a change in the *narh*. The great snowstorms at the beginning of December 1573 were used as a pretext by the bakers of the city to try to force an increase in the *narh* for bread, claiming that there was no grain. The sultan, however, remained unconvinced, stating that two days of snow and storms was not sufficient to cause any change in the *narh*, and banned them from hoarding grain and announcing that there was a shortage in an attempt to increase the prices.[48] *Narh* prices could also be brought down in times of particular hardship, in order to release the pressure on the people. In 1811 Mahmud II lowered the *narh* for bread from three *para*s for ninety *dirhem* of bread to two *para*s for eighty *dirhem*. The poor, in particular, were delighted and there was much praying for the sultan and for the continuation of his reign.[49]

The control of the *narh* was one of the duties of the grand vezir, who would tour the markets accompanied by various officials of state, inspecting the prices and quality, to the point of breaking open loaves in the bakeries to check that they were baked correctly. Ahmed I's grand vezir Ali Paşa gave particular importance to *narh*, and during his time in office bread and meat were abundant in the city. He himself continually toured the markets, *han*s and covered bazaars in disguise, to check that market prices and practices were being implemented correctly.[50] The sultans personally inspected the markets incognito, checking both availability and prices of foodstuffs. On one such trip, Selim III observed a riot in front of a bakery in Divan Yolu, when the crowd was unable to find bread to eat. He immediately instructed the grand vezir to find a solution, as this state of affairs was unacceptable, particularly in Ramazan.[51] Day-to-day

[48] Ahmet Refik, *Onuncu Asr-ı Hicrî*, p. 91, *hüküm* 26; Gerlach, *Günlüğü*, I, p. 110.
[49] Cabi, *Târihi*, II, p. 775. [50] Topçular Katibi, *Tarihi*, I, p. 375.
[51] Karal, *Hümayunları*, p. 105.

19. A caravansaray, in Schweigger, *Ein newe Reyssbeschreibung*, p. 40.

control was in the hands of the market inspector, who, according to the *Asafname*, should be a man experienced, honest and religious.[52] It was his job to control prices and the quality of the goods on sale, check that the animals were not overloaded and collect the various market taxes.

Infringement of the *narh*, either selling at a price other than the one established, at an incorrect weight, or at a quality below the fixed standard, was punishable, often very severely. Bakers who sold bread at an incorrect weight or of bad quality were hanged in front of their bakeries; on one occasion, according to rumour, Mahmud II, in the market in disguise, strung up a baker himself, an act for which he was greatly praised by the people. Greengrocers, fruit sellers and grocers could also suffer the same fate.[53] It was not acceptable for people to sell at the prices they wished, and any profit thus made would not be canonically legitimate.

The sultans also tried to control market practice by the use of a guarantor for sales. This system aimed to prevent stolen goods being

52 Kütükoğlu, "Lütfi Paşa Âsafnâmesi", p. 79.
53 Cabi, *Târihi*, I, pp. 597–8, II, pp. 919, 929, 947, 1005.

auctioned on the market, when the sales could be rigged for certain buyers, who would buy the goods at cheap prices, selling them on either after altering them slightly or as they were, at higher prices. A case of this type occurred in 1583, when 'servants and scoundrels' took goods to the market for auction without a guarantor. Murad III issued an order that no auctions were to take place without a guarantor and that no goods were to be bought from such people who did not have a guarantor. Those who sold, bought or auctioned without a guarantor were to be killed.[54]

The physical security of the market was very important. It had always been essential for the Ottomans to be able to guarantee safety to the merchants. The level of security in Ottoman lands had struck the Mamluk historian Ibn Hajjar many years before the conquest of Constantinople, when he reported the comment of Şemseddin, doctor to Bayezid I, according to whom security was so effective that no one would touch a fully laden camel whose owner had left it unattended.[55] Markets were policed and watchmen appointed. Shopkeepers on occasion paid for such watchmen, as was the case in Galata in 1501, when an order was issued for the hiring of a nightwatchman, to whom the shopowners were to pay one *akçe* per month, an obligation which was compulsory.[56] The security of the caravansarays was taken very seriously, and, according to the law code of Selim I, every morning, before the gates of the caravansaray were opened, the person in charge had to check that all goods were in place and that nothing was missing.[57]

Theft was punished very harshly. When, in 1591, thirty thousand to forty thousand *altın* (gold coin) and *kuruş* were stolen from the security safe of the old cloth market, all the market traders were arrested and tortured. The market was closed for fifteen days, while the *subaşı*, the *kadı* and the janissary *ağa* conducted a thorough search. When the money was ultimately found, concealed in a storage room under the shop of the son of a trader in musk and amber at the Kuyumcular Kapısı, both were arrested. The son confessed and was sentenced by the *kadı* to be tortured to death, a sentence from which he was reprieved by the sultan, who acceded to his request to be hanged without torture.[58] The extremity of the collective punishment of those who were in fact totally unrelated to the crime, together with the financial loss occasioned by the fifteen-day closure of the market, highlights the lengths to which the authorities would go in their attempts to

[54] Ülker, *Emir Defteri*, pp. 45–6, facsimile p. 27, *hüküm* 90.
[55] Halil İnalcık, *The Ottoman Empire: The Classical Age 1300–1600* (London, 2000), p. 89.
[56] Şahin and Emecen, *Ahkâm Defteri*, p. 88, *hüküm* 317.
[57] Yaşar Yücel and Selami Pulaha (eds.), *I. Selim Kanunnameleri (1512–1520)* (Ankara, 1995), pp. 35, 154.
[58] Selaniki, *Tarih*, I, pp. 231–2.

20. Street pedlar in Pera, in Amicis, *Constantinople*, p. 21.

ensure the security of the market and the level of the deterrent applied. Theft was therefore collectively to be avoided and it was in the interests of all merchants that it did not occur.

The severity of punishment was clearly effective. Writing in the sixteenth century, Heberer noted that theft was much less common in the Ottoman empire than it was in Christian countries, this being the result of the extremely severe punishments given for stealing.[59] The Venetian ambassador Alvise Contarini also recorded in his report to the senate after his return from Istanbul in 1641 that theft there was rare.[60] This was apparently true also for the nineteenth century, when Charles Pertusier commented on the security of the market, even arguing that too much contact with the Europeans had had a bad effect on the Turks' natural honesty.[61]

Although goods might be safe in the markets, women were not always so, for here, as elsewhere on the streets of the capital, they could be subjected to hassle, abuse and even kidnapping and rape; one young girl, out shopping in 1811 for muslin and silk with an old woman, narrowly escaped abduction when she became lost in the market and was approached by a janissary who tried to kidnap her at gunpoint.[62] Women were sometimes prohibited from wandering round openly in the markets among the men, as they were by the *şeyhülislam* Sunullah Efendi in 1599.[63] This was not, however, by any means always the case, and certainly in the nineteenth century they were keen shoppers in the Grand Bazaar and other markets of the city.[64] Even when they were prevented from wandering in the markets, their shopping was not necessarily affected, for there were both the street pedlars who passed by, selling water, liver, candyfloss, candies, *dolma*, roasted chickpeas, vegetables and even little poems which were very popular,[65] and the women who came to their houses bringing goods for sale, gossip and matchmaking services.

The pleasures of the market

For the people of the city, the market provided them not merely with the essentials necessary for survival, but at least for those who could afford such items, the luxury goods and enticing entertainments that made life bearable. The markets, the 'rendezvous of the idle as well as of the busy',[66] were a hive of buying and selling, window-shopping, wandering and pleasure-seeking. The great covered Grand Bazaar was

> a meeting place of the people of Istanbul, popular not just among the buyers and sellers, but also for those who wanted to kill time, dandies and well-off women of

[59] Heberer, *Köle*, p. 213.
[60] Alvise Contarini, 'Relazione di Costantinopoli de bailo Alvise Contarini', in Firpo, *Relazioni*, p. 337.
[61] Pertusier, *Promenades*, pp. 82–3. [62] Cabi, *Târihi*, II, pp. 787–8.
[63] Selaniki, *Tarih*, II, p. 826.
[64] Pertusier, *Promenades*, pp. 81–2; Murad Efendi, *Manzaraları*, pp. 46–7.
[65] Sadri Sema, *Hatıraları*, pp. 33, 272–4; Alus, *İstanbul*, pp. 289–91.
[66] Pertusier, *Promenades*, pp. 81–2.

21. Shop in the Grand Bazaar, in *Servet-i Fünun*, no. 587, p. 228 (from the private collection of Ebru Boyar).

Istanbul. It was an ideal environment for someone who wanted to know the street life of Istanbul and to observe it. Of course in the Grand Bazaar there were many places to eat, coffee houses, barber shops, *hamams* and fountains. There was no lack of wandering *simit* [bread in the shape of a ring], *kağıt helva* [pastry wafers] and sherbet sellers.[67]

Much of the cosmopolitan consumption of the capital revolved round what was either forbidden or frowned on by society, and perhaps because of this was particularly attractive. Here, too, the symbiotic nature of sultan and people was in evidence, with a careful balance being maintained between popular demand and governmental desire, where the demand was for consumption and the desire was for control.

It is often argued that the Ottomans avoided displays of wealth, fearful of attracting attention and consequent sequestration and dramatic fall from grace. It was not, however, a matter of concealment so much as one of display in certain areas and not in others. In contrast Europeans,

[67] Murad Efendi, *Manzaraları*, pp. 46–7.

the Ottomans did not in general exhibit their wealth in the form of houses or furnishings, a lack which puzzled European travellers like Lithgow, who commented on the absence of 'internall domestick furniture, or externall decorements of Fabricks palatiatly extended'.[68] One reason for this was fire, which 'could reduce many pretentious masters of emporia of wealth into miserable wretches'.[69] As Hayrullah Efendi noted during his travels in Europe in the 1860s, Europeans lived in stone-built houses and so did not spend their lives in constant fear of their homes burning down, as the Ottomans did, and were spared the terror of fleeing half-naked from their beds in the middle of the night as flames consumed their possessions. In consequence, their houses were lavishly furnished and their beds fixed structures, not rolled out at night and taken up in the morning.[70] The ever-present menace of fire no doubt made the display of wealth invested in houses and furnishings somewhat unappealing, particularly when a magnificent mansion, which had taken two years to build and furnish with great expense, could burn to the ground in just one hour, reducing the contents to ashes, as happened to the mansion of Selanikli Memiş Ağa in 1785.[71] It took a mere half an hour for flames to destroy the mansion of Hüseyin Avni Paşa, the ex-grand vezir, later assassinated, in 1876.[72] Although furnishings became increasingly fashionable at the end of the nineteenth century, with the change in consumer patterns stimulated by the increased appearance on the city's markets of European goods, fire, without doubt, continued to be a disincentive to excessive expense on furnishings, except for those who could afford to see such items reduced to ashes without undue concern. That this was the case is supported by the remarks of Rashid Rida, who, as late as 1910, noted that nothing had surprised him more during his stay in Istanbul than the great number of fires. Nearly every night people were put into panic by the cries of fire, which were designed to alert those who had a house or relations in the affected *mahalle* to rush there and grab any valuables they could carry away with them, for once a fire had broken out there was hardly time to rescue anything from the area.[73]

A lack of rich household furnishings did not, however, mean a lack of Ottoman interest in lavish display. For this, they turned to clothing and jewellery. In August 1577, Gerlach wrote:

[68] Lithgow, *Discourse*, p. 139. [69] Ahmed Vasıf Efendi, *Ahbâr*, p. 180.

[70] Hayrullah Efendi, *Avrupa Seyahatnamesi*, ed. Belkis Altuniş-Gürsoy (Ankara, 2002), pp. 29–30.

[71] Taylesanizade, *Tarihi*, p. 93.

[72] Ahmed Lütfi Efendi, *Vak'a – Nüvis Ahmed Lûtfi Efendi Tarihi, C. XV*, ed. M. Münir Aktepe (Ankara, 1993), p. 57.

[73] Rashid Rida, *İttihad*, p. 179.

The Turks are very interested in making displays with their outward appearances. They love to decorate themselves with clothes made from velvet, silk and cloth of silver thread and with jewellery ornamented with pearls and other valuable stones. You can see on some Turkish women jewels which alone are worth two to three thousand thalers which they wear on their hands and necks. They have made for themselves necklaces and bracelets ornamented with pearls and other valuable stones worth thousands of thalers. If a man has much money, he wants his wife and children dressed in an eye-catching manner. In the market they sell rings for five hundred to one thousand ducats to button shirts of armour. Our doorman is having a necklace and bracelet worth one thousand three hundred *thaler*s made for his daughter.[74]

This level of desire for display could reach ridiculous heights, where a man who could not find even a felt covering for his back or a rope to tie around his waist as a belt would dress his wife in a satin caftan and a girdle of silver and gold.[75] Some women were clearly very costly to maintain, the expenses of the wife of Tinyüz Halil Ağa costing him his job at the end of the eighteenth century. Tinyüz Halil Ağa, a high state official, requested leave not to be sent on campaign with the imperial army, a request which caused his exile to Rhodes. The reason for his desire to avoid going to war was his 'heart-stealing' mistress, then wife, İnce Hanım, who needed fifteen thousand *kuruş* a year merely to cover her expenses for her carriage for promenading.[76]

Wives and daughters became the objects upon which to drape rich fabrics and precious stones, in an ostentatious display of wealth. This, in turn, emphasised the lack of importance of the house for many as a symbol of money, for women were unseen there and any display largely pointless, at least for the male section of the population.

The desire to display wealth through clothing was not always the case, at least if Busbecq's account is to be believed. Busbecq wrote referring to the mid sixteenth century:

The dress of all has the same form whatever the wearer's rank; and no edging or useless trimmings are sewn on, as is the custom with us, costing a large sum of money and worn out in three days. Their most beautiful garments of silk or satin, even if they are embroidered, as they usually are, cost only a ducat to make.[77]

Busbecq was particularly impressed by Turkish clothing habits:

The Turks were quite as much astonished at our manner of dress as we at theirs. They wear long robes which reach almost to their ankles, and are not only more

[74] Gerlach, *Günlüğü*, II, p. 624.
[75] Develi, *Risale-i Garibe*, p. 28. [76] Ahmed Cavid, *Hadîka*, p. 195.
[77] Ogier Ghiselin de Busbecq, *The Turkish Embassy Letters of Ogier Ghiselin de Busbecq*, trans. Edward Seymour Forster (Oxford, 1968), p. 61.

22. *Kaymak* (clotted cream) shop, in Julia Pardoe, *The Beauties of the Bosphorus* (London, 1838), between pp. 34 and 35.

imposing but seem to add to the stature; our dress, on the other hand, is so short and tight that it discloses the forms of the body, which would be better hidden, and is thus anything but becoming, and besides, for some reason or other, it takes away from a man's height and gives him a stunted appearance.[78]

[78] Busbecq, *Letters*, p. 61.

A few decades later, however, things had apparently changed, as Gerlach's comments show. The great importance of dress as a symbol of wealth, and thus importance, is made particularly clear by one of the stories told about Nasreddin Hoca, a legendary figure whose life was, and is, used to illustrate humorously the realities of everyday existence. One day, Nasreddin Hoca was invited to a feast to which he went dressed in his everyday clothes. When he entered, he was ignored. He could not even find a place to sit. Very annoyed, he left, borrowed a fur caftan from his neighbour, put it on and thus dressed went back to the feast. As soon as he entered, everyone rushed up to him. He was given a great welcome and placed at the head of the table. Having understood why he was being treated in this way he started to give food to his caftan. Everyone was surprised and asked him what he was doing. 'Feeding my caftan', he replied.

While the population in many, if not all, periods, sought to display, the state set out to curb this, and a tussle developed between state control and popular consumption and lavish display. The sultan and his ministers were anxious to control such display for a variety of reasons, partly to ensure the social and religious status quo and to link expensive clothing to rank.

Clothes were used to mark the different religious groups, each being required to wear distinct garments or colours. Selim II issued orders about what non-Muslim men and women were to wear, and forbade them from dressing in clothing assigned to Muslims or in expensive garments.[79] Murad III sent public criers throughout the city in 1577, announcing that Christians and Jews who were subjects of the sultan were not to dress in clothes made from silk or fine woven cloth, but instead in garments of poorer quality cloth. Instead of elegant footwear, they were to put on simpler shoes worth half a thaler; their turbans were not to be of a high quality, and they were to wear stockings and gaiters, not long trousers. If the authorities caught a Christian or a Jew wearing a silk belt, the belt would be confiscated and the guilty individual hauled before a judge and given bastinadoes. If caught wearing a garment of silk, the same thing would happen, with the addition of a hefty fine. According to Gerlach, the reason behind Murad III's decree at that time was the sighting of a Jewish woman out on the streets two weeks before the announcement wearing jewels round her neck worth forty thousand ducats. Jewish men had also been seen out and about in garments of velvet and silk.[80]

[79] Ahmet Refik, *Hicri On İkinci Asırda*, p. 47, *hüküm* 6.
[80] Gerlach, *Günlüğü*, II, pp. 633–4.

Mustafa II banned Christians and Jews from wearing yellow, light, thin-soled boots or shoes, red broadcloth calpacks or Tatar calpacks, which were reserved for Muslims. They were instead to dress in black broadcloth calpacks and hats.[81] According to Selaniki, it was Mevlana Abdülkerim Efendi who was the man responsible for changing the dress code for the Jews and Christians in 1584, from blue and yellow turbans to red skullcaps and black hats.[82] This ban, forcing Jews and Christians to wear black hats, used up to that point only by European foreigners in the empire, was much resented by the Jews, who tried, unsuccessfully, to overturn the ruling by means of a bribe of thirty thousand to forty thousand florins. Forced therefore to adopt the new headgear, they promptly went down with inflammation of the eyes, head colds and headaches. Where before their heads had been enveloped in the many layers of a turban, they now only had a hat, which consisted of just one layer, to protect them.[83] At the end of the eighteenth century, Selim III decreed that Armenians were to dress in red hats and shoes, Greeks in black and Jews in blue.[84] Muslim dress was also controlled, Selim ordering that Muslims wear yellow turbans and shoes. He was not happy about the eminent *paşa*s, the style of whose turbans he found unacceptable.[85]

One of the main reasons for the state imposition of dress codes was to ensure social order, making sure that groups remained distinct and distinguished, and in their proper places. For Mahmud II,

> The people of Istanbul are divided into numerous categories and each category has its own clothing, and they should dress in this clothing and they should observe the established customs and everyone should know their place, and they should show respect, reverence and obedience to their superiors and the authorities. One group should not wear the costume of another.[86]

This was another reflection of the way in which the state saw its people in terms of groups and responded to them accordingly, seeking to control and command through mechanisms based on structured groups rather than individuals. Inappropriate dressing and ignoring of dress codes caused a breakdown in social order. Clothes therefore marked rank – furs, for example, being a mark of status. Wearing sable was the prerogative only of high-ranking officials and was given by the sultan as a mark of distinction. Sables were not, therefore, to be worn by others, however rich they might be. Following this logic, non-Muslims were prohibited from wearing expensive garments and restricted, at least in theory, to less costly

[81] Özcan, *Anonim*, p. 176. [82] Selaniki, *Tarih*, I, pp. 347–8.
[83] Gelibolulu Mustafa Ali, *Künhü'l-Ahbâr*, III, pp. 423–4.
[84] Karal, *Hümayunları*, p. 100. [85] Karal, *Hümayunları*, p. 102.
[86] Ahmet Refik, *Hicri On Üçüncü Asırda*, p. 11, *hüküm* 10.

clothing. For Selim III, ignorance of such regulations led to all people being equal. But it was essential that each group should be distinct from the others, and be dressed in such a way as to distinguish the members of different groups, whether such differences were religious or social or by rank. Guild members were to dress in the garments associated with their group, as were the military.[87] Mahmud II, too, was unhappy about disregard for such distinctions, and complained in the early years of his reign that no one was wearing what they were supposed to and that it was no longer clear who belonged to which group. No one was following the dress codes or taking any notice of them. This, he ordered, had to stop, and anyone, regardless of who they were, was to be punished if dressed inappropriately.[88]

There was another factor dictating the government's approach to the clothing of its subjects, and that was economic. Dressing extravagantly, or in imported rather than home-produced cloth, was seen at times as damaging to the economy of the empire or to the economic well-being of the people, who overspent on sartorial display and then suffered economic hardship. For Selim II, non-Muslims dressing in expensive clothes had the effect of increasing the cost of clothing for Muslims, thus pushing prices up.[89] Selim III noted, when imposing strict dress codes banning the wearing of extravagant materials, that it was important to save the people from expense.[90] During a discussion in the *divan* headed by the grand vezir İbrahim Paşa in 1597, on ways to rectify the economic problems facing the state, a decision was taken that people were not to dress extravagantly, as they were at present doing, nor to dress above their station.[91]

At the beginning of the eighteenth century, Ahmed III was annoyed to note that people were wearing clothes of broadcloth which was positively festooned with silver and gold thread, in contrast to the earlier habit of making only limited use of silver and gold. Now such cloth cost five hundred to six hundred *kuruş* and was worn even by those not from the high echelons of society. An imperial order was issued banning the wearing of silver- and gold-threaded open-work embroidery and the use of elaborate horse trappings by anyone except the sultan and vezirs. All were instead to dress in plain say broadcloth and use plain harnesses. For those people who were moderate by nature, according to the anonymous author of an eighteenth-century Ottoman history, this order brought great happiness.[92]

87 Karal, *Hümayunları*, p. 101. 88 Ahmed Refik, *Hicri On Üçüncü Asırda*, p. 11, *hüküm* 10.
89 Ahmet Refik, *Onuncu Asr-ı Hicrî*, p. 47, *hüküm* 6.
90 Karal, *Hümayunları*, p. 136. 91 Selaniki, *Tarih*, II, p. 706.
92 Özcan, *Anonim*, p. 293.

Overspending on expensive, showy clothing was also distinctly discouraged by Selim III, who ordered that, apart from the men of high office, those dressed in *şal* (material used for turbans) in Indian and European material, lynx, sable, ermine or any other expensive fur, and not wearing the clothes that they were supposed to wear according to the dress codes, would be punished. He announced that if he saw anyone wearing *şal* or rich fur jackets, except those entitled to wear sable, he would have them killed. He forbade the upper echelons from wearing sable, ermine, lynx and flower-patterned cloth, and the women from wearing clothes made from English cloth.[93]

When it came to women, the state had a further reason for controlling dressing, for women were always perceived as potentially dangerous, inciting disorder and causing unrest by their too open presence on the streets. It was therefore considered necessary to ensure that how they dressed was at all times appropriate and avoided excessive ostentation. Linked to this was the overriding economic concern for a balanced market, stability of prices and avoidance of excessive consumption, which applied equally to male fashion. One further factor influencing the government approach to female attire was the avoidance of innovation, to which the women of the capital were constantly attracted, tempted continuously to try out new fashions on their own persons.

The state issued constant directives over what women should and should not wear. Dress was to be appropriate, not over-ostentatious and not excessively expensive. It was certainly not to be revealing in any way whatsoever. Bans were issued forbidding the making of *ferace*s (long flowing outer garments) from English cloth, which was a fine material through which the garments underneath could be discerned. *Ferace*s made of Ankara cloth were also forbidden, for wearing a *ferace* made from this material was the equivalent of not wearing one at all. But despite this ban, women continued to dress in Ankara cloth *ferace*s and another ban was issued in 1792. The imams of the *mahalle*s were made responsible for ensuring that women did not dress that way and that no tailor made up *ferace*s of this material. Any tailor caught doing so would be hanged in front of his shop and the person who had ordered the garment would also be punished.[94] Large collars on *ferace*s were also found offensive by various governments, and in 1811 the watchmen of the *mahalle*s were instructed to announce that women were banned from wearing such collars or from dressing in inappropriately coloured *ferace*s.[95] Indeed, two years before, the governor Osman Paşa had cut off the collar of the

93 Karal, *Hümayunları*, p. 136.
94 Ahmet Refik, *Hicri On Üçüncü Asırda*, p. 4, *hüküm* 4.
95 Cabi, *Târihi*, II, p. 773.

ferace of a woman whom he had seen out, as he perceived the collar to be too large.[96] Selim III found women's headgear too long and their collars both long and of bright colours. This he banned, ordering that if any women were seen dressed like this, their collars and headgear were to be cut and they were to be warned.[97] Mahmud II also issued similar bans, and women caught in contravention of them were punished.[98]

Innovation in women's clothing was always frowned on and sternly discouraged. Murad IV, out in disguise, was appalled to see women on the streets dressed in new fashions and had criers announce that women were to wear the soft felt caps they had dressed in in the past and not in any new-fangled fashion. After this announcement, men took the new clothes away from their wives and punished them for incorrect dressing.[99] Innovation in fashion, however, could not easily be prevented, and led Ahmed III to issue another ban against it in 1726, in which he noted that, profiting from the absence from the capital of the sultan, who was in Edirne, some 'shameless' women had been going round decked out in the latest fashions, overdressed, imitating non-Muslim women in dress and hairstyle. Although this had already been banned, the prohibition had had no effect. Such women were having an undesirable effect on good Muslim women and leading them astray. They were pressuring their husbands to buy them the latest fashions, these 'immodest and immoral innovations'. Those men who could afford such things were being drawn into sin because they were wasting money on these unsuitable extravagances for their wives. Others who did not want to spend in this way, or those who could not afford to do so were now facing problems which could go as far as divorce. Old-style clothes had lost their popularity and this was adversely affecting the people of the market, for they were faced both with a loss of demand for their goods and with the need to sell the new fashions. The order therefore banned women from wearing big-collared *ferace*s or large head-covers. If they did so, their collars would be cut off and they could face exile. Tailors and ribbon makers who made up such garments would be punished. These regulations were to be presented to the women of the *mahalle*s by their imams.[100]

Failure to observe such clothing codes was taken seriously, for it was seen as a challenge to the sultan's authority and to the order in the city. Violation of the dress codes could lead to instant execution.[101] This was particularly pronounced in periods of difficulty, such as the reign of Selim

[96] Cabi, *Târihi*, I, p. 562. [97] Karal, *Hümayunları*, p. 102.
[98] Cabi, *Târihi*, I, pp. 564, 587–8, II, p. 772. [99] Topçular Katibi, *Tarihi*, II, p. 990.
[100] Ahmed Refik, *Hicri On İkinci Asırda*, pp. 86–8, *hüküm* 118.
[101] Taylesanizade, *Tarihi*, p. 419.

III, when the response of the sultan to transgressions was more dramatic than at other times. When Selim III, during one of his tours in disguise in 1789, came across a Greek Orthodox man wearing a long cloak of camlet and ermine fur, a caftan with flowers, *entari* (a loose robe) and yellow, light, thin-soled boots, he had the man killed on the spot.[102] Mahmud II could be equally severe, though not on every occasion. When touring near Balık Pazarı in disguise, Mahmud came across a young man wearing a *şal* on his head worth one thousand *kuruş*. He immediately had the *şal* removed and cut into pieces. He wanted to punish him further, but the women with him pleaded for leniency, explaining that he was young and that he was getting married that evening.[103] Overdressing could be lethal. In 1598, a man who dressed expensively and claimed to be the son of Selim II was caught and killed, so paying for his dressing-up, and his riding of an expensive horse, with his life, as Selaniki remarked.[104]

Despite such drastic punishments, dress codes were often ignored. The orders of İbrahim Paşa in 1597 had no effect;[105] those of Selim III had no impact, for the men of state preferred to wear foreign cloth instead of the home-produced product, as the sultan himself noted. Aggrieved, he complained to his grand vezir, pointing out that he himself always wore Istanbul and Ankara cloth, but his officials dressed in cloth from India and Iran. Their failure to dress in locally manufactured material undermined demand for local products.[106] That many sultans issued such dress laws further indicates that they were largely ineffective and often ignored. The order of Selim II was preceded by a similar one issued by Süleyman I.[107] Those promulgated much later by Selim III were followed by those of Mahmud II. In 1600, Sanderson had very little faith in the endurance of the order issued by Mehmed III, commenting in a letter he wrote at the end of March, ‘it is proclaimed about the citty that nether Jewe nor Greeke shall wear garment or chackchiers [breeches] of fine cloth; but this, I thinke, will not longe be observed’.[108]

Sometimes it was the excessive consumption of the state which angered the populace, rather than the other way round. The Lale Devri, the Tulip Age, which lasted from 1718 until the overthrow of Ahmed III in 1730, was a period of conspicuous extravagance and constant festivity, when Topkapı palace glittered with night-time revelries, and tortoises wandered through the gardens with candles attached to their backs. The inhabitants of the city resented this lavish extravagance bitterly, and this hostility

102 Taylesanizade, *Tarihi*, p. 419. 103 Cabi, *Târihi*, II, p. 753.
104 Selaniki, *Tarih*, II, pp. 779–80. 105 Selaniki, *Tarih*, II, p. 706.
106 Karal, *Hümayunları*, pp. 101–2. 107 Gerlach, *Günlüğü*, II, p. 634.
108 Sanderson, *Travels*, p. 202.

contributed to the Patrona Halil revolt in 1730, which saw the sultan deposed and the grand vezir executed.[109] İbrahim's absorption in his own entertainment and total lack of engagement with the many problems of the state caused fury among the *ulema*, janissaries and high-up officials, Hanefi Efendi even complaining to the *valide sultan* that things had reached such a point that the sound of drums, shawms, harps and lutes coming from the palace was throwing off the *müezzins*, who were unable to make the call to prayer correctly from the minaret of the Ayasofya mosque. This was, in any case, hardly the noise that should have been emanating from the palace at the time of prayer.[110]

Sultans were aware, though clearly some more than others, of the need to consider the impact of luxurious display, and Abdülhamid I called off the celebrations for the birth of his daughter Hibetullah Sultan in 1789, which occurred in the midst of a major shortage of bread and other foodstuffs.[111] The celebrations for the circumcisions of Abdülaziz's sons were cancelled in 1870 after the devastating fire in Pera.[112]

Rich clothes and jewels were not the only indulgences to be had in Istanbul. From the seventeenth century onwards, another luxury commodity began to make its appearance on the city's market and was adopted with gusto by Istanbul's inhabitants. This was tobacco, brought into the empire in 1600, according to Peçevi, by 'English infidels', who sold it as a treatment for diseases caused by dampness. Naima, who places its arrival a little later, in 1606, says that when it arrived from Europe it created a storm over whether it was or was not acceptable, but, regardless of this, it quickly became a fashionable addiction.[113] Having arrived, it was soon being used for purposes other than medicinal ones.

Some of those who were pleasure-seekers became addicted to it for pleasure and even those who were not pleasure-seekers, and even statesmen and men of science became addicted to tobacco. It was difficult to make anything out in the coffee houses because the smoking of the riff-raff there was so great that the smoke prevented people seeing one another. Their pipes never left people's hands, and they carried them with them in the streets and the market, and they smoked puffing smoke into each other's faces. They caused the streets and the *mahalle*s to smell. They wrote poems about smoking and read them aloud. In the end everywhere began to smell of smoke, people's houses, their turbans, their beards, even their undergarments, sometimes they burnt the carpets and felts on their floors, and everywhere was made dirty, and while sleeping the bad smell entered the brain. As if this wasn't enough, this habit also prevented people from working with their hands. So when you ask what is the delight and the use of this, they say this is just

109 Abdi, *Tarihi*, p. 26; Destari, *Tarihi*, pp. 2–3. 110 Naima, *Târih*, III, p. 1164.
111 Taylesanizade, *Tarihi*, p. 342. 112 Ahmed Lütfi Efendi, *Tarihi*, *C. XII*, p. 96.
113 Naima, *Târih*, I, p. 310.

an enjoyment, nothing else. There is no spiritual delight in this, so we cannot say that this is an enjoyment. Perhaps if watchmen in ships use it, it stops them falling asleep, in which case one cannot deny that it has a use. And in cases of damp, it dries things out. But for such a small usefulness, its use is not justified. By 1638 tobacco was so widespread that it is impossible to describe.[114]

Smoking might have been widespread, but all clearly did not know how to do it properly and the disgusting habits of some smokers caused great annoyance. There were those who

smoke in a sumptuously decorated room and spit behind the cushions of fine cloth and against the wall, may their mouths become desiccated. These ugly people press the tobacco into the pipes with their fingers and then wipe their fingers on their clothes, and they knock out their pipes on the candle plates and candle holders when there is a fireplace where they could do this, may their hands become paralysed. And [there are] those donkeys who when there is a fire in the hearth or the brazier light their pipes with the candle and drop tobacco onto it.[115]

For many a source of pleasure, tobacco was for others a source of great evil, and Peçevi was not alone in his condemnation. Claiming that tobacco had caused their ancestors to kill many people, the leaders of the rebels in 1703 even requested a ruling from the *şeyhülislam* banning the substance. He refused to ban it outright, saying that those who had killed for this reason were responsible for their own actions, which were contrary to the sharia, but he did agree to decree against the use of tobacco in public.[116]

Earlier, however, Murad IV had banned it altogether, together with coffee houses, so gaining lavish praise from Peçevi, for whom this act was 'such a great goodness and blessing for the people that it would not be enough if they thanked him until Judgement Day'.[117] Murad IV was a very determined anti-smoking sultan. He issued a ban on smoking, announcing that anyone caught doing so would be killed.[118] When, during one of his tours in disguise, he came across fourteen people, some of them state officials, sitting smoking, he had them killed. If he found any premises with tobacco, the place was raided and the owner killed. His reputation was such that, according to rumour, if during his tours in disguise at night he came across any sign of smoking in a house, he would climb up and check the chimney for any incriminating smell. In the end, people were so terrorised that, quite apart from abandoning totally any idea of smoking in public, they stopped going out at night altogether, not even for the night prayer.[119] But, Naima noted, such zealousness on the part of the sultan did not prevent smoking totally, because 'people do not accept what is

[114] Peçevi, *Tarihi*, I, p. 197. [115] Develi, *Risale-i Garibe*, p. 26.
[116] Özcan, *Anonim*, p. 271. [117] Peçevi, *Tarihi*, I, p. 197.
[118] Naima, *Târih*, II, p. 756. [119] Naima, *Târih*, II, p. 756.

right by force. Even if you slaughter them, they will not give up their addictions'.[120] A contemporary of Naima, Katip Çelebi, supported Naima's view about the uselessness of punishment. In fact, he even argued that forbidding something simply made it more attractive. Despite the harsh punishments imposed by Murad IV, people continued to smoke, carrying small pipes in their pockets and smoking whenever possible, particularly in the lavatory.[121]

Killing smokers was not the response of all sultans. Less dramatically, smoking could be disapproved of when indulged in near royal palaces, and thus by implication in the presence of the sultan, an action which seems to have been regarded as one showing a lack of respect. Mahmud II clearly saw it that way. When sitting one day in 1809 in Çinili Köşk, he caught sight of a man in his boat who, having just passed Beşiktaş palace, promptly lit up a pipe. Most put out, the sultan ordered inquiries to be made as to who the man was and having discovered that he was the chief secretary Naili Efendi, he gave instructions to the governor to warn him severely about his unacceptable behaviour. The governor did so and as a result Naili Efendi was very frightened.[122] That smoking near Topkapı palace was equally unacceptable, and at a much earlier period, is indicated by the disapproval directed by the anonymous author of the *Risale-i Garibe* at those who boarded boats at Ahır Kapı and started smoking before they had passed Sinan Paşa Köşkü, that is, before they were out of the confines of the Topkapı palace area.[123] Later, in the latter part of the nineteenth century, the upper echelons of society could light up as the boats left Istanbul, but eating candies or fruit was regarded as a shameful act, to be avoided.[124]

Government bans of tobacco were less to do with morality and more to do with fire, even Murad IV's ban being motivated for this reason, according to Katip Çelebi.[125] Şeyh Kadızade Efendi convinced the sultan, already much agitated after the colossal conflagration in 1633 which had devastated much of the city, that most fires were caused by those drunk evil-doers who sat smoking in the wine houses.[126] Smoking was regarded as the source of many destructive conflagrations in the city and the deaths of thousands by fire – the result, according to Tournefort, of Turks falling asleep in bed with lighted pipes, or of putting them out carelessly.[127] In 1788/89, Selim III was personally involved in such an incident when he

120 Naima, *Târih*, II, pp. 85–7. 121 Gökyay, *Kâtip Çelebi*, p. 265.
122 Cabi, *Târihi*, I, p. 518. 123 Develi, *Risale-i Garibe*, p. 23.
124 Abdülaziz Bey, *Osmanlı*, p. 244. 125 Gökyay, *Kâtip Çelebi*, pp. 260–1.
126 Naima, *Târih*, II, p. 756.
127 Peçevi, *Tarihi*, I, p. 197; Thévenot, *Voyages*, I, pp. 80–1.

went to a pavilion at Ok Meydanı, where he spent time talking to the *şeyh* of the *tekke* there, Fethizade Efendi. When he announced that he wished to leave, his attendants shook out their pipes in a great hurry. A flame from the bowl of one of the pipes flew into the curtains, which promptly caught fire. Amid cries of 'the curtains are burning, the curtains are burning', those present rushed forward to extinguish the flames. Fethizade Efendi made a sacrifice to thank God that the fire had not been worse.[128] A similar incident occurred in the Bab-ı Ali in 1809, when his servant, in charge of tobacco, shook out the pipe of the Reis Efendi, the minister in charge of foreign affairs, and left the room, closing the door. But the tobacco was still alight and a fire began. Fortunately, however, the ensuing fire was quickly put out.[129]

Despite the bans, tobacco smoking continued and such prohibitions had little effect. For its addicts, 'the taste and flavour of tobacco had no equal even in that of honey and sugar'.[130] In the end the government gave up, in part encouraged to do so, no doubt, by the enormous revenue that tobacco brought into the coffers, given that a very high percentage of the population smoked.[131]

Like tobacco smoking, the use of opium attracted hostile criticism and was in general disapproved of, if tolerated, by the society at large. As with so many aspects of Ottoman social life, morality was a flexible rather than a fixed concept. Much that was morally unacceptable or even religiously prohibited, such as drinking alcohol, smoking opium or homosexuality, could be tolerated if indulged in in small quantities or in private, concealed from public gaze or, in the case of opium, for medicinal purposes, as it was in hospitals.[132] Once a habit became conspicuous or clearly uncontrolled, it was condemned and severely punished.

Excessive opium consumption was harshly criticised by the anonymous author of the *Risale-i Garibe*, who was exceedingly given to hurling curses at many sectors of society whose conduct he found reprehensible. Those who took it soon began to see hallucinations and were even capable of having conversations with their own faeces.[133] Addicts started with small quantities the size of a lentil, but quickly moved up the scale to pieces the size of hazelnuts. Well known in their *mahalle*s, they would be followed round by crowds of tormenting children, who, aware of the addicts' craving for anything sweet, would present them with liver covered in sugar. One amusing pastime was to frighten them, something that was easy to do as they were fearful of any loud bang or sudden movement,

[128] Taylesanizade, *Tarihi*, p. 415.
[129] Cabi, *Târihi*, I, p. 515.
[130] Gökyay, *Kâtip Çelebi*, p. 267.
[131] Özcan, *Anonim*, p. 20.
[132] Barkan, 'Fatih Câmi', p. 329.
[133] Develi, *Risale-i Garibe*, p. 25.

which caused them to jump in panic. During the celebrations for the circumcisions of Ahmed III's sons, firecrackers were used to scare the addicts, causing those watching 'to laugh until they were out of breath'.[134] After a while, many would lose the taste of opium and would begin to add a type of poison, white mercury chloride, to increase the effect, a concoction which after a while killed them.[135] Addicts were conspicuous, weak and puny, pale, sad-faced and rickety.[136] Latifi described the reduced condition of the addict in a poem:

> His body has turned from thinness into a thread
> It has turned into a desiccated skeleton
> In his skin there is no trace of a drop of blood
> You think that it is a corpse, there is no sign of life
> The whites of his eyes and the colour of his face have turned yellow
> His teeth have rotted, some have turned black
> His mouth hanging open, his eyes vacant he dozes
> It is strange that while he dozes he talks deliriously.[137]

The accusation of using opium was employed as a slur on those who were causing trouble of one kind or another, and they were often referred to as opium addicts, whether true or not. One of the main figures in the janissary revolt of 1703, Torucan Ahmed, was described as an opium addict and a drunk;[138] those who went to Üsküdar to watch the fighting between the janissaries and the Celali rebels in July 1649 were called opium addicts by Evliya Çelebi;[139] and those who wrote to the sultan supporting popular protest over the failure to go on campaign in 1595 were described as high on opium by Selaniki.[140]

Regardless of social disapproval, however, the use of opium was widespread. According to Abdülaziz Bey, in the old days – that is, before the late nineteenth century – 80 per cent of the population of the city used it,[141] and opium extracts were given as tranquillisers to babies to make them sleep. Opium dens were well known and addicts openly frequented the little coffee shops opposite the Süleymaniye mosque. These shops were very small, holding no more than ten or fifteen customers each, and were always packed.[142] These were the shops seen by Baronne Durand de

[134] Seyid Vehbi, *Sûrnâme*, p. 24. [135] Abdülaziz Bey, *Osmanlı*, pp. 326–7.
[136] Baronne Durand de Fontmagne, *Kırım Savaşı Sonrasında İstanbul Günleri*, trans. İsmail Yerguz (Istanbul, 2007), p. 275; Abdülaziz Bey, *Osmanlı*, p. 327.
[137] Latifi, *Evsâf*, pp. 52–3. [138] Özcan, *Anonim*, p. 256.
[139] Evliya Çelebi, *(Gördüklerim)*, p. 208. [140] Selaniki, *Tarih*, II, p. 525.
[141] Abdülaziz Bey, *Osmanlı*, p. 326. [142] Abdülaziz Bey, *Osmanlı*, p. 326.

Fontmagne, in Istanbul after the Crimean War, who noted that the area was known as the addicts' market.[143]

Quite apart from any social ostracism the use of opium might occasion, opium was certainly a killer. The son of the famous sixteenth-century *şeyhülislam* Ebussuud Efendi, Mevlana Şemseddin Ahmed, himself an important member of the *ulema*, died in 1562/63 of too much opium and opium syrup consumption, which destroyed his stomach and intestine.[144] It could also kill for other reasons. The opium addiction of Murad IV's chief doctor, Emir Çelebi, brought his downfall by delivering an invaluable weapon into the hands of his arch-enemy at court, the *silahdar paşa* (the sultan's sword-bearer). By the judicious use of bribery, the *silahdar paşa* obtained information from the doctor's servant, who prepared his opium for him, about when the doctor took the opium and where he kept it – in a golden container concealed inside his trouser pocket. The servant revealed that if the doctor stayed any length of time in the presence of the sultan, he would excuse himself and go to the lavatory, where he would take his opium. Armed with this information, the *silahdar paşa* set his trap, waiting until the doctor left the sultan's presence and then informing the sultan of the reason for the doctor's departure. The sultan, whose suspicions had earlier been aroused but then allayed by the doctor's denial of any addiction, was annoyed. The *silahdar paşa* insisted, however, advising the sultan to check the doctor's pocket. 'If you do not find opium', he said, 'then I am a liar'. On the doctor's return, the container and ten *dirhem*s (approximately thirty-three grams) of opium were revealed. In an attempt to save himself, the doctor explained that the substance was a type of harmless, treated opium extract, whereupon the sultan insisted, since it was harmless, that the doctor eat it all on the spot. Despite the doctor's protestations that, even though harmless, consuming such a quantity all at once would be lethal, he was forced to eat it, and then to play several games of chess, to ensure, as the sultan explained, that he did not leave and get rid of the effects of the opium. After three games, and with the doctor clearly in a parlous condition, the sultan let him go. His students, having heard what had happened, had prepared his medicines. Waving them aside, the doctor said, 'if I have an enemy as strong as the *silahdar paşa*, then to die is better than to live'. He then drank a glass of very cold sherbet, a cold beverage being lethal if taken after that amount of opium, and died. The *silahdar paşa* had his own close ally appointed in the doctor's place.[145]

While opium was tolerated, if disapproved of, hashish was totally unacceptable and, in contrast to the opium dens, the places frequented by

[143] Fontmagne, *İstanbul*, p. 275. [144] Peçevi, *Tarihi*, I, p. 42.
[145] Naima, *Târih*, II, pp. 872–4.

hashish addicts were kept secret.[146] Hashish addicts were stronger, more vigorous and livelier than opium addicts, despite the fact that their bodies were shrivelled, their faces yellow and there was no light in their eyes.[147]

The use of hashish by some dervishes, roundly condemned by the author of *Risale-i Garibe*,[148] was a source of concern for the government in 1725, for under the influence of this drug such men hallucinated, and, as a result, many 'ignorant Muslims' were led to believe that these dervishes were religious and saintly figures. They thus began to attract followings, and beliefs that were contrary to Islam were becoming prevalent. Such heresy was regarded by the government as dangerous. In order to protect the population and get rid of this pernicious innovation, the majority of those caught in Istanbul were exiled, some were sent to the galleys and some imprisoned. Buying, selling and using hashish was banned.[149]

Opium and hashish were not the only dangerous intoxicants available to the inhabitants of Istanbul. *Boza*, a popular drink made from fermented millet, rendered those who drank too much of it prone to dropsy and gout, which affected their ability to walk and left them having to use crutches, this being the reason, according to Evliya Çelebi, why *boza* addicts were never attacked by dogs, for they always had a stick in their hands.[150] Just as was the case with opium, *boza* attracted the same combination of public disapproval and private tolerance. There were two types of *boza*: sweet (non-alcoholic) *boza*, which was permissible, and fermented *boza*, which was not, at least for Ebussuud, although Evliya Çelebi was more liberal and regarded it as permissible if not drunk to excess. For Ebussuud, or those like him, the problem of drinking was not merely a matter of alcoholic consumption. What was important was where and how the drink was to be consumed. Sitting around all day in a *boza* house, drinking – however innocent a drink – playing backgammon or chess and chattering, was not an acceptable way to pass time.[151] But this was what often happened, for *boza* addicts sat there drinking from sunrise to sunset.[152]

The *boza* houses were places frequented by the riff-raff, according to Gelibolulu Mustafa Ali, writing in the late sixteenth century, for the upper echelons did not condescend to go there, or if they did it was only to drink *boza* and have kebabs cooked, but not to spend time there like the regular

146 Abdülaziz Bey, *Osmanlı*, p. 326. 147 Abdülaziz Bey, *Osmanlı*, p. 329.
148 Develi, *Risale-i Garibe*, pp. 22, 35.
149 Ahmet Refik, *Hicri On İkinci Asırda*, pp. 83–4, *hüküm* 113.
150 Evliya Çelebi, *Seyahatnamesi, I Kitap*, pp. 312–13.
151 Düzdağ, *Ebussuûd Efendi*, p. 148, *hüküm* 720, pp. 147–8, *hüküm*s 716, 717.
152 Evliya Çelebi, *Seyahatnamesi, I Kitap*, p. 313.

habitués of these places. Gelibolulu warned his readers, 'The *boza* house is a place of the disreputable/ Do not drink its *boza*, do not lower yourself'.[153]

One location that was to become extremely popular in Istanbul, and where many were to while away hour upon hour, was the coffee shop. According to Peçevi, coffee first appeared in Istanbul in 1554, when two men, Hakem from Aleppo and Şems from Damascus, built a coffee shop.

> People who like to enjoy themselves and some of the literate elite started to come together there. Some of them read books and beautiful things, some played backgammon and chess, some brought new poems and discussed poetry and literature, and some spent more money bringing in friends and giving feasts. And it became so popular that dismissed officials, *kadı*s, *medrese* teachers and those who didn't have any work started to come to the coffee house, saying that there was no place where you could enjoy yourself so much, and it became impossible to find a seat. It became so famous that apart from government officials, even important people began to come and even imams, muezzins, blue-robed religious figures, and ordinary people became addicted to the coffee house. Nobody went any more to the mosques.[154]

Indeed, coffee and tobacco took up so much of people's time that, according to one poem, people found they had no time left to pray.[155] By the end of the century, according to Katip Çelebi, any religious attempts to ban coffee had had to be abandoned. Coffee was drunk openly everywhere and every street had a coffee shop. Because of the great attractions of the storytellers and dancers in the coffee shops, no one was going to work and there was no trading. People gossiped in the coffee houses and had opinions about everything, from the sultan to the beggar.[156] It was this aspect of the coffee house that made it so unacceptable to sultans like Murad IV, who not only banned them but even had such centres of sedition demolished.[157] The same reason had resulted in an earlier ban imposed by Ahmed I.[158] Sultanic bans, however, had little effect and coffee houses continued to flourish.

For some, the coffee house was a centre of sin. Vagabonds opened coffee houses to earn money, and in order to increase the number of customers they hired beardless boys to work for them. They filled cafes with entertainments and games, with backgammon boards and chess sets. Pleasure-seekers, worthless sinners and beardless youths assembled there

[153] Gelibolulu Mustafa Ali, *Mevâıdün*, p. 366.

[154] Peçevi, *Tarihi*, I, p. 196. Gelibolulu Mustafa Ali, *Mevâıdün*, p. 363, dates its arrival in Istanbul to 1552/53, while Katip Çelebi dates it to 1543 (Gökyay, *Kâtip Çelebi*, p. 267).

[155] Peçevi, *Tarihi*, I, p. 198, n. 1.

[156] Gökyay, *Kâtip Çelebi*, pp. 267–8.

[157] Naima, *Târih*, II, pp. 755–6.

[158] Naima, *Târih*, II, pp. 755–6.

to smoke different types of drugs and drink coffee. Comfortably settled and high on drugs and coffee, they played games and gossiped.[159]

By the early nineteenth century, the tendency to sit in the coffee shops during Ramazan instead of going to the mosque for the special Ramazan night prayer had become so pronounced that in 1809 people were actually banned from doing so, and coffee-house owners were warned. This did not produce quite the desired effect, for rather than being an opportunity for prayer, it became one for lucrative earnings, as officials used the opportunity the new order offered to extract bribes from those they seized and sent to Ağa Kapısı, who then had to pay heavily to be released.[160]

The great popularity of coffee and the enormous pull of the coffee house distressed the *ulema*, in particular Ebussuud, whose hostility to the beverage was so well known that people gossiped that he had sunk ships bringing coffee to the capital. Warnings were issued about the dangers of this pernicious liquid.

> The *ulema* said that the coffee house was a place of evil and that it was better to go to a wine house than to the coffee shop. The preachers tried to convince people not to go there and the muftis gave *fetva*s [rulings] stating that coffee was forbidden. During the time of Murad III they started to give warnings about the problems of coffee. But nobody listened. And they even opened secret coffee houses and the police could not do anything about it. The situation became such that the authorities gave up trying to warn people or to stop them going to the coffee houses and the muftis and the preachers began to say that it was permissible to drink coffee, and everyone, *ulema*, *şeyh*s, vezirs and important people, all drank coffee. It came to such a point that some of the great vezirs built coffee houses to make money and they were getting one or two gold pieces daily as rent.[161]

The coffee-house business was a very lucrative one, attracting even very high-up vezirs to invest in it, as Peçevi noted. Many *vakıf*s included coffee shops in their properties. Some of the tactics adopted by coffee-house owners were somewhat more entrepreneurial than others. In 1808, Kerim Çavuş, a janissary, built a very well-decorated and cared-for coffee house by the sea, on the jetty outside Karaköy Kapısı in Galata. Much of the decoration – the mirrors, silver water pipes, coffee cup containers and even canaries – were the unwilling gifts of those using the jetty, whom Kerim Çavuş accosted, demanding, 'Oi, where are the presents for my coffee house?' Forced not merely to contribute to the decoration, they were also obliged to have a coffee in Kerim Çavuş's coffee house, a pleasure which resulted in a sharp drop in the numbers frequenting the jetty. Finally, news reached the grand vezir Alemdar Mustafa Paşa, who

159 Düzdağ, *Ebussuûd Efendi*, p. 149, *hüküm* 724.
160 Cabi, *Târihi*, I, p. 591.
161 Peçevi, *Tarihi*, I, p. 196.

23. Coffee house on the jetty, in Pardoe, *Beauties of the Bosphorus*, between pp. 146 and 147.

ordered the grand admiral Seydi Ali Paşa to deal with the situation. Seydi Ali Paşa did so and the coffee house was demolished.[162]

Coffee fast became an essential element in the ritual of hospitality. As soon as a visitor arrived, coffee was produced.[163] Vezirs served it to their guests, it was drunk at official receptions, and ambassadors were served it when they were received by the grand vezir, as the Persian ambassador was in 1701, when the grand vezir offered him coffee and sherbet.[164] Even when cuts were made in expenses for receptions, coffee was left untouched.[165]

The coffee houses quickly became a great hit, popular with many circles of the population. According to Gelibolulu Mustafa Ali, coffee shops were frequented by the dervishes, by the intellectual circles who went there to talk and drink coffee, and by the poor who, having nowhere else to go on a limited budget, went there all the time. The janissaries and the *sipahi*s were to be found there from morning to night, gossiping away in every corner, and there were those who played backgammon and chess or who gambled for money.[166] By the late nineteenth century, every coffee house in Galata, and some in Pera, apparently always had a room at the back for gambling.[167]

There were coffee houses everywhere. Every jetty had one;[168] they were located near the mosques, in the Grand Bazaar and in the coffin makers' market in Üsküdar.[169] Coffee stoves were set up in government offices, sometimes with disastrous consequences. In 1788, the coffee stove of the secretary of the steward's office inside the offices of the grand vezir caught fire and resulted in the destruction of a considerable number of government offices, including those of the minister who dealt with foreign affairs, the petitions' office, various secretaries' offices, the correspondence office and the audience hall, as well as several houses and shops nearby.[170] Some years earlier, in 1786/87, a fire that broke out in a coffee shop in Galata reduced an entire *mahalle* to ashes, destroying a mosque, a *hamam*, shoemakers and timber merchants, two churches, wine houses and non-Muslim houses.[171]

Just like the barbers' shops where men sat all day, lolling and swinging their legs like little *paşa*s,[172] the coffee shops represented a

[162] Cabi, *Târihi*, I, p. 182. [163] Özcan, *Anonim*, p. 232.
[164] Özcan, *Anonim*, p. 162. [165] Ahmet Refik, *Hicri On Üçüncü Asırda*, p. 4, *hüküm* 5.
[166] Gelibolulu Mustafa Ali, *Mevâıdün*, pp. 363–4.
[167] Francis Marion-Crawford, *1890'larda İstanbul*, trans. Şeniz Türkömer (Istanbul, 2006), p. 72.
[168] Murad Efendi, *Manzaraları*, p. 69. [169] Taylesanizade, *Tarihi*, p. 192.
[170] Taylesanizade, *Tarihi*, p. 331. [171] Taylesanizade, *Tarihi*, p. 189.
[172] Develi, *Risale-i Garibe*, p. 34.

much-frequented gathering place, where men could idle away their time in chattering, gossiping, and, much more alarmingly for the government, complaining. Such seditious talk by one Armenian, who plotted together with others in a coffee shop near Sakka Çeşmesi, resulted in an imperial order for his execution. He was hanged in front of the coffee house, while others involved were exiled to Lemnos.[173]

For the government, any places like the coffee shops where men gathered were potential sources of trouble, not just of open plotting and seditious muttering, but also brawling or more serious clashes, often involving the janissaries. The dangerous nature of such establishments meant that they were often subjected to raids by the authorities. This pressure, not unnaturally, upset the coffee-house owners, who used the opportunity of the circumcision of Murad III's son Mehmed in 1582 to express their irritation over what they regarded as unjust behaviour. As part of the ceremony, each guild gave a performance related to their trade. In this case, the coffee-house owners performed a scene in which the security forces raided a coffee shop. The owners complained to the sultan that this sort of thing occurred often while their customers were sitting peacefully drinking their coffee, and they requested that he do something about it.[174]

While for the owners of *boza* houses, coffee was 'the wickedness of Yemen', it was wine that was 'the coquettish woman of the Rum'.[175] Wine houses were widespread throughout the city, as dangerous a threat to the *boza* trade as coffee houses were, and for this reason as hated by the *boza*-house keepers, who regarded both as bringing ill fortune to their own trade and destroying their livelihood. Wine houses were particularly common in Galata, an incomparable area for wine and prostitution according to Latifi, and proverbial for drinking and enjoyment.[176] With its 'wickedly luxurious'[177] wine houses, Galata for Evliya Çelebi meant wine house.[178] In the early sixteenth century, if Evliya Çelebi's figures are to be believed, there were six thousand one hundred wine houses in the city, of which one hundred were Jewish-owned. While those in Galata were owned by Greek Orthodox,[179] there were also Muslim owners who ran wine houses in different parts of the city.[180]

The use of wine, the 'whore whose name is mother of all vices',[181] was widespread even among the most eminent men of state. According to

173 Çeşmizade, *Tarihi*, p. 25. 174 Gelibolulu Mustafa Ali, *Sûr*, pp. 186–7.
175 Gelibolulu Mustafa Ali, *Sûr*, p. 188. 176 Latifi, *Evsâf*, p. 58.
177 Evliya Çelebi, *Seyahatnamesi, I Kitap*, p. 184.
178 Evliya Çelebi, *Seyahatnamesi, I Kitap*, p. 314.
179 Evliya Çelebi, *Seyahatnamesi, I Kitap*, p. 184. 180 Develi, *Risale-i Garibe*, p. 35.
181 Naima, *Târih*, I, p. 177.

common gossip, Osman Paşa, for example, a vezir during the reign of Murad III, was known for his addiction to alcohol and drugs, a reputation which worried the sultan, who wished to make him a vezir but was concerned about his drink problem. He therefore summoned the *paşa* and interviewed him for four hours, at the end of which he was very relieved, since he had seen no signs of addiction during the interview, as he would have over such a long period had the rumours been true. Peçevi noted tartly that the sultan could understand this because of his own familiarity with alcohol, adding that in fact the sultan was wrong, for he so flattered Osman (whom Peçevi did not like) that there was no need of alcohol because he was drunk on compliments.[182]

The government response to wine was in many ways reflective of the Ottoman approach to many social issues: on the one hand, it banned what was in any case religiously prohibited; on the other, it turned a blind eye to alcohol, allowing the wine houses to proliferate in the city. Well aware of the great financial implications of the trade, it taxed it heavily and made a great deal of money from it; and its officials supplemented their salaries both secretly and openly, by bribery related to its consumption. Added to this was the other very common Ottoman characteristic of total fluidity, for nothing was ever fixed, and the official policy fluctuated period to period, sultan to sultan. At some times, response to alcohol consumption was swift and brutal, culprits hanged, wine houses sealed and wine destroyed. At others, orders would be issued prohibiting the selling of wine to Muslims, but Christian wine houses were permitted, though Muslims were not to frequent them.[183] Even when it was banned – for example, between 1730/31 and 1790/91 – the tolerant attitude of the police authorities allowed for the slow establishment of new wine houses.[184]

On many occasions, sultans banned wine, as Süleyman I did,[185] a ban which some religious figures wanted continued under his son and successor Selim II.[186] Selim did ban it, as Murad III did in 1584, having previously banned wine houses only in Muslim areas.[187] It was banned in 1596 by Mehmed III,[188] when in Ramazan of that year all wine found in the wine houses was destroyed and the doors of the wine houses sealed, so rescuing the good people of Islam from this evil. Those caught drinking at

[182] Peçevi, *Tarihi*, II, p. 322. [183] Ahmed Cavid, *Hadîka*, p. 216.
[184] Ahmed Cavid, *Hadîka*, pp. 216–17. [185] Selaniki, *Tarih*, I, p. 52.
[186] Selaniki, *Tarih*, I, p. 52.
[187] Ahmet Refik, *Onuncu Asr-ı Hicrî*, p. 141, *hüküm* 8, pp. 146–7, *hüküm* 15, pp. 141–2, *hüküm* 9, pp. 50–1, *hüküm* 12.
[188] Selaniki, *Tarih*, II, p. 597; Ahmed Cavid, *Hadîka*, p. 215.

this point were severely punished. When a raid was conducted in an area where men and prostitutes were drinking and committing adultery, five women were hanged, one soldier beheaded and the salaries of two *sipahi*s cut.[189] It was banned yet again in 1613/14 by Ahmed I,[190] and in 1634 by Murad IV,[191] who had all wine houses closed. Murad adopted a tough line over this, as over many other things. If he came across any drunk during his tours incognito at night, he personally killed him. On one particular occasion, the victim, whom Murad had shot with an arrow, was saved by falling into the sea, where he was left for dead. Still alive, he later emerged from the waves, presumably safely after the departure of the sultan.[192] Mehmed IV banned it in 1670/71,[193] and it was again forbidden in 1689 by Süleyman II, when Küfri Ahmed Efendi, the tax collector on wine, was killed.[194] Selim III also struggled to ban it, with only limited success.[195] Selim took a firm line over alcohol consumption, informing the patriarch and the chief rabbi that Christians and Jews caught selling wine or *rakı* (arrack) to a Muslim would be killed without exception.[196]

What made it so hard to ban effectively, apart from its attraction as a pleasurable and forbidden beverage, was its ready accessibility, Istanbul being surrounded by wine-growing regions and inhabited by a very large non-Muslim and drinking population, with many wine houses, as well as, and more importantly, the enormous income to be made from the trade, legally or illicitly. It was this problem which undermined Selim III's efforts to ban it. In an attempt to prevent Muslims drinking, Selim issued an order for the closure of all wine houses in Istanbul, Bosphorus and the islands. The *bostancıbaşı*, on the other hand, had undermined this by giving permission for some wine houses in Bosphorus and for the bringing in of wine by boat, he himself taking a certain amount of money from each vessel. For this, the sultan had him removed from his job and exiled him to Rhodes. A new *bostancıbaşı*, Mehmed Ağa, was appointed and an imperial order issued, warning that there were to be no wine houses in Istanbul, Galata or Bosphorus, and that wine was not to be sold to the Muslims. Those who did so would be punished. This order, too, proved ineffective, for the secret sale of alcohol to the Muslims continued under the new *bostancıbaşı*, prompting yet another order from the sultan, much incensed and blaming the situation on the weakness and greed of the *sekbanbaşı*, deputy of the janissary *ağa*, and the ineffectual and weak administration.

189 Ahmed Cavid, *Hadîka*, p. 215; Selaniki, *Tarih*, II, p. 597.
190 Ahmed Cavid, *Hadîka*, pp. 215–16. 191 Naima, *Târih*, II, p. 792.
192 Naima, *Târih*, II, p. 792. 193 Ahmed Cavid, *Hadîka*, p. 216.
194 Ahmed Cavid, *Hadîka*, pp. 216–17; Özcan, *Anonim*, pp. 10–11.
195 Karal, *Hümayunları*, pp. 99–100. 196 Cabi, *Târihi*, I, p. 22.

This time the *sekbanbaşı* was to be replaced by a new one, Said Efendi, and there was to be no selling of wine to Muslims and no wine houses.[197]

Bans were not necessarily a favoured option, for they represented a considerable economic loss for the treasury. It was economic hardship which caused the abandonment of the prohibition on wine in 1688 and the imposition of a tax.[198] According to Ahmed Cavid, the ban imposed in 1613/14, during the reign of Ahmed I, cost the state dearly.[199] Economic necessity often forced a reversal of policy. Campaigns in Hungary drove the state into a cash shortage, which in turn forced the sultan to reverse the ban on wine imposed in 1595/96, since wine was such a lucrative source of income.[200] Again in 1687/88, the government once more allowed the wine trade, after banning it in 1670/71. The long military campaigns had so reduced the treasury that even gold and silver were collected from the imperial stables and the expenses were innumerable. Various options were considered, including debasing the *mangır*, a policy which had been adopted before when the state faced similar difficulties caused by long campaigns. It was also noted that before the 1670/71 ban, wine and *rakı* had been taxed and had brought in a substantial income for the state. The ban, it was argued, was impractical, since it did not prevent the wine trade. Christians and Jews continued to trade it, but now without paying tax. It was also pointed out that the quotas permitted for the embassies far exceeded what they needed for their own personal use, so the embassies were in fact making a profit selling off what they did not use. Had the tax been in place, the campaign expenses would not have been so crushing. As a result of this discussion, taxation was reimposed.[201]

Bans on wine hit not merely the treasury but also the local economy and those working for the state, for whom implementation of the prohibition brought in income. Wine houses were a stimulant to the local economy, for much local trade relied on them. In Galata, for example, the fish market sold many kinds of fish for those frequenting the wine houses. Fruit sellers too provided them with the best kinds of all types of fruit, while the alcohol sellers benefited, selling every kind of alcohol imaginable.[202] The police force earned a living from fees they collected from the wine houses. According to Gerlach, the position of *subaşı* was a lucrative one in which a person could quickly become rich,

> for when he comes across someone who is drunk he demands a payment of one to twelve ducats per head. Doing everything they can to avoid being thrown into

[197] Karal, *Hümayunları*, pp. 99–100. [198] Özcan, *Anonim*, p. 4.
[199] Ahmed Cavid, *Hadîka*, pp. 215–16. [200] Ahmed Cavid, *Hadîka*, p. 215.
[201] Ahmed Cavid, *Hadîka*, p. 216.
[202] Evliya Çelebi, *Seyahatnamesi, I Kitap*, p. 184.

prison, the men pay over the money. If young men are caught together with prostitutes, he takes the rings on their fingers, the tiaras on their heads, their jewels, the gold buttons on their clothes, whatever they have on them.[203]

Kara Hızır, the *subaşı* in the 1540s, certainly profited well from wine, for he collected one thousand *akçe*s from around one hundred to two hundred wine houses, but only registered twenty thousand to thirty thousand *akçe*s and pocketed the rest.[204] When, in 1577, a *subaşı* caught a Muslim man drinking in a wine house, he immediately seized him, mounted him on a donkey with two jugs hung round his neck and paraded him through the streets of the city, before fining him twenty ducats. The *subaşı* was himself subsequently arrested and the authorities called those with complaints against him to come forward. One of those who did so was the man who had been paraded around on a donkey, who now had his twenty ducats returned to him.[205] Acknowledgement of the loss of income led Selim III, after imposing a ban on wine, to order the creation of what was called 'a deadly poison substitute levy', to be paid monthly to the police, who made a living from the drunks they caught, fined and sent to Ağa Kapısı, and from the money they took from the wine houses.[206]

The banning of wine thus involved the state in considerable loss. In the case of the ban imposed by Selim III, the state lost out twice, forfeiting the income from taxation and incurring extra expenditure caused by paying out compensation in the form of the substitute levy to those who lost income as a result of the prohibition. The fact that Selim III had to make this concession gives a very good idea of the level of income collected by the state from the wine trade and its importance in the economy of the city.

Despite any economic loss, and even though by imposing bans the state was merely prohibiting what was already religiously forbidden, the state continued to fluctuate between economic necessity and no wine bans and harsh clampdowns and prohibitions. Clearly there was a religious element in government banning: sultans were motivated by religious duty, and for the *ulema* drinking was unacceptable. But what largely lay behind the bans, or the more minor attempts to curb consumption, was the need to maintain order, the fundamental motivation which spurred on the great bulk of government policy in the city. Drunkenness was dangerous, and sedition was worse, and both could be found in the wine houses. For some, however, there was another, if less plausible, explanation. According to Ahmed Cavid, who had it from

[203] Gerlach, *Günlüğü*, II, p. 522.
[204] Sahillioğlu, *H.951–952 ve E-12321 Numaralı Mühimme*, p. 216, *hüküm* 281.
[205] Gerlach, *Günlüğü*, II, p. 521. [206] Ahmed Cavid, *Hadîka*, p. 211.

a trustworthy source, gossip circulating among the Christians attributed the banning of wine in that period to the desire of the Muslims to massacre them, for all the Muslims, being stone-cold sober rather than drunk, would massacre all the Christians while they were at church for the Easter service. The fear was so great that the priests instructed their congregations to come to the churches, pray and leave again at once. When Easter day arrived, a *börek* (filled pastry) seller, who had given chase to some *mahalle* children who had stolen *börek*s from his stall, caught one of the offending boys outside the doors of the church. He struck the boy several resounding slaps, whereupon the culprit began to cry out. The nervous priest inside, already on edge, with his ears strained for the first sign of trouble, exclaimed in terror, 'Judgement Day has come, may God protect us', and promptly fainted clear away, emptying his bowels and, in Ahmed Cavid's perhaps not quite accurate account, making the inside of the church unclean.[207]

As was always the case with Ottoman authority, habits that were officially to be condemned were tolerated, provided they were not open or disruptive. If they occasioned disorder, however, such tolerance vanished. When Muslims drank openly to excess in the wine houses, cavorting with prostitutes there and, even worse, doing so in Ramazan and religious festivals, then there was a crackdown. When janissaries who had not drunk for a month during Ramazan threw themselves into drinking with renewed gusto during Ramazan *bayramı*, this open defiance of social norms could neither be accepted nor be seen to be accepted. Wine houses were potential places of sedition and riot, even more dangerous for order on the streets than the coffee houses. They were very popular with the janissaries, two-thirds of whom were wine-house goers, according to Ahmed Cavid, in the late eighteenth century.[208] Apart from the violence associated with them, they were an environment in which ideas threatening to both political and religious order could circulate. It was in the wine houses in 1527 that Molla Kabız, to be declared a heretic and executed, tried to spread his teaching that Jesus was the greatest of all the prophets.[209]

Regardless of the cause for them, bans on alcohol were often ignored or evaded, 'because evil and sedition triumph over human nature'.[210] Various ruses were employed during the reign of Selim III to bypass the

[207] Ahmed Cavid, *Hadîka*, pp. 225–6. [208] Ahmed Cavid, *Hadîka*, p. 218.

[209] Peçevi, *Tarihi*, I, pp. 71–2. See also Müneccimbaşı Ahmed Dede, *Tarihi*, II, pp. 528–9; Ahmet Yaşar Ocak, *Osmanlı Toplumunda Zındıklar ve Mülhidler (15.-17. Yüzyıllar)* (Istanbul, 1998), pp. 230–8.

[210] Ahmed Cavid, *Hadîka*, pp. 215–16.

prohibition. One man was caught carrying a nightingale in a cage. Inside the cage were intestines which he had filled with *rakı*. The police who stopped him realised from the weight of the cage that there was something amiss and examined it carefully. On discovering its concealed contents, they sent the man to Ağa Kapısı, where he managed to escape the death penalty due to string-pulling.[211] Others addicted to alcohol disguised themselves as non-Muslim women who sold goods door to door, and thus, in plain view, carried jugs full of alcohol into their own houses.[212] An itinerant Jewish tin-pipe seller made false compartments in his pipes, by soldering up several inches from the bottom, which he filled with wine or *rakı*. Apart from these specially adapted pipes, he also carried normal ones, in case there were genuine pipe customers and in order to disguise his real trade. If many customers appeared who wanted straightforward pipes, he would explain that those he had with him were already sold. This illicit trade in alcohol brought him in a good income.[213]

Some people turned to alcohol production as a way round the prohibition. Retorts were used to distil *rakı* and wine. Many used remote parts of their gardens for this, calculating that if caught they could claim that the equipment belonged to their gardeners.[214] Retorts began to sell in a way they never had before and soon none were to be found in the copper shops in the quarter of Beyazıt. It reached such a point that innocent customers who wished to buy a retort for a legitimate purpose were too ashamed to ask for one, fearful of the response of the sellers, who were known to snap, 'the drunkards have raided the retorts with the enthusiasm of one who wants be a wine-house keeper'.[215]

For many of the inhabitants of the city, the wine houses were a source of wonderful and extravagant entertainment. The taverns in Galata resounded to the sounds of revelry, full day and night with crowds of pleasure-seekers, drinking down the intoxicating mixtures concocted for them by the wine-house keepers, who added various substances to the wine, and listening to the singers and musicians who performed there.[216] The numbers involved could be very large, and the two hundred huge wine houses along the seashore and at Orta Hisar attracted five hundred to six hundred customers a night, all out to enjoy themselves to a degree that was beyond description, even for Evliya Çelebi.[217] Many were lured in by the encouragement of others, who whispered, 'Come to the wine house, there is no hypocrisy and

[211] Cabi, *Târihi*, I, p. 22. [212] Cabi, *Târihi*, I, p. 22. [213] Cabi, *Târihi*, I, p. 22.
[214] Cabi, *Târihi*, I, p. 22. [215] Cabi, *Târihi*, I, p. 22.
[216] Evliya Çelebi, *Seyahatnamesi, I Kitap*, p. 134.
[217] Evliya Çelebi, *Seyahatnamesi, I Kitap*, p. 184.

no dissimulation there', 'the wine houses seem stuffy from outside but there is a different delight and a different charm within'.[218]

The alluring and inviting wine houses had even more to offer than wine and music: they were also dens of prostitution. As Ahmed Rasim put it, speaking of his innocent youth: 'How could I know that prostitution was a lock and wine its key. In those days, neither *rakı* nor wine nor, God forbid, a prostitute were found in our houses'.[219]

Many of the young male dancers in the wine houses were prostitutes. Taking names like Jasmine, Gazelle and Morning Star, and leaving 'no stars in the sky and no flowers in the garden whose names they did not use',[220] these young men caused many to lose their families and their fortunes. The most famous in the late eighteenth century was Gerdankıran (meaning one who swings the head coquettishly), who destroyed many homes and reduced many merchants to penury.[221] Not all the pleasures in the wine house were pleasures forever. The regulars came and spent a good time there, leaving their worries behind them and talking to their hearts' content, as Evliya Çelebi wrote, but they lost their wealth and the wine-house keepers made great profits.[222] As one poem put it, 'In the wine-house of love I drank my fill/ I loved a beautiful boy dancer and I had my fortune stolen'.[223]

Male prostitutes were not restricted to the wine houses, but also to be found working the streets, as Gerlach noted in the 1570s:

> youths, dressed up in alluring clothing, pass in front of the houses of high-up gentlemen and they make great efforts to attract their attention and they behave in a far worse way than the most cheap women. These boys earn great amounts of money. A young man if he is beautiful can earn by selling himself twenty to forty or even fifty ducats and ensure that he is given beautiful clothes as well.[224]

Male prostitutes were more coquettish than female ones, according to Latifi, who wrote, 'Teasing, smiling and uttering sweet words/ In this, male prostitutes surpass females'.[225] 'Catamites who were flirtatious and disdainful in order to sell themselves to the customers',[226] they were very good at flirting and fawning and flattering, up to the point of capturing the object they were hunting, but ruthless and without compassion once the prey was caught.[227]

[218] Ahmed Cavid, *Hadîka*, p. 218. [219] Ahmet Rasim, *Fuhş-i Atik*, p. 79.
[220] Ahmed Cavid, *Hadîka*, pp. 216–17. [221] Ahmed Cavid, *Hadîka*, pp. 216–17.
[222] Evliya Çelebi, *Seyahatnamesi, I Kitap*, p. 315. [223] Ahmed Cavid, *Hadîka*, pp. 216–17.
[224] Gerlach, *Günlüğü*, II, p. 527. [225] Latifi, *Evsâf*, p. 49.
[226] Develi, *Risale-i Garibe*, pp. 35–6. [227] Latifi, *Evsâf*, p. 49.

Certain areas, in particular Galata and Cihangir, were known for prostitution.[228] According to Lithgow, there were more than four thousand brothels in the city, both Muslim and Christian.[229] In the late nineteenth century, despite the fact that brothels were still not legally recognised, leading madams and pimps were among the well-known and well-heeled figures of Istanbul. The police were well aware of the locations of the brothels and kept them under surveillance, but did not interfere unless there was a specific reason to do so.[230]

Prostitutes could work from brothels or, controlled by pimps, on the streets, or could operate on their own, giving appointments themselves and using their own houses.[231] Open spaces were also used. There were also secret places used for meetings between prostitutes and their clients, known in the nineteenth century as *koltuk*s. Other locations frequented by prostitutes were the barracks for migrant workers and sailors, and the janissary barracks – the janissaries being particularly eager customers.

Pimping was not an activity approved of by society and was roundly condemned by the anonymous author of *Risale-i Garibe*, who cursed those Christians who had a craft but did not follow it, or who could work as unskilled labour but did not choose to do so, but instead were pimps for women and boys, and also those Jews who brought boys and women for their customers and turned their houses into brothels.[232] For that author, to pimp was one of the worst jobs in the world, along with being a policeman, an usher in court and a tax collector.[233] Pimps in Galata were often Jewish,[234] but pimps and madams could also be Muslim and Christian.

Slaves could be pimped by their owners, such as Halil Ağa, who was eventually imprisoned in 1595 for this activity,[235] and slave dealers could at times run what amounted to a prostitution ring. Taking concubines from their owners on the pretext that they would sell them, the dealers instead handed them to soldiers and the like for a few days, after which the soldiers returned them and the dealers took the concubines back to their owners, claiming that they had not been able to sell them. This practice was banned in 1583.[236] But it clearly continued, for in the *narh* register of 1640, the list of slave dealers officially allowed to trade had been reduced from over one hundred to sixty, the reason being the unacceptable practice of many of the dealers, particularly the female traders, whereby they took concubines from

[228] Develi, *Risale-i Garibe*, p. 23. [229] Lithgow, *Discourse*, p. 155.
[230] Ahmet Rasim, *Fuhş-i Atik*, pp. 176–7; Abdülaziz Bey, *Osmanlı*, p. 333.
[231] Cabi, *Târihi*, II, p. 903. [232] Develi, *Risale-i Garibe*, p. 25.
[233] Develi, *Risale-i Garibe*, p. 25. [234] Evliya Çelebi, *Seyahatnamesi, I Kitap*, p. 184.
[235] Selaniki, *Tarih*, II, p. 546. [236] Ahmet Refik, *Onuncu Asr-ı Hicrî*, p. 46, *hüküm* 8.

their owners promising to sell them for a good price. They then handed the concubines over to the Polish and Moldavian embassies and to other rich infidels, who 'used' them for several days, paying a few *akçe*s to the dealer, and then returned them to the trader, who in turn took them back to the owners, claiming that no sale had been made. To ensure that this practice did not occur, the slave dealers listed in the *narh* register were all guarantors for each other. Were any of them to be caught acting in an unseemly manner, they would all be held collectively responsible.[237]

Prostitution was not something officially approved of. Tolerated if kept discreet, it was punished when openly practised, and was regarded by society at large as something which brought dishonour. It was certainly not acceptable among married men, nor in the upper echelons of society or even among the slightly better-off. In part, this was because, for them, there was an alternative: the slave market and the purchase of a concubine.

The slave market caused surprise for westerners, being a place where women and men were sold 'as Horses and other Beasts are with us'.[238] 'Heare likewise they sell many Christian slaves of all sects and adge, in manner as they sell thier horses, lookinge them in the eyes, mouth, and all other parts. This they doe every forenone, except Friday, which the Turks hould for thier day of rest'.[239] For Careri,

> the manner of selling them is odd; for after praying for the grand seignior, the seller holds the slave that is to be sold, by the end of a cloath, and on the other side, the crier goes proclaiming the price. He that has a mind to buy, uncovers the slave's face, and feels him or her, in several parts of the body, as we do in buying horses or asses.[240]

Looking carefully was probably important, for the women on sale were not always what they seemed. Displaying concubines with make-up was banned by Selim I.[241] Such a ban was clearly not that effective, for several centuries later, the author of *Risale-i Garibe* was cursing the slave traders who presented their slaves as better than they were by painting their faces.[242]

Prices of women could be very high. Beautiful young women could indeed cost a fortune, those bought for the harem at time of Selim III, for example, costing from eight thousand to twenty thousand French francs.[243] Very beautiful women, 'more beautiful than *huri*s and more exceptional than fairies… cost their weight in gold', and 'those with money who saw

237 Kütükoğlu, *Narh*, pp. 257–8. 238 Lithgow, *Discourse*, p. 136.
239 Sanderson, *Travels*, pp. 78–9. 240 Careri, 'Voyage', p. 72.
241 Yücel and Pulaha, *I. Selim Kanunnameleri*, p. 65. 242 Develi, *Risale-i Garibe*, p. 40.
243 'Voyage to Constantinople' [an article on *Picturesque Voyage to Constantinople and the Shores of the Bosphorus. From the Drawings of M. Melling…*], *La Belle Assemblée; or, Bell's Court and Fashionable Magazine*, issue 79 (1816), p. 334.

them ceased to think about money and instead regarded money as less important than lust'.[244] Not all could afford the prices, however, and men without money were reduced to going to the slave market to look at women whom they could not afford, and, unable to buy, 'had no other option than to go to bed every night alone and grasping their knees until morning'.[245] The practice of those who had no money but went daily to look at the girls in the slave market, pretending to be customers and examining the goods, was much disapproved of by the author of *Risale-i Garibe*.[246]

Not all westerners were driven by honest intent when buying on these markets. One such was Monsieur Nerack, a master gunner of a ship of Marseilles called the *Great Dolphin*, which docked at Galata for forty days in the early seventeenth century. Monsieur Nerack confided in Lithgow that he wanted, 'for Conscience and Merits sake', to redeem some poor Christian from Turkish slavery. Not interested in rescuing an old Christian, he preferred a virgin or young widow, driven by the desire 'to save their bodies underfloured with Infidels'. Unable to afford a virgin, he bought a widow, whom he promptly incarcerated and abused, intending to resell her afterwards. Lithgow, who, by threatening to inform first the ship's captain and then the French ambassador of Nerack's behaviour, forced him to free her, noted piously, 'this French Gunner was a Papist and here you may behold the dregs of his devotion, and what seven nights leachery cost him, you may cast up the reckoning of 36 Duckets'.[247]

By no means all those who frequented the slave markets were men like Nerack, and concubinage did not automatically equate with prostitution, its role being better illustrated by the story of Nuri Bey than by that of the French gunner. At the end of 1812, Nuri Bey, a seventeen- or eighteen-year-old landholder, bought a concubine in Üsküdar for seven thousand five hundred *kuruş*. Nuri Bey and the concubine got on very well together, but two months later both fell ill with plague. They lay together in bed unconscious. Whenever Nuri Bey regained consciousness he said to the concubine, 'Oh beautiful one, I have prepared my horse, I shall take you and we shall go together'. He would then lose consciousness again. The concubine would then regain consciousness and would say, 'My lord, my master, I have prepared my bundle, I will come with you'. In this way they lay for ten days and then died on the same day, their bodies buried within an hour of each other. All those who heard the story were deeply moved. The two young people had only been able to be together for fifty-five days and had died like Ferhad and Şirin, Arzu and Kanber, the tragic heroes of the most famous romances.[248]

[244] Latifi, *Evsâf*, p. 40. [245] Latifi, *Evsâf*, p. 40. [246] Develi, *Risale-i Garibe*, p. 40.
[247] Lithgow, *Discourse*, pp. 136–8. [248] Cabi, *Târihi*, II, p. 941.

6 Outings and excursions

One very important aspect of city life was promenading, the strolling around in the gardens and open spaces both within and just outside the city, being seen and viewing others, enjoying the flowers, feasting, boating and generally relaxing in the fresh air. On specific occasions – the nights of the month of Ramazan and the two religious festivals of Ramazan *bayramı* and *kurban bayramı* – people poured onto the streets in a carnival of enjoyment, decked out in their best finery, as they promenaded through the hectic and illuminated streets where the shops and coffee houses stayed open until dawn, their fronts festooned with laurel and lanterns, and were entertained by amusements from puppet plays to dancing.[1] In Ramazan, minarets were illuminated, lanterns strung between them forming different patterns, such as crescent moons in blazing lights, until they seemed as if covered from top to bottom in a shirt of fire.[2] The lighting of these lanterns announced the beginning of the festival.[3] This was in contrast to the rest of the year when, according to Balıkhane Nazırı Ali Rıza Efendi, referring to the late nineteenth century, 'there was no night life as there was in European cities', and 'after the evening call to prayer everybody was plunged into the repose of sleep in their houses'.[4]

One of the great attractions of these festivities, both for the populace, who enjoyed them immensely, and for the janissaries, who made money out of them, was the *bayram* swings, which, to Selaniki's disgust, resembled those at infidel fairs.[5] Four tall poles were set up in every square

[1] John Covel, 'Extracts from the diaries of Dr John Covel', in J. T. Bent (ed.), *Early Voyages and Travels in the Levant* (London, 1893), p. 152; Topçular Katibi, *Tarihi*, II, p. 1161.

[2] Schweigger, *Ein newe Reyssbeschreibung*, p. 175; Ahmet Rasim, *Şehir Mektupları*, ed. Nuri Akbayar (Istanbul, 2005), p. 321; Philippe du Fresne-Canaye, *Le Voyage du Levant de Philippe du Fresne-Canaye (1573)* (Paris, 1897), pp. 117–18; Quiclet, *Les Voyages de M. Quiclet à Constantinople* (Paris, 1664), p. 175; Leyla (Saz) Hanımefendi, *The Imperial Harem of the Sultans. Daily Life at the Çırağan Palace During the 19th Century*, trans. Landon Thomas (Istanbul, 1999), p. 172; Thomas Dallam, 'The Diary of Master Thomas Dallam 1599–1600', in Bent, *Levant*, p. 64.

[3] Özcan, *Anonim*, p. 199. [4] Balıkhane Nazırı Ali Rıza Bey, *Hayatı*, pp. 215–16.

[5] Selaniki, *Tarih*, II, p. 601.

24. Swings, in Schweigger, *Ein newe Reyssbeschreibung*, p. 194.

and main street, decorated with flowers and leaves of olive, daphne and other greenery, with pomegranates, lemons, candies and other delicacies placed among them. The structure was covered with a beautiful awning. Two people, one on either side, swung the rope on which the swing seat was positioned. There was a competition whereby the person sitting in the swing seat who could collect the most delicacies while swinging won the competition. Collecting money from those swinging, whom they charged at varying rates per push – sometimes at one *akçe* per push, sometimes one *akçe* for five, six or eight pushes – the janissaries earned a great deal of money.[6] They also forcibly extracted the cloth they used for swings from the richer elements of society, or were given it by the state.[7] There were also great wheels erected, where 'for each spoke they put a seat, fixed above two poles, like those in the

[6] Gerlach, *Günlüğü*, II, p. 535, I, pp. 118–19; Schweigger, *Yolculuk*, p. 194.

[7] Peçevi, *Tarihi*, II, p. 486; Gerlach, *Günlüğü*, I, pp. 118–19; Heberer, *Köle*, pp. 314–15; Schweigger, *Yolculuk*, p. 194; Naima, *Târih*, III, pp. 1354–5.

coxmpasses used for sailing, and the Turks sit on this, the wheel turning in such a way they remain always with their heads in the air'.[8]

Women participated in all these festivities in one way or another, at some periods more actively than at others, depending on the predilection of the current sultan and on the political stability of the period. One of the many European misconceptions about Ottoman history is the idea – no doubt inspired, in part at least, by the many travel accounts written, almost exclusively, by men – that Ottoman women were incarcerated in the harem, never to come out except to go to the *hamam*. But women clearly did go out: they visited friends and relatives; they went on picnics and promenades; they participated in sultanic pageantry; they certainly went shopping. The poorer ones worked as pedlars, going door to door selling goods, bringing gossip and matchmaking. They worked in the *hamam*s, laundries and in private houses; others worked as prostitutes. They went to mosques, to shrines and consulted *şeyh*s, spiritual figures not always as spiritual as they might have been, an activity roundly condemned by the author of the *Risale-i Garibe*, who had no time for those 'stupid men' who allowed their wives and daughters to go and listen to such people.[9] The fact that festivities could be cut short because of a perceived danger of too much female presence, or that orders could be issued banning women from appearing at certain *bayram*s or on specific occasions, such as the entry of the Iranian ambassador in May 1576,[10] clearly show that such a presence existed. The ruling by the *şeyhülislam* Ebussuud Efendi that it was acceptable for women to go out to public places, provided they carried themselves with dignity and in a virtuous manner, and were accompanied by a servant, is further evidence of women on the streets of the capital.[11] They were also travelling together with men on the boats between the old city and Galata, a journey whose pleasures were presumably few, for in 1583 the sultan ordered boats withdrawn from service due partly to the molestation of the female passengers.[12] In short, women were by no means only to be found in the harem, even if men such as the anonymous author of the *Risale-i Garibe* might have wished it that way, cursing as he did those 'cuckolds' who took their daughters out promenading on *bayram* days, those 'pimps' who allowed their wives out onto the streets on Fridays,

[8] Costantino Garzoni, 'Relazione dell'impero ottomano del senatore Costantino Garzoni stato all'ambasciera di Costantinopoli nel 1573', in Albèri, *Relazioni*, series III, I, p. 385.

[9] Develi, *Risale-i Garibe*, p. 28. [10] Gerlach, *Günlüğü*, I, pp. 289–90, 337.

[11] Düzdağ, *Ebussuûd Efendi*, p. 55, *hüküm* 154.

[12] Ülker, *Emir Defteri*, facsimile pp. 142 and 88, *hüküm* 272; Ahmet Refik, *Onuncu Asr-ı Hicrî*, pp. 41–2, *hüküm*s 6 and 7.

and those 'panders' who permitted their women to go to the pageants or festivities in the city.[13]

The fact that, without doubt, the male and female worlds were segregated and much socialising took place in single-sex environments – no decent woman, for example, ever appearing in the coffee shops or wine houses – does not mean that they did not participate in social life except behind the closed doors of the harem. While it is true that the nineteenth century saw a revolution in female freedom – a freedom fought against tooth and nail by some, such as the journalist Basiretçi Ali Efendi – women were out and about in the earlier centuries too, even if not spotted by European males in their often brief stays in the Ottoman capital.

That said, however, it would be a mistake to exaggerate the presence of women in public in Ottoman society, in a desire to redress the balance. The movement of women was restricted, partly as the result of concern over the perceived danger for social order that women, and indeed young boys, posed if they appeared too openly among the crowds. Much of the violence against women was perpetrated by the janissaries or the sailors, who, not surprisingly in such a major seaport, were often roaming the streets, and were frequently drunk. Reports that sailors in the market in Üsküdar were plotting to seize honourable women had Selim III hurrying off there in disguise. When he arrived, however, they had gone.[14] Sailors, Turkish or otherwise, were a menace not merely to honourable women but even to hardened Italian travellers like Careri, who was so terrified by them that he was forced to barricade himself into his room to protect himself from their attentions.[15] The janissaries were a constant threat to women and it could well be argued that one of the main beneficiaries of the massacre of the janissaries by Mahmud II in 1826 was the female population, for whom a major menace had been removed. It is perhaps this event that precipitated greater female presence in the public spaces of the city, which was to lead to a much higher profile for women as the decades went by.

The dangers of the street no doubt caused women, in particular in certain periods, to prefer the safety of the harem. This was certainly the case in the violent and chaotic times after the murder of Selim III, when women were too frightened to venture out.[16] In calmer times, however, women did go out and were, even well before the nineteenth century, a much greater public presence than is sometimes understood. One of the places to which they, and the male inhabitants of the city, went in droves was the many gardens which dotted Istanbul.

[13] Develi, *Risale-i Garibe*, p. 24. [14] Karal, *Hümayunları*, p. 97.
[15] Careri, 'Voyage', p. 77. [16] Cabi, *Târihi*, I, pp. 477, 484.

The garden

Nor indeed doth a *Turke* at any time shew himself to be so truely pleased, and satisfied in his sense, as he doth in the summer time, when he is in a pleasant garden. For, he is no soner come into it (if it be his own, or where he thinks he may be bold) but he puts off his uppermost Coat and laies it aside, and upon that his *Turbant*, then turns up his sleeves, and unbuttoneth himself, turning his breast to the winde if there be any: if not, he fans himself; or his servant doth it for him. Again, sometimes standing upon a high bank, to take the fresh air, holding his arms abroad (as a *Cormorant* sitting upon a rock doth his wings in sun-shine after a storm) courting the weather, and sweet air, calling it his soul, his life, and his delight; ever and anon shewing some notable signes of contentment: nor shall the garden (during his pleasant distraction) be termed other than *Paradise*: with whose flowers he stuffes his bosome, and decketh his *Turbant*, shaking his head at their sweet savors; and sometimes singing a song to some pretty flower, by whose name per-adventure his mistresse is called; and uttering words of as great joy, as if at that instant she her self were there present. And one bit of meat in a garden shall do him more good (in his opinion) then the best fare that may be elsewhere.[17]

One of the greatest pleasures for the Ottomans was the garden and Istanbul was awash with them, from the magnificent rolling lands of the Topkapı palace and the numerous imperial gardens inside and just outside the city, to the gardens of the rich which lay round their *yalı*s and the small patches of the poor and the window boxes set up outside their houses. The city itself was so full of gardens and cypress trees that from a distance it seemed to resemble more 'shepherds' huts in the middle of a leafy wood than a city',[18] an illusion echoed by Sandys, for whom the intermingling of the buildings and the lofty cypress trees seemed to present 'a City in a Wood to the pleased beholders'.[19] What greatly contributed to the marvellous aspect of the city was the mix of wooden houses, the domes of the mosques and the cypress trees, noted by the seventeenth-century travellers Jacob Spon and George Wheler,[20] and, several centuries later, by Albert Smith, who talked of the 'quaint' houses, the intermingled foliage and the graceful cypress groves which covered the slopes of the hills and stretched far into the distance.[21] The trees were everywhere, as Mrs Brassey noticed when she sailed into harbour on board her yacht *The Sunshine*.[22] Count Forbin was dazzled and delighted by his first view of the city,

[17] Bon, *Description*, pp. 5–6. [18] Fresne-Canaye, *Voyage*, p. 93.
[19] George Sandys, *Sandys Travailes* (London, 1658), p. 24.
[20] Jacob Spon and George Wheler, *Voyage d'Italie, de Dalmatie, de Grece, et du Levant fait aux années 1675 et 1676*, 2 vols. (Amsterdam, 1679), I, p. 170.
[21] Smith, *Constantinople*, p. 59. [22] Brassey, *Sunshine*, p. 51.

half-concealed by the cypresses of the palace gardens and by the sight of the light and sumptuous minarets enveloped in groups of trees.[23] The view of Istanbul, almost submerged in foliage, was so fine that Albert Smith noted, in an uncharacteristically positive vein, 'I had never been so strongly moved before but once – when I looked down upon London, by night, from a balloon'.[24]

Although the Ottoman Armenian Sarkis Sarraf Hovhannesyan had presumably never gazed at London from a balloon, he, like Albert Smith, was enchanted by the natural beauty of the city's surroundings. On both sides of the Bosphorus, the valleys looking onto the water were bright green lawns, carpeted everywhere with beautiful flowers of every colour in the spring. Even the two castles of Anadolu Kavağı and Rumeli Kavağı were adorned with gardens and orchards.[25]

The sultan and the garden

The sultans amused themselves in the many imperial gardens, such as those at Eyüp where they went walking, or at the pavilions at Belgrad just outside the city, situated in delightful woodland and adorned with natural avenues meandering through lofty groves of beech, oak, and chestnut.[26] They hunted at the Tokat garden on the Bosphorus at Beykoz, a garden that Süleyman I was said to be very fond of and where he built pools which resembled the waterfalls in Kağıthane and which were later repaired by Mahmud I in 1746.[27] Mehmed IV also liked Kağıthane, for he had a garden built there called Vidos Bahçesi, where he went to enjoy himself with his harem. Indeed, he apparently enjoyed himself very much, for 'there was a pool in front of Yüksek Çardak Köşkü. On the pretext of making them swim he would have the girls thrown in naked and take great pleasure in their pretence of screams and cries'.[28] Selim II liked to eat simple, light food and to drink at the Carabali gardens near Galata, which were full of fruit

[23] Forbin, *Travels*, p. 14. [24] Smith, *Constantinople*, p. 58.
[25] Sarkis Sarraf Hovhannesyan, *Payitaht İstanbul'un Tarihçesi*, trans. Elmon Hançer and ed. Ara Kalaycıyan (Istanbul, 1996), p. 55.
[26] I. B. Tavernier, *Nouvelle Relation de l'interior du serrail du Grand Seigneur* (Amsterdam, 1678), p. 257; Quiclet, *Voyages*, p. 213; Edmund Chishull, *Travels in Turkey and Back to England* (London, 1747), p. 44.
[27] Eremya Çelebi Kömürcüyan, *İstanbul Tarihi. XVII. Asırda İstanbul*, trans. and ed. H. D. Andreasyan (Istanbul, 1952), p. 51; Hovhannesyan, *Payitaht*, pp. 58–9.
[28] Eremya Çelebi, *İstanbul*, pp. 34–5.

25. Carabali gardens, in Schweigger, *Ein newe Reyssbeschreibung*, p. 127.

trees and great wide avenues flanked by tall cypresses and rosemary plants.[29] Süleyman II spent much of his time at the Fener Köşkü in Kadıköy, where he could 'enjoy his Amours, and wanton away his hours of leisure with his *Sultanesses*'.[30]

The sultanic garden par excellence was that of the palace of Topkapı, built by Mehmed II after the conquest of Constantinople:

around the palace were constructed very large and lovely gardens abounding in various sorts of plants and trees, producing beautiful fruit. And there were abundant supplies of water flowing everywhere, cold and clear and drinkable, and conspicuous and beautiful groves and meadows. Besides that, there were flocks of birds, both domesticated fowls and song-birds, twittering and chattering all around, and many sorts of animals, tame and wild feeding there. Also there were many other fine ornaments and embellishments of various sorts, such as he [Mehmed II] thought would bring beauty and pleasure and happiness and enjoyment. The Sultan worked all this out with magnificence and profusion.[31]

[29] Schweigger, *Ein newe Reyssbeschreibung*, p. 126.
[30] Chishull, *Travels*, p. 39. [31] Kritoboulos, *History*, p. 208.

Europeans marvelled at the richness, beauty and extent of the gardens of Topkapı palace.[32] For Baron Wratislaw, in Istanbul with the Habsburg embassy in 1591, the gardens of Topkapı were of such beauty that one would believe them to have been the habitation of goddesses, where sat the muses of poetry, music and the other beautiful arts, and where, in secluded corners, the philosophers lost themselves in contemplation.[33] These heaven-like gardens, as Peçevi called them,[34] large, spacious and extremely delightful, where 'luxury [was] the steward, and the treasure un-exhaustible', ran down to the sea.[35] Here there were all types of flowers and fruits, and many very pleasant walks, enclosed on each side by high cypress trees.[36] Pavilions were scattered throughout the grounds, and little flower gardens, rare trees and fruit trees abounded.[37] Extremely pleasant paths meandered through the gardens among the many cypresses and fruit trees, all in 'verrie comly and desent order'.[38] Apart from the outer gardens, the courtyards, too, were planted. The first court was adorned with charming walks and stately cypress trees, intermixed with smaller trees which produced excellent fruit.[39] The second court, full of cypresses and fountains,[40] also contained 'green grasse-plots in which the *Gazells* [i.e. roe deer] do feed, and bring forth young'. These, together with the delicate fountains and rows of cypress trees made it far more beautiful and pleasant than the garden of the first court, in the estimation of Ottaviano Bon.[41]

Marble fountains, in which the sultan, and indeed all Turks, took great delight, were a feature of Topkapı and were in such abundance

[32] Giovanantonio Menavino, *I cinque libri della legge, religione, et vita de'Turchi: et della corte, et d'alcune guerre del Gran Turco: di Giovanantonio Menavino Genovese da Vultri* (Venice, 1548), p. 90; Bassano, *Costumi*, f. 17r; Nicolay, *L'empire*, p. 127; Domenico, *Istanbul*, p. 20; Frédéric Lacroix, *Guide de voyageur à Constantinople et dans ses environs* (Paris, 1839), p. 25; Bon, *Description*, p. 5.

[33] A. H. Wratislaw, *Adventures of Baron Wenceslas Wratislaw of Mitrowitz* (London, 1862), p. 75; A. H. Wratislaw, *Baron W. Wratislaw'ın Anıları, '16. Yüzyıl Osmanlı İmparatorluğu'undan Çizgiler'*, trans. M. Süreyya Dilmen (Istanbul, 1981), p. 69.

[34] Peçevi, *Tarihi*, II, p. 442.

[35] Louis Deshayes Courmenin, *Voiage de Levant fait per le Commandement du Roy par le Sr. D. C.* (Paris, 1629), p. 167; Garzoni, 'Relazione', p. 393; Sandys, *Travailes*, p. 25; Bernardo Navagero, 'Relazione dell'impero ottomano del clarissimo Bernardo Navagero stato Bailo a Costantinopoli fatta in pregadi nel mese di febbraio de 1553', in Albèri, *Relazioni*, Serie III, I, p. 52. Lacroix, *Guide*, p. 26, described the gardens as 'vast'; Quiclet, *Voyages*, p. 209; Courmenin, *Voiage*, p. 167.

[36] Bon, *Description*, p. 5.

[37] Chishull, *Travels*, p. 45; Tavernier, *Nouvelle*, p. 257; Arnold von Harff, *The Pilgrimage of Arnold von Harff*, trans. and ed. Malcolm Letts (London, 1946), pp. 241–2.

[38] Dallam, 'Diary', p. 78.

[39] Dallam, 'Diary', p. 61.

[40] Quiclet, *Voyages*, p. 190; Sandys, *Travailes*, p. 25.

[41] Bon, *Description*, p. 9.

that almost every walk had two or three of them.[42] The basins were of different coloured marble and near each there was a little platform surrounded by balustrades. This area was covered with rich carpets and squares of brocade whenever the sultan walked there, and it was only then that the water was made to flow, something which gave great pleasure to the royal women who accompanied him.[43]

Apart from trees and flowers, the gardens were also populated by rare wild animals, who ran unimpeded through the grounds.[44] Deer, foxes, goats, sheep and Indian cows, as well as many types of birds, wild geese and ducks, gave pleasure both with their calls and singing and as targets for the sultan's gun. The English clergyman Edmund Chishull, who was in Istanbul in 1699, noted the presence of 'hens of *Grand Cairo*', who had blue gills and feathers curiously coloured with grey circles at the centre of which was a black spot.[45] Phillipe du Fresne-Canaye's attention was focused on the dogs:

> in all his gardens he [the sultan] keeps dogs, horses and hunting birds. His greyhounds are controlled with great care; each is tied at the ankle and has over him a white [cover]. They have long ears and fur, most of them have their tails, ears and paws painted which produces a very pretty effect.[46]

It was these gardens, and not the buildings of the palace itself, that made Topkapı so agreeable, at least for Thévenot, who was far more impressed by the grounds than by the architecture, which he regarded as nothing magnificent.[47]

The sultans showed considerable interest in the gardens of the palace and lavished considerable expense on them. They were copiously stocked, and flowers were ordered from all over the empire and beyond. Tulips arrived from Caffa, pomegranate trees from Aleppo and Diyarbakır, hyacinth bulbs from Uzeyr and from Maraş (both white and blue), and rose bushes wrapped in felt from Edirne.[48]

Such extensive gardens clearly required a considerable workforce. The number of gardeners varied wildly for the sixteenth century, from the figure of 200 given by Garzoni in 1573,[49] and the 300 to 400 reported by Daniello de'Ludovisi in 1534,[50] to the 800 referred to by Bernardo

42 Bon, *Description*, p. 5. 43 Tavernier, *Nouvelle*, pp. 261–2.
44 Harff, *Pilgrimage*, p. 241. 45 Chishull, *Travels*, p. 45.
46 Fresne-Canaye, *Voyage*, p. 90. 47 Thévenot, *Voyages*, I, p. 69.
48 Ahmet Refik, *Hicri On Birinci Asırda*, p. 3, *hüküm* 6, p. 9, *hüküm* 17; Ahmet Refik, *On Altıncı Asırda İstanbul Hayatı (1553–1591)* (Istanbul, 1935), p. 6, *hüküm* 14.
49 Garzoni, 'Relazione', p. 394.
50 Daniello de'Ludovisi, 'Relazione dell'impero ottomano riferita in Senato dal secretario Daniello de'Ludovisi a dì 3 giugno del 1534', in Albèri, *Relazioni*, Serie III, I, p. 13.

Navagero, Venetian *bailo* at Istanbul in the mid 1550s,[51] and the much higher figure of 1,000 reported by the Englishman Thomas Dallam.[52] Domenico refers to 3,000 gardeners working in the various palaces of the sultan in the city,[53] while Navagero reported that there were 2,000 gardeners tending the twenty imperial gardens in the city.[54] For the following century, European estimates ranged from 600 to 700,[55] to 3,000 reported by de la Croix,[56] to 20,000 given by Tavernier.[57] Tavernier, however, also reports that there were more than 10,000 gardeners to look after all the imperial gardens,[58] while Quiclet and Courmenin give figures of 7,000 to 8,000.[59]

Whatever the exact number, there were clearly many of them. In the sixteenth century, these boys, aged between fifteen and twenty,[60] were paid at a rate of either three or four *akçe*s per day,[61] or two *akçe*s per day plus clothing and handouts which the sultan gave them, particularly when he went hunting.[62] By the following century the rate was up to four to five *akçe*s per day.[63] Apart from the handouts, there was another perk to the job. Whoever found the first ripe fruit of whatever kind and presented it to his superior, who then took it to the sultan, received one thousand *akçe*s.[64] The gardeners' job was to 'doo nothinge but kepe the garthens in good order',[65] to pull out the weeds which 'hide in the garden', to brush and water, and to do all other things necessary for the conservation and beauty of the plants.[66] They were, according to de la Croix, divided into nine groups, distinguished from each other by a special turban or belt.[67] It was also the gardeners who provided those who rowed the brigantines of the sultan when he wanted to amuse himself fishing or promenading on the water.[68] Menavino, captured by the Ottomans around 1501, maintained that the gardeners could not read, as they only did gardening.[69] A century later, Quiclet too reported that they were not as well educated as other boys in palace service, nor as well fed, but stated that they did learn to read

[51] Navagero, 'Relazione', p. 52. [52] Dallam, 'Diary', p. 62.
[53] Domenico, *Istanbul*, p. 25. [54] Navagero, 'Relazione', p. 52.
[55] Quiclet, *Voyages*, pp. 209, 210; Courmenin, *Voiage*, p. 168.
[56] De la Croix, *Mémoires du Sieur de la Croix cy-devant secretaire de l'ambassade de Constantinople*, 2 vols. (Paris, 1684), I, 3rd letter, p. 146.
[57] Tavernier, *Nouvelle*, p. 261. [58] Tavernier, *Nouvelle*, pp. 30–1.
[59] Quiclet, *Voyages*, p. 210; Courmenin, *Voiage*, p. 168.
[60] Menavino, *Libri*, p. 98. [61] Menavino, *Libri*, p. 98.
[62] Domenico Trevisano, 'Relazione dell'impero ottomano del clarissimo Domenico Trevisano tornado Bailo da Costantinopli sulla fine de 1554', in Albèri, *Relazioni* Serie III, I, p. 130; Navagero, 'Relazione', p. 52.
[63] Quiclet, *Voyages*, p. 210; Courmenin, *Voiage*, p. 168. [64] Menavino, *Libri*, p. 98.
[65] Dallam, 'Diary', p. 62. [66] Menavino, *Libri*, p. 98. [67] De la Croix, *Mémoires*, p. 146.
[68] Tavernier, *Nouvelle*, p. 30. [69] Menavino, *Libri*, p. 98.

and write.[70] They were kept under strict control and not allowed to go into the city unless they were sent there to perform some task for the sultan.[71]

The head gardener was the *bostancıbaşı*, in control not merely of the gardens of Topkapı, but of all the other palace gardens.[72] In the sixteenth century he received a salary of two hundred *akçe*s per day, and a gift of clothes of velvet and brocade twice a year.[73] By the seventeenth century, his pay had increased to a daily rate of three hundred *akçe*s.[74] He was a man of great political significance, for, despite his title of head gardener, his role was that of commander of the imperial guard, often in charge of the execution of important figures, and he had both political and financial power.[75] What made him important was his access to the sultan, which gave him potential political influence.

Now the *Bustange Bashawe*, by reason the King talks much with him in the *Kaik* [boat] (at which time lest any one should hear what they say, the *Mutes* fall a howling like little dogs) may benefit, or prejudice whom he pleaseth, the *Grand Signor* being altogether ignorant of divers passages, and apt to beleeve any information, either with or against any subject whatsoever.[76]

The noise made by the rowers was also commented on by Sanderson, who noted that they 'often in their rowinge barke like dogs. The reason I knowe not, except it be when they heare him [the sultan] talke (to the Bustangiebassi, who sitts at the rudder) that they dare not harken to his talke'.[77]

It was the *bostancıbaşı* who held the helm of the imperial boat when the sultan went out for pleasure on the waters of the Bosphorus. Whenever the sultan wished to go into his garden, he had the *bostancıbaşı* summoned to accompany him and discussed with him whatever he wished to.[78] Held in high esteem by the sultan, the *bostancıbaşı* was courted by the *paşa*s, who knew full well that in speaking to the sultan he could throw in a word in favour of or against anyone.[79] His ability to do them 'good or evil' ensured him a regular supply of gifts.[80] Powerful and 'very experienced in the ways things are done in Istanbul',[81] he had, as Ottaviano Bon noted, 'a very eminent place; for

[70] Quiclet, *Voyages*, p. 210; Courmenin, *Voiage*, p. 168. [71] Quiclet, *Voyages*, p. 210.
[72] Menavino, *Libri*, p. 98; Dallam, 'Diary', p. 62; Tavernier, *Nouvelle*, pp. 258–9.
[73] Menavino, *Libri*, p. 98. [74] Bon, *Description*, p. 66.
[75] Quiclet, *Voyages*, p. 210; Courmenin, *Voiage*, p. 168.
[76] Bon, *Description*, pp. 145–6; Thévenot, *Voyages*, I, p. 69. [77] Sanderson, *Travels*, p. 89.
[78] Navagero, 'Relazione', p. 52. [79] Navagero, 'Relazione', p. 53.
[80] Tavernier, *Nouvelle*, pp. 30–1. [81] Navagero, 'Relazione', pp. 52–3.

26. The *bostancıbaşı*, in Paul Rycaut, *The History of the Present State of the Ottoman Empire* (London, 1675), between pp. 754 and 755.

he hath the keeping of all the *Grand Signors* garden houses, and steeres the Kings *Kaik*', and from this position he could rise to great heights.[82]

By the second half of the seventeenth century, the enormous power of the *bostancıbaşı* made him a figure both loathed and feared.

The *bostancıbaşı*'s control stretches over the whole city, both shores of the Bosphorus as far as Kağıthane, all the islands, from Florya to Yeşilköy and, on the Üsküdar side, from Kartal to Pendik. Travelling in his boat, he watches the

[82] Bon, *Description*, p. 67.

shores continuously. And, in the role of sultan's deputy, he rules everywhere as if it is his own domain. The *bostancıbaşı* tracks down brawls and homicides, captures notorious murderers and bandits and throws them into the dungeons located below Has Bahçe. The *bostancıbaşı* hearing a noise in the gardens immediately goes there and from the perpetrators he takes one hundred, two hundred or as much as five hundred gold pieces. When he comes upon drunk men and women or those who are rowdy, he takes them to the shore and does as much harm to them as he can. The *bostancıbaşı* does not have a bastinado so he has sticks used on the left and right legs of the men who are beaten. While those who are being beaten shout and scream he sits and drinks wine. They in vain beg for mercy crying out 'oh my sultan [i.e. the *bostancıbaşı*], help me in the name of the *padişah* [sultan]'. He orders 'turn them over' and sticks begin to rain down on their coccyx. When rich women who have gone to enjoy themselves in the gardens are caught, they are forced to save themselves by handing over their belts, their earrings and their bracelets. God forbid that the *bostancıbaşı* should come across male and female singers on the waters, for without asking any questions, he sinks their boats. The Greeks cannot enter the places of pilgrimage without paying a bribe, otherwise the *bostancıbaşı* becomes like a Tatar. Those who give the most money escape from his clutches; many flee to the mountains and the valleys fearing death. The shield of those who are caught is their backs and the soles of their feet.[83]

After this bleak picture of the brutality of the *bostancıbaşı*, Eremya Çelebi, an Ottoman Armenian writing in the seventeenth century, concludes, 'may God protect us all from the tyranny, the beating, the punishment and the dungeons of the *bostancıbaşı*', a man whose beatings were so severe that people had even become Muslim under the blows.[84] In this he apparently resembled the Mamluk sultan al-Mu'ayyad, who, in the early fifteenth century, had the Catalan consul and the merchant accompanying him beaten so severely that the merchant converted to Islam.[85]

There might be a large staff of gardeners and a very powerful *bostancıbaşı*, but not all Europeans were impressed with the horticultural results or agreed with Thomas Dallam's view that Turkish gardens were the best kept in the world.[86] The Turks, 'being as little skill'd in Gardening as in Architecture … are much more beholding to Nature for producing the Fruit, than to Art for Cultivating or dressing either Plants or Trees',[87] and despite the large numbers employed, their

[83] Eremya Çelebi, *İstanbul*, p. 56. [84] Eremya Çelebi, *İstanbul*, p. 57.
[85] Emmanuel Piloti, *L'Égypte au commencement du quinzième siècle d'après le traité d'Emmanuel Piloti de Crète (incipit 1420)*, ed. P.-H. Dopp (Cairo, 1950), p. 113.
[86] Dallam, 'Diary', p. 62.
[87] Guillaume-Joseph Grelot, *A Late Voyage to Constantinople* (London, 1683), pp. 43–4.

gardens 'hardly approach the neatness nor the embellishments of ours'.[88] Others made carping comments about the 'various and very despicable jets d'eau' and the trelliswork which produced 'a wretched effect'.[89] Indeed, the situation was so appalling that the walks of the upper garden were 'laid out in worse taste than the fore court of a Dutchman's house in the suburbs of Hague'.[90] Such gardens could clearly in no way be compared to the gardens of the Tuileries, Versailles, Fontainebleau, or with the gardens of certain private individuals in France, for, Grelot complained, they observed no order.[91] The outer gardens lacked ornament apart from fountains and several alleys of cypresses,[92] which were completely neglected and overgrown.[93] They were, in the words of the seventeenth-century English clergyman Edmund Chishull,

> rude and wild places, affording nothing that is entertaining, but that wherewith nature has furnished them, which is an admirable situation rising into convenient ascents, and capable of infinite improvement, it if were happily in the possession of a Christian prince.[94]

Chishull's annoyance that such gardens should find themselves in the hands of the Turks echoed the sentiments of Baron Wratislaw, who had remarked a century before that 'after gazing on everything thoroughly, and gathering nosegays of sweet-scented flowers, we sincerely lamented that this most beautiful spot, and the whole of this delightful region, should remain in the power of the Turks'.[95] Busbecq felt the same way about the numerous imperial parks situated in charming valleys which he saw on his way from Istanbul to the Black Sea. 'What homes for the Nymphs! What abodes of the Muses! What places for studious retirement!' And what a pity they were in Turkish hands, for 'the very earth … seemed to mourn and to long for Christian care and culture'.[96]

But despite the distress of various visiting Europeans, such gardens were very firmly in the hands of the Ottomans, and the sultan, his harem and his immediate family enjoyed themselves very much in their imperial

88 Tavernier, *Nouvelle*, p. 262. Such scepticism is also apparent in an article on Captain Frankland's travels, in which the author, after quoting from Frankland's comments on the gardens in Damascus, noted that 'Mr. Buckland denies the existence of gardens, and perhaps Captain Frankland has confounded uncultivated groves with rudely-kept parterres' (*Ladies' Museum*, 1 August 1829, p. 105).

89 'The Seraglio of the Grand Signior at Constantinople', *Ladies' Cabinet of Fashion, Music and Romance*, Saturday 1 March 1834, pp. 164–5.

90 'The Seraglio of the Grand Signior at Constantinople', *Ladies' Cabinet of Fashion, Music and Romance*, Tuesday 1 April 1834, p. 256.

91 Grelot, *Voyage*, pp. 77–8.

92 Courmenin, *Voiage*, p. 167; Quiclet, *Voyages*, p. 208.

93 Tavernier, *Nouvelle*, pp. 258–9.

94 Chishull, *Travels*, p. 45.

95 Wratislaw, *Adventures*, p. 75; Wratislaw, *Anıları*, p. 69.

96 Busbecq, *Letters*, pp. 39–40.

grounds. Here the sultans indulged themselves in such entertainments as archery, watching the training of birds of prey (a favourite pastime), sitting with their courtiers, listening to music and poetry, and eating and drinking. Many sultans were very fond of hunting. Murad III

> holds hunts in his garden, having had not only deer and goats but also wild boar, bears, and lions brought in, and standing at a window he watches his *acemi oğlan*s hunt. He also has birds of every kind brought there, and riding a horse through his garden he watches them fly; and in short, all the pleasures of the hunt which the other princes have in the countryside, he has within his palace and he enjoys them at his leisure.[97]

Deshayes de Courmenin, in Istanbul in 1621, also commented on the sultan's predilection for hunting:

> He [the sultan] sometimes has small hunts in his palace which are very pleasant. He has many live wild boars caught, which they bring there into a place enclosed by canvas. When he wants to give them the pleasure, he has the Sultanas, eunuchs, and others whom he likes the most brought there. He gives each wild boar the name of one of his enemies, such as the King of Spain, whom he calls the Signor of Spain, the Duke of Florence, the Grand Master of Malta, and others in this manner; and after he has killed them by shooting them with arrows he gives the assistants great trophies because they are very superstitious and they believe that it is an omen that the *Grand Seigneur* must destroy the princes whose names he has given to the wild boars. Afterwards he sends these boars pierced with arrows to the ambassador of the king, and sometimes to other ambassadors so that they can participate in the joy at the destruction of their common enemy.[98]

Some enjoyed rough-and-tumble entertainment, involving mutes, buffoons and water. Ahmed I took pleasure in having his mutes and buffoons row him up and down in a little boat on an artificial lake in the gardens of Topkapı. Here he liked 'to sport with them, making them leap into the water; and many times as he walks along with them above upon the sides of the lake, he throwes them down into it, and plunges them over head and ears'.[99] The amount of time sultans spent in such company led at least one Venetian, the *bailo* Gianfrancesco Morosini, to question just how good the life of the Ottoman sultan was, for the sultan spent almost his entire time in the palace surrounded by eunuchs, boys, dwarfs, mutes and slaves, which seemed to him almost as bad as the company of women.[100]

[97] Lorenzo Bernardo, 'Relazione dell'impero ottomano di Lorenzo Bernardo 1592', in Albèri, *Relazioni*, serie III, II, p. 352.

[98] Courmenin, *Voiage*, p. 175. [99] Bon, *Description*, p. 14.

[100] Gianfranco Morosini, 'Relazioni', in Albèri, *Relazioni*, serie III, III, p. 281.

The women of the harem also enjoyed themselves in the gardens, for one western traveller reported somewhat implausibly seeing the *valide sultan* and 'the four principle Sultanas, who were in high glee, romping and laughing with each other'.[101] Apart from romping happily, they also indulged in 'tearing up and destroying all the plants', a pastime which was their greatest pleasure, according to another European account,[102] which calls to mind the story of the red-turbaned maidens who at night warned the sleeping sultan of fires by tickling his feet. This vision of the women of the sultan's harem as destructive little vixens, was clearly a popular one with the British reading public in the nineteenth century, for yet another account from the popular press of the time refers to the women of the palace breaking the mirrors in the audience chamber of the *valide sultan* 'in their frolics'.

The mischief done in this way, by the Grand Signior's women, is so great, that some of the most costly articles of furniture are removed when they come from their winter apartments into this palace. Among the number was a large coloured lustre given by the Earl of Elgin; this was only suspended during their absence, and even then by a common rope.[103]

The populace and flowers

All Turks loved flowers, or so it seemed to Europeans who visited the empire.

One can scarcely believe how much the Turks love flowers, how they always have them in their hands and turbans, and value them as something sacred. And if the Grand Seigneur has any tree that pleases him more than the others, he plants under its shadow many flowers of all types and scents. And in all his gardens there is such a quantity of all kinds that merely by extending one's hand one gathers a mixed and varied bouquet of all the colours one can imagine. The alleys are lined with cypresses so high that their sight excites admiration; but they are narrow, for the Grand Seigneur always walks alone.[104]

Even Albert Smith, who hardly ever had anything nice to say about the Turks or Istanbul, was impressed. While Topkapı, whose gardens and stables were equally disappointing, might contain nothing very striking, and Ayasofya might not 'in any way, excite my astonishment', the Turks were, albeit 'in absence of all artistic impressions', great admirers of

[101] 'The Seraglio of the Grand Signior at Constantinople', *Ladies' Cabinet of Fashion, Music and Romance*, Saturday 1 March 1834, p. 161.
[102] *La Belle Assemblée; or, Bell's Court and Fashionable Magazine*, issue 79, p. 335.
[103] 'The Seraglio of the Grand Signior at Constantinople', *Ladies' Cabinet of Fashion, Music and Romance*, Tuesday 1 April 1834, p. 253.
[104] Fresne-Canaye, *Voyage*, pp. 87–8.

nature. 'Fields and forests, blue water and skies, sunny air and bright flower gardens, are the great sources of their happiness'.[105] Such care for and cultivation of plants was explained by Tournefort as being a religious duty, undertaken by the most devout Turks out of charity.[106] Flowers were sold on the streets of Istanbul on *bayram* days.[107] Men wore flowers in their turbans; even those who were unable to afford underwear still had a great wedge of flowers shoved onto their heads, to the disgust of the author of the *Risale-i Garibe*.[108]

This Turkish love of flowers was apparent even in the midst of conflict. During the Balkan Wars (1912–13), the American journalist H. G. Dwight, for whom the Turk's love of flowers was one of his most sympathetic traits, saw Turkish soldiers in a temporary camp laying out patches of turf and pansies round their tents. 'No man', he commented, 'likes a garden better than he. He never could put up with a thing like the city back yard or the suburban lawn of the New World. He is given to sitting much out of doors, he does not like to be stared at while he is doing it, and he has a great love of flowers'.[109]

In this period, at the end of the empire, the passion for flowers was evident in every aspect of Turkish life. Even if a house did not have a garden, its windowsills and balconies would have pots of carnations, roses, geraniums, fuchsias and basil. Every morning children took little bouquets of flowers for their teachers; people sent a beautiful carnation or jonquil in very delicate vases to sick friends.[110] Everyone, 'the chic gentlemen and the youths of Istanbul, summer and winter, all year long, everyday', wore a flower.[111] Even if, according to Dwight, the fashion of the buttonhole had not yet become universally adopted in Istanbul, nevertheless

> nothing is commoner than to observe a grave personage marching along with one rose or one pink in his hand – of which flowers the Turks are inordinately fond. Less grave personages do not scorn to wear a flower over one ear, with its stem stuck under their fez. As I always remember a fireman I once beheld who was not too busy squirting water at a burning house to stop every now and then and smell the rose he held between his teeth.[112]

105 Smith, *Constantinople*, pp. 313, 133, 135, 160.
106 Joseph Pitton de Tournefort, *A Voyage in the Levant*, 2 vols. (London, 1718), II, p. 65; Tournefort, *Relations*, II, p. 82.
107 Gerlach, *Günlüğü*, II, p. 534. 108 Develi, *Risale-i Garibe*, p. 37.
109 H. G. Dwight, *Constantinople. Old and New* (New York, 1915), p. 227.
110 From the notes of Münir Süleyman Çapanoğlu, in Reşad Ekrem Koçu, *Tarihte İstanbul Esnafı* (Istanbul, 2003), p. 67.
111 From the notes of Çapanoğlu in Koçu, *Esnafı*, p. 69.
112 Dwight, *Constantinople*, pp. 227–8.

The use of the flower motif, so evident in Turkish art, in ceremonial caftans, carpets and the celebrated marbled paper, *ebru*, is, of course, a standard Islamic theme, and Ottoman gardens were formed in an Islamic context. For the Islamic world, the garden was the symbol of paradise. Many verses in the Qu'ran speak of paradise as a garden full of flowing waters, a place of greenness and tranquillity, where the believers sit on luxurious carpets among the verdant luxury of paradise, surrounded by the cool waters of its many rivers and streams. The religious image of the garden is central to the Sufi tradition, where earth and water, flowers and trees represent unity with God and the purity of the soul. For the Sufi, the believer was one with the earth. As Said Emre wrote, 'the face of the earth is my flesh and my skin and the flowing water is my blood'.[113]

Said Emre was a follower of the thirteenth-century Turkish poet Yunus Emre, perhaps the most famous of Sufi poets, who used the imagery of the garden to express the oneness of the individual with God. Essential elements in Sufi imagery, which appear constantly in the poetry of Yunus Emre, were the rose and the nightingale, the rose being the beloved, and the nightingale, the lover, that is, God and the believer. The rose garden, too, was used by Yunus Emre to symbolise God, the *şeyh* or the beloved. In one of his poems he likens himself to a rose in a rose garden:

> Come, let us go together to my land where you will enter the garden
> There nightingales always sing and my rose garden never fades
> The roses of the gardens in my land are always in bloom
> My garden is cultivated, no rival can hurt my rose.[114]

The idea of the heavenly garden of water and greenness was reflected in the traditional Islamic garden pattern, where an essential element was water. In the Ottoman garden, too, water was a fundamental element, as was the cypress tree. Antoine Galland, in Istanbul in the 1670s, wrote that one of the differences between gardens in France and those in the Ottoman empire was that in France one watered the garden with a watering can, whereas in Turkish gardens there were conduits and little channels which took water everywhere and from which water was extracted under pressure.[115]

113 Mehmet Kaplan, *Türk Edebiyatı Üzerinde Araştırmalar. 1* (Istanbul, 1976), p. 146.
114 Kaplan, *Araştırmalar*, p. 143.
115 Frédéric Bauden (ed.), *Le Voyage à Smyrne. Un manuscript d'Antoine Galland (1678)* (Paris, 2000), p. 202.

However, while the Ottoman garden was situated within the world of the Islamic garden, it differed from it. Unlike the traditional order, seen in such classic examples as the gardens of the palace of Alhambra, for example, the Ottoman garden was much wilder, more natural, and had a functional aspect to it. It was to be both decorative and productive. Where the Islamic garden was constructed and ordered, the Ottoman garden adapted itself to the site, using what was there and moulding itself round the features of the landscape. Thus, while many traditional Islamic palace gardens had straight, artificial channels of water running through formally laid out gardens, those of the Ottomans more often tended to use an already present stream or river, around which the garden was designed, as was the case with the palace of Edirne. This aspect struck Baron Wenceslas Wratislaw when he visited the gardens of Topkapı, where he saw 'most delightful spots, many kinds of bowers, most pleasant parterres and lawns, delightful vales, flowing streams, and an abundance of groves, not so much artificially constructed by men, as growing spontaneously by nature'.[116] Such lack of formality was not always appreciated by European travellers, Chishull describing all the gardens of the sultan as being 'only a Confusion of Trees growing as they were planted, without any Order or neatness, like so many petty Wildernesses'.[117] While French gardens were embellished with alleys and flowerbeds, those of the Turks had practically no adornment, 'apart from what nature gives them'.[118]

It was not only the natural, unconstructed aspect of the Ottoman garden which made it different from both the more formal classical Islamic layout and the grand gardens of Europe, but also its functionality. The Ottoman garden was a mixture of flowers and vegetables, fruit trees and cypresses. This system of planting both for pleasure and for food puzzled the Europeans, who did not like the intrusion of such functionality among the beauties of a garden. Careri's eye was drawn to the abundance of lettuces,[119] while de la Croix warned his readers that instead of the beautiful flowerbeds and attractive alleys one might expect, there was a confusion of cypresses, small squares of fairly common flowers, and quantities of cucumbers, pumpkins, watermelons and herbs.[120] Courmenin noted that instead of flowerbeds, the outer gardens of Topkapı were planted with vegetable gardens and herbs,[121]

[116] Wratislaw, *Adventures*, pp. 74–5; Wratislaw, *Anıları*, p. 69.
[117] Chishull, *Travels*, p. 39; the one exception being the garden of one of the sultan's summer houses at Kadıköy.
[118] Bauden, *Galland*, p. 201. [119] Careri, 'Voyage', p. 76.
[120] De la Croix, *Mémoires*, I, 3rd letter, p. 146.
[121] Courmenin, *Voiage*, p. 167; Quiclet, *Voyages*, p. 208.

and Tavernier expressed surprise at the spaces between the alleys in the palace gardens being used as kitchen gardens, vegetable plots and orchards. Here there were strawberries and raspberries in abundance and great square gardens of melons and cucumbers. It was the cucumbers that were in the greatest abundance, for

> the Levantine are very keen on [them]. Most often they eat them without peeling them, after which they drink a glass or water. In all Asia it is the normal food of the poor for three or four months, and when a child asks for something to eat, instead of giving him bread as in France or elsewhere, in the Levant he is given a cucumber which he eats raw, straight from being picked. Working men and those who get very tired like the camel drivers and those who look after horses and mules in the caravans make a kind of salad with their cucumbers similar to that which we would give to our horses.[122]

A fellow Frenchman, Antoine Galland, also commented on the Turkish predilection for cucumbers, as well as for great quantities of raw greenery, which 'one never eats in France unless it is cooked and accompanied with a good sauce'.[123] The delicious little cucumbers known as Russian cucumbers, and the cherries grown in the gardens and the orchards around Rumeli Hisarı, were very famous, while the productive gardens of the Büyük Göksu stream reared a long and delicious type of aubergine, which became renowned in the city.[124]

The Turks relished not only cucumbers but were, for Salomon Schweigger, great fruit eaters, who enjoyed eating oranges, pomegranates, figs, lemons, melons, mulberries, apples, pears and cherries, instead of drinking wine.[125] This is perhaps not surprising, in view both of the amount of fruit to be found in the Ottoman garden and of the high reputation of the fruit grown in the empire. Aleppo produced wondrous grapes and the best watermelons in the world, according to one mid-sixteenth-century Venetian source.[126] The Venetian *bailo*, Ottaviano Bon, was sure that neither the sultan, nor the women of the palace, nor the servants could ever want for fruit, it always being present in such abundance and such variety. Produced either in the sultan's own gardens or elsewhere, it was taken every morning to the palace. These fruits were 'excellent good; especially figs, grapes, peaches, and *Caoons* [melons]'.[127] Thomas Dallam was most impressed:

[122] Tavernier, *Nouvelle*, pp. 258–9. [123] Bauden, *Galland*, p. 192.
[124] Hovhannesyan, *Payitaht*, p. 61. [125] Schweigger, *Ein newe Reyssbeschreibung*, p. 123.
[126] 'Relazione anonima della Guerra di Persia dall'anno 1553 e di molti altri particolari', in Albèri, *Relazioni*, Serie III, I, p. 221.
[127] Bon, *Description*, pp. 132–3.

> every oda [room or kiosk] or corner hath som exelente frute tre or trees growing in them, allso thar is greate abundance of sweete grapes, and of diverse sortes; thar a man may gather grapes everie Daye in the yeare. In November, as I satt at diner, I se them gather grapes unpon the vines, and theye broughte them to me to eate. For the space of a monthe I Dined everie day in the Surralia, and we have everie day grapes after our meate; but moste sartain it is that grapes do grow thare contenually.[128]

Such production was not merely for home consumption and for feeding the sultan and his household. Vegetables and fruit grown in the royal gardens which were surplus to requirement were sold to the public, as were flowers, which were sold to shops in the city. In the sixteenth century, surplus fruit from the Topkapı gardens was apparently sold in the square in front of the palace,[129] and in the seventeenth century at a special market in the city selling only the sultan's fruit.[130] It apparently sold very well and was in great demand. Those who bought it often sent it to 'great personages' as presents, 'for it is extraordinary good, and so artificially piled up in baskets, by the *Bustangees* [the gardeners], that for the beauty of it, it oftentimes proves more acceptable then a gift of greater price'.[131] Flowers, too, were sold. It seems that at the end of the sixteenth century, there were more than a hundred shops selling off the surplus flowers, a number that authorities felt to be excessive. According to Busbecq, Rüstem Paşa, sultan Süleyman's grand vezir and son-in-law, 'neglected no source of revenue, however small, even scraping together money by selling the vegetables and roses and violets which grew in the Sultan's gardens'.[132]

The income from such sales was spent on the expenses of the sultan's table, it being, according to Tavernier, a custom for the Ottoman rulers to use the revenue of their gardens 'for the maintenance of their table and for their mouth alone',[133] a phrase also used earlier by Menavino.[134] Every Friday the *bostancıbaşı* gave an account of the sales of the garden produce to the treasury officials.[135] This habit of selling off the produce of the royal gardens seemed odd to Schweigger, but, he explained, the sultan saw no problem in trading in these items,[136] the reason being, according to Menavino, that the sultan regarded such income as 'well earnt and not from the sweat of poor men'.[137] From Bon's description, however, the revenue was not always spent solely on feeding the sultan, for the ruler could choose to

[128] Dallam, 'Diary', p. 62. [129] Menavino, *Libri*, p. 98. [130] Bon, *Description*, p. 133.
[131] Bon, *Description*, p. 133. [132] Busbecq, *Letters*, p. 30.
[133] Tavernier, *Nouvelle*, p. 257. [134] Menavino, *Libri*, p. 98.
[135] Quiclet, *Voyages*, p. 211. [136] Schweigger, *Ein newe Reyssbeschreibung*, p. 123.
[137] Menavino, *Libri*, p. 98.

spend it in other ways. It was his 'cebe akcesi', his pocket money, which he 'gives ... away by handfuls, as he sees occasion, to his *Mutes* and *buffones*, at such times as they make him sport'.[138]

Gardens were an integral part of everyday Turkish life and all were interested in growing flowers. The *şeyhülislam* Ebussuud Efendi, for example, was well known for his great passion for flowers. He successfully cultivated three kinds of jonquil, one white and two yellow, which were named after him.[139] There were gardens everywhere, and Istanbul was full of large gardens surrounded by walls, 'on which cats usually jump and assemble'.[140] Spon and Wheler noted that there was hardly a house without a garden in Gelibolu,[141] and Mrs Brassey, many centuries later, was struck by the endless houses and gardens they sailed by on their way into harbour in Istanbul.[142] The coastline stretching northwards towards the Black Sea was peppered with innumerable palaces and kiosks,[143] which were very popular for they appealed to the Turks' 'musing humour'.[144] All were surrounded by lovely gardens,[145] while at Üsküdar, on the Asian side, the cypress groves and leafy terraces,[146] and the very fine walks, all shaded with cypresses, pine, fir, oak, ash, lotus, horse chestnut, cherry, beech and other trees, greatly pleased the eye.[147] For the Venetian ambassador, Andrea Badoaro, who went to Istanbul in 1573, the hills above Pera offered the most delightful and most satisfactory hunting that one could enjoy in the world.[148] It was this prodigious number of gardens and the mass of greenness from the cypresses and other trees which contributed to the pleasing confusion of various colours that charmed the eyes of all who approached the city.[149]

In the second half of the seventeenth century, the European shores of the Bosphorus were dotted with

> an infinite number of villages, *yalı*s and palaces. The rich enjoy themselves here and promenade by the delightful waters. The shores are as a garden completely adorned with trees of every sort. They are excellent places for excursions. These grassy meadows, valleys and mountain pastures full of plane trees, laurels, cypresses, wine-coloured Judas trees, evergreen stone pines and the elegant

[138] Bon, *Description*, p. 133.
[139] Registered in *Netayicülezhar* of Übeydi Efendi written in AH 1110, Koçu, *Esnafı*, p. 63.
[140] Wratislaw, *Adventures*, p. 75; Wratislaw, *Anıları*, p. 70.
[141] Spon and Wheler, *Voyage*, I, p. 160. [142] Brassey, *Sunshine*, p. 52.
[143] Brassey, *Sunshine*, p. 65. [144] Grelot, *Voyage*, p. 71. [145] Brassey, *Sunshine*, p. 65.
[146] Smith, *Constantinople*, p. 60. [147] Covel, 'Diaries', p. 168.
[148] Andrea Badoaro, 'Relazione dell'impero ottomano di Andrea Badoaro stato ambasciatore a Costantinopoli per la confermazione della pace col Turco l'anno 1573', in Albèri, *Relazioni*, Serie III, I, pp. 352–3.
[149] Grelot, *Voyage*, p. 59.

cypresses are blessed with abundant waters for man, for the flocks of sheep and for the sultan's dairy farms. The people, from spring to the end of November, come to enjoy themselves in these places of endless beauty.[150]

As with the palace gardens, other gardens, too, were both functional and recreational, for the growing of fruit and vegetables was essential for general household economy. Every house had a garden and everyone stocked and decorated his garden according to his means.

Flowers, trees, green vegetables, fruit ... there was no house which did not have one or two rose bushes, a bower of jasmine, an arbour of bunches of pendulous blue flowers. No garden could be without one or two fig trees, pear, cherry, plum and quince trees. The greater the wealth of the owner, the more the garden was transformed into a paradise.[151]

The *yalı*s which lined the Bosphorus in the nineteenth century generally had a small garden in the front overlooking the water, but it was behind the house, hidden from view, where the main, large gardens were to be found. These well-cultivated and cared-for gardens were a focal point of the household, where the family spent much time and where they relaxed and enjoyed themselves. They consisted of a flower garden and, behind it, a section for vegetables and fruit, and an area for seedlings and cuttings used to stock the gardens. There were also greenhouses, heated in winter, where lemon and orange trees were placed when the weather became cooler. The whole garden was surrounded by a wall covered in thick ivy. Behaviour in these gardens was governed by strict etiquette. Snapping off flowers, catching fish or running after the animals, trampling on the grass or over the flowers were all unacceptable and forbidden.[152]

These *yalı* gardens, with their arbours of honeysuckle and jasmine, were a riot of flowers, and the variety of plants grown in them was considerable. Abdülaziz Bey, a member of a wealthy and well-established Istanbul family, who wrote his memoirs of the late nineteenth century, refers to thirteen different types of roses, twenty-one different varieties of hyacinth, twenty different types of tulips and twenty different types of jonquil that could be found in the *yalı* gardens.[153] Such gardens provided the house-owners with the many flowers they used for the bouquets that they sent to each other. Such bouquets had different names, according to their shapes. For wedding nights, bouquets in the shape of hearts were prepared. The cultivation of flowers was taken very seriously, and in Istanbul there were people famous for growing and

[150] Eremya Çelebi, *İstanbul*, p. 50. [151] Sadri Sema, *Hatıraları*, p. 37.
[152] Abdülaziz Bey, *Osmanlı*, p. 218. [153] Abdülaziz Bey, *Osmanlı*, pp. 219–22.

selling certain types of flowers, such as the rose-grower Gülcü Hacı, the hyacinth-grower Sümbülcü Aziz and the carnation-grower Karanfilci Ziya. People would go to certain gardens – those of Aşçı Şakir and Turfandacı Ali, for example – to buy specific flowers or plants.

Apart from flowers, the *yalı* gardens also had a wealth of trees, although by this time the cypress, traditionally the most important tree of an Ottoman garden, was no longer popular. The oleander, too, was unpopular, and indeed was not planted in the gardens, for it was held to bring bad luck. This was due to the traditional belief that it was a tree that grew in hell. Topiary was very much in fashion, and great care was taken over pruning and shaping the boxwoods. Just as in imperial gardens, water was a feature of these gardens too. There were fountains and marble pools in which swam fish of different colours, and even small artificial streams with little bridges over them. Often there were little kiosks by the pools, and wooden benches covered in cushions were set up in different parts of the gardens.

Both men and women enjoyed these gardens. Women frequented them particularly after the afternoon prayer, when the sun's effect was less strong, or on nights with a full moon. At such times, women wandered around the gardens, or swung on the swings set up for them in suitable places, sang and enjoyed themselves. In summer, and on summer nights when there was a full moon, people sat in the little pavilions and played musical instruments and sang. The pavilions were furnished with cages of canaries. To enhance the surroundings, the gardens were furnished with peacocks and green-headed ducks and ruddy shelducks. White rabbits were brought from the islands and released into the gardens, for people enjoyed seeing them hopping through the plants. In the evenings, the people of the house liked to watch the gardeners, dressed in their aprons and carrying colourful watering cans, while they watered the gardens. This was a pleasure not restricted to the rich owners of the *yalı*s on the Bosphorus, Courmenin reporting that the sultan often promenaded round his garden and took pleasure in watching the gardeners at work.[154] The beauty of these gardens depended on the gardeners and choosing one was a matter of great importance, for it was essential to find a man with the requisite skill and experience.[155]

While the palaces and the *yalı*s all had gardens, they were by no means the only places in the city where gardens were found. Throughout the empire, mosque courtyards, too, provided a refuge for believers, not only to pray in but also to socialise in, and their gardens were often

[154] Courmenin, *Voiage*, p. 169. [155] Abdülaziz Bey, *Osmanlı*, p. 218.

27. Graveyard at Üsküdar, in Walsh, *Scenery of the Seven Churches*, between pp. 12 and 13.

rich with old and magnificent trees, such as the very stately and very pleasant tall cypresses and pines which John Covel saw in the mosque gardens near İzmir.[156] Graveyards were green spaces of tranquillity. The importance of green and its association with paradise encouraged the desire for trees and flowers in the graveyards. It is believed that any green plant over or on a grave will aid the soul of the dead by decreasing the effect of the first punishment after death before going to the other world. The old graveyards in Istanbul were in areas of the city with magnificent views, such as Eyüp, Zincirlikuyu or Aşiyan, and were also, like the mosque courtyards, the sites of the oldest trees.

Open spaces and pleasure gardens

The Turks' love of nature often took them beyond the confines of the garden and into the open spaces so popular for picnics and promenades. Such sites were everywhere, throughout the empire – along the corniche at İzmir, for example, a very popular area for walking and taking the air in the summer,[157] and in many places just outside Istanbul. The pleasure gardens were very popular with all sectors of society. They could be extensive or limited to the shade under a tree, such as the very large plane tree described by John Covel near the Edirne Kapı, which had 'a square green bank cast up about it, and a very noble fountain by. Here in sommer many come to take their *spasso* [promenading] and recreation in the shade (which that tree casts), sitting upon carpets with tobacco, coffee, and pure water'.[158]

Different areas had different reputations and offered different attractions. The pleasure garden of Yahya Efendi in Beşiktaş, for example, had many large trees, and people visited it for the beautiful birdsong of the golden orioles, blackbirds, horned owls, chaffinches, greenfinches, reedlings and nightingales.[159] In the white cherry and chestnut season, people went to Akbaba Sultan garden, a one-day journey from Istanbul, leaving from the Beykoz jetty in thousands of carriages.[160] The most famous was Kağıthane, known to the Europeans as Sweet Waters, at the tip of the Haliç (Golden Horn). Its uniqueness was such that even though there were other such locations, nothing since the foundation of the Ottoman state had ever come to match the pure pleasure of gathering together at Kağıthane. Not to have seen it meant not to have seen anything in the world, or so Evliya Çelebi's friend explained to him

[156] Covel, 'Diaries', p. 141. [157] Tavernier, *Voyages*, pp. 86–7.
[158] Covel, 'Diaries', p. 176. [159] Evliya Çelebi *Seyahatnamesi, I Kitap*, p. 192.
[160] Evliya Çelebi, *Seyahatnamesi, I Kitap*, p. 209.

when he inquired about the place. Intrigued, Evliya Çelebi decided to go there and see for himself. Forking out forty gold pieces, he bought two sheep and much food and drink, and set off to enjoy the pleasures of Kağıthane with a group of close friends. Erecting a tent near the water, they spent two months there. They were not alone, for the area was covered with around three thousand other tents, large and small, belonging to the high echelons of society, to the idle rich and the pampered sons of influential families. What little ground was left was covered by kilims and other coverings, seven thousand to eight thousand of them spread out on both sides of the river. The scene was such that it called to mind the encampment of a marauding army. At night, the whole area was illuminated by lanterns, candles and torches; music was played, fireworks were shot into the sky and guns and cannon were fired. On fine days, acrobats performed, magicians did their tricks and wrestlers demonstrated their skills. All enjoyed themselves watching the spectacles or amusing themselves in other ways, for 'there was no limit to the lovers and the beautiful fresh-faced youths swimming in the river at Kağıthane. The lover and the beloved wandered around together openly embracing. Day and night friends in every tent invited each other to great feasts and had deep conversations'.[161] Not everything about Kağıthane, however, was so idyllic, for the waters of Kağıthane concealed the roots of plants growing on the banks of the river which would entwine themselves around the feet of unsuspecting swimmers, who, exclaiming, rather impractically, 'the king of the sea has caught me', would drown in fear.[162]

During the Lale Devri, the Tulip Age in the early eighteenth century, Kağıthane was known as Sadabad and came to be associated particularly with enjoyment, beauty, relaxation and, to an extent, forbidden pastimes and behaviour that was not socially acceptable, but could be concealed in the natural expanses of Kağıthane. One of the most famous of Ottoman poets and court poet of Ahmed III, the sultan of the Lale Devri, was Nedim, whose poetry symbolised the luxury and beauty which the age sought to create, the laxity of morals, the praising of ease and the decadence of life. For him, the gardens of Sadabad were the ultimate haven, an escape to a life of beauty, ease and moral fluidity.

Let us give pleasure to this unhappy heart
Come, my waving cypress, let us go to Sadabad
The three-oared boat is ready at the jetty
Come, my waving cypress, let us go to Sadabad

[161] Evliya Çelebi, *(Gördüklerim)*, pp. 328–31.
[162] Evliya Çelebi, *Seyahatnamesi, I Kitap*, p. 207.

Let us laugh, let us dance, let us enjoy this world to the full
Let us drink the waters of paradise from the fresh fountain
Let us see the waters of life flowing from the dragon
Come, my waving cypress, let us go to Sadabad

Let us stroll beside the pond
Let us come and wonder at the sight of this heavenly mansion
Let us sing, let us recite
Come, my waving cypress, let us go to Sadabad

Let us take leave from your mother as if to go to Friday prayer
Let us for one day say farewell to cruel destiny
Let us wander to the jetty through the hidden streets
Come, my waving cypress, let us go to Sadabad

You, and I and a musician who excels
And, if you allow it, Nedim, who is madly in love
Let other friends be happily left behind for today
Come, my waving cypress, let us go to Sadabad.[163]

Nedim's poetry later came to be taken to represent all that was considered unacceptable about the age – the decline in standards of behaviour and the perceived moral crumbling of the state, against which the grandees revolted. Writing about sixty years later, Ahmed Cavid described Nevşehirli Damad İbrahim Paşa as a man who, while attending to his own amusements, allowed the flourishing of gangs, and who, while killing good warriors, was a friend of the infidels. This was a man who was addicted to the pleasures of Sadabad.[164] The extent to which Sadabad became associated with the corrupt and excessively liberal and lavish rule of Ahmed III was made clear by its destruction just after Mahmud I came to the throne, when he ordered public criers to announce to those who had pavilions there that they were to demolish them at once. Within three days of this order, all Sadabad was in ruins.[165] It was not, however, destroyed for ever, and its position as a foremost pleasure garden was to continue.

According to Balıkhane Nazırı Ali Rıza Bey, who wrote about Istanbul life at the turn of the nineteenth century, Kağıthane was popular because it was very near the city, and one could even walk there from Beyoğlu.[166] It was an area where there were streams, the sea, meadows and forests, in short, 'all the blessings of nature which people love'.[167]

[163] Köprülüzade Mehmet Fuat, *Eski Şairlerimiz. Divan Edebiyatı Antolojisi* (Istanbul, 1934), p. 575.
[164] Ahmed Cavid, *Hadîka*, p. 37. [165] Abdi, *Tarihi*, p. 45.
[166] Balıkhane Nazırı Ali Rıza Bey, *Hayatı*, pp. 110–16.
[167] Balıkhane Nazırı Ali Rıza Bey, *Bir Zamanlar İstanbul* (Istanbul, n.d.), p. 213.

28. Kağıthane, in Pardoe, *Beauties of the Bosphorus*, frontispiece.

The area was extensive, indeed sufficiently large to accommodate one-third of the population of Istanbul at any one time. A place particularly popular on Fridays, the weekly holiday, and Sundays, when it was generally frequented by Christians,[168] the Kağıthane season started from 9 March, after which it slowly became livelier and livelier, reaching a peak with the festival of *Hıdırellez* (6 May, popularly taken as marking the beginning of spring). Later, with the mowing of the meadows, the season began to decline and the days for excursions to Kağıthane passed.[169]

At nights, Kağıthane was a delight. People rowed under the full moon on the waters of Kağıthane, singers sang and musicians played. Sultan Abdülaziz used to spend the spring in Sadabad Kasrı (Sadabad Mansion) in Kağıthane in the first years of his reign. He made appearances among the crowd, who greeted him with cries of 'Long live the sultan!'[170] Indeed, part of the attraction of going to Kağıthane in the second half of the nineteenth century was to catch a glimpse of

[168] Balıkhane Nazırı Ali Rıza Bey, *Hayatı*, p. 111.
[169] Alus, *İstanbul*, p. 30.
[170] Balıkhane Nazırı Ali Rıza Bey, *Hayatı*, p. 112.

Abdülaziz, for the sultan liked to pass time there and held his Friday prayer there.[171] At this time, Kağıthane was the best of Istanbul's pleasure gardens. It was a Tower of Babel, where you could find characters 'of all kinds and all varieties, from every social class, from every nation and from every type'.[172] It was packed with people and entertainment.

The arbours of saplings thatched with dried boughs follow the curve of the river; the picnic parties spread rugs or matting on the grass, partaking strange meats while masters of pipe and drum enchant their ears; then groups of Turkish ladies, in gay silks, dot the sward like tulips; then itinerant venders of fruit, of sweets, of nuts, of icecream, do hawk about their wares; then fortune-tellers, mountebanks, bear tamers, dancers, Punch and Judy shows may be seen; boats pass and repass on the river like carriages on the Corso. Most of them are *sandal*s of the smarter kind. But once in a while the most elegant craft in the world skims into sight – a three-oared caïque, with a piece of embroidered velvet, whose corner tassels trail in the water, thrown over the little deck behind the seat. The *kaïkji*s [boatmen] are handsome fellows, in fuller white cotton knickerbockers than you can imagine, in white stockings, in shirts of crinkly Broussa gauze and short sleeveless jackets embroidered with gold.[173]

Departure from Kağıthane offered quite a spectacle in itself, and foreigners and embassy staff would even come in rowing boats to watch.[174] It was not just foreigners who enjoyed this performance. Many women and children from the circles of the population who could not go to Kağıthane followed it from the jetties of Fener, Ayakapısı and Cibali. Here they squatted down on their heels and munched on the stale food of the most common pedlars while they followed the spectacle. Where they sat was always filthy with heaps of rubbish, and dogs sniffing, rummaging about and snarling at each other. These alternative entertainment areas were commonly known as 'Bitli Kağıthane', lice-ridden or lousy Kağıthane.[175]

Kağıthane, or Sadabad, was in many ways the quintessential pleasure garden. It symbolised the place of pleasures, enjoyment and ease, sometimes tinged with a slight whiff of disapproval as ease melted into sloth; it was pleasure garden par excellence. It was 'Anatolia's Sadabad' which the early twentieth-century writer Refik Halit Karay described in his short story *The Peach Orchards*, about a small Anatolian town to which a troublesome official had been exiled by Abdülhamid II. Initially enthusiastic, the official had sought to do his job effectively and had been horrified by the behaviour of his colleagues, who, in the heat of the

171 Balıkhane Nazırı Ali Rıza Bey, *İstanbul*, p. 203. 172 Alus, *İstanbul*, p. 29.
173 Dwight, *Constantinople*, pp. 145–6. 174 Balıkhane Nazırı Ali Rıza Bey, *İstanbul*, p. 115.
175 Balıkhane Nazırı Ali Rıza Bey, *İstanbul*, p. 116.

summer, set off on donkeys from the office early in the morning for the peach orchards located outside the town. They passed the day there, lying in the cool under the trees before mounting their donkeys and returning in the early evening. Incensed, the official would watch the dust cloud each day as the donkeys trotted slowly back and forth. By the end of the story, the official, too, would mount his donkey and pass the long, hot summer days under the branches of the peach trees. For

> here was Anatolia's Sadabad. As in the original Sadabad, musical instruments played continuously, professional dancers performed, and poetry was read and written. Most of the liquor-prone administrators and officials were poets. They wrote poems in the style of Nedim, discussed meter and mysticism, and talked about the whirling dervishes and other mystic orders. Their lives passed sweetly in talk and music. These pleasure-loving officials refrained from meddling in things which would bring them trouble. They virtually made the town their own, put up houses, opened pools and built arbours. Naturally, most of these were men whom the previous ruler had not regarded favourably and had been sent here as punishment. Without hope of promotion, they attached no importance to official matters and looked to their own amusement.[176]

Despite Karay's somewhat scornful representation of 'Anatolia's Sadabad', such places were central to the lives of the people. There were many pleasure gardens in Istanbul. There were places on the islands, Büyükada and Heybeliada, others on the Anatolian side, in Fenerbahçe, Kalamış, Haydarpaşa and Çamlıca. Çamlıca was popular among the upper elements of society, where Fazıl Mustafa Paşa, the brother of Khedive Ismail of Egypt, known as 'Mısırlı', the Egyptian, used to host parties. The first garden party and masquerade were given during the reign of Sultan Abdülaziz in his mansion at Çamlıca. It was to Çamlıca that 'connoisseurs of pleasure' came each year from Aksaray and Küçük Pazar. On one occasasion, the *valide sultan*, the mother of Mahmud II, seeing them there, asked who they were. On being told that they were the people who came from Aksaray and Küçük Pazar to enjoy themselves there for a couple of days each year, she invited them to appear before her. They danced for her and as a reward she ordered the *bostancıbaşı* to provide them with meat, rice and other foodstuffs to enable them to stay a few days longer.[177] Istanbul craftsmen frequented the beautiful meadows of Hünkar İskelesi, where they relaxed by the water. Here they set up tents and spread out carpets, danced and stretched out on the green grass, turning the whole place into a festive encampment.[178]

[176] Refik Halit Karay, 'The peach orchards', in Fahir İz (trans. and ed.), *An Anthology of Modern Turkish Short Stories* (Minneapolis and Chicago, 1978), pp. 78–86.

[177] Cabi, *Târihi*, I, p. 540. [178] Hovhannesyan, *Payitaht*, p. 58.

29. Going on an excursion, in Amicis, *Constantinople*, p. 237.

30. Fenerbahçe, in Salih Erimez, *Tarihten Çizgiler* (Istanbul, 1941), [p. 23].

Outside Istanbul, there were pleasure gardens at Kağıthane, Kasımpaşa, Makriköy (modern Bakırköy) and Ayastefanos (modern Yeşilköy), and along the Bosphorus there were popular spots at Kavacık and Kanlıca, around Beykoz and in the meadows of Küçüksu and Göksu. Women went about in their carriages at the famous Göksu and Küçüksu pleasure gardens. Later, the carriage excursions came to be replaced by boat trips taken by women with parasols in multi-coloured *ferace*s and gorgeous gowns, and men dressed in the latest fashions.[179] Küçüksu Köşkü was built there for Sultan Mahmud I. Sultan Abdülmecid later had it replaced by another pavilion, built for him by Nigosos Balyan, a member of the Balyan family of architects, another member of which, Karabet Balyan, built Dolmabahçe palace. On the European side, there were other places along the Bosphorus, at Sarıyer, Tarabya, Bebek, and in Beşiktaş, Ihlamur, and Zincirlikuyu.[180] It was to such places along the shores of Bosphorus, adorned with mansions, that the populace of Istanbul flocked in spring and summer, to promenade and to amuse themselves, to see and to be seen,[181] to eat, drink, sing and generally disport themselves.[182] Such places were also wonderful sources of gossip. All tongues wagged about the famous courtesan Rana, as she was rowed in her boat along the Bosphorus to the famous pleasure garden Kalender, much frequented by the rich. This was a place where 'the aristocratic ladies, the wives of famous men, the sons of *paşa*s and the spendthrift heirs of rich men, satisfied their need to see and be seen by each other … and to gossip'.[183]

Promenading and picnicking was not restricted to dry land. At night, especially when there was a full moon, the Bosphorus became awash with little boats, as people rowed out onto the waters from their *yalı*s. Sometimes special, large boats were hired for parties to float up and down the Bosphorus, accompanied by singers and musicians, and to admire the full moon. On these occasions, the Bosphorus was bathed in the sound of music coming from the boats of the many different groups. 'When they played or sang very beautiful songs, the musical instruments on the nearby boats immediately fell silent and people listened until they had finished. There were no inappropriate cries of "well done", "God bless you" or "bravo". Everyone listened politely and with pleasure. They watched, the instruments were played and they sang

179 Balıkhane Nazırı Ali Rıza Bey, *Hayatı*, p. 125. 180 Abdülaziz Bey, *Osmanlı*, pp. 297–8.
181 Balıkhane Nazırı Ali Rıza Bey, *Hayatı*, pp. 119–33.
182 Abdülaziz Bey, *Osmanlı*, pp. 291–8; Balıkhane Nazırı Ali Rıza Bey, *İstanbul*, pp. 200–18.
183 Refi' Cevad Ulunay, *Eski İstanbul Yosmaları* (Istanbul, n.d.), p. 10.

songs'.[184] On these nights the water was so crowded that Abdülaziz Bey related, 'I have heard from those who saw it with their own eyes that the boats which rode out at full moon to the point between Kayalar and Kandilli, which is the narrowest point between the two shores, so filled the Bosphorus that it was possible to cross it by jumping from one boat to the other'.[185]

Meals of fresh fish from the Bosphorus, stuffed lamb, fresh vegetables and *börek*, summer desserts, ice cream, sherbets and *meze*s, were prepared for these night-time excursions. They were eaten not on the boats but at well-known pleasure gardens along the Bosphorus, at İç Göksu, Paşa Bahçesi and Kalender, frequented by the upper echelons of society.

Display was an important aspect of the pleasure gardens, the seeing and the being seen. For some, this was paramount, and any amount of discomfort was to be endured in order to promenade. Fenerbahçe, for example, was practically invisible in the summer for the clouds of dust that rose over it, despite the municipality's constant watering of the roads. In less than ten minutes, the ground which had been wetted was once again dry, and a dust haze blotted out the horizon. Dust stung the eyes, blinding the promenaders, whose teeth crunched constantly on the little gritty particles. It even worked its way through into people's underwear. 'Dust, dust, dust', remarked Sermet Muhtar Alus, who was amazed by the astonishing resistance to these typhoons of dust displayed by all those who frequented the place, from the upper echelons of society to the lowest. 'If Monsieur Pasteur were alive and had a bird's eye view of this spectacle for just a second, he would drop dead on the spot!'[186]

Alus was quite clearly not a fan of promenading, regarding not merely the activity itself but even the journey to a pleasure garden as a thoroughly ghastly ordeal. The expedition to Kayışdağı on the Anatolian side of the Bosphorus, a popular picnic site nearer the city than the more beautiful Alemdağı, was undertaken

> engulfed in dust, in a carriage thrown about over rocks and stones, juddering and shuddering, hopping and lurching. Part of the journey is uphill. The animals' tongues hang out, the drivers lead the horses, their chests bare, their eyes weeping from the dust … the elderly female passenger who has had a stroke thinking of getting home and putting her feet in hot water, the gentleman wetting his handkerchief and putting it on his head, the middle-aged woman talking about the stiff neck she has got from the draught she is in, the other woman complaining that 'all the kohl round my eyes is running', the younger man

[184] Abdülaziz Bey, *Osmanlı*, pp. 290–1.
[185] Abdülaziz Bey, *Osmanlı*, p. 290. [186] Alus, *İstanbul*, p. 44.

stretching his hand into the basket and shoving a *yalancı dolma* [grape-leaves stuffed with rice and stewed with oil] into his mouth, and exclaiming 'the oil in this food is bitter', the youngest woman right at the back of the carriage showing a pink handkerchief signifying 'my heart is yours' to the young man in the carriage behind which almost seems to be following them, completely exhausted and after great difficulty they arrive under the trees of Kayışdağı. Each person who totters to a place under these trees is as a patient who has come out of hospital and is returning home to convalesce.[187]

Despite any hardships endured in reaching them, the pleasure gardens offered women in the nineteenth century more freedom than they had ever had before. Although women were not allowed to promenade in places where men went, or were only allowed to have excursions on certain days during the reign of Mahmud II, this began to change under the rule of his successor Abdülmecid.[188] Women now began to appear in public much more and to take a more conspicuous role in social life. But, although allowed out in a way unheard of in earlier centuries, they were still very restricted when it came to communication with members of the opposite sex. Women and men thus resorted to a coded language.

A parasol in the rowing boat! It explains what the person wants to say. For example, if it is bent a little to one side, it means 'I am annoyed with you', if it is bent over further, 'I am really angry', if it completely covers the face, it means 'you will not see my face again', 'I don't want to see you, have you still not understood?', if it swings hard from right to left, it signifies 'don't stay, pass by', 'return, go', if it falls slightly to the front, it is in the place of a greeting, 'welcome, sir', if it falls a lot, 'my heart has beaten again', if it goes to the back, it means 'oh!', if it leans all the way over backwards, 'what a state I am in, see me and have pity!', if it is held to the side, 'oh, how fine, what happiness this is!', if it is opened and closed, it means 'not tonight, tomorrow', if it is closed and stays so, 'we will make an appointment for the following day'.[189]

With all this freedom, women were becoming obstreperous, at least in the eyes of some of the male members of Ottoman society. Among them was the sultan Abdülmecid, who did not approve of the behaviour of the women of his family, who, like many others, so enjoyed the promenades.[190] 'My daughters', he noted with much displeasure, 'have been going around at night in the full moon. No daughter of mine will wander around under the full moon at night. I will repudiate them. The behaviour of these rogues [i.e. the men who allowed this

[187] Alus, *İstanbul*, p. 85. [188] Balıkhane Nazırı Ali Rıza Bey, *İstanbul*, p. 131.
[189] Ahmet Rasim, *Fuhş-i Atik*, p. 201. For his account of coded language in general, see pp. 198–204.
[190] Leyla (Saz) Hanımefendi, *Harem*, pp. 145–9.

behaviour] is a disgrace'.[191] Abdülmecid promptly removed his son-in-laws from their government posts as a punishment for their inability to control their wives.[192] Some royal son-in-laws certainly did lose control, for just after the 1908 Revolution, two of the daughters of Murad V, Hatice Sultan and Fehime Sultan, divorced their husbands and married men they had seen and liked in the pleasure gardens.[193]

For some, the changes of the *Tanzimat*, the period of reform which began in 1839, and the relative emancipation of women, encouraged a view that they were more disreputable than they had been in the past. The fact that women could now promenade with men in the pleasure gardens gave rise, according to Ali Rıza Bey, to 'a natural instinct, that is men being carried away by the new trend of looking at and enjoying looking at women, and women at men'.[194] This situation led to many incidents contrary to public morality.[195] In 1861, the government published a document setting out what was, and what was not, acceptable, and listing the punishments for behaviour that transgressed the law. 'It is an old tradition', the document ran, 'for the people to go to pleasure gardens. It is natural that the government will expect those who go to adopt an honourable and seemly conduct. It is unacceptable for people who frequent such places to behave in any other manner, or act in any way against the laws of the state'.[196] Women and men could not sit together. Certain areas were only open to women on certain days, others were out of bounds for Muslim women. It was forbidden to pass any kind of sexual comment directed at women, or to drink alcohol. Those who drank or caused any kind of affray would be punished. These rules applied to all, without exception.[197]

In fact, the presence of women, which was so to disturb Abdülmecid in the second half of the nineteenth century, was a source of consternation to many much earlier. The author of the eighteenth-century *Risale-i Garibe* heartily disapproved of those men who allowed their women, faces unveiled, to wander about in boats during the cherry season.[198] Even worse were those 'pimps', a word he used liberally and apparently applied to a high percentage of the male population of Istanbul, who actually accompanied their wives and daughters on pleasure jaunts, going with

[191] Ahmed Cevdet Paşa, *Ma'rûzât*, p. 13. [192] Ahmed Cevdet Paşa, *Ma'rûzât*, p. 13.
[193] Nahid Sırrı Örik, *Bilinmeyen Yaşamlarıyla Saraylılar*, ed. Alpay Kabacalı (Istanbul, 2006), p. 37.
[194] Balıkhane Nazırı Ali Rıza Bey, *Hayatı*, pp. 131–2.
[195] Balıkhane Nazırı Ali Rıza Bey, *Hayatı*, p. 132.
[196] Balıkhane Nazırı Ali Rıza Bey, *İstanbul*, pp. 218–19.
[197] Balıkhane Nazırı Ali Rıza Bey, *İstanbul*, pp. 218–19. [198] Develi, *Risale-i Garibe*, p. 36.

them in the summer to Kağıthane or to buy candyfloss at the jetties, or those 'donkeys' who went with them at grape time to the Bayram Paşa garden.[199]

Women going to pleasure gardens led, in 1752, to complaints being made to the sultan, who in turn ordered the *bostancıbaşı* to look into the matter. It appeared that with the beginning of spring, women were going by carriage from Üsküdar to Kısıklı, Bulgurlu, Çamlıca and Nerdübanlı. Others were going from Beykoz to Tokat, Akbaba, Derseki and Yuşa, for pleasure and promenading. But they were not comporting themselves appropriately and this was causing the abandonment of restraint and many shameful acts. In consequence, women were banned from going to such places, either by carriage or by any other means, and the *bostancıbaşı* was warned to keep the situation under constant scrutiny.[200]

It was not just women whose behaviour might be open to question in the pleasure gardens. Such places were danger zones of disorder, for it was here that men would drink and bring dancing girls. There was the ever-present danger of unruliness, socially unacceptable behaviour or violence, much harder to detect and control in these wide open spaces than in the confines of the city streets and drinking houses. Fighting could be fatal, as it was in 1597 when a fight broke out at Çizmeci Tekkesi, a favourite pleasure ground for people from Tophane and Galata, who gathered there to talk and drink wine. In the fight, more than twenty people were injured and three people died on the spot, two dying later as a result of their injuries.[201] Fighting was also a problem for the gardeners of a garden belonging to the *vakıf* of Selim II, who in 1583 petitioned the sultan Murad III over a second gate which had been opened into the garden. As a result, cattle dealers and similar lowlifes had begun to come into the garden to drink wine and take the vegetables without paying. There were many fights and all this was very damaging to the *vakıf*. If the new gate was not closed, the gardeners argued, there would be more trouble. The sultan accepted the petition and ordered the *subaşı* to close the gate.[202]

Far worse could occur in the remoter reaches of the pleasure gardens. In 1809, a group of women, including the wives, daughters and concubines of important officials, set off in three carriages, accompanied by the carriage drivers, to pick cherries at an orchard in Üsküdar. When they were there, a group of ruffians appeared, beat the drivers senseless and

199 Develi, *Risale-i Garibe*, p. 24.
200 Ahmet Refik, *Hicri On İkinci Asırda*, pp. 174–5, *hüküm* 210.
201 Selaniki, *Tarih*, II, p. 677.
202 Ülker, *Emir Defteri*, p. 69, facsimile p. 42, *hüküm* 133.

31. Dancer at pleasure ground, in Erimez, *Tarihten Çizgiler*, [p. 19].

seized the women. Keeping them all in the orchard overnight, they raped them. The women decided among themselves to keep what had happened secret. They were, however, staying in the house of the wife of the ex-harbour master Kaşorti Bey who, as she was ill, had not gone with them and was much alarmed when they did not return that evening. She extracted some information about the rapes from the children who were with them and the female slaves. Gradually the whole story came out. One of the women who was newly married was divorced by her husband and promptly went mad. An investigation was begun among the riff-raff in Üsküdar. They denied the rapes, saying that they had many, good prostitutes available so had no need to do this. The result of the investigation drew a blank and no culprits were found.[203]

Such dramatic events, as well as more minor incidents – brawling, drinking or merely lax morality – meant that the security of such areas was taken very seriously. It was extremely important to the sultans that the population be able to enjoy themselves in the pleasure gardens, but

[203] Cabi, *Târihi*, I, pp. 476–7.

that they do so within limits and while behaving appropriately, as the *bostancıbaşı* noted during the brief period of Alemdar Mustafa Paşa's control at the beginning of Mahmud II's reign.[204] Bad behaviour led to stern warnings about unacceptable conduct, as well as strict measures that reduced the popularity of certain disreputable locations. The once very fashionable İncir Köyü, on the Anatolian side of the Bosphorus, lost its former popularity after the *bostancıbaşı* took firm measures as a result of the frequent disgraceful conduct and immoral goings-on there.[205]

Such conduct could bring severe punishment. In the early nineteenth century, Çamlıca was a very popular venue, especially among the non-Muslims, who used to hire summer houses or go and visit family and friends there. Such a free-and-easy atmosphere developed that non-Muslim men were able to enjoy themselves under the full moon with their wives until very late at night, the women uncovered and the sexes mixed. This was apparently tolerable, as long as no scene was made. But then certain non-Muslims started to take prostitutes there. On one occasion, a couple of non-Muslim men brought a prostitute, telling those who asked who she was that she was the wife of one of them. Everybody knew full well, however, what she was. Retribution was swift, the man who claimed that she was his wife receiving six hundred blows and being fined two hundred and fifty *kuruş*. The following day, women were banned from being present in such places after a certain hour at night.[206]

Womanisers like Nuri Bey, one of the sons of rich and influential fathers who were to be the target of ridicule and disdain in so many novels of the late nineteenth century, were warned when their behaviour went beyond the bounds of propriety. Nuri Bey's habit of sitting very close to women in the pleasure gardens drew the attention and disapproval of the *bostancıbaşı*, who warned him, saying, 'if men were to sit near your women, you would no doubt be deeply indignant. When gentlemen like you behave like this, what can be said to ruffians and disreputable men?' Nuri Bey was later exiled to a post outside Istanbul for his unacceptable conduct.[207]

Despite, or because of, such moral laxity, and the relative freedom which the open spaces offered to the population, the pleasure gardens were always well frequented. At the hub of Ottoman social fabric, they were places of entertainment, relaxation, secret communication and

[204] Cabi, *Târihi*, I, p. 210. [205] Hovhannesyan, *Payitaht*, pp. 59–60.
[206] Cabi, *Târihi*, I, p. 210. [207] Cabi, *Târihi*, II, pp. 958–9.

32. Separation between the sexes, in Erimez, *Tarihten Çizgiler*, [p. 39].

blatant social display. Harder to police than the city itself, they were spaces which gave an opportunity for the stretching of the often strict moral code which restricted male–female communication, and which provided a greater laxity for socialising in general. They were, throughout the life of the empire, an essential element of everyday life.

The impact of Europe

Over the centuries, European ideas about gardens came more and more to influence Ottoman concepts. The effects of this can be seen as early as the Lale Devri, which began in 1718. The first Ottoman ambassador to France, Yirmisekiz Mehmed Çelebi, who was sent to Paris in 1720, wrote extensively about the gardens in France. Charmed by being presented with spring flowers such as violets and hyacinths wherever he stayed as he travelled from Toulon to Paris,[208] he was also very taken by the gardens at Bordeaux castle, whose commander apparently had a great love of flowers, for he had grown a mass of Cretan tulips from seed.[209] Saint-Cloud, to which he was invited by the Duc d'Orleans, had a very good garden, where fountains shot columns of water high up into the air, which, catching the reflections of the sunlight, created rainbows. Everywhere there were little water spouts in the shape of dragons' mouths, which, when they flowed, were a sight to behold.[210] Yirmisekiz Mehmed Çelebi also visited the gardens of Versailles, which he toured in a two-wheeled open carriage,[211] and those of Marly, which prompted him to comment that 'the charming subtlety of the saying "the worldly prison of the faithful is the paradise of the infidels" became apparent'.[212] It was in this period that the grand vezir of Ahmed III, Nevşehirli Damad İbrahim Paşa, built in two months a palace with fountains at Kağıthane.[213]

The impact and influence of European gardens on Ottoman taste can be seen clearly in the wall decorations of the room of Selim III's mother in Topkapı palace, which dates to the end of the eighteenth century. By the nineteenth century, this influence was not limited to paintings, but was now very much in application. The nineteenth-century palaces built in European style were embellished with European-style gardens, as is evident in the contrast between those of Dolmabahçe palace and those of Topkapı. Such influence was not limited to the palaces, but was apparent, too, in the gardens of the rich.

The concept of open space in the city changed also, as did ideas on what a city should look like. The sultan, the government and the mayors of Istanbul were staunch supporters of such changes, which imitated European models,[214] and the second half of the nineteenth century, in particular, saw a considerable drive to modernise Ottoman cities, especially, of course, Istanbul. One feature of this modernisation was the introduction of public parks within the city. Abdülhamid II hired the famous French city planner, Joseph Antoine Bouvard (1840–1920), then inspector general of the architectural department of the city of Paris, to redesign the old city. Bouvard's plans, based firmly on a very European understanding of the city, included a new Beyazıt square and

[208] Şevket Rado (ed.), *Yirmisekiz Mehmet Çelebi'nin Fransa Seyahatnamesi* (Istanbul, 1970), p. 26.
[209] Rado, *Yirmisekiz*, p. 26. [210] Rado, *Yirmisekiz*, pp. 58–60.
[211] Rado, *Yirmisekiz*, pp. 62–4. [212] Rado, *Yirmisekiz*, p. 66.
[213] Hovhannesyan, *Payitaht*, p. 34.
[214] Zeynep Çelik, *The Remaking of Istanbul. Portrait of an Ottoman City in the Nineteenth Century* (Berkeley, Los Angeles, London, 1993), pp. 52–3.

French-style parks which dominated the entire space. Although very much liked by the Ottoman bureaucracy, the necessary funds could not be found, and Bouvard's plan, like various other projects proposed by European city planners, remained unimplemented.[215]

Having a park within the city was considered a symbol of European lifestyle. 'If you go through any European city small or large', wrote Şerafeddin Mağmumi, a doctor and member of the Committee of Union and Progress, when describing the Pencio Garden in Rome at the end of the nineteenth century, 'you will certainly see several such public parks, gardens and woods. The parks and gardens are not merely for the provision of pleasure but health and vitality. The people go in for free, wander about and enjoy themselves. Their children, toddlers and teenagers come and play'.[216] The first parks were established within the more Europeanised parts of the city, in Taksim and Tepebaşı. To ensure order and discourage those whose presence was unwanted, an entrance fee was charged for the parks there, which were mostly frequented by the Levantine and foreign population of the city. The very European flavour of such public parks is apparent in Mrs Brassey's account of the public garden that she went to after landing at Tophane. Here, 'the band was playing, and all the European rank and fashion of Constantinople were assembled'.[217] Another park was laid out at Çamlıca, due largely to the initiative, not this time of the sultan, but of another imperial figure, the brother of the khedive of Egypt who owned a mansion there.

After the Young Turk Revolution in 1908, the approach to establishing parks became more egalitarian. Several were opened in other parts of the city and entrance was free. Cemil Paşa (Topuzlu), mayor of Istanbul before the First World War, a well-known doctor and the sultan's private physician, who had been educated in France, was an ardent supporter of such public parks. 'There were', he explained in his memoirs, 'no public gardens in which the people could get some fresh air. Since entrance to the parks such as Tepebaşı and Taksim was not free, poor people were unable to receive any benefit from them. The garden established in Çamlıca at Üsküdar was in ruins and was only good for grazing sheep'.[218] Şerafeddin Mağmumi, too, complained about the lack of any public garden for which entrance was free, obliging the

[215] Çelik, *Istanbul*, pp. 110–25.

[216] Quoted in Baki Asiltürk, *Osmanlı Seyyahlarının Gözüyle Avrupa* (Istanbul, 2000), p. 547; Şerafeddin Mağmumi, *Bir Osmanlı Doktorunun Seyahat Anıları, Avrupa Seyahat Hatıraları*, ed. Nazım H. Polat and Harid Fedai (Istanbul, 2008), pp. 289–90.

[217] Brassey *Sunshine*, p. 52.

[218] Topuzlu, *Hatıralarım*, pp. 114–15.

people of Istanbul to go to the graveyards of Edirne Kapı and Karacaahmet in order to promenade and get fresh air.[219] Motivated largely by concerns for public health, 'because my profession was that of a doctor', Cemil Paşa's first thought when he became mayor was 'to construct gardens for the people and especially the children, to enable them to take the air'.[220] With pressure from Cemal and Talat Paşas, two of the key political figures of the era, Cemil Paşa managed to persuade the sultan to donate land belonging to Topkapı palace for the establishment of a public park. This was Gülhane park, in old Istanbul, the traditional, conservative and Muslim-dominated quarter of the city.

Cemil Paşa thus provided the ordinary people with a park, and even with a French designer, for it was the French landscape gardener Monsieur Deruvan, already in Istanbul as head gardener at the palace, who laid out Gülhane park. Not only was the designer French, but the trees were French, too. Approximately twenty thousand different species of trees were imported from France and planted in the garden.[221] In addition to these French features, Cemil Paşa also introduced novelties in the park, such as a stage for musical performances by military bands on Fridays and Sundays, sandpits for children and puppet shows. In two years, the municipality spent six thousand gold coins on the park.[222]

But for all the novelty, the traditional values still had to be accommodated. Parks might become a feature of Istanbul, but mixing of the sexes was still some way off, as Mrs Brassey noted. 'There were some public gardens opened the other day, to which the Turkish ladies went with their husbands. This was speedily stopped by imperial edict'.[223] Her experience was shared some years later by Cemil Paşa.

> On the day [they opened the Gülhane park] men and women wandered round it together. Enver Paşa, who was very conservative, did not like it. The next day he informed me in a fiercely worded memorandum that I must forbid women going into the park. I went to the war ministry to see Enver Paşa about this. He was sitting beside Cemal Paşa. I informed him that I could not carry out his wishes. Immediately Cemal Paşa intervened. 'Since Cemil Paşa is thinking of women taking the air, appoint a separate day especially for them. We can assure you that men and women will go into the park together in the future', he said. One month later Cemal Paşa fulfilled his promise. But I then began to receive unsigned letters full of insults from various conservative people. If we compare the thought of that period with our mentality today [referring to the 1950s] it is possible to see with pleasure and pride the great difference between them.[224]

[219] Quoted in Asiltürk, *Avrupa*, p. 547. [220] Topuzlu, *Hatıralarım*, p. 132.
[221] Topuzlu, *Hatıralarım*, pp. 130–1. [222] Topuzlu, *Hatıralarım*, p. 137.
[223] Brassey, *Sunshine*, p. 69. [224] Topuzlu, *Hatıralarım*, p. 136.

While gardens, open spaces and the city parks of the nineteenth century offered the populace a pleasure zone in which to disport themselves, such recreation was not restricted to the outdoors, for there was another location frequented by one and all which was central to the life of every citizen throughout Istanbul's existence as Ottoman capital, and that was the public baths.

7 The *hamam*

> If the Western world boasts of her grand and magnificent buildings such as those in Washington, Philadelphia, and New York, Turkey also boasts of her baths, which are well known throughout the world. Baths are some of the greatest institutions in the Turkish Empire.[1]

Perhaps one of the most important axes of social life in Istanbul was the *hamam*. Far more than merely a place of washing, the *hamam* provided men and, in particular, women with a social space where many of the important rituals of life took place. It enabled them to be clean in the way they wished, providing services that made it the equivalent of a modern beauty salon and health spa all rolled into one. It was where neighbours and friends could meet and socialise, enabling women, whose social relations were more limited than those of men, to mix with women not from their immediate family circle. There, after careful scrutiny, they could choose the brides for their sons and brothers; brides were washed before their weddings; and babies were taken for ablutions in their first outing, forty days after their birth. A place of chitchat, gossip and political grumbling, it was also a multi-ethnic and multi-religious space, a quintessential element in the lives of the people of the city, without which their everyday existence would have been inconceivable.

It is hardly surprising, therefore, that the *hamam*, along with a mosque and a market, was one of the first buildings erected by the Ottoman sultans after the conquest of any urban space. Mehmed II ordered the construction of splendid and costly baths shortly after his conquest of Constantinople, as part of his plan for the building up and beautifying of the city, 'for the benefit and needs and comfort of the inhabitants'.[2] If any town lacked a *hamam*, this absence was something exceptional and needed explanation. Evliya Çelebi attributed the absence of a *hamam* either to the backwardness of the town[3] or to the presence of a Christian

[1] Basmajean, *Life*, pp. 148–9. [2] Kritoboulos, *History*, 55, p. 105.
[3] Robert Dankoff, *An Ottoman Mentality. The World of Evliya Çelebi*, with an afterword by Gottfried Hagen (Leiden and Boston, 2004), p. 50.

majority. The town of Pınarhisar in Bulgaria thus had only one small *hamam*, because the majority of the population was Christian and therefore did not wash, while the Muslim population of the town had baths in their houses and did not need a public bath.[4]

Istanbul had many *hamam*s, indeed an infinite number according to Bassano.[5] Schweigger talks about the existence of more than 150 *hamams* in the city in the late 1570s,[6] du Fresne-Canaye more than 100 in 1573,[7] while Domenico mentions more than 220.[8] In the following century, Sandys noted that every main mosque in Istanbul had a bath attached to it,[9] a view reiterated by Bon in the same period.[10] Evliya Çelebi, whose figures are notoriously unreliable, listed by name 124 *hamam*s in the city[11] and gives a figure of 151 for those belonging to *vakıf*s, of which most were double *hamam*s, making a total of 302, according to his calculations. This, he notes, is a small number for such a large city, but adds there were 14,536 private *hamam*s belonging to the vezirs and the richer elements of society. He further notes that while he was away from the city, a further 17 *hamam*s were built.[12] De la Croix, writing in 1671, refers to more than 60 *hamams* in the city.[13] The Ottoman Armenian İnciciyan referred to 48 *hamam*s in Topkapı palace alone at the end of the eighteenth century,[14] and Lacroix gave a figure of 300 for Istanbul around the 1830s.[15]

Many *hamam*s were *vakıf* property, for they had the twofold advantage of religious purpose and economic viability. A *hamam* performed an important religious function by providing the population with a place in which to wash. Cleanliness was an essential element in Ottoman society. It had religious significance and ablution formed, and forms, an integral part of the ritual of prayer. As the popular Turkish saying puts it, 'cleanliness comes from belief'. It was also a guaranteed money-spinner, for its centrality in the life of the city ensured its constant use. An important part of many *vakıf* holdings, it was integral to the economic life of the city, giving employment and stimulating trade in related services and in the production of needed commodities and materials. Both men and women worked in the *hamam*s in various capacities: as *tellak*s (bath attendants), *natır*s (attendants in a women's bath), porters, casual labourers and stokers in the boiler rooms. These men and women worked under the

4 Dankoff, *Mentality*, p. 69. 5 Bassano, *Costumi*, f. 2v.
6 Schweigger, *Ein newe Reyssbeschreibung*, p. 116. 7 Fresne-Canaye, *Voyage*, p. 93.
8 Domenico, *Istanbul*, p. 2. 9 Sandys, *Travailes*, p. 25. 10 Bon, *Description*, p. 182.
11 Yüksel Yoldaş-Demircanlı, *İstanbul Mimârisi İçin Kaynak Olarak Evliya Çelebi Seyâhatnâmesi* (Istanbul, n.d.), pp. 376–428.
12 Evliya Çelebi, *Seyahatnamesi, I Kitap*, pp. 138, 136–7.
13 De la Croix, *Mémoires*, I, 3rd letter, p. 132. 14 İnciciyan, *İstanbul*, p. 23.
15 Lacroix, *Guide*, p. 22.

authority of the bath-keepers, female in the case of the women's *hamams* and male for the men's. The bath-keepers ran the baths and were figures of great authority, held in high esteem by those working there and to whom they referred 'as if to a judge'.[16] Many people found employment in the *hamams*, the Bey *hamam* in Beyoğlu in Istanbul, for example, employing fourteen people, five *tellaks*, three *natırs*, one casual labourer, one stoker and four porters, according to a mid-seventeenth-century court register.[17] Evliya Çelebi referred to two thousand *tellaks* and one thousand *natırs* working in the *vakıf hamams*.[18]

Apart from employment within the *hamam* itself, the *hamam* sector created demand for commodities such as towels, *hamam* bowls, *peştemal* (cloth used for covering the body), special clogs used in the *hamam* which were often beautifully ornamented, and clay which was sold in the *hamam* to be used by both women and men for softening skin, removing dead skin and dandruff, cleaning grease from the skin and opening the pores.[19] Ash from the stokeholes was used to produce ink and was in great demand. In consequence ownership of the ash could become a matter of dispute. According to early eighteenth-century legal rulings, in two cases of dispute between a bath-keeper, who rented the *hamam*, and the administrator of a *vakıf* which owned the *hamam* in question, ownership of the ash was granted to the bath-keeper.[20] The *hamams* also stimulated other, related trades. Evliya Çelebi, for example, refers to five hundred launderers working in three hundred laundries, and twenty people working in ten shops specialising in the removal of spots.[21]

The social importance of the *hamam* meant that its regulation was a matter of significance for the state, which interested itself in regulating the affairs of the *hamam* and in ensuring its efficient and hygienic running. A quintessential place of ablution, it was important that the *hamam* itself be kept clean. In the early sixteenth century, Selim I issued orders that officers were to check that the bath-keepers kept their baths clean and hot, and the water warm. The *tellaks* were to work quickly and to be expert in shaving heads, and the razors they used were to be sharp. The *natırs* were to keep the *peştemals* clean. Those who did not abide by these orders were

16 Gelibolulu Mustafa Ali, *Mevâıdün*, pp. 355–6.
17 Reşad Ekrem Koçu, 'Bey Hamamı', in Reşad Ekrem Koçu (ed.), *İstanbul Ansiklopedisi* (Istanbul, 1961), V, pp. 2637–8.
18 Evliya Çelebi, *Seyahatnamesi, I Kitap*, pp. 290–1.
19 Abdülaziz Bey, *Osmanlı*, p. 300. This is presumably the same substance referred to by Sandys, *Travailes*, p. 54.
20 Abdürrahim Efendi Menteşzade, *Fetâvâ-yı Abdürrahim Efendi, I-II* (Istanbul, 1827), II, pp. 551, 553–4, quoted in Tahsin Özcan, *Fetvalar Işığında Osmanlı Esnafı* (Istanbul, 2003), p. 222.
21 Evliya Çelebi, *Seyahatnamesi, I Kitap*, p. 290–1.

to be heavily punished.[22] The *tellak*s and *natır*s offering services in the *hamam* – the washing and scrubbing, shaving and plaiting of hair, a service charged according to the length of the hair – had, according to the *narh* register for 1640, to dress in clean *peştemal*s of silk thread. They were not to ask for tips, especially from the poor and from those from outside the city. Nor were they to hassle the customers. The *natır*s were to plait hair correctly, and not crookedly, while *tellak*s when shaving were to place *peştemals* round the necks and across the chests of their customers, to ensure that nothing ran down over them. The *tellak*s were to show respect to the customers and to give them clean, dry *peştemal*s.[23] Despite such regulations, not everyone was happy with the service they received. The author of the *Risale-i Garibe* cursed the bath-keepers who kept their baths cold and the towels and *peştemal*s dirty.[24] He was (as he so often was) displeased about other aspects of the service in the *hamam*: the *tellak*s provided over-hard scrubbing and the *natır*s gave wet *peştemal*s.[25] Those who failed to run a clean establishment could be ordered to do so. A case taken to court by customers complaining about the dirty conditions of a *hamam* at the beginning of the eighteenth century resulted in a ruling that the bath-keeper should be instructed to keep his *hamam* in a proper state.[26]

Bath-keepers could also be condemned for failure to deal respectfully with their customers. In 1874, Ali Efendi complained in his column in the newspaper *Basiret* of the lack of respect shown in the Istanbul *hamam*s towards Ottoman soldiers, who risked their lives to protect the state. On seeing soldiers coming into the baths, the bath-keepers treat them rudely, 'saying "there is no water" or "the water is cold" and then giving them wet *peştemal*s and towels'.[27] The reason for such hostility, according to Ali Efendi, was the reduced entrance fee of only twenty *para* which the soldiers paid. This behaviour was unacceptable and Ali Efendi called on the authorities in Istanbul to do something about it.

Ali Efendi based his complaints not just on the inherent disrespect shown towards the proud defenders of the nation, but also on the health implications involved. Apart from any insult, 'wet *peştemal*s and towels make people ill'.[28] There was also the danger of contagious disease. This aspect of the need to control the hygiene of the *hamam* developed towards the end of the nineteenth century, with the increasing awareness of the importance of the prevention of the spread of disease. Public health

[22] Yücel and Pulaha, *I. Selim Kanunnameleri*, pp. 67, 119, 200–1, facsimile 43b–44a.
[23] Kütükoğlu, *Narh*, pp. 260–1. [24] Develi, *Risale-i Garibe*, p. 40.
[25] Develi, *Risale-i Garibe*, p. 40.
[26] Yenişehirli Abdullah Efendi, *Behcetü'l fetâvâ maa'n nukûl* (Istanbul, 1266), p. 559, quoted in Özcan, *Fetvalar*, p. 217.
[27] Basiretçi Ali Efendi, *Mektupları*, p. 378. [28] Basiretçi Ali Efendi, *Mektupları*, p. 378.

became a matter of government concern in a way it had not been in previous centuries, reflecting the growing part government was coming to play in the daily lives of the empire's citizens and in the shifting perceptions of what its role was. In consequence, the *hamam* became subject to health checks for the purpose of the prevention of contagious diseases such as syphilis, which was widespread in the late nineteenth and early twentieth centuries. Described by the population as the affliction which 'wanders from house to house',[29] syphilis decimated many areas of Anatolia, and certain regions even had hospitals dedicated solely to the treatment of syphilis patients. In 1898, the *Şura-i Devlet*, the Council of State, drew up regulations for syphilis health checks to be applied to social places where men gathered, such as barbers, coffee houses and *hamam*s, which were believed to be environments conducive to the spread of the disease. Employees were subject to monthly health checks and owners were to keep the utensils they used clean and hygienic.[30] A later regulation of 1915 applied to the province of Kastamonu, which had a particularly high incidence of syphilis. Those working in the *hamam*s were subject to regular syphilis checks, and any who were found to have the disease were to be 'removed from their jobs and sent for compulsory treatment'.[31] Bath-keepers were instructed to 'wash the *hamam* equipment frequently with soap and boiling water. The equipment used by one client was not under any circumstances to be given to another without first being cleaned'.[32]

Some bath-keepers offered a somewhat less official service, allowing the poor to spend the winter in the boiler rooms of the *hamam*s. In the nineteenth century, children who had ended up on the streets for various reasons, orphaned, turned out of their homes, or as a result of general delinquency, were permitted by 'good-natured and compassionate' bath-keepers to pass the winter in the stokeholds, which effectively became homeless shelters, and thus performed a further welfare function, largely conducted by the *vakıf* institution rather than the state. Very small children there were given clothes for religious festivals by various charitable people, while others donated their children's old shoes and clothes. They were given leftover bread and food as charity in Ramazan by the mansions surrounding the *hamam*s. The most crowded and most famous among the *hamam*s for this was Gedik Ahmed Paşa *hamam*. There was a definite hierarchical order in the stokeholds; those children who had been there

[29] Ahmed Şerif, *Anadolu'da Tanîn*, ed. Mehmed Çetin Börekçi (Ankara, 1999), I, p. 416.

[30] 11 Mayıs 1314: Başbakanlık Osmanlı Arşivi, Istanbul, Y. A. RES. 99–32.

[31] Clause 32 in 'Kastamonu Vilayetinde Teşkil Olunacak Memleket Hastahaneleri ve Seyyar Heyet-i Tıbbiye Hakkında Nizamname' in *Düstur*, 2nd edn (Dersaadet, 1330), II, pp. 337–8.

[32] Clause 35 in 'Kastamonu', p. 338.

longest and so had the most senior rank slept on sheepskin rugs nearest the furnace, with the others ranged according to rank at increasing distance from it, down to the newest arrivals by the door. If there were any sick children among them, they were put to sleep by the furnace. These children, who were called *külhanbeyleri*, *beys* of the stokehold, helped the stokers, carrying logs, throwing out the ash and keeping the area clean. They developed their own coded language, with special words and accent.[33]

The provisioning of winter shelter was an act of charity which many approved of, and indeed the author of *Risale-i Garibe* condemned those who did not allow the poor and destitute to winter in such places.[34] This was not, however, the attitude taken by Selim III, who ordered that young urchins were not to be allowed into the stokeholds, while older urchins were to be dispatched to work in the dockyards.[35] It would also appear that the use of *hamams* as living quarters by those coming into the city from outside without work, who were regarded as disruptive trouble-makers, was a problem for Mahmud I, whose janissary *ağa* rounded them up, loaded them onto boats and sent them to Üsküdar.[36]

Not only was the state concerned about the conditions within the *hamams*, but also about security on the way to and from them. As always, the state was preoccupied with matters of order and security, and the excessive presence of women on the streets was always regarded as a potential cause of disorder, prompting Mahmud II to cancel the festivities for his daughter's birth in 1809, for example.[37] For this reason, the state took strict precautions about what was acceptable in the vicinity of the *hamams*, and along the routes which women took to get there. The concern for order was not just the result of the presence of women, for the problems which might arise in relation to women applied equally to young boys, who could also be targets of unwanted attentions on the streets of the capital. Selim I issued instructions that men were not to gather and sit outside the *hamam* or on the roads leading to the *hamam*.[38] Men were not to go 'a child in one hand, a bundle in the other' up to the *hamam* door, as if assisting their wives, a socially unacceptable action and one which was construed as invasion of female space, whatever the implied justification.[39] Nor was there to be loitering, and thus ogling, concealed or otherwise, on the street nearby. That such unseemly behaviour was a problem is graphically demonstrated by the judgement issued in 1594 in response to the

33 Abdülaziz Bey, *Osmanlı*, pp. 324–5. 34 Develi, *Risale-i Garibe*, p. 40.
35 Karal, *Hümayunları*, p. 96. 36 Aktepe, 'İstanbul'un Nüfus Mes'elesi', pp. 10–12, 18.
37 Cabi, *Târihi*, I, pp. 515–16.
38 Yücel and Pulaha, *I. Selim Kanunnameleri*, pp. 37, 92, 157, facsimile 7b.
39 Develi, *Risale-i Garibe*, p. 24.

rather enterprising commercial profiteering from this male desire for the sighting of women. Various private houses had been converted into *boza* houses in the *mahalle* of Koca Nişancı Bey. Here they began to make *boza* and to attract male customers, who gathered at these houses. Ripping out the wooden boards of the houses nearby, men even began to cook kebabs. The local police official was bribed weekly to turn a blind eye to these illegal goings-on. Happily settled with their *boza* and kebabs, men watched the women passing by innocently on their way to the *hamam*. The result was disruptive. Groups of men gathered in the street to leer at the good Muslim women, who, not suprisingly, were deterred from going to the *hamam*. The sultan promptly banned the making of *boza* in the *mahalle*, and anyone caught doing so was to be imprisoned or sent to the galleys.[40]

In 1576, the people of various *mahalle*s were so incensed by such problems that they went to the Istanbul *kadı* to complain. Non-Muslims in these *mahalle*s had started to open wine shops in their houses, and drunkards from these places were molesting women going to the *hamam* and men going to the mosque for the evening and the night prayer. The situation was such that men, deterred by this aggression, were not going there to pray. In response to this petition, the sultan ordered that all wine houses on main roads, roads leading to *hamam*s, round *mescit*s and in areas with a Muslim majority should be demolished.[41]

It was not just men whose behaviour in the vicinity of the *hamam* was under scrutiny; inappropriate female comportment would also cause censure. Indeed, any going-out by women, whether to the *hamam* or elsewhere, was to be conducted decently. The famous sixteenth-century *şeyhülislam* Ebussuud ruled on the matter, stating that a woman who went out to the *hamam* or to a public area was a 'virtuous' woman, if she behaved in an honourable and dignified manner and was accompanied by a servant.[42] The danger of unseemly female behaviour was clearly felt keenly by their husbands, whose honour would be stained by any unsuitable actions of their wives. One husband, before going on pilgrimage, notified his wife that were she to go to the *hamam* or a wedding, or be seen by any non-related male, this would cause her to be divorced on the spot. To underline this, he wrote these stipulations down on a piece of paper and fixed the paper to the wall of his house. The ruling of the *şeyhülislam* Ebussuud on the matter was that were his wife to violate these conditions in her husband's absence, then she would indeed be divorced in the absence of her husband.[43]

[40] Ahmet Refik, *Hicri On Birinci Asırda*, p. 18, *hüküm* 35.
[41] Ahmet Refik, *Onuncu Asr-ı Hicrî*, pp. 141–2, *hüküm* 9.
[42] Düzdağ, *Ebussuûd Efendi*, p. 55, *hüküm* 154.
[43] Düzdağ, *Ebussuûd Efendi*, p. 54, *hüküm* 147.

Many upright citizens were equally concerned about the honour of their women when it came to visiting the *hamam*. In a court case from the early eighteenth century, a group of men complained that female members of their families could be seen entering the *hamam* from the windows of a nearby house. The men wished to have the offending windows boarded up, but the judge ruled against them.[44] It was not even permissible for women in a village to be seen through the windows of the dressing room of a *hamam*.[45] One case involved a plaintiff protesting that the stock of wood piled up beside the *hamam* could be used by a man to climb up and see over into the plaintiff's property, where his women lived. The plaintiff petitioned the court to order the removal of the wood, unsuccessfully.[46]

Regardless of any moral rectitude on their way to the *hamam*, women could be the victims of sexual violence once inside. Those people who had complained to Murad III in 1576 further protested about the drunks from the wine houses entering the women's *hamam* and of one man who had even cornered a woman in one of the small rooms in the *hamam*. The other women had come to her aid but were unable to remove him and had to call in outside help to expel him from the *hamam*.[47] In 1809, in a period of total political chaos, during which people did not venture out onto the streets for fear of being attacked, a woman was seized by force from the Alaca *hamam* by armed porters and then raped in a room above a butcher's shop just opposite the *hamam*. This incident created a huge scandal and horror among the populace.[48] The enormity of the violence was magnified by the fact that the woman had been taken from a *hamam*, where of all places she should have expected to be safe, and around which the state took so much care to enforce order. The fact that this violation happened there indicates the level to which the government had lost control in this period, unable to protect the female population, and the degree to which there was lawlessness and uncontrolled violence on the streets of the capital.

While cleanliness was central to the *hamam*, the *hamam* itself was far more than merely a communal bath. It was a social hub, a central pillar of Ottoman social make-up. It was where many of the major ceremonies of life were celebrated. Babies and mothers were washed there on the fortieth day after the birth of the baby. This was traditionally the baby's first outing. Their washing was accompanied by special prayers, and the

[44] Menteşzade, *Fetâvâ-yı Abdürrahim Efendi*, II, p. 576, quoted in Özcan, *Fetvalar*, p. 214.

[45] Çatalcalı Ali Efendi, *Fetâvâ-yı Ali Efendi*, 2 vols. (Istanbul, 1312), II, p. 256, quoted in Özcan, *Fetvalar*, p. 214.

[46] Menteşzade, *Fetâvâ-yı Abdürrahim Efendi*, II, pp. 575–6, quoted in Özcan, *Fetvalar*, p. 214.

[47] Ahmet Refik, *Onuncu Asr-ı Hicrî*, pp. 141–2, *hüküm* 9.

[48] Cabi, *Târihi*, I, p. 490.

washing itself followed a certain ritual order. Relatives and neighbours were invited, festivities were laid on and dancing girls and musicians hired for the event.[49] The *hamam* was used in order to find suitable brides, the women scrutinising possible candidates for their sons or brothers, not merely judging them physically, but also checking out their manners and behaviour. This was one of the few social spaces in which women, who were neither related nor close neighbours, could come together and could thus view a wider field of potential wives. Matchmakers would sit on the *divan* of the bath-keeper under their veils and *ferace*s and carefully watch the girls entering and exiting the tepidarium. Those washing in the *hamam* were aware of who they were. The matchmakers would learn from the bath-keeper whether the girls they liked were married or single, and would then get the addresses of the unmarried girls from her in order to pay them a visit later.[50]

The *hamam* also played a part in wedding ceremonies, and an essential part of a girl's dowry was the *hamam* set, including good-quality embroidered bath towels, a special kind of wooden clogs, which were ornamented with silver threads, and a *hamam* bowl. The *gelin hamamı*, the bath of the bride, was held a few days before the wedding and involved the female members of both families, together with their relatives and neighbours. They washed the bride and sang religious hymns and sad traditional folksongs. They would also dance.[51] Women often spent an entire day in the *hamam*, in an endless round of washing, eating and chatting. The food was an essential part of the pleasures of the *hamam*. Food typically included stuffed vine leaves, meatballs, cheese *börek*, pickles, nuts, even salami and *pestil* (thin strips of dried fruit pulp), as well as various cakes and desserts.[52]

The *hamam*s could be crowded. In this case, women sometimes reserved places. The grandmother of Haris Spataris, an Istanbul Greek who moved to Athens during the Turkish War of Independence, did so by sending the grocer's boy ahead to announce that she would be coming and to reserve a place for her family members to change in.[53] The grandmother of Spataris's contemporary, İrfan Orga, sent a maid to arrange

49 Balıkhane Nazırı Ali Rıza Bey, *Hayatı*, p. 5.

50 Münevver Alp, 'Eski İstanbul Hamamları ve Gezmeleri', *Türk Folklor Araştırmaları*, no. 179 (June 1964), pp. 3423–5, reprinted in İ. Gündağ Kayaoğlu and Ersu Pekin (eds.), *Eski İstanbul'da Gündelik Hayat* (Istanbul, 1992), pp. 57–8.

51 Lady Mary Wortley Montagu described such a *gelin hamamı*, which she likened to 'the spithalamium of Helen by Theocritus', *Letters*, pp. 134–5.

52 Haris Spataris, *Biz İstanbullular Böyleyiz! Fener'den Anılar 1906–1922*, trans. Iro Kaplangı (Istanbul, 2004), p. 219; İrfan Orga, *Portrait of a Turkish Family* (London, 1950), p. 18.

53 Spataris, *İstanbullular*, p. 217.

with the bath-keeper both for a place to change and for a space within the *hamam* at which to wash.[54] Not everyone could reserve spaces beforehand. Often the old women of the family, accompanied by children, were sent to the *hamam* early in the morning, in order to be there at the time the *hamam* opened, for they were the ones who had no duties at home and so were free to go. It was then their job to find a suitable place in the *hamam* and reserve it for the family members who would come later. They reserved these spaces by sitting firmly in one section and placing their *hamam* bowls in another. The pressure to secure space could be intense and fights could break out. This could even lead to blows, some women wrapping their *hamam* bowls in their *peştemal*s and beating their opponents with them. It was sometimes not just a matter of securing a space in a crowded *hamam*, but of securing the best place, such as the basin with the hottest water in the *hamam*, or that with the fastest-running water, or that furthest from the door, and thus less cold, or, for some, one of the little rooms off to the side.

In many ways, the *hamam* was a microcosm of the world outside, reflecting the social divisions and political upheavals of the society beyond its walls. It was a setting for political discussion and complaints about the conduct of state affairs, a setting so well known that spies were active there, listening out for seditious mutterings, which were then reported to the authorities. Such reports could lead to arrests, as was the case in 1809, when women who had been discussing the government were seized.[55] Even the divisions among the janissaries, which resulted in open and often extremely violent fighting between members of different regiments, could be played out in the *hamam*s, this time among the wives, who, hurling abuse at each other, fought among themselves, fighting the wives of janissaries from other regiments. In true janissary spirit, such fights could be very aggressive, with the free use of *hamam* bowls and clogs.[56]

Just as the *hamam* thus reflected political differences, it also reflected social divisions. Selim I ordered that the *peştemal*s which were given to non-Muslims were not to be used for Muslims; those *peştemal*s used by non-Muslims were to be marked with a sign.[57] These regulations were repeated in those issued in 1640, which stipulated that non-Muslims, both male and female, were to be distinguished from Muslims by wearing a special marker, a ring, on their *peştemal*s. They were to change in a different place, were not to be given clogs, and had to wash at separate spots.[58] Thus, although all religions went to the same *hamam*s, the distinction

[54] Orga, *Portrait*, p. 17. [55] Cabi, *Târihi*, I, p. 392. [56] Cabi, *Târihi*, I, p. 507.
[57] Yücel and Pulaha, *I. Selim Kanunnameleri*, pp. 67, 119, 200–1, facsimile 43b–44a.
[58] Kütükoğlu, *Narh*, p. 261.

between them was maintained, at least in theory. The state was always concerned to maintain order through clear status division, with each group knowing its place, a concept that was applied to all divisions of society, whether religion-, guild- or function-related. However, the issuing of orders did not mean that they were always obeyed or that they were a faithful reflection of reality on the ground. Just as the frequent issuing of dress codes indicates that they were not in fact implemented, so, too, perhaps, did the strictures of division in the *hamam* not necessarily mean that such division was strictly observed in the noisy commotion of the *hamam*. At the beginning of the twentieth century, although they changed their clothes in separate places, Muslims and non-Muslims shared the same space for washing.[59] This social mixing comes out clearly in Basmajean's description: 'in the exterior [bath] everything is calm. Here is a Christian smoking in his bed; there in the corner is a Mohammedan praying on his carpet, a little beyond another, with a beard reaching to his middle, reading the Koran, while near by is a Jew performing his toilet'.[60]

There was, however, strict separation between the sexes. Male children went to the *hamam* with their mothers up to a certain age, which was defined not according to age, but rather according to the appearance of the boy. At a certain point, remarks such as, 'why didn't you bring your father too?' were made by the bath-keeper, and the boy's time in the women's *hamam* was brought to an abrupt end. In his memoirs, İrfan Orga, who was born in 1908, recalled that boys of five years old could be considered too old to go to the women's *hamam*. He himself, however, was protected by his grandmother, whose strong character prevented any adverse comment from either the bath-keeper or the other customers.[61] A contemporary of Orga's, Spataris, reported that boys went to the women's *hamam* until they were seven, when, 'according to the Muslim understanding they became adolescent, that is they started to be interested in women',[62] and women began to regard such boys as an alien male presence in the baths. When Spataris himself reached the age of seven, he was expelled from the *hamam* to which he went regularly with his mother.[63] This was a disappointment for him, for when he began to go with his father to the men's *hamam* he found nothing interesting there.[64]

Many middle- and upper-class men had baths in their own houses, but most of them preferred to go to the public baths.[65] They did not, however,

[59] Spataris, *İstanbullular*, p. 217; Orga, *Portrait*, p. 19. [60] Basmajean, *Life*, p. 150.
[61] Orga, *Portrait*, p. 17. [62] Spataris, *İstanbullular*, p. 216.
[63] Spataris, *İstanbullular*, p. 216. [64] Spataris, *İstanbullular*, p. 216.
[65] Edward William Lane, *An Account of the Manners and the Customs of the Modern Egyptians*, 2 vols. (London, 1836), II, p. 36.

go just anywhere. The *hamam* had to have certain qualities in order to appeal to them. First of all, it had to have good-quality water, it had to be wide enough for one not to hit one's head, it had to be near where one lived but, importantly, not in an area where single men were living. There should be no workers or day labourers among its customers. The *hamam* and its towels had to be clean. If the *hamam* had all this, then they would go to it.[66]

The centrality of the *hamam* in everyday life is highlighted by its appearance in the *Karagöz*, the traditional and extremely popular shadow play, one of the main entertainments in Ottoman society which was performed particularly during the month of Ramazan. One such *Karagöz* was set in the *hamam*.[67] Writing in the mid seventeenth century, Evliya Çelebi refers to a *Karagöz* performance in which the main character of the shadow play, Karagöz, was removed naked from a *hamam*, tied up with the roll of skin which had been peeled off him during his scrubbing.[68] An early Republican version of a play called 'The play in the Double *Hamam* or Karagöz gets beaten' has survived and may well be that which Evliya Çelebi saw.[69] As it was a popular entertainment, it clearly needed to reflect people's everyday experiences in order to be both believable and funny, and thus gives a good idea of the *hamam*, at least at this period. The first part of the play consists of an account given by Hacivad to Karagöz about his wife's trip to the *hamam* and the behaviour of Karagöz's wife there, and highlights the social divisions in Ottoman society. Hacivad represented the better-off, better-class man, while Karagöz was much more of a common character. This social division comes out in the depiction of the contrast between the reception in the *hamam* by the *natır* and the bath-keeper of Hacivad's wife and daughter, who are shown much respect and given clean seats, and that of the 'filthy dirty, cheap and common' wife of Karagöz. While Hacivad's wife and daughter changed into their silk *peştemal*s, which they took out of their *hamam bohça*s (bundles containing the things necessary for the *hamam*), Karagöz's wife wore only her dirty, old *peştemal*. Hacivad's wife and daughter were led to their washing area, where, without any display of manners, Karagöz's wife plonked herself down too and began to wash. Hacivad's wife and daughter were 'mortified with embarrassment'.

[66] Abdülaziz Bey, *Osmanlı*, p. 299.

[67] The same theme appears in *orta oyunu*, the traditional theatre; Abdülaziz Bey, *Osmanlı*, p. 403.

[68] Evliya Çelebi, *Seyahatnamesi, I Kitap*, p. 310.

[69] Muhittin Sevilen, 'Çifte Hamamlar Oyunu Yahut Karagöz'ün Dayak Yemesi', in Muhittin Sevilen, *Karagöz* (Istanbul, 1969), pp. 92–112. Muhittin Sevilen, known as Hayali Küçük Ali, was one of the last great masters of traditional Turkish shadow theatre.

33. Women fighting in a *hamam*, in Erimez, *Tarihten Çizgiler*, [p. 24].

Karagöz's wife's behaviour continued to cause embarrassment, for, when a bowl of delicious pickles arrived, sent by Hacivad for his wife and daughter, she seized the bowl and, sitting comfortably on the hot central massage slab with the pickles beside her, began to eat with gusto, smacking her lips and shovelling them down with relish. A pregnant woman approached. 'I really fancy a bit of pickle', she said, 'would you give me some?', but Karagöz's wife did not even give a morsel to the poor woman and instead smacked her lips even harder. Hacivad was very angry about Karagöz's wife's behaviour, for he considered himself a cut above the common Karagöz family and felt that his family had been insulted by her vulgarity. Karagöz, however, laughed merrily throughout his account, interjecting comments about his wife's cleverness.

The second part of the play revolves around the economic aspect of the *hamam* and introduces Çelebi, the well-off owner of the double *hamam* (a *hamam* with one side for women and the other side for men), who was in discussion with Hacivad. Hacivad was to open and take over the running of the *hamam*, and now began to take on staff. The newly hired stoker arrived, promising to produce a great deal of heat for the *hamam*, which would make the customers very pleased. Hacivad next went to speak to Kilci Baba, the old man who sold the clay. Kilci Baba was singing a folksong. 'Oh bath-keeper, which beauties come to this *hamam*?/ My beloved with her fingers hennaed comes/ Without her the world becomes small/ Buy clay, girls, buy clay!' He brought clay of such good quality that it was 'like henna', and filled the *hamam* storage space. Next, Hacivad took on a female bath-keeper and two *natırs*, but then learnt that the *natırs* were not on speaking terms. He resolved to make peace between them. The two arrived singing a song: 'The door of the *hamam* was struck/ Inside there was a gathering/ The bath-keeper fell in love with the stoker'. Hacivad asked the girls, 'What has happened [between you]? Did you kill each other's mother and father?' Although the two had rowed bitterly and fought hard, they now decided to make up. Kissing, they went happily together into the *hamam*.

Karagöz's role in the play revolved around trying to get into the women's section of the *hamam*. He was evicted each time, once after being beaten with wet *peştemals* by the *natırs*, and was thrown out naked onto the street. The play ends with the discovery of an illicit mixed party in the women's *hamam*, the door between the male and the female sections having been opened and the men having entered, undetected by those outside. Karagöz set fire to the *hamam*, the scene of such disgraceful behaviour. When Hacivad appeared and asked who had burnt down the *hamam*, Karagöz answered that he had done it because 'it is not a *hamam*, it is a den of iniquity'. 'In that case', replied Hacivad, 'let it be so'.[70]

The *hamam* through European eyes

Of all the aspects of Ottoman life which fascinated and intrigued an often remarkably ignorant European audience, the *hamam* was the most important. European observers were intrigued by what they perceived as the Turks' total addiction to cleanliness, and were driven to flights of fancy about activities within the *hamams*, or to howls of horror at the scrubbing and limb-twisting that professional washing involved. For the majority of western travellers, and for almost all of those who never set foot in Istanbul, the *hamam* represented the 'orient', the 'exotic' par excellence, for 'there is, perhaps, no luxury throughout the luxurious East more perfect, or more complete, than the Baths', nothing which so embodied a scene from the *Thousand and One Nights*.[71] It was the bath that most fascinated and intrigued them and which fed their fantasies about the East. As in so many aspects of European understanding of Ottoman

[70] Sevilen, 'Çifte Hamamlar', p. 112. [71] Pardoe, *Beauties of the Bosphorus*, p. 13.

society, much of what the Europeans reported about the *hamam* was inaccurate or incorrect, a reflection of their own perceptions and the desire to fulfil the fantasies of their readership. Regardless of reality, they are amusing as accounts and for the picture they give of the European traveller's encounter with the Turkish culture of cleanliness.

'The Turks are devoted to washing their hands, their feet, their necks and all the body, including parts which I am ashamed to mention'.[72] So wrote Theodore Spandounes in the early sixteenth century, reflecting a common European amazement at the extraordinary Turkish devotion to washing. Indeed, according to the Habsburg ambassador Busbecq, the Turks 'hate uncleanliness of the body as though it were a crime, and regard it as worse than impurity of the soul; hence their frequent ablutions'.[73] It is not surprising, therefore, that the Frenchman Grelot regarded the Ottomans as a nation that affected cleanliness like no other,[74] or that his fellow Frenchman Tournefort was convinced that they spent a great part of their lives washing.[75] This, Tournefort explained, was related to religion, having been commanded by the Prophet. He himself found such linking of cleanliness to religion 'ridiculous'.[76]

European travellers such as Thévenot were struck not only by the numbers of baths, but also by their magnificence and beauty.[77] The large baths were well and richly made, while the luxurious baths were 'constructed of the finest marble of inestimable value, with fountains and various channels of fresh water in front of the bath, and many of them are hot'.[78] They were seen as the chief ornament of the town which served all, regardless of rank or religion.[79] Sandys regarded the public baths as being second to the mosques for the excellence of the buildings.[80] Even Grelot, so hard to please in most ways, was impressed. There were, he said, a great number of baths, all over the empire, 'and some not inferior to the ancient *Thermae* of the *Roman* Emperours',[81] a viewpoint echoed by Sanderson:

> The citie is also full of a number of very fa[i]re banies, as well publique as private, which, in imitation of the auntient Greeks and Romaines, ar built and contrived with great industry, sumptuousness, and expence almost incredible. Besides those of the Great Turks seraglio, his women, and bassaies, the most of the common sorts ar bewtified with pillors, banks, and pavements of divers and rare colored marble. Faire they ar, and very great, with plenty of water.[82]

72 Spandounes, *Origin*, p. 134. 73 Busbecq, *Letters*, pp. 119–20.
74 Grelot, *Voyage*, p. 187.
75 Tournefort, *Voyage*, II, p. 66; Tournefort, *Relations*, II, p. 85.
76 Tournefort, *Voyage*, II, p. 65; Tournefort, *Relations*, II, p. 85.
77 Thévenot, *Voyages*, I, p. 94. 78 Bassano, *Costumi*, f. 2v.
79 Tournefort, *Voyage*, II, p. 66; Tournefort, *Relations*, II, pp. 85–6.
80 Sandys, *Travailes*, p. 54. 81 Grelot, *Voyage*, p. 187. 82 Sanderson, *Travels*, p. 78.

34. Cooling room in a *hamam*, in Pardoe, *Beauties of the Bosphorus*, between pp. 14 and 15.

Baths were for everyone, of whatever type and whatever religion,[83] rich or poor,[84] and people went to them regularly, at least once a week according to Thévenot,[85] often twice a week, according to

[83] Tournefort, *Voyage*, II, p. 65; Tournefort, *Relations*, II, pp. 85–6.
[84] Thévenot, *Voyages*, I, p. 99. [85] Thévenot, *Voyages*, I, p. 99.

Sandys.[86] Women went often, twice, and even three or four times, and certainly never less than once a week,[87] for, according to Thévenot, Turkish women were very clean, having neither filth nor hair on their bodies.[88] This was not the case, apparently, in Cairo later, for Lane wrote that while many men went to the bath twice a week, women went less frequently.[89] There were baths for men, baths for women, or the same bath for both, in which case they had separate hours, men in the mornings and women (plus young children) in the afternoons, or were on alternate days.[90] They were not expensive, the entrance charge being minimal.[91] In the seventeenth century, the charge was apparently only three or four *akçe*s.[92]

What happened in the baths was a source of great curiosity for European visitors, many of whom wrote eagerly of the pulling and stretching, the turning backwards and forwards of the bathers' limbs,[93] the cracking of the bones[94] (the *coup de grâce* of the massage)[95] and the other intricacies of treatment in the baths. They were often impressed, if alarmed, for they acknowledged that 'as to the washing and scrubbing of men, the *Turks* have a particular dexterity'.[96] Apart from rubbing, stretching and cleansing the skin with a piece of rough grogram, the bath attendants also shaved the heads and bodies of the men, or removed body hair using *rusma* (a depilatory powder) and unslaked lime. Women used an ointment made from earth from Chios, which left their skin soft, white and shining, and freed their faces from wrinkles – at least according to Sandys.[97] According to Thévenot, *rusma* was much used by the men to remove hair, and was a source of considerable revenue for the sultan.[98]

Not all Europeans enjoyed the bathing experience, and some were not prepared to try it at all as it required undressing, certainly something that put off Bertrandon de la Broquière when invited to the baths at Adana in the 1430s.[99] Lacroix referred to the 'far from agreeable sensations' caused by the massage and warned that the strangeness of the operation could

86 Sandys, *Travailes*, p. 54.
87 Bassano, *Costumi*, f.5v; Bauden, *Galland*, p. 194; Thévenot, *Voyages*, I, p. 174.
88 Thévenot, *Voyages*, I, p. 174. 89 Lane, *Customs*, II, p. 36.
90 Lane, *Customs*, II, p. 36; Tournefort, *Voyage*, II, p. 66; Tournefort, *Relations*, II, p. 86; Thévenot, *Voyages*, I, p. 99; Grelot, *Voyage*, p. 189.
91 Lane, *Customs*, II, p. 36.
92 Tournefort, *Voyage*, II, p. 66; Tournefort, *Relations*, II, p. 86; Sandys, *Travailes*, p. 54; de la Croix, *Mémoires*, I, 3rd letter, p. 132.
93 Grelot, *Voyage*, p. 191; Sandys, *Travailes*, p. 54.
94 Tournefort, *Relations*, II, p. 87; Tournefort, *Voyage*, II, p. 66.
95 Lacroix, *Guide*, p. ii. 96 Grelot, *Voyage*, p. 190.
97 Sandys, *Travailes*, p. 54; Spon and Wheler, *Voyage*, I, pp. 198–9.
98 Thévenot, *Voyages*, I, p. 98.
99 Bertrandon de la Broquière, *The Travels of Bertrandon de la Brocquière*, trans. Thomas Johnes (London, 1807), p. 171.

cause somewhat disagreeable surprises.[100] Tournefort felt, when he first 'fell into the hands' of the bath attendants, that all his joints would be dislocated.[101] Such cracking of the bones produced, according to Thévenot, a sensation rather alarming to an inexperienced person.[102] Albert Smith was far more forthright, for he underwent 'a dreadful series of tortures, such as I had only read about as pertaining to the dark ages', and was convinced that his last minute had come and that death by suffocation would finish him off.

> I do not know that I ever passed such a frightful five minutes, connected with bathing, nervous as are some of the feelings which that pastime gives rise to. It is very terrible to take the first summer plunge into a deep dark river, and when you are at the bottom, and the water is roaring in your ears, to think of dead bodies and crocodiles; it is almost worse to make that frightful journey down a steep beach, in a bathing machine, with a vague incertitude as to where you will find yourself when the doors open again: but nothing can come up to what I suffered in my last extremity, in this Constantinople bath. Thoughts of Turkish cruelty and the sacks of the Bosphorus; of home, and friends, and my childhood's bowers – of the sadness of being murdered in a foreign bath – and the probability of my Giaour body being eaten by the wild dogs, crowded rapidly on me.[103]

Perhaps Wraxall had had a similar experience, for he wrote, 'suppose now, my dear reader, that you accompany me to a Turkish bath; – but no, I should not like to practice such cruelty upon you; you had better stay at home'.[104]

Other Europeans were more positive and were more able to understand why the Turks went to the baths for sheer delight,[105] apart from other considerations of health, cleanliness or religion,[106] or sex, for Harff reported that 'when a man wishes to sleep with his wife she goes before midday to the bath, and the husband after midday, and he gives the wife three aspers as bath-money'.[107] The baths were even, for some Europeans, a relaxing experience and, at least for Sandys, 'restoreth to the wearied body a wonderful alacrity'.[108] Théophille Gautier found that after a *kese* (a vigorous rubbing of the skin with a rough cloth) in the *hamam* he visited in Istanbul, 'long gray [*sic.*] rolls... peel[ed] from the skin, in a manner astounding to a European convinced of the cleanliness of his own person'.[109] By the nineteenth century, the European was

[100] Lacroix, *Guide*, p. ii. [101] Tournefort, *Relations*, II, p. 87; Tournefort, *Voyage*, II, p. 66.
[102] Thévenot, *Voyages*, II, p. 41. [103] Smith, *Constantinople*, pp. 101–2.
[104] Lascelles Wraxall, 'A week in Constantinople', *Bentley's Miscellany*, 39 (1856), p. 306.
[105] Sandys, *Travailes*, p. 54. [106] Thévenot, *Voyages*, I, p. 94.
[107] Harff, *Pilgrimage*, p. 244. [108] Sandys, *Travailes*, p. 54.
[109] Théophille Gautier, *Constantinople*, trans. Robert Howe Gould (New York, 1875), pp. 236, 233–5.

perhaps becoming less convinced of the cleanliness of his own person. The importance of hygiene, in particular in relation to the spread of disease, was becoming more recognised and, in consequence, the bath came to be viewed in a very positive light. Cleanliness came to be seen, in the words of the popular saying, as next to godliness, and the establishment of bath-houses regarded as 'a great step towards the purification of the mind and the achievement of moral superiority'.[110] In 1857, at a meeting of the British Association in Dublin, Dr Edward Haughton promoted the Turkish bath as 'a pleasure free from vice and a luxury which was not injurious'.[111] Some of the baths established in Ireland even served coffee and *çubuks* (long tobacco pipes) to complete the Eastern experience.[112]

This link between hygiene and health was made by some well before the nineteenth century. In the seventeenth century, Thévenot felt that the great use the Turks made of the baths effectively protected them from diseases.[113] Grelot, too, thought there was a connection between the healthy Ottoman and the bath, for he argued that the baths were the reason why the Ottomans were not so subject to diseases as the Europeans. Nothing was more wholesome than the baths, if used in moderation; moderation, however, being the key, for, as with 'all sorts of Physick', medicine should only be used in case of necessity, otherwise it became more prejudicial than advantageous to health. Baths should thus, he said, be frequented no more than once a month. The Turks, however, persisted in using them almost every day with dire consequences, for 'their brains are thereby so over moisten'd, that they are generally troubled with a continual Rheume in their eyes'.[114]

Apart from the virtues of cleanliness, there were other virtues displayed in the baths, one of which was modesty. According to Sandys, men went to the baths in the mornings, and women in the afternoon, unlike the Romans, who 'did ordinarily frequent them together: a custome, as they say, continued in Switzer-land at this day, and that among the most modest'.[115] Bassano warned that in undressing it was very important 'not to show any dishonest part because those who are without respect are beaten and thrown out of the bath'.[116] Writing two hundred years later, Tournefort also noted the need for care, since thoughtless undressing resulted in punishment. If such carelessness was by design, a severe

[110] Teresa Breathnach, 'For health and pleasure: the Turkish bath in Victorian Ireland', *Victorian Literature and Culture*, 32/1 (2004), p. 163.
[111] Breathnach, 'For health', pp. 163–4. [112] Breathnach, 'For health', p. 160.
[113] Thévenot, *Voyages*, I, p. 99. [114] Grelot, *Voyage*, p. 188.
[115] Sandys, *Travailes*, p. 54. [116] Bassano, *Costumi*, f.2v.

beating was administered,[117] for seeing what one should not see was a great crime.[118]

As with cleanliness itself, this aspect of the baths also appealed to some European visitors. It certainly attracted the German Protestant priest Salomon Schweigger, who felt that his own co-nationals would benefit from a similar attitude to unnecessary displays of the flesh.

Men and women had separate baths. In the bath they cover themselves in a very modest way. In contrast, Germans behave in a shameless manner in this regard, almost as if they particularly wish to show their intimate parts, or, as I myself have seen in Venice, the men enter the bath completely naked. The Turks wrap around themselves a cover made from blue linen which goes round their hips twice and reaches to the ground. We Christians should take these barbarians as an example from the point of view of good behaviour and morality.[119]

In one respect, however, German behaviour was distinctly superior: the lack of lust.

The thing which the Turks and the Greeks cannot believe is that, although we Germans sit, women and men side by side on the same bench in the washing places almost naked, this does not lead to any excess, importunity, prostitution or adultery. I think that the jealous Greeks, Turks, Spanish, Italians and other peoples of races addicted to lust cannot imitate us from this point of view.[120]

Although Germans may not have lusted, the imagination of many European men ran wild over the activities within the confines of the female Turkish bath. For many, the women's baths were filled with voluptuous females and 'many girls of extraordinary beauty brought together by various chances from every quarter of the world'.[121] European male visions of female *hamam*s filled the frames of many paintings, by artists such as the Irish portrait painter Charles Jervas, whose work would have been greatly improved by actual experience in the opinion of Lady Mary Wortley Montagu. 'I had wickedness', she wrote in a letter of 1 April 1717, describing her visit to a *hamam* in Edirne, 'to wish secretly that Mr Gervase could have been there invisible. I fancy it would have very much improved his art'.[122]

Luigi Bassano was convinced that the women's baths were dens of iniquity and that women washing each other there led to unsavoury practices.[123] Sandys agreed: 'much un-naturall and filthy lust is said to be committed daily in the remote closets of these dark-some *Bannias*: yea

[117] Tournefort, *Voyage*, II, p. 66; Tournefort, *Relations*, II, p. 86.
[118] Thévenot, *Voyages*, I, p. 95. [119] Schweigger, *Ein newe Reyssbeschreibung*, p. 115.
[120] Schweigger, *Ein newe Reyssbeschreibung*, p. 115. [121] Busbecq, *Letters*, p. 120.
[122] Montagu, *Letters*, p. 59. [123] Bassano, *Costumi*, f. 5r.

women with women; a thing un-credible, if former times has not given thereunto both detection and punishment'.[124]

Oddly, Sandys immediately follows this with the remark that 'they have generally the sweetest children that ever I saw; partly proceeding from their frequent bathings, and affected cleanlinesse'.[125] Some, including Bassano, argued that sometimes women did not in fact go to the baths at all, but used a trip there as an excuse for leaving the house to go elsewhere, for men did not allow them to go out otherwise.[126] Grelot, too, noted this tendency, for he remarked that men who had baths in their own houses were thus able to prevent their wives from 'gadding abroad' under the pretence of going to the baths.[127]

Not all were so suspicious, other Europeans regarding the *hamam* as an 'innocent pleasure' for the women, a 'diversion they take great pleasure in'[128] where they 'chatted among themselves together without any constraint, and they passed there hours more enjoyable than they did in their own homes'.[129] Going to the baths was a source of great pleasure for the women of Egypt. There they frequently had entertainments and were often 'not a little noisy in their mirth'.[130] Women put much effort into their trips to the *hamam*, at least according to Tavernier, describing the women of Aleppo, for they would spend an entire week preparing food to take there.[131] The bath was, in the words of Ubicini, a fundamental pleasure for Ottoman women, obligatory on Fridays and a social extra on other days. There they passed half a day eating, drinking and enjoying themselves.[132] In the baths, 'the very paradise of Eastern women',[133] they conversed, worked, drank coffee and sherbet or lay 'negligently… on their cushions while their slaves (generally pretty girls of seventeen or eighteen) were employed in braiding their hair in several pretty manners'.[134] They busied themselves with 'colouring their Locks, the nails of their toes and fingers, with the powder of an herb which the *Arabians* call *Elhanna*, the Turks *Alkana*, which makes them look red, and gumming and dying the hair of their eyelids, to render themselves more amiable to their Spouses'.[135] They went, according to Grelot, 'more out of wantonness than necessity; it being the chief place where the Gossips meet and spend

124 Sandys, *Travailes*, p. 54. 125 Sandys, *Travailes*, p. 54. 126 Bassano, *Costumi*, f. 5v.
127 Grelot, *Voyage*, p. 192. 128 Montagu, *Letters*, p. 134.
129 Tournefort, *Voyage*, II, p. 67; Tournefort, *Relations*, II, p. 88.
130 Lane, *Customs*, II, p. 44.
131 Jean-Baptiste Tavernier, *Les Six Voyages de Jean Baptiste Tavernier Ecuyer Baron d'Aubonne, en Turquie, en Perse, et aux Indies*, 2 vols. (Paris, 1679), I, p. 151.
132 J. H. A. Ubicini, *1855'de Türkiye*, 2 vols., trans. Ayda Düz (Istanbul, 1977), II, p. 104. Ubicini refers to Lady Mary Wortley Montagu's account of the baths on pp. 104–5.
133 Pardoe, *Beauties of the Bosphorus*, p. 15. 134 Montagu, *Letters*, pp. 59–60.
135 Grelot, *Voyage*, p. 190.

the Afternoons in tattling and junketing'.[136] Indeed, for the female population, the bath was, as Lady Mary Wortley Montagu shrewdly noted, 'the women's coffee house, where all the news of the town is told, scandal invented'.[137]

Going to the baths was not an entertainment that husbands could oppose, for 'the men who have any complaisance for their wives, do not refuse them these innocent Diversions'.[138] Perhaps the reason for this was less related to kindness of nature than to fear of divorce, for, at least according to Tournefort, 'too much Constraint makes them sometimes seek Reasons for Divorce'.[139] Women could not divorce their husbands, he explained, unless they failed to furnish them with what they needed: bread, rice, coffee and the money to go twice a week to the baths. If the husband did not provide them with one of these, the woman could go to the *kadı* and demand a divorce.[140]

While the Europeans found much about the *hamam* and the washing practices peculiar, if not downright unpleasant, Mehmed Enisi experienced a rather similar feeling when, as an intern in the French navy in 1895, he went to a Turkish *hamam* in Nice. Although he took the whole experience in good spirit, he found it quite impossible not to twitch and flinch every time one of the strange, long-handled brushes was applied to his skin.[141]

Regardless of any European perplexity or suspicion, the *hamam* was a cornerstone of Ottoman daily life, an essential part of socialisation, particularly for women. It provided a space for religious ablution, an area of general cleanliness for a society which, except for the richer echelons, had no other access to such facilities, and a setting for social exchange, where important life events were marked and where people who otherwise could not socialise together could meet. It was a source of gossip, of brides and of diseases. It could even, in the words of Karagöz, be a den of iniquity. In short, it was a quintessential part of Ottoman life. It was also a largely unchanging one, for its centrality and popularity was as true for the early days of the empire as it was for the nineteenth century.

136 Grelot, *Voyage*, p. 189. 137 Montagu, *Letters*, pp. 59–60.
138 Tournefort, *Voyage*, II, p. 67; Tournefort, *Relations*, II, p. 88.
139 Tournefort, *Voyage*, II, p. 67; Tournefort, *Relations*, II, p. 88.
140 Thévenot, *Voyages*, I, p. 178.
141 Mehmet Enisî, *Bir Denizcinin Avrupa Günlüğü - Avrupa Hatıratım*, ed. N. Ahmet Özalp (Istanbul, 2008), pp. 173–5.

8 The nineteenth century

During the nineteenth century, Istanbul was to witness many changes that were to alter the lives of its citizens. New fashions arrived from Europe, new political ideas and concepts of state began to permeate the political circles of the capital, and even views on how a city should be laid out altered. Yet for all this innovation, Istanbul remained the lively, disorganised, chaotic and dynamic metropolis it had always been, and novelties arrived, were absorbed and became part of the Ottoman fabric just as they always had. What was different was the increasing political and financial weakness that delivered the empire into the rapacious hands of western imperialism, which squeezed ever tighter round the Ottoman windpipe until, with the First World War, all hope of survival was gone.

The traditional city

While much changed in the life of the city during the nineteenth century, much remained the same. Fire and plague constantly assailed the population of the late Ottoman empire and drove them to distraction.[1] *Mahalle* life continued much as it always had: those who sat behind the steamed-up windows of the coffee house in their *entari*s

> were grandsons of those in the [nearby] graveyard. Only the waters of their water pipes moved while the people themselves seemed less mobile than those gravestones. All frozen and insensible like the Seven Sleepers, they seemed untrammelled by cares. Their little mosque was just next door, their graveyard was there, the grocer and the butcher were near, the baker came every day, the water seller brought the water and God even provided them with neighbours.[2]

For many contemporaries, the city streets were a nightmare. The roadway in Pera was 'paved with all sorts of ragged stones, jammed down together without any regard to level surface; and encumbered with dead rats,

[1] Saraçoğlu, *Hatıralar*, p. 138.
[2] Celâl Esat Arseven, *Seyyar Sergi ile Seyahat İntibaları*, ed. N. Ahmet Özalp (Istanbul, 2008), pp. 116–17.

35. A coffee house in Üsküdar, in Amicis, *Constantinople*, p. 380.

melon-rinds, dogs, rags, brickbats, and rubbish, that had fallen through the mules' baskets, as they toiled along it'.[3] Narrow and windy and badly made, the roads of the city were littered with rocks which stuck up at menacing angles from their surfaces.[4] They were full of potholes and open drains, and when it rained they turned into impassable quagmires, the drains and ditches filled with water and pedestrians fell into them.[5] Pavements were non-existent or unusable – it was even hard sometimes to distinguish if there was one or not.[6] On cold days, the mud froze and passing phaetons threw up clouds of icy mud, which not only dirtied the passer-by but also caused considerable pain.[7] Road maintenance was unheard of,[8] drains and ditches were constantly being opened and then not filled in, broken pavements remained unmended, all of which was a matter of much concern for the new mayor of Istanbul in 1912, Cemil Paşa (Topuzlu).[9] Not surprisingly, progress along city streets was not easy and many Ottomans complained.

Even in the central and busiest streets, progressing along the thoroughfare is a very difficult job for those who are not skilful or do not know how to play hopscotch. If

[3] Smith, *Constantinople*, p. 66. [4] Basmajean, *Life*, p. 145.
[5] Ahmet Rasim, *Şehir*, pp. 197–8.
[6] Sadri Sema, *Hatıraları*, p. 101; Basmajean, *Life*, p. 145. [7] Ahmet Rasim, *Şehir*, p. 346.
[8] Sadri Sema, *Hatıraları*, p. 101; Murad Efendi, *Manzaraları*, pp. 48–9.
[9] Topuzlu, *Hatıralarım*, p. 129.

the weather is slightly rainy, every street, every alley becomes a sea of mud. You will find a stone, step on it, cling on, and then leap from there onto another stone. You will find something sticking out, and launch yourself at it. But what will happen depends on luck. If the thing you thought was a solid protruding object is in fact a pile of mud, you have had it. You will sink into it from head to toe.[10]

The complaints of the writer Sadri Sema echoed those made several decades earlier by Basiretçi Ali Efendi, who bemoaned the fact that any solution to the appalling condition of the streets of Istanbul still eluded the authorities. Channels and ditches continued to be opened for various purposes and then not filled in. The dangers to the pedestrian were obvious.

Even recently some sewage drains were opened in Büyükkaraman in the Fatih district and remained open for a period. At night many people fell into them. I even know a member of the *ulema* who fell in and was injured and went to hospital. They have since been closed and now a few more ditches have been opened on a street in Tavşantaşı leading from Beyazıt to Kumkapı.[11]

The pavements along this street had been repaired only once in years and they were now in a state of complete disrepair. This, combined with the open ditches, made the street completely impassable, even in the daytime. At night the position was even more dangerous because there was no light, since the lanterns that had been there before had been removed, perhaps, Basiretçi Ali Efendi suggests, as an economy measure. He asked the authorities that if the drains were to remain open, then at least the lanterns should be reinstated in order to prevent poor wretches from having to pay bonesetters as a result of injuries received from pitching into the drains in the dark.[12]

Those who did not have trouble in the streets of the capital were the dogs who trotted about, unconcerned by potholes, ditches or lack of pavements. While every human competed in a sycophantic display of salutation of ministers' carriages along the Bab-ı Ali street, the centre of government, the dogs strolled up and down, with their heads held high. They 'turned their backs, stuck out their tongues, held their tails in the air, frisked about, rolled around and played together'.[13]

'Dogs', Haris Spataris noted, 'were a part of the life of Istanbul'.[14] They were everywhere and attracted the attention of every visitor to the city.[15] 'I do not believe', wrote Basmajean, 'that there is another city in the world

[10] Sadri Sema, *Hatıraları*, p. 101. [11] Basiretçi Ali Efendi, *Mektupları*, p. 365.
[12] Basiretçi Ali Efendi, *Mektupları*, p. 365. [13] Sadri Sema, *Hatıraları*, p. 158.
[14] Spataris, *İstanbullular*, p. 62.
[15] Sadri Sema, *Hatıraları*, p. 160; Basmajean, *Life*, p. 143; Vicente Blasco Ibañez, *Fırtınadan Önce Şark. İstanbul 1907*, trans. Neyyire Gül Işık (Istanbul, 2007), p. 55.

36. Dogs, in Amicis, *Constantinople*, p. 131.

where there is such an immense crowd of dogs'.[16] Man gave way to dogs, and not the other way round.[17] Albert Smith was forced to pick his way among the scores of them as they lay in the streets;[18] Mrs Brassey tumbled over them at every step;[19] Spataris's driver had to get down from the carriage and gingerly draw a dog to the side of the road by pulling gently on his tail in order to pass.[20] Not only did they sprawl across the highways, but they also barked. Nights were made hideous by the noise,[21] and the 'yelping, howling, barking, growling, and snarling, were all merged into one uniform and continuous even sound, as the noise of frogs becomes when heard at a distance'.[22]

Despite their incessant noise, their total dominance of the public highway and their street fighting, the dogs were viewed with sympathy, at least by some. People gave them bread and the rich left money for them in their wills,[23] a charitable custom Thévenot had noted several centuries earlier.[24] The best hotel in Pera, the Pera Palas, took care of these animals, and a positive army of dogs could be seen at the end of the century, lined up outside the hotel, waiting for their rations.[25] These 'mildest of God's creatures', as H. G. Dwight perhaps somewhat surprisingly described

[16] Basmajean, *Life*, p. 143. [17] Basmajean, *Life*, p. 143.
[18] Smith, *Constantinople*, p. 64. [19] Brassey, *Sunshine*, p. 56.
[20] Spataris, *İstanbullular*, p. 62. [21] Brassey, *Sunshine*, p. 53.
[22] Smith, *Constantinople*, p. 95. [23] Basmajean, *Life*, p. 144.
[24] Thévenot, *Voyages*, I, p. 159. [25] Spataris, *İstanbullular*, p. 62.

them,[26] had their own *mahalle*s, where they set up their sultanates, not straying out of them for fear of fights. Here, they attached themselves to individual families, protecting the house and respectfully giving way on the street to the women and children of the household as they returned home. The family fed them, looked after their puppies and gave the dogs names, which were then used by the people of the *mahalle*.[27] The dogs were even regarded as assets to society, for they 'assaulted burglars, wounded mischief makers, and caught womanisers'.[28] They helped Abdülhamid's police force because they, too, followed strangers in the *mahalle*s; and both Mrs Brassey and Sadri Sema noted their assistance to the street cleaners in clearing up rubbish from the streets.[29] There was one other, though somewhat tangential, way in which the dog population could perform a social service, for there was, in the view of Basmajean, 'no more favourable city for Dr. Pasteur to practise his new cure of hydrophobia than the city of Constantinople'.[30]

Other facets of life also remained unaffected by the innovations of the new century; festivals continued as they always had and children continued to enjoy them to the full.

> It was above all for the children that the *bayram*s, *şeker bayramı* [Ramazan bayram] and the four-day *kurban bayramı*, of Istanbul in the old days were, in the true meaning of the term, happy periods in which hours of pleasure, gaiety, hope and joy chased after each other. School holidays, new clothes from head to foot, pockets full of shiny, new *kuruş* and 50-piaster coins like horseshoes.[31]

Children, decked out in their new clothes bought for *bayram*, took their pocket money which they had been saving up well before Ramazan and, putting it together with the money given to them by the adults at *bayram*, spent it in great excitement on the big swings, revolving wheels and merry-go-rounds which were set up in different parts of the city. In some places, boys hired little donkeys and cart-horses, which pleased them greatly, or the little carts which the animals pulled. Here were sold all sorts of different sweets and candies and foods which children loved. 'In short … in every part of Istanbul time was spent and enjoyed in the pleasure of buying and eating sweets, *simit* [a round bread ring with sesame seeds], biscuits and Turkish delight'.[32]

It was particularly in Ramazan that the traditional shadow play, the *Karagöz*, was performed in the coffee houses. But it was another form of

[26] Dwight, *Constantinople*, p. 389. [27] Sadri Sema, *Hatıraları*, p. 157.
[28] Sadri Sema, *Hatıraları*, p. 158.
[29] Sadri Sema, *Hatıraları*, p. 158; Brassey, *Sunshine*, p. 59. [30] Basmajean, *Life*, p. 144.
[31] Saraçoğlu, *Hatıralar*, p. 250. A *kuruş* was a piaster coin.
[32] Abdülaziz Bey, *Osmanlı*, p. 267.

popular theatre, the *orta oyunu*,[33] which had its roots among the Jews who came from Spain to the empire at the end of the fifteenth century, which came into its own in the nineteenth century, producing famous figures such as Hamdi and İsmail Dümbüllü, as unforgettable at the end of the century as they are in Turkey today.[34] People of every class flooded to see these performances, which were also put on at the circumcisions of the princes and at the weddings of the sultan's daughters, and were sometimes given as private performances in the palace for the sultan and the people of the harem.[35] While these traditional entertainments had been popular for many centuries, what changed in the nineteenth century was their audience, or at least one section of it, for now women were able to attend. Women watched the performances seated in areas separated off from the male audience by latticework screens.[36]

The content of these traditional plays, as was the case with 'The play in the double *hamam*', was often either explicitly or implicitly vulgar. Such lewdness shocked the Frenchman Jean Thévenot, who was much embarrassed by a puppet show he saw when staying as a guest in a house in Crete. For the entire three hours of the performance, the wife of his host, who had settled herself down comfortably behind a carpet hung up as a screen at the entrance to the salon where the men were seated, did not move, watching 'without shame' the 'immoral' goings-on of the main character, Karagöz. He found himself astounded that she was not discomforted by such open jokes.[37] Thévenot's disapproval was echoed by Basiretçi Ali Efendi, who complained of the same thing some two hundred years later. This self-appointed messenger on moral matters wrote in his newspaper column about the performance of an *orta oyunu* in Bayrampaşa, to which people flocked and to which he himself went:

> if you ask me what kind of a play it was, well as you know it was one of those plays in which men get caught with women. I don't know about the others but I myself was much vexed during the time I sat there. For the play does not benefit the spectators, rather it may even corrupt their morals! Inside there were pure-hearted and tender young girls and virtuous and chaste women. The dialogue was such as to shock even decent men. If it so shocks men then just think what it does to women![38]

[33] *Orta oyunu*, also known as *zuhuri kolu*, *meydan oyunu*, *taklit oyunu*, *kol oyunu* or *han kolu*, was a traditional form of theatre performance. It involved two main characters, Kavuklu and Pişekar.
[34] Metin And, *Türk Tiyatrosunun Evreleri* (Ankara, 1983), pp. 109–11.
[35] And, *Evreleri*, pp. 110–12; Leyla (Saz) Hanımefendi, *Harem*, p. 25; Alus, *İstanbul*, pp. 65–8.
[36] Alus, *İstanbul*, p. 65. [37] Thévenot, *Voyages*, I, pp. 95–6.
[38] Basiretçi Ali Efendi, *Mektupları*, p. 165.

It was not only the bawdy *Karagöz* and *orta oyunu* that the population flocked to see. Storytellers, the *meddah*, continued to recite their stories taken from epics and traditional tales and from the trivia of everyday life in the nineteenth century, as they had for centuries.[39] *Mani* and *semai* (types of folk poetry) were performed and epic poems recited in coffee houses known as the *semai kahveleri*, which were particularly popular with the *tulumbacı*s.[40] Minstrels, known as *kahvehane şairleri* (coffee-house poets), men who came to the city from the provinces, performed in certain coffee houses.[41] These minstrels played *saze*s (long-necked stringed instruments) and recited poems.[42]

Apart from the numerous coffee houses, where people not only drank coffee but were also entertained by songs and poems, Istanbul was also provided with another very popular venue, the *meyhane*, the wine house, also known as *şerbethane* and found in many areas of the city, such as Kumkapı, Samatya, Cibali, Üsküdar, Kadıköy and Galata. Since they were places of illicit drinking, they did not openly advertise their presence, but used the traditional sign of a piece of an old mat attached to their doors or windows. On going in, the first thing to strike the eye was a counter on which there were wine and *rakı* glasses and water glasses, together with various *meze*s. Wine and *rakı* bottles were lined up on the shelves. Wooden tables were set up round the room, with low wicker chairs beside them. Apart from the drink in the *meyhane*, food was served or brought in from outside by the customers, who came with fruit in season and even fish to be cooked there. Poems continued to be written about the *meyhane*s in this century, as they had been in the past.[43]

While watching popular entertainment, attending popular festivities and drinking in the coffee shops and wine houses, much of the population sought to protect their often difficult lives in the traditional way, visiting religious shrines, using holy water, warding off the evil eye and placing curses on their enemies. People believed in vampires and ghosts and took precautions against them.[44] Divination of dreams was very important, as were all types of chance events. Even the twitching of people's eyes had a significance.[45] A belief in fate dominated all. 'All the inhabitants of these countries, both Christian and Musulmans',

[39] Balıkhane Nazırı Ali Rıza Bey, *Hayatı*, pp. 162–4; Sadri Sema, *Hatıraları*, pp. 252–3; Abdülaziz Bey, *Osmanlı*, pp. 395–8.

[40] Musahipzade Celal, *Eski İstanbul Yaşayışı* (Istanbul, 1946), pp. 101–4.

[41] Abdülaziz Bey, *Osmanlı*, pp. 452–3. [42] Abdülaziz Bey, *Osmanlı*, pp. 452–3.

[43] Selim Nüzhet Gerçek, *İstanbul'dan Ben de Geçtim*, ed. Ali Birinci and İsmail Kara (Istanbul, 1997), pp. 111–14; Abdülaziz Bey, *Osmanlı*, pp. 306–9; Balıkhane Nazırı Ali Rıza Bey, *Hayatı*, pp. 178–83.

[44] Abdülaziz Bey, *Osmanlı*, p. 374. [45] Abdülaziz Bey, *Osmanlı*, p. 365–6.

according to Ubicini, 'have a blind belief in destiny which leads them to infer every event, and even every action of their lives, to the direction of a fixed and immutable fate'.[46]

The population of Istanbul, particularly the vast majority of the women, went to shrines such as Miskinler Tekkesi, lit candles, made vows and tied pieces of cloth to the shrine. They went to wishing wells, the most famous of which was at Eyüp, and to *ayazma*s, fountains or springs such as Balıklı, sacred to the Ottoman Greek population, to which those from other religions also went and from which they collected bottles of water. All these visits were to bring about cures for their illnesses, the fulfilment of their wishes or the restoration of what they had lost.[47] It was believed that 6 May, St George's day for the Greek Orthodox and Hıdırellez (Hızırilyas) for the Muslims, celebrated as the coming of spring, would bring blessings. Hızırilyas Baba, dressed in robes 'woven with pink, yellow, red and purple spring flowers', and whose 'white-bearded, luminous face was caressed by the edge of the cloth, shining fresh emerald green like the spring meadows, which envelopes his red conical hat', would bring abundance and good luck, that is good husbands, to girls.[48]

An almost daily preoccupation then, as indeed it is today, was *nazar*, the evil eye, in which the vast majority of society believed.

> The dominion of *nazar* is present from the cradle to the grave. It touches the twenty-day-old innocent babe, whose soul leaves its body. It touches the ten-year-old child who then goes down with smallpox. It touches the twenty-year-old young man who then falls impotent on the first night of marriage. It touches the grey-haired man who is then swept to the other world by a stroke. It is the same for women. Headaches, toothaches, backaches, aching kneecaps, all from *nazar*. It is *nazar* which makes one squint, which makes one unable to climb Zeyrek hill without having to stop ten times, which makes the person who before could shovel down half a tray of *börek* now unable to finish two slices of bread.[49]

Dominant it might be, but the population did not remain paralysed before it, but took precautions. They wore the blue bead which is now one of the tourist symbols of Turkey; they carried chickpeas wrapped in blue cloth, or black cumin, they wore *nazar* amulets. They muttered a wealth of *nazar* prayers. They even poured lead (a popular method of

[46] J. H. A. Ubicini, *Letters on Turkey: An Account of the Religious, Political, Social and Commercial Conditions of the Ottoman Empire*, 2 vols. (London, 1856), II, p. 318.

[47] Sadri Sema, *Hatıraları*, p. 292; Balıkhane Nazırı Ali Rıza Bey, *Hayatı*, p. 64; Abdülaziz Bey, *Osmanlı*, pp. 366–72; Dwight, *Constantinople*, pp. 332–41.

[48] Musahipzade Celal, *Yaşayışı*, pp. 89–90; Sadri Sema, *Hatıraları*, pp. 342–3; Dwight, *Constantinople*, pp. 341–4.

[49] Alus, *İstanbul*, p. 132.

getting rid of *nazar* and its effects was to pour hot lead into a pan full of cold water, held above the covered head of the afflicted person), both against *nazar* and against illness.[50] Sometimes they did not restrict themselves to precautions designed to ward off the evil eye, but adopted more proactive means for dealing with difficulties and dangers, and assuring a correct direction for the course of events in their lives. For this they turned to magic.

The practice of magic was widespread. For every trouble there was a magic remedy: an amulet to make you more attractive to the person you desired, donkey tongue fed to irritable men to make them calmer, water which had run off the elbows of a devout man during his ablutions before prayer secretly administered to a man too given to alcohol in order to make him teetotal. If the amulet of attraction was not working, there was another, if somewhat less convenient, remedy to which one could turn for greater potency: first, urinate on sugar and then add it to the coffee served to the person one wished to attract. As well as bringing people together, there was also magic for splitting them up. One of the best-known methods to destroy relations between man and wife was to smear pig fat on the clothes of the man. More extreme, and fatal, ends could also be obtained. Death could be brought about by driving seven or forty-one needles into a piece of soap and throwing it into a well.[51]

There were many experts who were believed to be able to do, or undo, magic. Such people were so popular that 'the space before their doors was full of mansion carriages, their … rooms packed with all sorts of people',[52] for all classes, from the highest echelons to the lowest, had recourse to magic. Even the sultan was not immune. According to Ahmed Cevdet Paşa, Sultan Abdülaziz's mother was convinced that the reason for her son feeling ill was that magic had been performed against him. Having understood this, she then fell into the hands of various mischief-making *şeyh*s, behaviour which caused gossip among the people. She even went as far as having a meaningless prayer read by the preachers during the Friday prayer in various mosques in Istanbul. Tongues wagged even more and people began to whisper that the sultan was suffering from melancholia or that he was displaying signs of madness. Such rumours so worried the grand vezir Fuad Paşa that he reprimanded the major-domo of the sultan's mother over the issue.[53]

[50] Alus, *İstanbul*, pp. 133–4; Balıkhane Nazırı Ali Rıza Bey, *Hayatı*, pp. 7–9.
[51] Alus, *İstanbul*, pp. 134–5; Abdülaziz Bey, *Osmanlı*, p. 361.
[52] Alus, *İstanbul*, p. 135. See also Balıkhane Nazırı Ali Rıza Bey, *Hayatı*, pp. 57–64; Sadri Sema, *Hatıraları*, pp. 256–60; Abdülaziz Bey, *Osmanlı*, pp. 369–73.
[53] Ahmed Cevdet Paşa, *Ma'rûzât*, p. 54.

37. Arrest of those in *entari*s (loose robes), in Erimez, *Tarihten Çizgiler*, [p. 6].

Not all were so drawn to magic and superstition. İrfan, the young hero of Hüseyin Rahmi Gürpınar's early twentieth-century novel *Kuyruklu Yıldız Altında Bir İzdivaç* (A Marriage under a Comet), was a great believer in the scientific thought and positivism of Europeans. He strove to explain Halley's comet to the women of the *mahalle* in which the novel was set. Due to pass near the earth in 1910, it was popularly believed that it would strike the world and usher in doomsday. İrfan showed one of these women a picture of the comet in one of his scientific books. The women's interpretation, however, remained firmly rooted in tradition and the description of it by one woman was more comprehensible than any positivist interpretation that İrfan could offer. 'Should I call it a mermaid', she asked her neighbours, 'or should I describe it as an Ankara goat or as a Van cat? Such a fringed head, slanting eyes like an almond … luminous hair as if of combed white linen … reaching down to the heel'.[54]

[54] Hüseyin Rahmi Gürpınar, *Kuyruklu Yıldız Altında Bir Evlenme. Kaderin Cilvesi*, ed. Kemal Bek (Istanbul, 2005), pp. 30–1.

The changing city

As in any dynamic metropolis, the city and its population were constantly changing, accepting new fashions and modifying old traditions. But much of what was new was simply absorbed within what was already there, an accretion to centuries-old tradition, and on some levels much remained the same. While the nineteenth century produced many İrfans – men and women affected by positivist thought who avidly followed the latest intellectual trends and read the European press – many people continued to think and live like the *mahalle* women in Hüseyin Rahmi's novel. Many preferred to wear their traditional clothing and continued to spend time in their traditional pursuits. For some, wearing loose robes, *entari*, was much more pleasant than any newfangled fashion. Such traditional garments allowed a nice gentle breeze to blow up the legs, and they were in so many ways much more convenient than the European style of dressing.[55] For others, however, the *entari* represented backwardness and had to go. Almost as soon as he assumed his post as governor of Üsküdar in 1909, Cemal Bey, later Cemal Paşa, who had himself been a keen wearer of traditional clothing, frequenting the coffee houses in his *hırka* (a type of woollen jacket) before his political rise,[56] issued an order banning men from going to coffee houses or the market dressed in *entari* and *hırka*s. But it proved impossible to enforce this regulation, for although the police arrested those dressed in this manner, the absence of a legal dress code meant that there were no grounds to hold them on and they had to be released immediately. Dressed in their *entari*s and *hırka*s, they simply went in the front door of the police station and, still dressed the same way, processed out through the back door.[57]

Nevertheless, this was a century of innovation. Much change was not violent, or a break with the past, but a matter of new forms moulded to old shapes. In came new forms of entertainment, the dance halls, the European theatres and the sea *hamam*s, but these innovations were modelled, changed, smoothed and eased into a comfortable Ottoman version, which appealed more to the society into which they had seeped. The European-style dance halls were very popular with Levantines and foreigners, or those who liked to pass their time in Beyoğlu, the Europeanised quarter of the city, but the common people still much preferred to dance the traditional *halay* and *sirtaki* during public festivities, to watch the dances of the gypsies or to listen to *fasıl* (traditional music) and drink *rakı*.[58] European-style

[55] Sadri Sema, *Hatıraları*, p. 82. [56] Sadri Sema, *Hatıraları*, p. 82.
[57] Sadri Sema, *Hatıraları*, pp. 82–3.
[58] Alus, *İstanbul*, pp. 105–10; Abdülaziz Bey, *Osmanlı*, pp. 330–1.

38. Sea *hamam*, in Erimez, *Tarihten Çizgiler*, [p. 34].

theatres were successfully opened in Şehzadebaşı and in Beyoğlu. While the form was new, the plays put on there were those which appealed to the traditional tastes of an Ottoman audience, melodramas full of tragedy, unrequited love and cruel fate. Plays such as *La Dame aux camelias* were very much enjoyed by the Istanbul upper classes.

Popular theatre, too, was affected by the changing habits of the century, for it could now move out of the coffee houses and onto the stage. There were now the thriving and popular theatres of Kel Hasan and Abdi, where the actors improvised comedy. As each performance was improvised, being based only very loosely on a set storyline, the play presented differed from night to night, and it was the ever-changing comic improvisation that the audience came to see. Before the play began, female cabaret singers would appear in what were, for that time, revealing costumes, and, amid wolf-whistles and shouted encouragement, would dance and sing.[59] Active audience participation did not end with the departure of the girls,

[59] Alus, *İstanbul*, pp. 61–4.

but would continue throughout the play, which was performed to the accompaniment of a constant barrage of comments.[60]

Not just the theatre, but even the *hamam*, that quintessential Turkish institution, felt the winds of change. Following the developing European fashion of bathing in the sea, the *hamam* took to the water, where it transformed itself into a sea *hamam*. This new variety of *hamam* became very popular at various locations along the Bosphorus and Haliç (the Golden Horn), both considerably cleaner then than they are today. While the rich had their own boathouses, attached to their *yalı*s, from which they bathed, the less well-off frequented the new, noisy, bustling and boisterous sea *hamam*s and took to the beaches in droves. There was much commotion, splashing around and horseplay: pushing people into the sea, spraying water around and generally frightening those who did not know how to swim.[61]

Sea *hamam*s consisted of bathing huts surrounding a small enclosed area of sea, large enough for three or four people to 'flap their arms around in',[62] and screened off by a wooden fence. Such 'hovels' or 'sea shanties', as Sadri Sema disparagingly called them,[63] were made of wood. Swimming was, in theory, restricted to this screened-off section of water, but many men prised away the boards and swam off into open water. In those *hamam*s made specifically for women, the fence that screened off the area ran down into the water, to prevent the risk of unwanted ingress or egress. A policeman sitting on a seat at the entrance to the *hamam* kept guard and intimidated any boat which came into the vicinity.[64] His presence, however, was not always enough to fend off the gaze of curious males, and the sounds emanating from the women's *hamam* excited the interest of the ever-present men. Few women had the courage to evade the enclosure and swim out into the open water, but those who did became the focus of great interest. On one occasion, a woman from one of the foreign embassies, who, for that reason, had a more cavalier attitude to the authorities, swam out from the fence of the women's *hamam* at Fenerbahçe and into the open sea. The men in the neighbouring male *hamam*, regardless of age, all followed her with binoculars.[65]

Men did not merely watch women, but curious crowds watched all swimmers, regardless of sex or age. This practice excited much agitated disapproval from upright citizens such as Basiretçi Ali Efendi, who complained vociferously about it. In 1873, a police announcement appeared

[60] Alus, *İstanbul*, pp. 46–55; Saraçoğlu, *Hatıralar*, pp. 176–81, 188–91, 199–203.
[61] Ahmet Rasim, *Şehir*, p. 20. [62] Sadri Sema, *Hatıraları*, p. 337.
[63] Sadri Sema, *Hatıraları*, p. 337. [64] Saraçoğlu, *Hatıralar*, pp. 111–12.
[65] Alus, *İstanbul*, pp. 47–8.

in the newspapers warning against unwarranted staring at bathers. Swimming, it explained, was something undertaken for concerns of health. People should enter the sea and come straight out again after this treatment. There was to be no loitering or lolling around at the water's edge. But, the announcement went on, some people were not following this code of behaviour and instead regarded swimming as a form of pleasurable entertainment or an amusing excursion, and were lying about for hours watching the other bathers, conduct which disturbed the young men who came to swim. Basiretçi Ali Efendi was very pleased with this police response, but unhappy with the result. 'I must say', he wrote despondently, 'those watching the swimmers have not taken any notice whatsoever. They don't just give annoyance to the young but even to old, bearded men like me. As soon as a man goes into the water, people fix their eyes on him, following him backwards and forwards as if they were harpooning fish'.[66]

The sea season began, according to Sermet Muhtar Alus, at the end of May,[67] or, in the more poetic definition of Ahmed Rasim, when the first watermelon skin fell into the sea.[68] Bathing became an enormously popular pastime with people from every class. Many customers came in the mornings, although the demand increased considerably after the afternoon call to prayer. But the peak point was Sundays. Then the crowds were so great that 'if you threw a needle it would not fall to the ground'.[69] This was the day on which the non-Muslims of the area did not go to work, but went instead to the sea.

Although they might be on the sea, the sea *hamam*s in many ways resembled the more conventional *hamam*s. Those who worked there were called bath-keepers. Women and men had their separate areas placed next to each other, or, if there was only one sea *hamam*, they were assigned different times. Women used them in the mornings and men in the afternoons and evenings, up to midnight.[70] The most esteemed customers were treated with especial favour by the bath-keeper, just as they were in normal *hamam*s, and were granted the best bathing huts.[71] The slow rhythm of the *hamam* was retained and people spent many hours there, regarding the whole thing as much more a social activity than anything related to sport or exercise. Men entered the sea dressed in 'long-legged, white underwear down to their feet, or with *peştemal*s wrapped round their waists'.[72] There was 'none of that stripping

[66] Basiretçi Ali Efendi, *Mektupları*, pp. 169–70. [67] Alus, *İstanbul*, p. 46.
[68] Ahmet Rasim, *Şehir*, p. 43. [69] Alus, *İstanbul*, p. 47.
[70] Sadri Sema, *Hatıraları*, p. 337. [71] Alus, *İstanbul*, p. 47.
[72] Saraçoğlu, *Hatıralar*, p. 112.

on the shore and hurling yourself, plop, into the sea as there is today',[73] for such shameless displays were forbidden and swimming in the open sea banned, though many ignored this prohibition and dived in regardless.[74]

Those who adapted too freely to the new *alafranga* (European) mode of bathing were either mocked or disapproved of. They certainly attracted attention.

It is clear at first glance who is going to the sea. I don't know, but have you never noticed? An *alafranga* cap generally on their heads, cotton shirt, a screw thread or knobbed pointed tie, a light coloured jacket, at the waist a belt which brings to mind gym buckles, tight, light trousers, coloured socks, shoes like chic overgrown slippers, with a *hamam* set tied with a belt in one hand, a yellowish cloth parasol in the other. If you add a pair of goggles to this, you will see one of the *alafranga* divers going into the sea. They do not smoke *nargile*s [water pipes] at the *hamam*, they do not sit around much. After lighting and putting out a cigarette, pulling on a tiny pair of underpants, and wandering around pretending to dry sweat off themselves with a towel, plop, they throw themselves into the bottom of the sea.[75]

After swimming in various styles, they come out from the sea, pour

a bowl of fresh water on their heads, dress and go home. They eat that type of meal, is it 'dejöne' [dejeuner] or 'dine' [diner]? They take a little nap. Changing their clothes they go off to work. This arrangement is not too arduous. It merely requires dressing seven times and undressing eight times at the same hour in the mornings and in the evenings – surely a small inconvenience! But it certainly does not appeal to me.[76]

There were not many who wore small bathing shorts, and those who did were either *alafranga* Ottomans or Europeans. Those working at the European embassies swam in clothing which, although not totally appropriate to the sea habits of Istanbul, was hardly outrageous. Nevertheless, 'they caused those watching to pucker up their lips and say "what shameless infidels!"'[77]

While many innovations were thus 'Ottomanised', other aspects of society were changed in a more radical sense. Muslim women became freer, and those from the upper echelons of society became more educated, had foreign governesses, spoke French and played the piano. But communication between the sexes was still conducted within strict boundaries, and women still wore veils, even if they were thin. Decoration became all the rage: 'from the sultan to the most minor member of society all became addicted to ornamentation and splendour'.[78] What people ate, how they

[73] Alus, *İstanbul*, p. 47. [74] Sadri Sema, *Hatıraları*, p. 337.
[75] Ahmet Rasim, *Şehir*, p. 19. [76] Ahmet Rasim, *Şehir*, p. 19.
[77] Saraçoğlu, *Hatıralar*, p. 112. [78] Balıkhane Nazırı Ali Rıza Bey, *Hayatı*, p. 241.

39. Advert for Kemal Ömer's haberdashery in Vezneciler, in *Servet-i Fünun*, no. 587 (supplement), p. 40 (from the private collection of Ebru Boyar).

ate, what they read, how they moved around the city and what they wore were all transformed by the impact of imported modes and fashions.

For contemporaries, the Crimean War marked a turning point in the consumption patterns of the city. Ahmed Cevdet Paşa described the French and English soldiers who came to Istanbul in this period as spending money like water. The Istanbul traders profited from this unexpected turn of events and made considerable sums of money.[79] The arrival of the French and English had a further effect, according to Ali Rıza Bey, for it brought Ottomans and Europeans into face-to-face contact and increased Ottoman interest in everything European. All the latest fashions could be found in the shops of the capital. Parasols, starched-collared shirts, perfumes, collars, handbags, bow ties, socks, gloves, corsets, shawls, canes, wallets and purses, ties, sock suspenders, brush and comb sets, watches, soaps and lavender water, for example, were all sold, in the shop in Vezneciler.[80]

Not everything western arrived from the West. European tastes and fashions, which so seduced the people of Istanbul, came also in roundabout ways through different peripheral parts of the empire. Abbas, the khedive of Egypt, and his entourage purchased costly mansions and *yalı*s on the shores of the Bosphorus and decorated them in European style. Hidiv Kasrı (the khedive's mansion) is still standing today on Çamlıca, one of the most beautiful hills of the city. Spurred on by this Egyptian display, the notables of Istanbul began to compete with them, and the women of these families imitated Zeynep Hanım, the daughter of Muhammed Ali Paşa, the de facto ruler of Egypt until his death in 1849.[81]

Although the streets in Istanbul might not have changed over the centuries, the way one moved about the city certainly did. Out went the horse and in came the phaeton and the carriage, for now mounting a horse was considered ugly and inappropriate for a European state.[82] As the popular saying had it, 'to go about in a phaeton makes a man proud'.[83] Every notable household began to buy or hire phaetons or carriages, and women started to promenade more frequently in them. For those not so well-off, the tram became a normal form of transport. The standard of service differed from area to area and was reflected in the age of the carthorse pulling the tram. Young horses were assigned to the expensive and modern area of Şişli. Three years later they were moved on to Aksaray, after another three years to Azapkapı, and after two years in Azapkapı they were taken to Topkapı for one year. Finally they were sent to Samatya. If they were still going after this, they were given for free to donkey drivers and carried loads around the city.[84] Driving trams in the narrow, steep streets of the city was often dangerous, and in some places stopping them was impossible. In such places the tram company hired *vardacı*s, men who

79 Ahmed Cevdet Paşa, *Ma'rûzât*, p. 8.
80 *Servet-i Fünun, Tevcihat ve Havadis Kısmı*, no. 577, 6 Sefer 1320/15 May 1902, p. 34.
81 Ahmed Cevdet Paşa, *Ma'rûzât*, p. 7. 82 Ahmed Cevdet Paşa, *Ma'rûzât*, p. 6.
83 Sadri Sema, *Hatıraları*, p. 54. 84 Ahmet Rasim, *Şehir*, p. 316.

ran in front of the trams blowing horns to warn people to get out of the way. For very steep streets, where the trams needed extra horses to pull them up, temporary stables were located to provide additional animals. A groom waited there and when a tram arrived, he attached either one or two horses, depending on the steepness of the road. Travelling up the hill with the tram, he detached the extra horse or horses at the top and then returned with them to the bottom to wait for the next tram.[85]

Trains, too, were an important innovation. This symbol of progress brought in the tourists, who took the Orient Express to the exotic city of Istanbul, where they stayed at the Pera Palas hotel, or other hotels, constructed especially to fulfil their oriental fantasies. It promised to open up the empire for economic development, enhancing its ability to compete in the world market. And it carried pilgrims to Mecca. The Hamidian Hijaz railway, the new way of travelling on pilgrimage, was described as 'the greatest work of charity'. It was 'the blessed line', an auspicious and laudable achievement for all Muslims that would continue to be of benefit 'as long as the world existed'.[86]

The bicycle might not have been quite as blessed or beneficial as the Hijaz railway, but it certainly made a splash in Istanbul society. Indeed, as Alus explained, writing in the 1930s, 'it is no exaggeration to say that the enthusiasm about the bicycle then was something like the excitement about aviation today'.[87] It had high-ranking fans, such as the navy minister and commander of the fleet Hüseyin Rami Paşa, who was said to be much taken with the 'velosiped', as the bicycle was then known.[88] One of its most ardent fans was İbnülcemal Ahmed Tevfik, who wrote an account of his bicycle trip from Istanbul to Bursa in 1900. For him, the bicycle was 'Beauty created by intelligence/ Nimble, and submissive and without caprice/ It makes the East wind jealous by its speed'.[89] His adoration is clear in his assurance that whoever rode a bicycle was automatically drawn to it by a tight bond of love. He had a preacher's enthusiasm in his desire to convert the population into a nation of bicycle riders. For him, the bicycle was far more than a mere means of exercise and body building. It was a way of achieving a long road in a short time without feeling tired. It was a vehicle for making friends.[90] For many, it was a means of enjoyment. The

[85] Talu, *Anılar*, p. 259.
[86] *Servet-i Fünun*, no. 592/593, 19 Ağustos 1318, special issue for the anniversary of the accession of Abdülhamid. The French title of the special issue was *Numéro Spécial Servetifinun Publié pour les travaux du chemin de fer de Hédjaz-Hamidié.*
[87] Alus, *İstanbul*, p. 142. [88] Alus, *İstanbul*, p. 142.
[89] İbnülcemal Ahmet Tevfik, *Velosipet ile Bir Cevelan. 1900'e Doğru İstanbul'dan Bursa'ya Bisikletli Bir Gezi*, ed. Cahit Kayra (Istanbul, 2006), p. 102.
[90] İbnülcemal Ahmet Tevfik, *Velosipet*, pp. 103–4.

young went to the pleasure gardens on bicycles and whirled around there, spinning about in myriad displays of cycling skill.[91]

The panache and speed of this new machine from Europe did not appeal to everyone. Ahmed Rasim wrote about it with a mixture of mockery and suspicion in his newspaper column. While out walking with a friend, he wrote, he had seen one approaching through a cloud of dust:

> calling to mind a quick, blinding flash of lightening, a strange vehicle emerged, pursued by some of the aggressive dogs who constantly wander around in our streets and attack strange animals and even people … In front a wheel, a body bent straight in a straight line at a tangent to the circumference of the wheel, beyond that another wheel moving without stopping … The changeable evening wind incessantly blew into one's face the dust whipped up by the turning of the front wheel of the *velosiped* and the running of the barking dogs. His [the rider's] body was covered in filth, his underarms soaked right through to his lungs and his liver.[92]

The bicyclist, owner of this unprepossessing appearance, swept past Ahmed Rasim and his companion with speed and pride and shortly after fell off, the bicycle crashing to one side, the rider to the other. Feeling a little guilty, for he remarked that they must have put the evil eye on the bicycle to make the wretched man fall off at such speed, Ahmed Rasim could not help laughing as he approached the man to offer his help. But falling off this machine was not the true horror; nor was the exhaustion brought on by such energetic cycling. It was having to wrestle it upright again and carry it home.[93]

The bicycle was not merely dangerous for its rider. It was in fact a positive menace for society. 'Do not underestimate the bicycle', Ahmed Rasim warned, for 'it has many vices'. The bicycle had a role in evils such as theft, pursuit and the seduction of women and girls. Thank God that the population was familiar with the well-known incident which had occurred recently in Beyoğlu, when the daughter of a wealthy man had been whisked off to Büyükdere by a bicyclist. This, Ahmed Rasim reminded his readers, was one of the latest contributions of the bicycle to Istanbul life.[94]

It was not just Ahmed Rasim who understood the arrogance of the cyclist and his propensity for accidents. All Istanbul was aware of it and people like the famous Şamran Hanım sang about it, bemoaning the bicycle's antics and its encounter with a telegraph pole:

> Oh my knee, oh my leg
> What will I do on Friday?
> What a contrary machine

[91] Ahmet Rasim, *Şehir*, p. 24; Alus, *İstanbul*, pp. 143, 145–6.
[92] Ahmet Rasim, *Şehir*, pp. 22–3. [93] Ahmet Rasim, *Şehir*, pp. 22–3.
[94] Ahmet Rasim, *Şehir*, pp. 23–4.

I will kick it to pieces
It was not my fault
It was the telegraph pole
I warned it so much
But it stayed where it was
Jump, jump
Jump the ditch
Hey, hop, hop, hop
Take care, watch out
Tight jacket, chic turnout
Watch out driver!
Simit seller watch out for your stall.[95]

For those with more money there was another new machine, the car. At first, the number of cars to be seen on the streets of the capital could be counted on the fingers of one hand. According to Alus, Zehyirzade Ahmet Paşa's daughter drove to Fenerbahçe in one of the first cars to be introduced into Istanbul. It terrified all the animals, horses shied and there was chaos.[96] By the beginning of the twentieth century, the situation had developed to such an extent that the sultan Abdülhamid felt it necessary to introduce measures against traffic problems, and in 1908 he ordered that precautions should be taken in order to prevent car accidents in places such as Şişli, Kağıthane and Üsküdar.[97]

The sea was not left behind in the transport innovation that was sweeping the city. Until the nineteenth century, people had crossed the Bosphorus on the *pazar kayıkları*, described by Alus as 'sea buses'.[98] These *pazar kayıkları* were

public boats which could take forty to fifty people on them … Some of these boats were donated by philanthropic owners and were worked at the jetties to which they belonged, their profits being used for good works. Men sat at the head of the boat, and women at the back. A rower worked each of the five or six pairs of oars, which had a handle the thickness of a man's body. Just as they transported the customers backwards and forwards to the jetties on both shores of the Bosphorus, so they also carried foodstuffs.[99]

Pazar kayıkları were now largely replaced by ferries, which came to be one of the symbols of Istanbul, although the former continued to exist and were used for carrying commercial goods that were not accepted by ferries.[100]

95 Reşad Ekrem Koçu (ed.), *İstanbul Ansiklopedisi* (Istanbul, 1961), V, p. 2822.
96 Alus, *İstanbul*, p. 45.
97 Vahdettin Engin (ed.), *Sultan Abdülhamid ve İstanbul'u* (Istanbul, 2001), p. 137.
98 Alus, *İstanbul*, p. 257. 99 Musahipzade Celal, *Yaşayışı*, p. 181.
100 Spataris, *İstanbullular*, p. 57. See also Cengiz Orhonlu, 'İstanbul'da Kayıkçılık ve Kayık İşletmeciliği', in Orhonlu, *Araştırmalar*, pp. 90–1.

40. Ferries, in Erimez, *Tarihten Çizgiler*, [p. 24].

Planned by the grand vezir Fuad Paşa and Ahmed Cevdet Paşa when on vacation at the hot springs in Bursa, the first ferry company, *Şirket-i Hayriye*, was established as a joint stock company in 1851.[101] There were two ferry companies, *Şirket-i Hayriye* and *İdare-i Mahsusa*, the former controlling the lines on the Bosphorus, and the latter running ferries going to Kadıköy and the islands. The ferries, whose numbers were written both in *alafranga* and *alaturka* numbers (i.e. in Arabic and Latin script) and which were equipped with paddle wheels, were well-proportioned, beautiful boats, with chimneys like the heads of shawms.[102] Although beautiful, they were never on time. Travel on them was not always a pleasant experience, particularly in rough seas. The Kadıköy ferries lurched from side to side so much that the passengers suffered from seasickness, and when vomiting in Ramazan ruined their fast. Ahmed Rasim sarcastically noted that most of the people of Kadıköy no longer bothered to get up for *sahur* (the meal in the early morning before daybreak in Ramazan), for they knew that their fast would not survive the day.[103]

[101] [Ahmed] Cevdet Paşa, *Tezâkir 40-Tetimme*, ed. Cavid Baysun (Ankara, 1991), pp. 44–5.
[102] Alus, *İstanbul*, p. 270. [103] Ahmet Rasim, *Şehir*, p. 348.

Despite such drawbacks, passengers supported their own ferry companies as football fans of today support their teams. They composed poems to praise their company and to satirise their rivals, and traditional poems were adapted to fit. Satirical ditties such as 'these ferries which are on the sea are never repaired', or 'these ferries are on the sea but they don't sail', were hurled at the boats of the *Şirket-i Hayriye.* Its supporters replied, poking fun at the age of the ferries of *İdare-i Mahsusa*: 'By respecting the old, one does not hurt the feelings of old men'.[104]

For some, the ferry became almost a second home, particularly in winter, when the number of passengers travelling to the islands was small. Those who did travel, such as the passengers to and from Büyükada in the late 1890s – among whom were Ercümend Ekrem Talu and his brother on their way to school – formed a happy band of brothers, playing cards and backgammon, making tea, chatting and telling jokes as they journeyed to Istanbul in the mornings. The return trip was accompanied by similar entertainments, with the addition of *mezes* and alcohol. The passengers spent five hours a day together, travelling back and forth from the island and the city. When asked where he lived, the leader of this group of passengers, the doctor Şemsi Molla, replied, 'on the island ferry'.[105]

Just as the way of moving about the city changed, so too did people's taste in food and drink. Running water was brought to the city from the nearby lake of Terkos. People were not, however, as pleased with this innovation as one might have imagined, for it was believed that this lake was full of all kinds of carcasses.[106] Turks were very fussy about the water they drank and it was something they could put much time and money into, at least in the estimation of Alexander van Millingen, son of the Istanbul doctor Julius van Millingen. For the Turk, good drinking water should, he said, come from rock, fall from a height, be lukewarm, flow fast and strong, be sweet, come from deserted plateaus and flow south–north or east–west.[107] According to Murad Efendi, the quality of water was as important to Ottomans as that of wine was to westerners.[108]

Canned food arrived from Europe, along with sweets of various kinds, and beers from Munich and Bavaria appeared on the table of the sultan Abdülhamid II.[109] Ahmed Cevdet Paşa, who was by no means always a fan of the new ways, wrote disparagingly about one of his acquaintances, who

[104] Ahmet Rasim, *Şehir*, p. 350; Saraçoğlu, *Hatıralar*, p. 44.
[105] Talu, *Anılar*, pp. 262–3, 278–9.
[106] Hagop Mintzuri, *İstanbul Anıları (1897–1940)*, trans. Silva Kuyumcuyan and ed. Necdet Sakaoğlu (Istanbul, 1993), p. 103.
[107] Alexander van Millingen, *Constantinople* (London, 1906), pp. 220–1.
[108] Murad Efendi, *Manzaraları*, p. 56.
[109] Balıkhane Nazırı Ali Rıza Bey, *Hayatı*, p. 346.

would not leave the dinner table without first eating Roquefort cheese. The hero of Hüseyin Rahmi Gürpınar's novel *Şıpsevdi* (The Susceptible Man), Meftun Bey, was so fond of French food that he instructed his cooks about French recipes. Such instructions were not, however, well understood. Canned mushrooms which were a garniture for food posed a problem to the cook Zarafet, who could not remember what she was supposed to do with them, and was further confused by the fact that the Turkish word *mantar* meant both mushroom and cork, asking herself, 'What will I do with these corks? I forgot to ask. Into what part of the meat will I stuff them?'[110] Zarafet was the only cook who had sufficient patience to listen to the *alafranga* recipes of Meftun Bey, and the stamina to wash the forty or fifty plates a day required for such culinary performances. But, despite her efforts, for she persevered, nothing she produced was pleasing to him.

The change in eating habits was reflected in what was served in restaurants catering for those who wanted a more European cuisine. One such restaurant was Sponik in Beyoğlu, described by Ahmed Rasim as a pseudo-European restaurant, popular with those with pretensions.

> Those who are not European but affect European ways and those who are fed up with *alaturka* food but whose budgets are limited, are all here. For the fixed menu is only six *kuruş*. There are four types of food and wine. Going in, taking off your fez or hat, showing your hair which has been especially combed half an hour earlier, they immediately think that you are European. Fish, pastries come one after the other. Don't even ask about the clinking of knives and forks, the mindless chatter of those types of Europeans, the clattering of plates. If the water in the jugs stays one week more, the croaking of little yellow frogs, peculiar to Terkos will be heard. It is that clean![111]

Cutlery changed and imported European spoons replaced the old Ottoman ones produced from boxwood, tortoiseshell, coconut wood, ebony, rhinoceros horn, buffalo horn, ox claws, coconut shells, with handles of coral or mother-of-pearl. Such utensils were made by the spoon makers in Beyazıt, at a place known as Kaşıkçılar Kapısı (the spoon makers' gate), who were only one of the many groups of artisans who suffered from the increasing domination of European manufactured goods in the empire.[112] Fingers fell from fashion and were replaced by the fork, introduced to the palace in 1860 according to Leyla Hanım, who passed much of her childhood in the harem of Çırağan palace in that period.[113]

While what the Ottomans ate with changed, so did what they sat on to do so. As was always the case, change was frequently not as hard and fast

[110] Hüseyin Rahmi Gürpınar, *Şıpsevdi*, ed. Kemal Bek (Istanbul, 1995), p. 67.
[111] Ahmet Rasim, *Şehir*, p. 206. [112] Balıkhane Nazırı Ali Rıza Bey, *Hayatı*, p. 245.
[113] Leyla (Saz) Hanımefendi, *Harem*, p. 143.

41. Advert for the furniture shop Maison Psalty, in *Servet-i Fünun*, no. 591 (supplement), p. 149 (from the private collection of Ebru Boyar).

as it is sometimes presented, and there was often a mixing of new and old, and an adaptation of a modern fashion to a traditional way of life. As in any society, not everyone appreciated innovation.

Before, we had three corner cushions in our rooms. When we were loading them to go to our country houses for the summer or to our winter houses, we put them into sacks and loaded them onto the *pazar kayıkları*. But now we had got used to loading sofas and chairs instead of cushions and these sofas and chairs got broken on the journey and needed repairing and so our expenses went up. We had acquired *alafranga* dinner services. But we had not been able to give up the old tableware for *iftar* [the meal breaking the fast during Ramazan]. Although all these sorts of things had increased expenses, when salaries did not increase, the people did not know what to do.[114]

[114] Ahmed Cevdet Paşa, *Ma'rûzât*, p. 10.

42. Advert for Singer sewing machine, in *Servet-i Fünun*, no. 591 (supplement), p. 148 (from the private collection of Ebru Boyar).

Despite any such expense, there was an increasing demand that was met by shops such as Maison Psalty in Beyoğlu which catered for the changing tastes in furniture and accessories, selling goods imported from Europe and making things to order in their factory. They sold drawing-room, bedroom and dining-room furniture, chairs, curtains, beds, mirrors and cloth.[115] Shops also catered for other requirements. The Singer sewing machine became increasingly popular and several shops in different parts

[115] *Servet-i Fünun*, *Tevcihat ve Havadis Kısmı*, no. 591, 17 Cemaziyelevvel 1320/21 August 1902, p. 149.

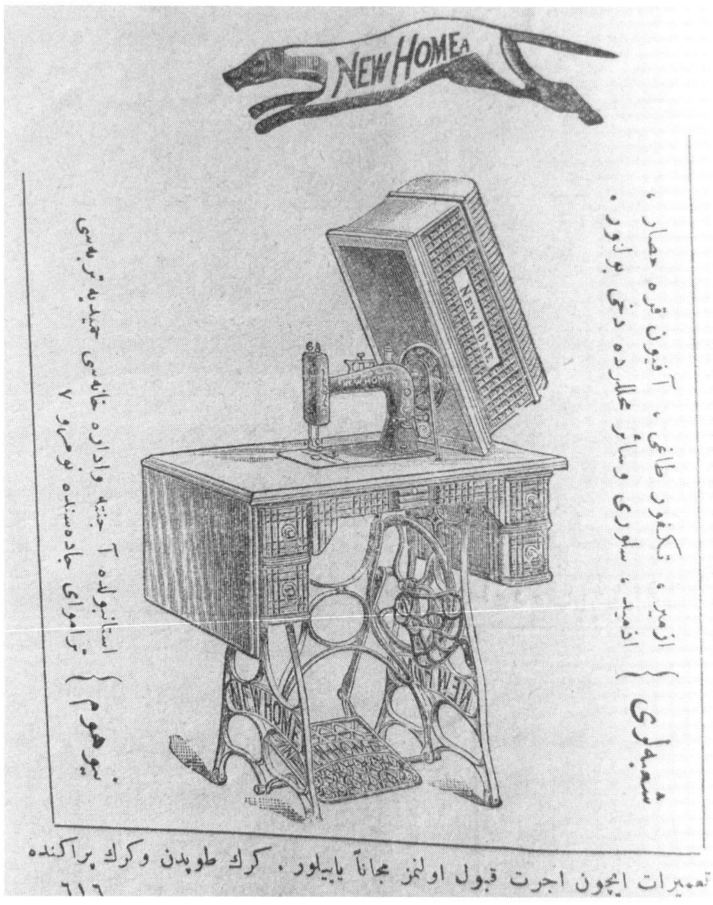

43. Advert for New Home sewing machine, in *Servet-i Fünun*, no. 591 (supplement), p. 149 (from the private collection of Ebru Boyar).

of the city started to sell it. Not only did they market the machine, but they also gave free lessons in how to use it.[116] Singer had its rivals. The American sewing machine, New Home, was also sold in Istanbul and orders were taken for it from the provinces. The New Home had an added advantage in that it came with free lessons and free servicing.[117]

116 *Servet-i Fünun, Tevcihat ve Havadis Kısmı*, no. 590, 10 Cemaziyelevvel 1320/14 August 1902, p. 140 and no. 591, 17 Cemaziyelevvel 1320/21 August 1902, p. 148.

117 *Servet-i Fünun, Tevcihat ve Havadis Kısmı*, no. 591, 17 Cemaziyelevvel 1320/21 August 1902, p. 149.

Changing patterns of consumption were evident also in fashion and in the lifestyle of the women of Istanbul which changed with the introduction of more and more *alafranga* modes and styles. Among wealthy families it became fashionable to have their daughters taught French, to give them piano lessons and to hire foreign governesses for them. While in the earlier part of the century 'a woman who possessed the slightest knowledge of reading or writing was certain to be regarded with an evil eye by her companions, and marriage for such a phenomenon was almost out of the question',[118] their education became more important, and in the last quarter of the nineteenth century, schools for girls were opened by the government. Basmajean noted that 'there is great enthusiasm now for the education of girls as compared with former years', although it was still regarded as less important than that of boys.[119] Women received education in western and Turkish music and the harem orchestra played both, including tunes from *William Tell* and *La Traviata*, which were very popular in those days in Istanbul.[120] Leyla Hanım noted that 'there were pianos pretty much everywhere in the Serail [Çırağan Palace] and in the rooms which were not too close to the apartments of the Sultan or of a *kadın* [wife], one could play the piano and sing in moderation.'[121]

Foreign governesses flooded into the capital. Adverts appeared in the newspapers for governesses from Paris or Germany, who knew French or German, played the piano well, gave good lessons, taught embroidery and gave music lessons, who 'in short knew many things and were desirous of teaching'.[122] However, there was also opposition to the use of foreigners to educate Muslim children. Abdülhamid expressed his displeasure in an order issued in 1901. European and local women, the order noted, were being hired as governesses. They were all Christian and were hired by Muslim households. Muslim children were then left in their care, and their education was placed in their hands. Such children moved on to Christian schools. They were therefore forgetting their own culture and their own religion. Further, Muslim girls were going out in their carriages with their Christian governesses, visiting the Christian quarters and wearing revealing garments. 'This', the order concluded, 'is causing comment'. Abdülhamid's Muslim subjects were warned to avoid this kind of lifestyle.[123] Basiretçi Ali Efendi was also hostile to the exclusive use of foreigners, giving an example of a Turkish woman he knew, who, despite being better qualified than the foreign governess and speaking four or five foreign languages, was unable to find employment, either because her

[118] Ubicini, *Letters*, II, p. 305. [119] Basmajean, *Life*, p. 179.
[120] Leyla (Saz) Hanımefendi, *Harem*, p. 55. [121] Leyla (Saz) Hanımefendi, *Harem*, p. 59.
[122] Basiretçi Ali Efendi, *Mektupları*, p. 101. [123] Engin, *Abdülhamid*, doc. 14, p. 162.

44. Veil, in van Millingen, *Constantinople*, frontispiece.

advert did not bring results or because, being Turkish, she was perceived as not being capable.[124]

Such hostility did not have a significant impact on the use of foreign governesses, nor, therefore, on the education of the daughters of the rich. Agitation about their appearance had an equally small effect as it continued to change under the impact of European fashion.

[124] Basiretçi Ali Efendi, *Mektupları*, p. 101.

In this period [1867], the young ladies and young girls had completely abandoned the old dresses with three tails or trains and the baggy pants underneath; fashion now demanded shirts with a single train which was caught up and attached to the belt – there were now petticoats instead of *şalvar*s or the baggy pants previously worn. The headdresses had also changed with the times and now usually matched the costumes; there were earrings with jewels, medallions and elaborate hairstyles, garnished with precious stones.[125]

Ottoman women were very affected by the visit of the empress Eugénie, the wife of Napoleon III. They followed the latest fashion from the French fashion magazines[126] and were swept away by 'a craze for *everything* French'.[127]

It was after the visit of the Empress Eugénie that the women of the palace and the wives of the high functionaries copied as nearly as they could the appearance of the beautiful Empress. They divided their hair in the middle, and spent hours in making little bunches of curls. High-heeled shoes replaced the coloured *babouches* [slippers]; they even adopted the hideous crinolines and abandoned forever those charming Oriental garments, the *chalvar* and the *entari* which they considered symbols of servitude, but which no other fashion has been able to equal in beauty.[128]

Women changed the thicker cloth they had traditionally used for their *ferace*s (long flowing outer garments) for a much thinner material. They changed their yellow boots of morocco leather for shoes with trimmings of imitation gold thread, which they wore with thin, white socks. They began to use thinner veils and they turned covering themselves into a method for making themselves more alluring,[129] a trend appreciated by Ali Rıza Bey, who commented that 'the veils of our women, which were a means of ornamenting the face rather than concealing it, became finer. How charming the colourful *ferace*s looked! And these finer veils were unable to obscure the beauty [behind]'.[130] With his habitual sarcasm, Wraxall, too, noted the change in the style of veils, for 'once on a time the veil covered the whole of the face, so that only the eyes were free, and the poor women did not use a pocket-handkerchief, because they could not find the way to their noses'.[131] He was far from complimentary about Turkish women, for he describes them all as waddling like ducks.[132] What women wore and what they wanted to wear had thus changed. Women now cried

125 Leyla (Saz) Hanımefendi, *Harem*, p. 212.
126 Tahsin Nâhid and Şahabeddin Süleyman, *Ben … Başka!*, ed. Sibel Ercan (Istanbul, 2004), p. 39.
127 Zeynoub Hanoum, *A Turkish Woman's European Impressions*, ed. Grace Ellison (London, 1913), p. 98.
128 Zeynoub Hanoum, *Impressions*, pp. 97–8.
129 Balıkhane Nazırı Ali Rıza Bey, *Hayatı*, pp. 107–8.
130 Balıkhane Nazırı Ali Rıza Bey, *Hayatı*, p. 108.
131 Wraxall, 'Constantinople', p. 308. 132 Wraxall, 'Constantinople', p. 308.

45. The *tango çarşaf* (thin burka), in Erimez, *Tarihten Çizgiler*, [p. 53].

out, in the words of the popular verse, 'I am young and so I of course want/ A red *ferace*, a thin veil and gloves'.[133]

These charming *ferace*s were slowly replaced by the *çarşaf* (the burka), brought to Istanbul from Syria by the wife of Suphi Paşa, who was then governor there. Despite being banned several times, the adoption of the *çarşaf* proved impossible to stop, for the women of Istanbul liked this new fashion and abandoned the *ferace* for it. The *çarşaf* did not stay in its original form, but rapidly went through various changes. Brightly coloured *çarşaf*s, before made from the silks of Damascus, Aleppo and Baghdad, began to be made from cloth imported from Europe. During the Balkan Wars the *tango çarşaf*, a thin and much more revealing garment than the traditional *çarşaf*, appeared. As its name, *tango*, meaning a loudly

[133] Balıkhane Nazırı Ali Rıza Bey, *Hayatı*, p. 108. For more on the fashion of the nineteenth century, see Musahipzade Celal, *Yaşayışı*, pp. 121–41.

dressed woman, implies, this new *çarşaf* was considered too racy in some quarters, in particular by elderly women.[134]

It was not just the old women who were unhappy. For many men, the changes in female apparel were going too far. The women of Istanbul were heading firmly in the wrong direction. They now had a freedom unknown in earlier centuries and, despite the western perception of the Muslim woman locked secretively away in the harem, they were frequently to be seen on the streets of the capital. In fact, according to Basmajean, one saw more Muslim than Christian women on the streets. It was always possible to find hundreds of Muslim women on the shores of the Bosphorus, walking about in their white lace veils, laughing and smoking cigarettes with a freedom not common among the Christian women.[135] Writing in the Istanbul newspaper *Basiret* in 1873, Ali Efendi declared:

> I regret to say that we see that the majority of Muslim women have become addicted to ornamentation to a degree beyond the sufferance of their husbands. Now a veil costing one gold coin has appeared in Beyoğlu and has been sold in a box. Parasols with fringes have become esteemed and apparently cost three *lira*. Moreover, the *ferace* cannot be found for less than seven or eight hundred [*lira*]. Whatever it takes, buy it, and hire a carriage for an excursion every week ... Isn't it better to buy a parasol for eighty *kuruş*, although even this is too much, instead of a veil for one *lira* or a parasol for three *lira*? Would this not produce the same effect? It is forbidden among us for women to make themselves up and go out onto the streets. They are to look good only for their husbands in their own homes. This is enough for women.[136]

Ebüzziya Tevfik Bey, an important literary figure of late nineteenth-century Istanbul, also complained about the Europeanisation of Ottoman women:

> The pretence by our cultured, urban women of today to imitate [European fashions] in such ways as trying to transform their *ferace*s into a coat with the desire of looking like the outfit of European women, attempting to make their hair under their head covers fit the European fashion, and to walk only with short and tiny steps, is not pleasing. For, as there was a walk special to the women of every religious community, so too did the women of Islam have a very beautiful style of walking, slow, swaying the hips. What a pleasing gait it was.[137]

Several years later, in 1877, Basiretçi Ali Efendi complained in his column in *Basiret* about the inappropriate dressing of Muslim women and requested that the police department deal with the problem. After a period of improvement the situation had again worsened, and, according to Ali

134 Musahipzade Celal, *Yaşayışı*, p. 133; Saraçoğlu, *Hatıralar*, p. 146.
135 Basmajean, *Life*, p. 172. 136 Basiretçi Ali Efendi, *Mektupları*, pp. 142–3.
137 Balıkhane Nazırı Ali Rıza Bey, *Hayatı*, p. 109.

Efendi, even had dangerous religious implications. 'I wonder', he wrote, 'if as the holy month of Ramazan is approaching, this [immodest dressing] is preparing to draw us into sin'.[138]

The sultan himself, Abdülhamid, was much concerned about the increasingly unsuitable dressing style of the Muslim women whom he saw on the streets in his infrequent excursions from Yıldız palace. The *çarşaf*s had become merely ordinary dresses, the *ferace*s had turned into sleeveless capes, the veils had become too thin. He issued an order that this should not occur. Further, women were not to wear coats or short, tight-waisted jackets which imitated military styles.[139] To make his disapproval clear and to underline the seriousness of the situation, he wanted this order to be published in the newspapers, thus ensuring that as many people as possible saw it. He also wished personally to check the order before it was released by the government.[140] It was not only the sultan and the press who passed comments on the unsuitability of female dress. Even men on the street made 'insinuating, ill-bred remarks at Muslim women whom they met on the ferry, on the bridge, at the market, on the street or in pleasure gardens'.[141] Old women did not content themselves with passing nasty comments about beautifully dressed women, but even attacked them physically.[142] This conduct much distressed Cemal Paşa, who had, he said, hated it since childhood. When he became governor of Istanbul in 1912, he set out to eradicate such behaviour, which he regarded as undermining the government. Having announced that he would exile men and women caught behaving in this manner, he promptly expelled four or five people from the capital. This firm action had immediate results and such incidents ceased. This, Cemal Paşa wrote in his memoirs, was 'a very healthy step taken in the direction of freedom of women in Istanbul'.[143]

It was not just women who were drawn to the new fashions, for the world of clothes was changing for men also. In 1829, Mahmud II introduced a clothing reform. The robe and turban were now replaced for all officials, except members of the *ulema*, by the frock-coat and trousers. The fez, a headgear from the Maghreb which had been introduced as the compulsory headgear for the military the year before, was now made compulsory for all male officials. It became such an integral part of the Ottoman dress code that no Ottoman gentleman could function without one. Indeed, while it

138 Basiretçi Ali Efendi, *Mektupları*, p. 602.
139 Engin, *Abdülhamid*, doc. 15, p. 163 (1904.i.12).
140 Engin, *Abdülhamid*, p. 55 (1904.i.15).
141 Cemal Paşa, *Hatıralar. İttihat ve Terakki, I. Dünya Savaşı Anıları*, ed. Alpay Kabacalı (Istanbul, 2001), p. 32.
142 Cemal Paşa, *Hatıralar*, p. 33. 143 Cemal Paşa, *Hatıralar*, pp. 32–3.

was possible to travel to Europe with only one pair of trousers, one jacket and a couple of pairs of underwear in your luggage, it was essential to take at least three or four fezes with you.[144] A fez became almost glued to the Ottoman head. In official places, a Muslim taking off his fez was totally unacceptable. For this reason, Hayrullah Efendi did not remove his while visiting the grave of Napoleon in 1863, and noted that even if asked he would not have done so, as it would be 'a violation of good manners'.[145] Fezes could not be removed in government offices, even in the hottest weather when sweat ran drop by drop down the faces of the wearers, staining them with little rivulets of dye in the case of cheap fezes.[146]

By the turn of the century, not wearing the fez was a source of scandal. Enver Paşa, the war minister and one of the triumvirate in charge of the government at the time of the outbreak of the First World War, warned the mayor of Istanbul, Cemil Paşa: 'I hear that you have not been wearing your fez in the office, which is a government office. This is giving rise to gossip and such behaviour is unbecoming to you'.[147] Although the fezes were mostly imported from outside the empire, from Tunisia and Austria (according to 1897 statistics, the Ottoman empire spent 20.9 million *kuruş* on importing fezes and hats),[148] some were produced in the fez factory in Istanbul.[149] In 1908, when Austria-Hungary annexed Bosnia-Herzegovina, Austrian goods were boycotted, among them fezes, the ultimate symbol of Ottomanism. The symbolic significance of this headgear was such that there was intense opposition to Mustafa Kemal Atatürk's order banning the fez and replacing it with the hat in the new Turkish Republic in 1925.

Some men took to the new *alafranga* fashions with excessive enthusiasm, going to extreme lengths in the dandification of their appearance, or so it seemed to their critics. Chic men wore gleaming shoes, starched shirts and perfectly shaped fezes, whose colour, shape and tassel length changed according to the fashion of the day. Everything about them glittered; their cigarette cases, their pocket watches and even the frames of their glasses shone. They carried gold-, silver- or nickel-handled canes in their gloved hands and wore flowers in their buttonholes. Their faces gleamed with such close, smooth shaves that 'even a fly would slip off'. Their moustaches were powdered and lotioned, their tips waxed, and their eyebrows shaped and blackened with kohl. They combed their hair and the tassels of their fezes

144 Hayrullah Efendi, *Seyahatnamesi*, p. 39. 145 Hayrullah Efendi, *Seyahatnamesi*, p. 114.
146 Sadri Sema, *Hatıraları*, p. 460. 147 Topuzlu, *Hatıralarım*, p. 136.
148 Stanford J. Shaw and Ezel Kural Shaw, *History of the Ottoman Empire and Modern Turkey*, vol. II, *The Rise of Modern Turkey 1808–1975* (Cambridge, 1977), p. 238.
149 Sadri Sema, *Hatıraları*, p. 459.

with equal care, and applied lotions such as violet water and lilac water to their hair, and lavender water to their clothes. With their pomaded moustaches, dyed beards and smooth cheeks, they promenaded under parasols to protect themselves from the sun and prevent any unpleasant bronzing of the skin. On their heads they wore red-, purple- and cherry-coloured fezes, their tassels flying in the wind.[150]

Fashion shifted fast and every Ramazan produced a new style for the man-about-town. With a considerable hint of mockery, Ahmed Rasim gave the Ramazan fashion for that year. 'For those of you who want to know', he wrote, 'you can refer to this list':

> fezes are to be black, with a large tassel hanging down half a centimetre shorter than the fez. Hair is to be dyed a dark, roasted Brazilian watery coffee colour and reach the bottom of the ear lobe. The back of the hair is to be gathered up slightly and to be slightly curly. The fez is to be worn slightly to the left, giving the face a spherical triangle shape. Eyebrows are to be brushed upwards. Eyelashes are to be tinged with kohl, eyes to be slightly closed. Cheeks are to be softened with pink powder. Moustaches are not to be blunt nor sharp-pointed. On the upper lip, the moustache is to be in a straight line. The line running from the nose to the lip is to be visible. Lips are to be, as usual, red. Teeth are not to be seen when laughing, or even yawning. The double chin will be double and not triple and will not force flesh up visibly into the face anymore than the corset pushes fat upwards, making it visible. The collar is to be stiff and straight. The tie is to be a purplish brown colour, the overcoat black, with tiny spots of blue and puffy shoulders, the waistcoat open and with double buttons. Trousers are to be a dark black and the trouser legs narrower. Shoes are to be polished and laced, socks, a light yellow.[151]

In his novel *Şıpsevdi*, Hüseyin Rahmi mocked the pretentious foppery of the affected *alafranga* man.[152] He was by no means against the introduction of European ways and was all in favour of learning foreign languages and adopting new ways that would benefit the empire, but this did not mean for him mindless and superficial aping of the ways of Europe. 'Some people think I wrote this novel to mock and belittle *alafranga*-ness. But this is a totally incorrect view and wrong. It is necessary to separate the affectation of applying *alafranga* from the belief in truth and progress'.[153]

According to Hüseyin Rahmi, there were three types of pretentious *alafranga*. One type consisted of those who came from privileged

150 Alus, *İstanbul*, p. 20; Ahmet Rasim, *Şehir*, pp. 138, 508–9; Sadri Sema, *Hatıraları*, pp. 81, 85.
151 Ahmet Rasim, *Şehir*, pp. 328–9.
152 The initial title when he began to publish it in serialised form in the newspaper in 1901 was *Alafranga*, but this was subsequently changed to *Şıpsevdi* when it was published as a book just after the 1908 Revolution.
153 Gürpınar, *Şıpsevdi*, p. 24.

backgrounds, learnt French from childhood, lived well and later had government jobs in Europe or were able to develop their knowledge of Europe in other ways. Most of them were known there, not because of their personal values but because of their family name. These people spoke very good French, were expert horsemen and were masters at gambling. They were 'salon men', middle-ranking socialites. But not one of them could understand Ottoman interests or defend the rights of the empire in a diplomatic setting. They brought nothing to the empire apart from social skills such as chic, gambling, dancing and being good conversationalists. Such men were of no use. 'What we need from *alafranga* is not only those poses, gestures and dress. Even monkeys have the ability to imitate gestures and demeanour in a very superficial way'.[154] The second type of *alafranga* men were those who married European women and lived in Beyoğlu. These 'half Levantines' came from families who were like a double-sided cloth, one side European, the other Ottoman.

The third type of *alafranga* man was the pretentious fop who dressed in the latest fashion and talked constantly about his time in Paris. This type was represented by Meftun Bey, the main character in the novel *Şıpsevdi*, 'who lived in winter in Horhor and in summer in Erenköy, but whose mind was always in Beyoğlu'.[155] Meftun Bey was

> an intellectual lightweight … with gerry-built knowledge, scant, forced and always stolen from a 'savoir-vivre' understanding … his behaviour is imitative, always false, soulless. His complaints are about the beating of the stick of the *mahalle* nightwatchman in the streets at night; dogs barking; the sounds of *boza* sellers following on each other's heels; *alaturka* guests who put their tobacco cases and cigarette holders in their pockets and wear nightshirts and *şam hırka*s [woollen jackets, usually yellow, with wide sleeves and open collars] and who appear after dinner in the evenings; the *fasıl* [classical Turkish music] band. The things he finds shameful: those who wear galoshes, those who eat couscous from street vendors, those who read Ottoman books and newspapers. Habits [of Meftun Bey]: to have his nails cut by a sort of blacksmith for human beings; to say with great difficulty even those words which are easy to say in Turkish; to forget sometimes the most used idioms … to use French proverbs in a conversation, whether or not related to the subject … to whistle pieces from opera during a conversation when he becomes bored.[156]

Fictional characters like Meftun Bey represented a type of man to be found all over Istanbul, such as the 'Büyükdere Monsieur' described by Ahmed Rasim. Chic, with a poor command of French, his rudeness was a

[154] Gürpınar, *Şıpsevdi*, p. 29. [155] Gürpınar, *Şıpsevdi*, p. 75.
[156] Gürpınar, *Şıpsevdi*, pp. 74–5.

particular source of irritation to Ahmed Rasim. He was a man of affectation and pretension, who,

jumping in his mind from Paris, passing mentally through Vienna, casting a glance at Berlin, having seen a map of the Italian cities of Milan, Rome and Naples, having sent a regretful sigh in the direction of London, having read about the American provinces such as New York, Washington and Philadelphia during the time of the exhibitions from guidebooks, had actually only been as far as İzmir and promenaded up and down the corniche.[157]

Another author to poke fun at the pretentious Ottoman fop was the well-known novelist Recaizade Mahmud Ekrem, a leading figure in the late nineteenth century of the new genre in Ottoman literature, the *Edebiyat-ı Cedide* (New Literature). In his novel *Araba Sevdası* (The Carriage Affair), one of the first Ottoman novels to be written, the main character, the well-heeled Bihruz Bey, a *paşazade*, son of a *paşa*, symbolises all the excesses of this superficial Europeanisation of the nineteenth century.

Working with initial enthusiasm for five or six months in a government office, without mastering even the reading of a paragraph in French, Bihruz Bey, with the many words and phrases he had learnt by ear, truly showed a great ability in imitating the behaviour, costume, demeanour and gestures of the most *alafranga* young man. Being an only child, Bihruz Bey had been brought up to be very spoilt. His father's wealth and riches were ever available for whatever his son wanted, and on top of this his tendencies coming from the exigencies of youth were never opposed. After a while, therefore, Bihruz Bey went very infrequently to the office. On the days he did not go there he spent time in Beyoğlu or other places for never-ending reasons such as having his hair cut, ordering clothes from the tailor, having his measurements taken at the shoemakers. On Fridays and Sundays, after half an hour of lessons with his teachers, he used to leave home and wander around the various popular haunts until evening … After coming to Istanbul, he had diverted himself with three things: one, to drive a carriage, two, to wander around more luxuriously dressed than all the other *alafranga* men, three, to speak in French to the barbers, shoemakers, tailors and waiters in the bars. Bihruz Bey resides in the family mansion in Süleymaniye in winter and their summer house in Küçük Çamlıca in summer. There was no place of amusement in vogue among the sons of the rich such as he where this gentleman was not to be found, dressed in the latest fashion in a four-wheeled carriage drawn by a pair of horses, sometimes black, sometimes grey, with only an ornamented bench and a place for the groom behind. In the depths of winter, upon seeing the weather lifting, Bihruz Bey, wearing a tight, thin jacket in order not to spoil his elegant appearance and with only a velvet cover on his knees in order not to conceal his finery, would burn with enthusiasm to drive along the main street of Beyoğlu and the roads of Kağıthane, trembling in the fiercest north-east wind. On hot summer days in temperatures of thirty or thirty-five degrees he would show the same enthusiasm on the roads of Çamlıca, Haydarpaşa and Fenerbahçe,

[157] Ahmet Rasim, *Şehir*, p. 86.

burning and boiling under the fiercest of suns. But this torment was considered by him the greatest pleasure. Wherever Bihruz Bey went, wherever he was to be found, his aim was not to see and be seen, but only to be seen.[158]

Bihruz Bey was not the only Ottoman caught up in a burning desire to display. As Balıkhane Nazırı Ali Rıza Bey noted, all the people of Istanbul had become addicted to ornamentation and splendour.[159] Display was the essential element in one of the quintessential Ottoman pastimes, the *piyasa*, the promenade. In places such as Direklerarası, Fenerbahçe, Kağıthane and Çamlıca, people rode up and down in their phaetons, strutted and strolled along the pavements in the latest fashions, exchanged pleasantries, flirted discreetly using various coded signals – many involving handkerchiefs which were dropped or removed from pockets or waved. Not all advances were so subtle, for some men, unable to distinguish among the women who under their black veils were young and who were old, resorted to pinching them. In response, the women wielded their parasols, delivering a sharp whack on their attacker. Parasols did not always fall on the rightful victim and pinching could be used for other purposes than locating young girls. On one such occasion, Ercümend Ekrem Talu was responsible for an assault on an innocent passer-by. In a great hurry and unable to get past two women in front of him, he pinched the arm of the younger one and then quickly altered his course. The older of the two women swung round. Seeing behind her an elderly (and entirely innocent) gentleman, she hit him firmly over the head. 'Aren't you ashamed, you bearded oaf? With your huge beard like a sack, aren't you ashamed of assaulting a girl who is young enough to be your granddaughter?'[160]

All types of women, from those of the sultan's harem to the prostitutes working for the well-known pimp Acem and the famous madams of the period, Hürmüz, Kaymak Tabağı and Cihanyandı, indulged in the *piyasa*, parading up and down in their phaetons. They were followed by those of chic men, either at a discreet distance or from very close at hand, such carriages going so far as almost to ram them as the men sought a glimpse of their female occupants, or even an exchange of messages or, more daringly, a letter.[161]

It was not merely a matter of how you looked at the *piyasa*, but how you arrived. In the same way as clothes were significant, it was equally important to be seen in a good phaeton. If you did not own one, it was essential to hire one from the right place, outside Pera Palas in Beyoğlu, or from Sultan Mahmud Türbesi (Divan Yolu) or Şehzade mosque. Not only did the carriage have to look good, but so did the driver, who had to be smart

[158] Recaizade Mahmud Ekrem, *Araba Sevdası* (Istanbul, 1985), pp. 16–18.
[159] Balıkhane Nazırı Ali Rıza Bey, *Hayatı*, p. 241.
[160] Talu, *Anılar*, pp. 64–5. [161] Talu, *Anılar*, p. 64.

and well dressed. If the driver was not suitably turned out, he would be told to go and change before his carriage would be hired. Having selected the carriage or phaeton, one then had to check it thoroughly to make sure there were no problems. After all these preliminaries, one was ready to hire the vehicle. Prices varied between two and three *mecidiye*. If the carriage cost three, then the driver was more experienced and a better quality of man. The carriage would also be clean. If it was cheaper, the driver would not be of the same calibre. He might have one shoulder higher than the other, be a little rough, chat needlessly with the passengers and be too familiar. Requesting a cigarette from the passengers, he would put it behind his ear. When the carriage stopped, he would give the horses bags of fodder – all 'shameful things that will make those in the carriage perspire in embarrassment'.[162]

The pleasure of the *piyasa* was not always apparent.

> Do you know what carriage promenading meant? … Imagine a row of carriages, two abreast, in some places where the road is wide, three abreast, stretching along the route from in front of the mosque to Beyazıt. Pack it so tight that the heads of the animals touch the backs of the carriages in front. It was so slow that progress was with the patience of Job, one step every ten, fifteen minutes, maximum two. In some places you could often wait half an hour. As in all places where carriages were to be found, there was a great variety. There were those from the palaces [with their passengers] in their veils, *ferace*s and the eunuchs of the harem, the families of the palace household, the sons and son-in-laws. Magnificent mansion carriages, luxurious hired carriages, broken-down carriages held together by the springs and bits of string and drawn by half-dead horses.[163]

Sometimes promenading was practically impossible due to the crush of people jostling for position on the pavements in their finery. Direklerarası was a favourite location for display. Here the street was jam-packed with a heaving mass of people, wearing furs, coats, boleros, jackets, purple, red, yellow and dotted *çarşaf*s, *hırka*s, *haydari*s [sleeveless jackets worn by dervishes] and *cübbe*s [gowns], capes and light overcoats. In their hands they carried worry beads, walking sticks and parasols. They were so densely packed together that it was impossible to tell if they were actually moving. 'The scowling and the smiling, the mocking and the too familiar, the flatterer and the coquette … Young and old, the lower classes and the upper classes' were all there, employing their red handkerchiefs in a game of subtle seduction, opening and closing their veils, laughing and displaying in the heady pursuit of the *piyasa*.[164]

[162] Alus, *İstanbul*, p. 30. [163] Alus, *İstanbul*, p. 38.
[164] Ahmet Rasim, *Şehir*, pp. 327–8.

The *piyasa* offered one of the few spaces for flirting, however controlled, and it was here that covert communication between the sexes reached its peak in a language of gesture and implication:

> making signs with the eyes and eyebrows, winking one eye, making as if wiping your face with a handkerchief, smelling the handkerchief with which you have just wiped your face, sighing deeply, and placing your hand over your heart. Placing your hand on your temple and half-closing then closing your eyes means 'I am dying for you', unbuttoning of one or two buttons of the waistcoat means 'my heart is palpitating, I cannot bear this beating'. If you have a cigarette in your mouth, even if it is newly lit, and you take it from the corner of your mouth and hurl it away, this is because women do not like addiction to tobacco any more than its smell. To call over a beggar and give him a few coins demonstrates your compassion and generosity. To be busy looking at the posters outside Manakyan's theatre is a sign of liking romantic themes such as *La Dame aux camelias* or *Countess Sara*. To screw your face up in front of Kel Hasan's theatre is a sign of detestation and dislike of buffoonery. Greeting a well-dressed gentleman in the carriage of a rich house by buttoning up your jacket and bending deeply from the waist, your left hand resting on your stomach, your right hand coming up to touch first your lips and then the forehead in a salute implies that you have an acquaintanceship with the upper classes.[165]

The 'modern' city

The dynamic and chaotic city of Istanbul did not appeal to all its inhabitants. Many of the intellectuals and politicians of the period wanted to change it, to create a 'modern' city comparable to those of Europe in design, order and modernity. Cemil Paşa complained that the city was a total mess and did not represent anything European, with no order and no hygiene. He compared Istanbul at the beginning of the twentieth century to a city of the Middle Ages.[166] The sultans were no longer contented with their palaces. Until the late eighteenth century, the palaces were planned according to the model of independent courtyards, with the harem and *selamlık*, the male section, arranged around them. They consisted of a series of separate, but connected, buildings. In the nineteenth century, the traditional Ottoman understanding of the palace was abandoned with the building of Mahmud II's palace, which was replaced by Çırağan palace in 1859. Mahmud was apparently a great fan of the European palaces and much less so of the traditional Ottoman ones. What attracted him to the plan for the palace of Beşiktaş was 'the assurance that it was thoroughly European'.[167] When his court architect attempted to assure him that the

[165] Alus, *İstanbul*, p. 40. [166] Topuzlu, *Hatıralarım*, p. 118.
[167] Pardoe, *Beauties of the Bosphorus*, p. 17.

46. Kel Hasan, in Erimez, *Tarihten Çizgiler*, [p. 70].

splendour of Topkapı was unrivalled by any palace in Europe, he replied angrily that

> none, save a rogue or a fool, could class that place [Topkapı] ... hidden beneath high walls, and amid dark trees, as though it would not brave the light of day; with these light, laughing palaces, open to the free air, and the pure sunshine of heaven. Such would I have my own; and such shall it be.[168]

Under Mahmud II's successor, Dolmabahçe palace became the residence of the sultan. Topkapı palace was abandoned totally. The multistorey European-style palaces continued to be built on both shores of the Bosphorus – Çırağan and Yıldız on the European side and Beylerbeyi on the opposite, Asian side. The most important interior feature of these palaces was their gigantic staircases imitating the European style.

[168] Pardoe, *Beauties of the Bosphorus*, p. 19.

47. Eminönü, in Barth, *Konstantinopel*, p. 164.

On some occasions, European criticism over the appearance of the city had a direct impact. Abdülhamid II was particularly stung by criticism he read in the western press. Summoning his ambassador to France, Salih Münir, he showed him one offending article:

this has been bothering me … It is the translation of an article written on Istanbul by a European traveler. Some of his accusations are wrong and unjustified, but others are true. For example, he criticizes us vehemently for not planning and improving the places that catch a traveler's eye, such as the Eminönü Square, the Karaköy Square, and the Galata Bridge; for neglecting the coast from Sarayburnu [Topkapi palace] to Yedikule [Golden Gate], which could be made even more attractive than the shoreline of Nice and that of the Italian seaside cities; and for not cleaning and repairing the streets of the city. What can we say against these well-founded words? We should either silently accept all the guilt and yield to every accusation or we should clean, embellish, and rebuild our capital. You are the perfect person to handle this matter. You have been living in Europe, you are familiar with it, and you have seen embellished cities, you know of beautiful things and of engineering. I bestow upon you the responsibility to bring here the experts from France.[169]

Following the sultan's orders, Salih Münir contacted Joseph Antoine Bouvard, the inspector general of the architectural department of the City of Paris, the city which was so influential in forming many of the tastes of the nineteenth-century Ottoman elite, and asked him to prepare a master plan for Istanbul. Bouvard's plan was a bold one which envisaged changing many of the major public spaces in the centre of the city. It was not implemented, however, due to lack of funding.[170]

How foreigners saw the city was thus important for Abdülhamid. According to an order from Yıldız palace, Abdülhamid had heard from one of his informants that poor migrants had built tin shacks in Kumkapı in the area around the train tracks. These shacks were now the first view of the city that visitors had as they arrived in Istanbul by train. This was a first impression that Abdülhamid feared would be lasting. Such ugliness undermined the considerable efforts that had been made to beautify those parts of the city seen by foreigners, many of whom came into the capital along this train line, a line which represented a door opening onto the capital of the empire. Abdülhamid therefore ordered that these shacks be removed and the people transferred to a different location, where houses would be built for or rented to them.[171] As part of the preparations for the arrival of the German Kaiser Wilhelm II, Istanbul was spruced up. Fences were built along the route he was to take, to prevent him seeing anything unattractive.[172]

When he became mayor of Istanbul in 1912, Cemil Paşa's 'first job was to investigate the reasons for the neglected condition of the city which had gone on for many years, to diagnose its illness and then try to find a solution to this'.[173] His aim was to make Istanbul into what he regarded as a modern city. In this he was very influenced by the European model, having lived in France himself when studying surgery at university in Paris. He brought twenty Italian road workers and their masters to build modern roads and pavements in the city; invited two English engineers, who had already built the sewage system in Cairo, to build the sewage system in the capital; and

[169] Quoted in Çelik, *Istanbul*, p. 110. [170] Çelik, *Istanbul*, pp. 110–24.
[171] Engin, *Abdülhamid*, doc. 28, p. 176 (1893.iii.22).
[172] Yusuf Akçura, *Hatıralarım* (Ankara, 2005), p. 62. [173] Topuzlu, *Hatıralarım*, p. 118.

requested a large German firm to prepare a city plan for Istanbul.[174] He brought in three experts in municipal cleanliness from Paris and Brussels to be inspectors in charge of the cleanliness of Istanbul,[175] and himself went to Bucharest to investigate how they conducted city cleaning, for he took Bucharest, which he regarded as the Paris of the Balkans, as an example of a clean city. Apart from experts, Cemil Paşa also imported European materials, such as the cement he had shipped from England, to be used in the widening of a bridge over the railway which passed by Topkapı and in building a jetty stretching to Fener on the shore.[176]

While men such as Cemil Paşa attempted to alter the city plan, widening the roads, moving away from construction in wood to construction in more long-lasting and fire-resistant brick, and removing the many little alleys ending in cul-de-sacs which made policing the city so difficult and access for firefighters almost impossible, others, such as the famous nineteenth-century architect Kemaleddin, complained. For Kemaleddin Bey, such changes altered the face of the city for the worse and destroyed the beauty inherent in the old, winding streets, and the dignity given to the city by its old and beautiful buildings.[177]

Beyoğlu: the foreign quarter of Pera and Galata

One area of the city more than any other became associated with the influx of European fashions and with the rapidly changing mores of many of its citizens. This was Beyoğlu, the 'foreign' quarter of Istanbul, so different in the eyes of the more traditional and conservative elements of society that it was referred to by some as Frengistan, the land of the Europeans, just as it had been four centuries before by Tursun Bey. With its theatres, nightclubs, departmental stores, cafes, wine houses, bookshops stocking European books and magazines, brothels and foreign embassies, it was a magnet to all those who wanted to escape the controls of the more staid society of the old city, who wanted to imbibe a more 'European' atmosphere, to shop for the latest European fashions and acquaint themselves more fully with those radical political ideas of which Abdülhamid so disapproved.

This was the quarter where the innovations from Europe were first introduced. Gas lamps came first to Beyoğlu, whose streets were lit from 1856 by gas from the *Gazhane*, the gashouse, of the palace at Dolmabahçe.[178] The first tram to go into operation in the city ran in

[174] Topuzlu, *Hatıralarım*, p. 130. [175] Topuzlu, *Hatıralarım*, pp. 126–8.
[176] Topuzlu, *Hatıralarım*, p. 137.
[177] İlhan Tekeli and Selim İlkin (eds.), *Mimar Kemalettin'in Yazıları* (Ankara, 1997), pp. 107–20.
[178] Balıkhane Nazırı Ali Rıza Bey, *Hayatı*, p. 189.

STREET IN GALATA

48. Street in Galata, in Hutton, *Old Capital of the Empire*, p. 223.

Beyoğlu. The first underground – indeed one of the first in the world – was built by the Frenchman Eugène Henri Gavand in 1875 to connect Karaköy, down by the water, to İstiklal Caddesi, the main street of Galata up on the hill above the sea. This underground line, known now as Tünel, is still in operation. It was the only underground in the city until the introduction of the new metro system in the early 2000s. The people of Beyoğlu were the first to see the new medium of film when, in the autumn of 1895, Edison's kynetoscope-phonographe was established in one of Pera's shops. It was followed by cinematograph showings in the Sponeck Beer House there.[179]

First and foremost, it was an area that buzzed. Everyone, from all classes, all the notable figures of Istanbul and many well-known personalities from the upper echelons of society,[180] flocked across the bridge over the Haliç (the Golden Horn) to promenade, to relax in the coffee shops, to shop in the noisy, bustling Cadde-i Kebir, la Grand Rue de Pera, today's İstiklal Caddesi, and to go to *apukurya*, the carnival. Always lively, it was on Friday and Sunday nights, as people returned from Kağıthane, and on carnival nights that the crowds were so great on Cadde-i Kebir that 'if a needle was thrown it would not fall to the ground'.[181] *Apukurya* actually had a religious significance, for *Apokreá* was the name for the second Sunday before Lent, 'the day of farewell to meat, which for the religious it actually is'. For many, however, it was when 'the gaieties of Carnival' were at their height.[182] Although the festivities of *apukurya* were held mostly in Christian populated areas, such as Fener, Kumkapı and Kurtuluş, it was the cosmopolitan, religiously and ethnically mixed Beyoğlu that was its true centre.

Its arrival was signalled by the appearance in the shop windows of Bon Marché, Pazar Alman and Karlman of carnival costumes and masks, called *mucunu* in Greek and *yüzlük* in Turkish.[183] When *apukurya* began, masqueraders filled the streets to overflowing.[184] All were caught up in the excitement and even the most lethargic became exuberant.[185] Groups of masqueraders wandered the streets indulging in various forms of buffoonery. The grinding and gurgling noises of the barrel organ, the bray of the shawm and the clash of the small double drum filled the air. Clowns in conical hats and inside-out jackets, their faces daubed with flour and their cheeks painted scarlet, pranced among the crowds. Men with saddles on their backs, grass on the saddles, horseshoes tied to their hands and wearing donkey-head masks cantered about, shaking their heads, braying and kicking their legs up high in the air.[186] The wild excitement and excessiveness of carnival drew all into it, and the extravagance entranced the inhabitants of Beyoğlu who indulged in it to the full.

Entertainment was not restricted to the buffoonery of the streets. Carnival balls were held in the most 'in' places in Beyoğlu, where heaving

[179] Nijat Özön, *Karagözden Sinemaya. Türk Sineması ve Sorunları*, 2 vols. (Ankara, 1995), I, p. 17.

[180] Alus, *İstanbul*, p. 21. [181] Alus, *İstanbul*, p. 20. [182] Dwight, *Constantinople*, p. 324.

[183] Saraçoğlu, *Hatıralar*, p. 210.

[184] Saraçoğlu, *Hatıralar*, p. 211; Ahmet Rasim, *Fuhş-i Atik*, pp. 138–66.

[185] Ahmet Rasim, *Şehir*, pp. 176–7.

[186] Quoted from Sermet Muhtar Alus, in Saraçoğlu, *Hatıralar*, p. 212.

crowds danced until morning.[187] The dance halls, coffee houses which offered musical entertainment, nightclubs, beer houses, all were jam-packed. As well as revellers, such crowds attracted those intent on less innocent entertainment, for carnival was accompanied by a multitude of pickpocketing, stealing and brawling. Many became the victims of irritating practical jokes, passing their time, for example, in constant scratching after having been sprayed with itching powder.[188]

Although many were content to pass the entire night in a riot of entertainment in the various establishments of Beyoğlu, not everyone who spent the night there did so by choice. In the evening, the bridge linking Galata to Istanbul was raised. There was no fixed time for this. It could happen suddenly and without warning during the last call to prayer. Despite the presence of two elderly nightwatchmen, who were often half asleep, and two ropes strung along both ends of the bridge, there were accidents as people plunged headlong into the black water, unaware in the dark of the non-existence of the bridge. The son-in-law of Mazhar Paşa, the mayor of Istanbul, for example, plummeted into the sea, together with his brougham, and was never seen again.[189] This was perhaps why many chose to pass the night in various hotels in Galata if they could not make it to the bridge before nightfall, or wandered around the streets until morning.[190]

A centre for nocturnal activity and carnival, Beyoğlu was also, for many, the place to shop. Here were to be found European-style shops selling goods imported from Europe. Many of the shops were kept by Italians, Greeks and Frenchmen, and many English articles were displayed for sale:

> stockings, cotton prints, cutlery, and blacking. In one window was a number of *Punch*, with one of Mr Leech's clever cuts, attracting the puzzled gaze of some Levantines; at a corner was a sign-board, with 'Furnished apartments to Let' painted on it; and on the wall of a small burying-ground a Turk sat with a tray of Birmingham steel pens on cards.[191]

Even the women of the palace were attracted by such shops, for Leyla Hanım commented that 'the Great Bazaar of Istanbul in those days had an importance which it has lost since the opening of the new shops and stores in Pera'.[192]

These shops in Pera provided the elite and wealthy circles of Istanbul's population with goods coming from Europe. They frequented such shops

[187] Ahmet Rasim, *Şehir*, p. 179 and quoted from Sermet Muhtar Alus in Saraçoğlu, *Hatıralar*, pp. 213–14.

[188] Ahmet Rasim, *Şehir*, p. 413.

[189] Alus, *İstanbul*, p. 272.

[190] Ahmet Rasim, *Şehir*, p. 197.

[191] Smith, *Constantinople*, p. 69.

[192] Leyla (Saz) Hanımefendi, *Harem*, p. 150.

as the famous departmental store Bon Marché, the famous fashion and perfume shop, Bon Ton, and bought their household furnishing from Cosma Vuccino and partners, experts in decoration and furniture, their clothing in Tiring Mağazası,[193] and their sewing machines from the Singer shop. They browsed through the books at Hristodulos bookstore, frequented by the Galatasaray students;[194] and had their photographs taken at Febus, a photographer's shop owned by Boğos Torkulyan, who specialised in photographing the rich and famous.[195] A branch of the exclusive Chemiserie Universelle, the shirt shop of Papadopulo and Leonlides, with branches in London and Paris, was also to be found in La Grande Rue de Pera. There were fur shops, watch shops and jewellers, the children's and men's clothing shop Mayer, which had various branches in the area, the Paris ve Londra Mağazaları (the Paris and London shops) and the İngiliz Pazarı (the English market), selling household goods, porcelain and lamps and the other latest goods imported from France and England. These shops advertised their wares in the newspapers – both Turkish and those in other languages – and their clientele were thus well informed about the new products imported from Europe which they could find in the enticing shops of Beyoğlu.[196] It was here, too, that the elite could while away their time in Lebon Pastahanesi (cafe)[197] or in the many dance halls, such as the Pera Palas ballroom, the Jardin des Fleurs and Casin de Péra, which provided their customers with food, drink and music and hired out the necessary ball-dresses.[198]

Pazar Alman and Bon Marché were both important departmental stores, where being seen was as important as the shopping. Sermet Muhtar Alus regarded Bon Marché as 'more crowded and less classy than Pazar Alman',[199] an opinion shared by Ahmed Rasim, who felt that there was a lack of manners in Bon Marché and who for this reason hated going there. He was, however, 'amazed at the politeness which I see at Pazar Alman', where 'everything is in its proper place'.[200] Despite this, Bon Marché attracted people in droves:

> the most crowded place was in front of Bon Marché. Those going in bumped into those coming out. It was customary to queue to get in. It was counted a great victory to give way to women with all sorts of poses and to obtain a thank you. Add to this heaving throng the beggars, porters, flower sellers, one or two Ottoman Greeks selling dogs. Then imagine the mansion carriages stretched out end to end along the pavement. Now, this was Beyoğlu's most teeming place.[201]

[193] Alus, *İstanbul*, p. 16. [194] Alus, *İstanbul*, p. 15. [195] Alus, *İstanbul*, pp. 17–18.
[196] Nur Akın, *19. Yüzyılın İkinci Yarısında Galata ve Pera* (Istanbul, 1998), pp. 220–5.
[197] Alus, *İstanbul*, p. 16. [198] Akın, *Galata ve Pera*, p. 259.
[199] Alus, *İstanbul*, pp. 16–17. [200] Ahmet Rasim, *Şehir*, p. 194.
[201] Alus, *İstanbul*, pp. 23–4.

Its customers were from every class, its personnel superior:

everyone, from the most chic and polite to the school pupils and the apprentice girls of the dressmakers and the hat makers, all would be going in one door of this establishment and coming out of the other. How quaint the well-dressed Ottoman Greek man working in the perfume department! With his face powdered and his moustaches dressed, his fawning over the madams and mademoiselles was quite beyond description. They hung on his every word; he, on the other hand, affected a mixture of coquetry, pompousness and disdain. If he granted a little favour, it was only the flicker of a smile! The special features of Bon Marché were many. News was given that the customer was going to pay money at the till by shouting in French: Suasant [soixante] piyastr, alakes! [a la casse] Kenz! [quainze]. Duz edemi! [douze et demi] … sometimes a discordant tune *Dans havanez* with false notes, sometimes a *Hamidiye Marşı* [a Hamidian March], at other times the folksong *Üsküdar'dan Gelirken* [While Coming from Üsküdar] were heard from a musical instrument, echoing around the surroundings, and, from the place where there were phonographs, the sounds of a reinforced pipe, a plastic whistle, a lamb, a cow were heard, and from time to time a Greek 'Yarummi' or an İzmir folksong boomed out.[202]

Bon Marché was sometimes a source of unexpected delights. According to gossip, Nureddin Paşa, married to Zekiye Sultan, the daughter of Abdülhamid II, met a beautiful Ottoman Greek woman outside the shop. Some time later she became his mistress. This was not apparently a wise decision on her part for, although urged to divorce her husband by her father, Zekiye Sultan did not want to give Nureddin Paşa up and, so it was rumoured, the mistress was murdered by the sultan's men.[203]

Nearby was a postcard shop. According to Alus, acquaintance with the rather good-looking owner ensured one the opportunity to withdraw into an empty corner of the establishment where, looking around furtively, one could obtain cards of half-naked women. 'It was a victory to get hold of a picture in which the women's breasts and arms were slightly more visible than usual'.[204] Near the Galata Tower was Stampa's, the shop which, according to Albert Smith, had everything.

We came home through Galata, as usual, and this day I was introduced to another great feature of Constantinople, and more especially a Frank one; I allude to Stampa's shop. Everybody knows Stampa; in fact, he may be considered as the embodiment of Pera and Galata; and not to have met him would have shown a want of connexion and investigation, which ought to preclude anybody speaking of Constantinople as a place they were acquainted with. Stampa is not an Englishman, but he speaks our language like a native; so does his son, who

[202] Alus, *İstanbul*, p. 18. The name of the song should actually be *Üsküdar'a Gider İken*, still a very popular song taught to students learning Turkish.

[203] Talu, *Anılar*, pp. 190–201. [204] Alus, *İstanbul*, p. 16.

> was educated in London; so does everybody you find about his establishment, whether they belong to it or not. His shop is a marvellous depôt of everything you want. He supplies you, with equal readiness, with a pot of Atkinson's bear's grease, or a bottle of Tennant's pale ale, a packet of Gillott's peas, a dozen of Day and Martin's blacking, or a box of Holloway's Pills. You want some Harvey's sauce – you find it at Stampa's; you do not know the address of some merchant in Galata – Stampa will tell you directly; you are uncertain about the different departures of the steamers – Stampa has all the information at his fingers' ends, or if he by chance has not, his clever son is a walking Bradshaw. For good razors (of which I hold Heiffor's Sheffield ones, at a shilling, to be the best, and accordingly recommended him to lay in a stock for future demands), solar lamps, cutlery, London ink, pasteboard, pins and needles, Stilton cheeses, gutta percha, otto of roses, sponge, Windsor soap, and Howqua's mixture, there is no shop like Stampa's.[205]

With all its European influence, its fashions, modes and ideas, Beyoğlu represented to many what the skimpy bathing shorts of the infidels disporting themselves on the shores of the Bosphorus did: moral decline and the seeping influence of shameful infidel ways. It was Frengistan. Indeed, it had long been the quarter for the foreigners. The Genoese were granted their trading settlement here by the Byzantine emperor Michael VIII after his reconquest of the city from the Latins in 1261. It was this quarter that they surrendered to Mehmed II in 1453 as his forces stormed Constantinople. This was the area from then onwards of the foreign consuls, the churches and the synagogues. The churches here, and nowhere else, were permitted to ring their bells. It was to Beyoğlu that the foreigners gravitated in the First World War, and where the occupiers spent their time and money after the defeat of 1918. For the passionate nationalists of the early Republic it was the viperous nest of those who had failed to support the National War of Liberation, of those who had, through their greed and self-interest, chosen to collaborate with a corrupt and morally bankrupt regime and its foreign masters. It was a dangerous Frengistan, not merely separate and different from the rest of the city, but a poison within the heart of Istanbul. In Salahaddin Enis's 1923 novel, *Zaniyeler* (The Adultresses) set in Beyoğlu during the First World War, all decadence and immorality was displayed here, the quarter where the German commanders, the Ottoman bureaucrats, the aristocrats, the army officers and the Levantines gathered together in the theatres and restaurants, spending their illicit war gains, drawn together by their shared desire to exploit the war-torn country.[206] All the wickedness and immorality of an occupied city was reflected in the novel *Sodom ve Gomore*

[205] Smith, *Constantinople*, pp. 126–7.
[206] Selahattin Özpalabıyıklar (ed.), *Türk Edebiyatında Beyoğlu* (Istanbul, 2000), pp. 85–91.

(Sodom and Gomorrah), written by Yakup Kadri Karaosmanoğlu and published in 1928. Here, as in *Zaniyeler* of Salahaddin Enis, Beyoğlu was the tainted and traitorous centre for the occupying powers – the French, Italian, British and even the Russians – and for those happy to collaborate with them.[207]

This foreignness had made Beyoğlu something separate, almost alien, to the rest of the city for centuries. In 1718, Lady Mary Wortley Montagu had described the area to Lady Bristol as wholly inhabited by Frank Christians. Together they 'make the appearance of a very fine town, are divided from it by the sea, which is not above half so broad as the broadest part of the Thames'.[208] Her remark was echoed centuries later by Rashid Rida in 1910, who commented on the huge gulf between Istanbul and Beyoğlu, though the distance between them was only a matter of minutes.[209] Perhaps the Haliç may not have been as broad as the Thames, but this waterway separating Beyoğlu from the rest of the city was apparently almost impassable, for

> the Christian men are loathe to hazard the adventures they sometimes meet amongst the levents or seamen (worse monsters than our watermen) and the women must cover their faces to go there, which they have a perfect aversion to do. 'Tis true they wear veils in Pera, but they are such as only serve to show their beauty to more advantage, and which would not be permitted in Constantinople. Those reasons deter almost every creature from seeing it, and the French Ambassadress will return to France, I believe, without ever having been there.[210]

Almost a hundred and fifty years later, Ahmed Cevdet Paşa commented on the isolation of Beyoğlu from Istanbul and related a conversation he had had with the French ambassador. Upon being corrected over his belief in the existence of clergy in Islam, the French ambassador commented, 'I have lived in Istanbul for a long time, but I have not apparently been able sufficiently to learn about it'. Ahmed Cevdet Paşa noted this startling lack of knowledge of Islam exhibited even by a European representative in the Ottoman empire and went on to say:

> You lived in Beyoğlu. You could not have learnt about the conditions of the Ottoman empire or even of the spirit of Istanbul properly. Beyoğlu is an isthmus between Europe and the Islamic lands. From here you see Istanbul through a telescope, but the telescopes which you used were always warped.[211]

Its foreignness was often perceived as dangerous and was the focus of much tut-tutting and moral disapproval. For Abdülhamid II it was a

[207] Yakup Kadri Karaosmanoğlu, *Sodom ve Gomore* (Istanbul, 2005).
[208] Montagu, *Letters*, p. 126. [209] Rashid Rida, *İttihad*, p. 151.
[210] Montagu, *Letters*, p. 126.
[211] Cevdet Paşa, *Tezâkir 21–39*, Cavid Baysun (ed.) (Ankara, 1991), pp. 103–4.

source of dangerous publications. Although often regarded as the censor sultan par excellence, Abdülhamid's approach to the press was far more nuanced than it is usually given credit for.[212] However, he certainly did revert to banning foreign and critical publications wherever possible and preventing such subversive material from seeping into the country. But in this he was often thwarted by the irritatingly uncontrollable Beyoğlu, whose bookshops provided young radicals with all the reading material they wanted.[213] Prohibition was not an easy policy to pursue, as was noted by Sadri Sema, an employee of the ministry of internal affairs whose job it was to write orders banning newspapers.

> Was this prohibition useful in any way? Absolutely not. Every young man who heard of the prohibition of a book or a newspaper, every intellectual, even some among the common people, due to their [aroused] curiosity, sought these newspapers and books in the booksellers of Beyoğlu and read them.[214]

Banned books came easily into the country via the foreign post,[215] which functioned outside Ottoman state control, and then popped up on the back shelves of the Beyoğlu bookshops, which were mostly run by non-Muslims.[216] The Ottoman elite did not even need to bother going to a bookshop to purchase banned books, for these could also be found in the clubs of Beyoğlu where the clientele was largely foreign. Ottomans entering such clubs were kept under surveillance by the government, which could do little else about them.[217]

For the grandmother of Ahmet İhsan Tokgöz, the well-known magazine owner and publisher, Beyoğlu was a source not of dangerous publications, but of dangerous immorality. She had but one dislike: 'to cross the bridge to the other side'.

> My grandmother, like other women of her time, did not count the other side, Galata and Beyoğlu, as part of our country. When she heard that I had gone to Beyoğlu with my aunt's son, she wailed: 'oh woe! they have taken the boy to Frengistan'.[218]

[212] Ebru Boyar, 'The press and the palace: the two-way relationship between Abdülhamid II and the press, 1876–1908', *Bulletin of the School of Oriental and African Studies*, 69/3 (2006), pp. 417–32.

[213] Ebru Boyar, 'Engelhardt from censorship to icon: the use of a European diplomat's history in Ottoman and Turkish historiography on the *Tanzimat*', *Eurasian Studies*, 3/1 (2004), pp. 91–7.

[214] Sadri Sema, *Hatıraları*, p. 12.

[215] 1308 Cemaziyelevvel 3: Başbakanlık Osmanlı Arşivi, Istanbul, Y. PRK. ZB. 10–58.

[216] Server İskit, *Türkiyede Neşriyat Haraketleri Tarihine Bir Bakış* (Istanbul, 1939), pp. 113–16.

[217] Süleyman Kâni İrtem, *Abdülhamid Devrinde Hafiyelik ve Sansür. Adülhamid'e Verilen Jurnaller*, ed. Osman Selim Kocahanoğlu (Istanbul, 1999), p. 267.

[218] Ahmet İhsan, *Matbuat Hatıralarım. 1888–1923. Birinci Cilt Meşrutiyet İlânına Kadar 1889–1908* (Istanbul, 1930), p. 25.

49. The Galata bridge, in Cochran, *Pen and Pencil in Asia Minor* (London, 1887), p. 277.

She was not alone in her concern for the well-being of boys who crossed the bridge to the seducing streets of Beyoğlu. Schoolmasters felt the same. Pupils at Darüşşafaka, an important boarding school in Istanbul established for orphans and poor but successful pupils, including Ahmed Rasim, were left in no doubt about the matter.

On every free day, he [the school master] collected us together in the school hall and after giving us various pieces of advice, he would give us orders such as do not cross to Galata or Beyoğlu, or, even if you are from there, do not wander around the back streets of the area, do not go to theatres or cafes with music, wear your jackets buttoned up and your trousers belted up round your waists, you will not carry bundles or large packets in your hands.

After such a lengthy list of admonitions about the area, the boys naturally became more and more intrigued by it. 'I wonder what kind of an area Galata and Beyoğlu is that it is forbidden to go there', they asked themselves. 'This warning awakened curiosity in every one of us. We started to ask each other. We had a friend called Ahmed who was from Galata. We said to him "What kind of an area is your quarter?"'[219] Ahmed explained, describing in detail the delights of the quarter, the drums, the music, the theatres. His description was so enticing that Ahmed Rasim inevitably wished to enter this 'forbidden land', which he did, going with Ahmed to a theatre. Others from the school also went, but not all were as lucky as Ahmed Rasim. One school mate was arrested by the police there while drinking 'arpa suyu' – beer, or, literally, barley juice. He was brought back to school and punished severely by the schoolmaster.[220]

Worse things even than drinking 'arpa suyu', and thus becoming an infidel, could befall those who strayed.

Casinos and nightclubs, decorated with lust-provoking pictures, low-class cafe chantants … opened daily in Galata and Beyoğlu and were open until the morning. The attraction of our youth to 'alafranga' increased. They had got very used to consuming champagne, cognac and whisky and to bottles containing liqueurs with various fruity and flowery smells and decorated with gilded labels. The brothels, full of local and foreign women, increased day by day. Carnival times especially produced a stream of idle drifters who flowed over to Galata and Beyoğlu. Mansion carriages and hired carriages transported the young men there with all speed, splashing mud in all directions. It became the custom for people to pack the dancing halls and the nightclubs and to stay there until dawn. The decked-out girls of the brothels drugged minds with the

[219] Ahmed Rasim, *Matbuat Hatıralarından: Muharrir, Şair, Edip* (Istanbul, 1342/1924), pp. 13–14.
[220] Ahmet Rasim, *Fuhş-i Atik*, pp. 16–17.

scent of lavender which they put on themselves and allured hearts with their vivaciousness. With the incentive of love and affection, and the provocation of jealousy, men thus became capable of anything. This led to many disasters one after the other. Even worse, an important section of our people was caught up by the evil of gambling which spread its tentacles into every part of Istanbul. Rich young men dedicated their capital, servants their wages, the mass of artisans and labourers their earnings to the merrymaking of Galata and Beyoğlu.[221]

It was due to the immoral ways of Beyoğlu that wealthy men of Istanbul lost their money, their health and their honour. 'The old "Turkish strength", at one time proverbial among the Franks, existed no longer. Our brave lads, their cheeks ruddy with health, huge, tall and strong, were eaten away and destroyed by gonorrhoea and syphilis. Our country became home to a generation of sick men'.[222]

It was to combat this sexual immorality and prostitution for which Beyoğlu was famous that the government established its first health checks in Istanbul on prostitutes there, carried out under the control of the Sixth Division, the administrative unit in charge of the Beyoğlu region. This establishment of health controls signified the change in the government's attitude to prostitution, for although it had always existed, it had never before been acknowledged. Now however, it was accepted, taxed and controlled.[223] The first venereal disease hospital was established in Beyoğlu in 1879, the Nisa Hastanesi for women.[224]

While men's moral fibre was sapped by the temptations of Beyoğlu, so women too were seduced by the Beyoğlu life, although to a lesser extent. To the horror of Basiretçi Ali Efendi, Muslim women were 'tripping around [Beyoğlu] from morning to night in their carriages, in clothes unsuitable to the honour and precepts of Islam, among foreigners, up and down in a totally coquettish manner'.[225]

Such behaviour, he wrote in his column in *Basiret*, was contrary to the essence of Islam, to its 'purity, modesty, custom and honesty', and he called on the authorities to take precautions against Muslim women from various important families of Istanbul crossing the bridge to Beyoğlu.[226] Quite who was responsible for this state of affairs was a matter of debate. According to the newspaper *İbret*, responsibility lay

[221] Balıkhane Nazırı Ali Rıza Bey, *Hayatı*, p. 191.
[222] Balıkhane Nazırı Ali Rıza Bey, *Hayatı*, p. 191.
[223] Ebru Boyar, 'Profitable prostitution: state use of immoral earnings for social benefit in the late Ottoman empire', *Bulgarian Historical Review*, 1–2 (2009), forthcoming. For the regulations applied to Beyoğlu, see Osman Nuri Ergin, *Mecelle-i Umur-ı Belediyye*, 6 vols. (Istanbul, 1995), VI, pp. 3296–306.
[224] Bedi N. Şehsuvaroğlu, *İstanbul'da 500 Yıllık Sağlık Hayatımız* (Istanbul, 1953), p. 74.
[225] Basiretçi Ali Efendi, *Mektupları*, p. 21. [226] Basiretçi Ali Efendi, *Mektupları*, p. 21.

not just with the police force, but also with the men who allowed their women to go freely to Beyoğlu. Ali Efendi agreed. What, he asked, are we to do as a society 'if a man can accommodate this shameful and base situation, which forms part of his comprehension of civilisation, into his understanding of patriotism, and therefore does not prevent these hussies from enjoying themselves [there]'.[227] Despite Ali Efendi's strictures, the situation did not improve, and when he visited Beyoğlu to see for himself what precautions had been taken against the unsuitable promenading of women, he was most displeased to find that nothing had changed. In fact, it had got worse.

> The cigarettes, the sign language [used between the sexes], the scandalous behaviour were all several times worse than they had been before ... Frank, Greek, Armenian and Jewish women also wandered around in Beyoğlu. Do they make facial gestures like monkeys? Have you ever seen this? What kind of lack of patriotism is this that our women commit scandalous acts no other nation would accept? For this reason a great sin has fallen on the community of Islam.[228]

What was happening in Beyoğlu involving the women of the Muslim community was, for Ali Efendi, a matter of public morality and one that had to be dealt with by the state. Ali Efendi's campaign appears to have borne fruit, for several months later, in March 1872, he informed his readers of the order issued by a high-up official banning Muslim women from going to Beyoğlu and from wandering around there unless they had some specific business.[229]

It was this immorality, which many equated with Europe and which was seen as a hallmark of the western, modern and Europeanised Beyoğlu, that was so abhorrent to men like Ali Efendi. 'If the meaning of civilisation is immorality', he stated firmly, 'then we do not want that civilisation'.[230] While echoing Ali Efendi's disgust, Balıkhane Nazırı Ali Rıza Bey blamed the present state of moral decline on the Ottomans' mindless aping of the West. 'Today, one section of the people of this nation lies groaning in the hospitals, one section in the prisons, and one section under the talons of poverty. Well, the results of blindly imitating western civilisation have brought us to this point'.[231]

Beyoğlu was the gateway to 'civilised' Europe, the quarter of the city, with its cosmopolitan structure, its Parisian cafes and ballrooms, through which the European world could be accessed. But it was also the quintessential symbol of moral decline, awash with all the defects and impurities of

[227] Basiretçi Ali Efendi, *Mektupları*, p. 109. [228] Basiretçi Ali Efendi, *Mektupları*, p. 114.
[229] Basiretçi Ali Efendi, *Mektupları*, p. 128. [230] Basiretçi Ali Efendi, *Mektupları*, p. 114.
[231] Balıkhane Nazırı Ali Rıza Bey, *Hayatı*, p. 192.

European culture, a sin city which brought ruination to the good Muslim and stripped him of his health, wealth and faith. Here was where the Ottoman *alafranga* fop felt most at home. Good men, such as Rakım Efendi, the hero of Ahmed Midhat's novel, *Felatun Bey ile Rakım Efendi* (Felatun Bey and Rakım Efendi), educated in European languages and European science and learning, kept their Ottomanness and their culture and did not frequent the backstreets of Beyoğlu. Bad ones, such as Felatun Bey, the foil to Rakım Efendi and anti-hero of the novel, denied their Ottomanness and blindly imitated European ways. Rakım Efendi was the ideal Ottoman, who took what was useful from European civilisation but not its immorality. In contrast, Felatun Bey, who even introduced himself to the foreigners in Beyoğlu as Platon, the European equivalent of his name, sowed the seeds of his own destruction by squandering all his wealth on an actress in Beyoğlu. His friend, Rakım Efendi, on hearing about Felatun's fall, was very distressed and told his friend Jozefina, who tried to console him: 'oh, my poor, dear Rakım ... Is it your job to be sorry for all the idiots of the world? Platon Bey was hardly a child. Even the children understood that he would finish his money in Beyoğlu'.[232]

It was impossible not to know what would happen to you in Beyoğlu, for even popular songs explained it. One of the most popular, sung by the famous singer Peroz Hanım, ran:

> It is very nice to wander in the Beyoğlu *piyasa*
> I was stripped like an onion
> Here, see my emptied pockets
> Wow, wow, wow, I was really done
> What a pity, I realised too late.[233]

While Beyoğlu was symbolic of Europeanisation in all senses, a world of both technological and intellectual innovation, of fast-changing fashion, more relaxed social interaction, as well as of moral depravity, it became the stage for more than mere adulation or mere condemnation of the ways of the West. It also became the setting for a fightback, a place where Europe could be taken on on its own terms, and be beaten, where the Ottoman elite found an opportunity to prove themselves as 'civilised' in the eyes of the Europeans who labelled them 'barbarians'. In Safveti Ziya's *Salon Köşelerinde* (In the Corners of the Salon), published in 1905, the main character, Şekip Bey, aimed to

[232] Ahmet Midhat Efendi, 'Felatun Bey ile Rakım Efendi', in Ahmed Midhat Efendi, *Bütün Eserleri Romanlar I. Dünyaya İkinci Geliş Yahud İstanbul'da Neler Olmuş; Felatun Bey ile Rakım Efendi; Hüseyin Fellah*, ed. Kazım Yetiş, Necat Birinci and M. Fatih Andı (Ankara, 2000), p. 133.

[233] Koçu, *İstanbul Ansiklopedisi*, V, pp. 2708–9.

prove himself, an Ottoman Turk, to be as good as any European by his ability to dance perfectly according to European fashion in the Pera Palas ballroom.

> I dressed myself with great attention ... what can I do? When I go to places such as these I want us, us Turks, to attract attention with our elegance, our behaviour, our upright stance, our good manners and our good breeding. I want those who see a beautiful woman dancing with a man in a fez to stop for a moment and say 'how well that young Turk waltzes!'[234]

Miss Lydia Sunshine, an Englishwoman who visited Istanbul and met Şekip Bey there, complimented him after their first waltz: 'but how well you waltz. An extraordinary thing for a Turk!' Far from being complimented, Şekip Bey was annoyed.

> Why must a thing which is normal for a European be extraordinary for a Turk? You can be sure Mademoiselle that there are now many young men in my country who are just as sensitive, with just as much of a moral upbringing and just as educated as the Europeans, perhaps even more so.[235]

Well aware of their image in Europe, the Ottomans spent much of the later nineteenth century struggling against the constant barrage of criticism from the Europeans, who largely regarded them as uncivilised and trammelled by a religion that was inimical to progress. From their cosmopolitan, dynamic and fast-changing capital, where innovation mixed and moulded to form part of the Ottoman social fabric, they looked at the world to the West and were not always impressed by what they saw.

[234] Safveti Ziya, *Salon Köşelerinde*, ed. Nuri Akbayar (Istanbul, 1998), p. 14.
[235] Safveti Ziya, *Salon Köşelerinde*, p. 19.

Beyond the city

> [Istanbul] is a city surrounded by places for promenade, a city which gives joy to the heart, a place which gives relief to the soul. In truth it is not a city but a world of its own, or a great country embracing seven hills which resembles seven climes of Ptolemy. For one *mangır* a man may cross to the other side [Galata] to see Frengistan [Europe]. Those who have not seen Algeria and Tunisia find consolation if they go to Kasımpaşa.[1]

An ornament of the world, a meeting point of nations beyond compare which afforded the delights of Europe and the pleasures of Asia,[2] Istanbul contained the splendours of the universe,[3] all the world within its walls. Some even went as far as to say that to see Istanbul was to see heaven,[4] and for Latifi his arrival in Istanbul certainly produced that effect, for he 'like Adam while seeking heaven in the skies found it on earth'.[5] For Yahya Kemal Beyatlı, writing in the twentieth century,

> If there were a second life
> And a return one day from the other world
> And every soul were set free into the universe
> And could according to its pleasure find a place to settle
> If fortune were to turn to me and graciously grant a star as my
> abode
> This favour would leave me cold
> I would want to return to Istanbul.[6]

No amount of worldly travel or intellectual investigation could reveal a capital as great anywhere on the face of the earth, so people told Murad IV,

[1] Solakzade, *Tarihi*, I, p. 273.
[2] Lithgow, *Discourse*, p. 130; 'The Seraglio of the Grand Signior at Constantinople', *Ladies' Cabinet of Fashion, Music and Romance*, Saturday 1 March 1834, p. 165; Murad Efendi, *Manzaraları*, p. 43; Oğulukyan, *Ruznamesi*, p. 20; Han Melik Sasanî, *Payitahtın Son Yıllarında Bir Sefir*, trans. Hakkı Uygur (Istanbul, 2006), p. 119; Solakzade, *Tarihi*, I, p. 274; Marion-Crawford, *İstanbul*, pp. 10–12; Rashid Rida, *İttihad*, p. 149; Careri, 'Voyage', p. 69; King Abdullah (Kral Abdullah), *Biz Osmanlı'ya Neden İsyan Ettik?*, trans. Halit Özkan (Istanbul, 2006), p. 17.
[3] Latifi, *Evsâf*, p. 7.
[4] Quoted from the famous Iranian poet and writer Mirza Habib Isfahani, in Sasanî, *Sefir*, p. 119.
[5] Latifi, *Evsâf*, p. 7. [6] Yahya Kemal, *Aziz İstanbul*, p. 67.

50. View of Istanbul, in Pardoe, *Beauties of the Bosphorus*, between pp. 112 and 113.

assuring him that even though they had studied many thousands of Arabic and Persian histories and had talked to those who had lived for one hundred and twenty and even one hundred and fifty years and had voyaged much, and even though they had themselves travelled for seventy or eighty years, and seen many castles and great cities, they had never seen one to touch the magnificent capital of the Ottoman empire.[7] It was quite simply the seat of the sultanate, as Süleyman I put it, no other city, not even the recent conquests of Baghdad or Buda, bearing comparison.[8] It was for the great Ottoman statesman of the nineteenth century, Fuad Paşa, one of the four pillars of the state, an essential element in what made the empire.[9]

Magnificent, violent, rich and powerful, it was the canvas and the backdrop to the projection of might, both for the benefit of the city's inhabitants, the people of the provinces and the foreigners from the world beyond. The inhabitants both participated in and were the target audience of the pageantry of pomp and splendour which so impressed and sometimes frightened the ambassadors of the foreign powers. The centre of the world for many who lived there, life beyond the city seemed tasteless, undesirable and well-nigh impossible. To leave Istanbul was like a fish leaving water,[10] and exile from it a fate worse than death.[11]

For the British, too, the dominant occupier in 1920, the capital seemed a city that could not be left,[12] they themselves refusing to do so even after the creation of the Republic and the establishment of a new capital, clinging obstinately to their embassy in the heart of Beyoğlu and refusing to follow the other nations as they set up embassies in Ankara, more pragmatically accepting the realities of the new world.

In the end, however, the capital which could not be left was abandoned and a new era begun. The desertion of Istanbul was not just pure politics, for psychologically many intellectuals were prepared for such an exodus, scarred by the repression of the reign of Abdülhamid II and moulded in the cauldron of exile. For many, the early 1900s saw the development of a simmering love–hate relationship with Istanbul which was to explode after the First World War, as the capital became identified with the man whom many saw as the spineless quisling sultan, co-operating with the British and surrendering everything in a bid to retain his throne. One of the most famous intellectuals of the era, who was to have a great influence on both the Committee of Union and Progress leaders and Mustafa Kemal Atatürk,

[7] Evliya Çelebi, *Seyahatnamesi, I Kitap*, p. 217.
[8] Peçevi, *Tarihi*, I, p. 74.
[9] [Ahmed] Cevdet Paşa, *Tezâkir 1–12*, Cavid Baysun (ed.) (Ankara, 1991), p. 85.
[10] Ahmet Cevdet Paşa, *Ma'rûzât*, p. 51.
[11] Özcan, *Anonim*, pp. 232–3.
[12] *The Times*, 4 February 1920 and The National Archives, London, CAB/24/97.

was Tevfik Fikret. His poem *Sis* (Fog), published in 1901, is a devastating denunciation of the state of the capital where everything was corrupt, advancement came by kissing feet and the only freedom the people had was that of being able to breathe. The contradictions in his feelings for the city encapsulate beautifully the mood of the times. The city was shameless, without honour, a whore, but one who still retained her attraction:

> Oh Decrepit Byzantium, Oh great bewitching dotard
> Oh widowed virgin of a thousand men
> The fresh enchantment in your beauty is still evident
> The eyes that look at you still do so with adoration.[13]

By 1923, even if such adoration remained, the realities of the post-First World War world required a new beginning. Istanbul was left behind, a magnificent and stunning city still, but no longer the capital, which from now on was to be the quintessentially Anatolian city of Ankara.

[13] Tevfik Fikret, *Rübâb-ı Şikeste*, ed. Kemal Bek (Istanbul, 2007), pp. 370, 371.

Select bibliography

Newspapers and magazines

Belfast Newsletter
La Belle Assemblée; or, Bell's Court and Fashionable Magazine
Bell's Life in London and Sporting Chronicle
Bentley's Miscellany
Children's Friend
Glasgow Herald
John Bull
Ladies' Cabinet of Fashion, Music and Romance
Ladies' Museum
Manchester Weekly Times
The Satirist; or The Censor of the Times
Servet-i Fünun
The Times

Primary sources

5 Numaralı Mühimme Defteri (973/1565–1566), 2 vols. (Ankara, 1994).

Abdi, *1730 Patrona İhtilâli Hakkında Bir Eser Abdi Tarihi*, ed. Faik Reşit Unat (Ankara, 1943).

Abdülaziz Bey, *Osmanlı Âdet, Merasim ve Tabirleri*, ed. Kazım Arısan and Duygu Arısan Günay (Istanbul, 2002).

Ahmed Cavid, *Hadîka-ı Vekāyi'*, ed. Adnan Baycar (Ankara, 1998).

Ahmet Cevdet Paşa, *Ma'rûzât*, ed. Yusuf Halaçoğlu (Istanbul, 1980).

(Ahmed) Cevdet Paşa, *Tezâkir 1–12, 13–20, 21–39, 40-Tetimme*, ed. Cavid Baysun (Ankara, 1991).

Ahmet İhsan, *Matbuat Hatıralarım. 1888–1923. Birinci Cilt Meşrutiyet İlânına Kadar 1889–1908* (Istanbul, 1930).

Ahmed Lütfi Efendi, *Vak'a-nüvis Ahmed Lûtfi Efendi Tarihi, C. X–XV*, ed. M. Münir Aktepe (Ankara, 1988–93).

Ahmet Midhat Efendi, *Bütün Eserleri. Romanlar 1- Dünyaya İkinci Geliş Yahud İstanbul'da Neler Olmuş; Felatun Bey ile Rakım Efendi; Hüseyin Fellah*, ed. Kazım Yetiş, Necat Birinci and M. Fatih Andı (Ankara, 2000).

Ahmed Rasim, *Matbuat Hatıralarından: Muharrir, Şair, Edip* (Istanbul, 1342/1924).

Fuhş-i Atik (Istanbul, 2005).
Şehir Mektupları, ed. Nuri Akbayar (Istanbul, 2005).
Ramazan Sohbetleri (Ankara, 2007).
Ahmet Refik, *Hicri On İkinci Asırda İstanbul Hayatı (1100–1200)* (Istanbul, 1930).
Hicri On Birinci Asırda İstanbul Hayatı (1000–1100) (Istanbul, 1931).
Hicri On Üçüncü Asırda İstanbul Hayatı (1200–1255) (Istanbul, 1932).
On Altıncı Asırda İstanbul Hayatı (1553–1591) (Istanbul, 1935).
Onuncu Asr-ı Hicrî'de İstanbul Hayatı (1495–1591) (Istanbul, 1988).
Ahmet Rıfat, *Tasvir-i Ahlak. Ahlak Sözlüğü*, ed. Hüseyin Algül (Istanbul, n.d.).
Ahmed Şerif, *Anadolu'da Tanîn, I*, ed. Mehmed Çetin Börekçi (Ankara, 1999).
Ahmed Vâsıf Efendi, *Mehâsinü'l-Âsâr ve Hakâikü'l-Ahbâr*, ed. Mücteba İlgürel (Ankara, 1994).
Akçura, Yusuf, *Hatıralarım* (Ankara, 2005).
Albèri, Eugenio (ed.), *Relazioni degli ambasciatori veneti al senato durante il XVI secolo*, serie III, 3 vols. (Florence, 1842–55).
Alus, Sermet Muhtar, *30 Sene Evvel İstanbul. 1900'lü Yılların Başlarında Şehir Hayatı*, ed. Faruk Ilıkan (Istanbul, 2005).
Amicis, Edmond di, *Constantinople* (Paris, 1883).
Andreasyan, Hrand D., 'Celâlilerden Kaçan Anadolu Halkının Geri Gönderilmesi', in *Ord. Prof. İsmail Hakkı Uzunçarşılı'ya Armağan* (Ankara, 1988), pp. 45–53.
Arıkan, V. Sema (ed.), *III. Selim'in Sırkâtibi Ahmed Efendi Tarafından Tutulan Rûznâme* (Ankara, 1993).
Arpad, Burhan, *Perde Arkası. Türk Tiyatrosundan Anılar...*, ed. Ahmet Arpad (Istanbul, 2001).
'Bir İstanbul Var idi' (Istanbul, 2003).
Arseven, Celâl Esat, *Seyyar Sergi ile Seyahat İntibaları*, ed. N. Ahmet Özalp (Istanbul, 2008).
Aşıkpaşazade, *Die Altosmanische Chronik des Ašıkpašazade*, ed. Fredrich Giese (Leipzig, 1929, reprinted Osnabrük, 1972).
Atıl, Esin (ed.), *Levni ve Surname: Bir Osmanlı Şenliğinin Öyküsü* (Istanbul, 1999).
Balıkhane Nazırı Ali Rıza Bey, *Bir Zamanlar İstanbul* (Istanbul, n.d.).
Eski Zamanlarda İstanbul Hayatı, ed. Ali Şükrü Çoruk (Istanbul, 2001).
Barbaro, Nicolò, *The Diary of the Siege of Constantinople 1453*, trans. J. R. Jones (New York, 1969).
Barkan, Ömer Lütfi, 'Ayasofya Camii ve Eyüp Türbesinin 1489–1491 Yıllarına Âit Muhasebe Bilânçoları', *İstanbul Üniversitesi İktisat Fakültesi Mecmuası*, 23/1–2 (1962–63), pp. 342–98.
'Fatih Câmi ve İmareti Tesîslerinin 1489–1490 Yıllarına Âit Muhasebe Bilânçoları', *İstanbul Üniversitesi İktisat Fakültesi Mecmuası*, 23/1–2 (1962–63), pp. 239–341.
and Ekrem Hakkı Ayverdi (eds.), *İstanbul Vakıfları Tahrîr Defteri 953 (1546) Târîhli* (Istanbul, 1970).
Barth, Hermann, *Konstantinopel* (Leipzig and Berlin, 1901).
Basiretçi Ali Efendi, *İstanbul Mektupları*, ed. Nuri Sağlam (Istanbul, 2001).
Basmajean, G. Y., *Social and Religious Life in the Orient* (New York, 1890).
Bassano, Luigi, *I costumi et i modi particolari de la vita de Turchi, descritti da M. Luigi Bassano da Zara* (Rome, 1545).
Bauden, Frédéric (ed.), *Le voyage à Smyrne. Un manuscript d'Antoine Galland (1678)* (Paris, 2000).

Baykal, Bekir Sıtkı, 'Osmanlı İmparatorluğunda XVII. ve XVIII. Yüzyıllar Boyunca Para Düzeni ile İlgili Belgeler', *Türk Tarih Kurumu Belgeler*, 4/7–8 (1967), pp. 49–77.

Belgrano, L. T., 'Documenti riguardanti la colonia genovese di Pera', *Atti della Società Ligure di Storia della Patria*, 13 (1877–84), pp. 99–317.

Beyhan, Mehmet Ali (ed.), *Saray Günlüğü (1802–1809)* (Istanbul, 2007).

Bon, Ottaviano, *A Description of the Grand Signor's Seraglio or the Turkish Emperours Court* (London, 1650).

Brassey, Anna, *Sunshine and Storm in the East* (London, 1880).

Brocquière, Bertrandon de la, *The Travels of Bertrandon de la Brocquière*, trans. Thomas Johnes (London, 1807).

Burian, Orhan, *The Report of Lello Third English Ambassador to the Sublime Porte* (Ankara, 1952).

Busbecq, Ogier Ghiselin de, *The Turkish Embassy Letters of Ogier Ghiselin de Busbecq*, trans. Edward Seymour Forster (Oxford, 1968).

Cabi Ömer Efendi, *Cabi Târihi*, 2 vols., ed. Mehmet Ali Beyhan (Ankara, 2003).

Cafer Efendi, *Risāle-i Mi'māriyye. An Early-Seventeenth Century Ottoman Treatise on Architecture*, ed. Howard Crane (Leiden, 1987).

Careri, Giovanni Francesco Gemelli, 'A voyage round the world by Dr John Francis Gemelle Careri in six parts. Part I containing the most remarkable things he saw in Turkey', in John Churchill (ed.), *A Collection of Voyages and Travels* (London, 1732), IV, pp. 1–103.

Celal Esad, *Eski Galata ve Binaları* (Istanbul, 1329).

Cemal Paşa, *Hatıralar. İttihat ve Terakki, I. Dünya Savaşı Anıları*, ed. Alpay Kabacalı (Istanbul, 2001).

Cenab Şahabeddin, *Hac Yolunda*, ed. Nurullah Şenol (Istanbul, 2004).

İstanbul'da Bir Ramazan, ed. Abdullah Uçman (Istanbul, 2006).

Chishull, Edmund, *Travels in Turkey and Back to England* (London, 1747).

Cochran, William, *Pen and Pencil in Asia Minor* (London, 1887).

Courmenin, Louis Deshayes, *Voiage de Levant fait per le Commandement du Roy par le Sr. D.C.* (Paris, 1629).

Covel, John, 'Extracts from the diaries of Dr John Covel', in J. T. Bent, *Early Voyages and Travels in the Levant* (London, 1893), pp. 101–286.

Çeşmizade Mustafa Reşid, *Çeşmî-zâde Tarihi*, ed. Bekir Kütükoğlu (Istanbul, 1959).

Dallam, Thomas, 'The diary of Master Thomas Dallam 1599–1600', in J. T. Bent (ed.), *Early Voyages and Travels in the Levant* (London, 1893), pp. 1–98.

Dei Crescenzi, Crescenzio, 'Letter di Costantinopoli del 1615. A un amico', in Michele Giustiniani, *Lettere memorabilia dell'Abbate Michele Giustiniani, Patrizio Genovese de' Sig.ri di Scio. Parte II* (Rome, 1699), no. XVII, pp. 65–72.

Defterdar Sarı Mehmed Paşa, *Zübde-i Vekayiât, Tahlil ve Metin (1066–1116/1656–1704)*, ed. Abdülkadir Özcan (Ankara, 1995).

Destari, *Destârî Sâlih Tarihi. Patrona Halil Ayaklanması Hakkında Bir Kaynak*, ed. Bekir Sıtkı Baykal (Ankara, 1962).

Develi, Hayati (ed.), *XVIII. Yüzyıl İstanbul Hayatına Dair Risale-i Garibe* (Istanbul, 1998).

Domenico, *Domenico's Istanbul*, trans. M. J. L. Austin and ed. Geoffrey Lewis (Wiltshire, 2001).

Doukas, *Historia Byzantina*, ed. I. Bekker (Bonn, 1843).
Decline and Fall of Byzantium to the Ottoman Turks, trans. H. J. Magoulias (Detroit, 1975).
Dumont, Jean (Sieur de Mont), *A New Voyage to the Levant* (London, 1705).
Düstur, 2nd edn (Dersaadet, 1330) II.
Düzdağ, M. Ertuğrul, *Şeyhülislâm Ebussuûd Efendi Fetvaları Işığında 16. Asır Türk Hayatı* (Istanbul, 1972).
Dwight, H. G., *Constantinople. Old and New* (New York, 1915).
Engin, Vahdettin (ed.), *Sultan Abdülhamid ve İstanbul'u* (Istanbul, 2001).
Ergin, Osman Nuri, *Mecelle-i Umur-ı Belediyye*, 6 vols. (Istanbul, 1995).
Erimez, Salih, *Tarihten Çizgiler* (Istanbul, 1941).
Evliya Çelebi b. Derviş Muhammed Zılli, *Evliya Çelebi Seyahatnamesi. Topkapı Sarayı Bağdat 304 Yazmasının Transkripsiyonu-Dizini. I Kitap*, ed. Orhan Şaik Gökyay (Istanbul, 1995).
Evliya Çelebi Seyahatnamesi, vol. IV, ed. Yücel Dağlı and Seyit Ali Kahraman (Istanbul, 2001).
Seyahatname (Gördüklerim) Evliya Çelebi, ed. Mustafa Nihat Özön and Nijat Özön (Istanbul, 2005).
Fatih Mehmet II Vakfiyeleri (Ankara, 1938).
Firpo, Luigi (ed.), *Relazioni di ambasciatori veneti al senato*, vol. XIII, *Costantinopoli (1590–1793)* (Turin, 1984).
Fleet, Kate, 'The treaty of 1387 between Murad I and the Genoese', *Bulletin of the School of Oriental and African Studies*, 56/1 (1993), pp. 13–33.
Fontmagne, Baronne Durand de, *Kırım Savaşı Sonrasında İstanbul Günleri*, trans. İsmail Yerguz (Istanbul, 2007).
Forbin, Count, *Travels in Greece, Turkey and the Holy Land in 1817–18* (London, 1819).
Frankland, Captain Charles Colville, *Travels to and from Constantinople in the Years 1827 and 1828* (London, 1829).
Fresne-Canaye, Philippe du, *Le Voyage du Levant de Philippe du Fresne-Canaye (1573)* (Paris, 1897).
Galland, Antoine, *Journal d'Antoine Galland pendant son séjour à Constantinople (1672–1673)*, ed. Charles Schefer (Paris, 1881).
Gautier, Théophille, *Constantinople*, trans. Robert Howe Gould (New York, 1875).
Gelibolulu Mustafa Ali, *Câmi'u'l-Buhûr Der Mecâlis-i Sûr*, ed. Ali Öztekin (Ankara, 1996).
Mevâıdün-Nefâis fi-Kavâıdil-Mecâlis, ed. Mehmet Şeker (Ankara, 1997).
Gelibolulu Mustafa Âlî ve Künhü'l-Ahbâr'ında II. Selim, III. Murat ve III. Mehmet Devirleri, 3 vols., ed. Faris Çerçi (Kayseri, 2000).
Künhü'l-Ahbār. C.II., Fatih Sultan Mehmed Devri 1451–1481, ed. M. Hüdai Şentürk (Ankara, 2003).
Georgievitz, Bartholomeus, *The Rarities of Turkey Gathered by One that was Sold Seven Times as Slave in the Turkish Empire…* (London, 1661).
Gerçek, Selim Nüzhet, *İstanbul'dan Ben de Geçtim*, ed. Ali Birinci and İsmail Kara (Istanbul, 1997).
Gerlach, Stephan, *Türkiye Günlüğü 1573–1576*, 2 vols., trans. Türkis Noyan (Istanbul, 2007).

Gökyay, Orhan Şaik (ed.), *Kâtip Çelebi. Hayatı, Kişiliği ve Eserlerinden Seçmeler* (Istanbul, n.d.).
Gölpınarlı, Abdülbaki (ed.), *Yunus Emre Hayatı ve Bütün Şiirleri* (Istanbul, 2006).
Gregoras, Nikephoros, *Nicephori Gregorae Byzantina Historia*, 3 vols., ed. L. Schopeni (Bonn, 1829).
Grelot, Guillaume-Joseph, *A Late Voyage to Constantinople* (London, 1683).
Guer, Jean-Antoine, *Moeurs et usages des Turcs*, 2 vols. (Paris, 1747).
Gürpınar, Hüseyin Rahmi, *Kuyruklu Yıldız Altında Bir Evlenme. Kaderin Cilvesi*, ed. Kemal Bek (Istanbul, 2005).
Şıpsevdi, ed. Kemal Bek (Istanbul, 2005).
Muhabbet Tılsımı, (Istanbul, 1928).
Harff, Arnold von, *The Pilgrimage of Arnold von Harff*, trans. and ed. Malcolm Letts (London, 1946).
Hasan Beyzade Ahmed Paşa, *Hasan Bey-zâde Târîhi*, 3 vols., ed. Şevki Nezihi Aykut (Ankara, 2004).
Hayrullah Efendi, *Avrupa Seyahatnamesi*, ed. Belkis Altuniş-Gürsoy (Ankara, 2002).
Heberer, Michael, *Osmanlıda Bir Köle. Brettenli Michael Heberer'in Anıları 1585–1588*, trans. Türkis Noyan (Istanbul, 2003).
Hoca Sadettin Efendi, *Tacü't-Tevarih*, 5 vols., ed. İsmet Parmaksızoğlu (Ankara, 1999).
Hovhannesyan, Sarkis Sarraf, *Payitaht İstanbul'un Tarihçesi*, trans. Elmon Hançer and ed. Ara Kalaycıyan (Istanbul, 1996).
Hutton, William Molden, *Constantinople. The Story of the Old Capital of the Empire* (London, 1904).
Ibañez, Vicente Blasco, *Fırtınadan Önce Şark. İstanbul 1907*, trans. Neyyire Gül Işık (Istanbul, 2007).
Ibn Battuta, *The Travels of Ibn Battuta*, 2 vols., trans. and ed. H. A. R. Gibb (Cambridge, 1962).
Ibn Taghribirdi, *Al-Nujūm al-Zāhira fī mulūk Misr wa al-Qāhira* (Cairo, 1389/1970).
History of Egypt 1382–1469. Part II, 1399–1411 A.D. Translated from the Arabic Annals of Abu L-Mahasin ibn Taghri Birdi, trans. and ed. William Popper (Berkeley and Los Angeles, 1954).
Imber, Colin, *The Crusade of Varna, 1443–45* (Aldershot, 2006).
İbn Kemal, *İbn Kemal Tevârih-i Âl-i Osman, VII. Defter*, ed. Şerafettin Turan (Ankara, 1991).
Kemal Paşa-zâde Tevarih-i Âl-i Osman, X. Defter, ed. Şefaettin Severcan (Ankara, 1996).
İbn Kemâl Tevârih-i Âl-i Osmân, VIII. Defter, ed. Ahmet Uğur (Ankara, 1997).
İbnülcemal Ahmet Tevfik, *Velosipet İle Bir Cevelan 1900'e Doğru İstanbul'dan Bursa'ya Bisikletli Bir Gezi*, ed. Cahit Kayra (Istanbul, 2006).
İbrahim Peçevi, *Peçevî Tarihi*, 2 vols., ed. Murad Uraz (Istanbul, 1968).
İnalcık, Halil, 'Adâletnâmeler', *Türk Tarih Kurumu Belgeler*, 2/3–4 (1965), pp. 49–145.
and Mevlud Oğuz (eds.), *Gazavât-ı Sultân Murâd b. Mehemmed Hân. İzladi ve Varna Savaşları (1443–1444) Üzerine Anonim Gazavâtnâme* (Ankara, 1978).
İnciciyan, P. Ğ., *XVIII. Asırda İstanbul*, trans. and ed. Hrand D. Andreasyan (Istanbul, 1956).

İsazade, *'Îsâ-zâde Târîhi (Metin ve Tahlîl)*, ed. Ziya Yılmazer (Istanbul, 1996).
İz, Fahir (trans. and ed.), *An Anthology of Modern Turkish Short Stories* (Minneapolis and Chicago, 1978).
Jacopo de Promontorio, *Die Aufzeichnungen des Genuesen Iacopo de Promontorio-de Campis über den Osmanenstaat um 1475*, ed. Franz Babinger (Munich, 1957).
Kantemir, Dimitri, *Osmanlı İmparatorluğu'nun Yükşeliş ve Çöküş Tarihi*, 2 vols., trans. Özdemir Çobanoğlu (Istanbul, 2005).
Kara Çelebizade Abdülaziz Efendi, *Ravzatü'l Ebrâr Zeyli (Tahlîl ve Metin) 1732*, ed. Nevzat Kaya (Ankara, 2003).
Karal, Enver Ziya (ed.), *Selim III'ün Hat-tı Hümayunları – Nizam-ı Cedit – 1789–1807* (Ankara, 1988).
Karaosmanoğlu, Yakup Kadri, *Sodom ve Gomore* (Istanbul, 2004).
King Abdullah (Kral Abdullah), *Biz Osmanlı'ya Neden İsyan Ettik?*, trans. Halit Özkan (Istanbul, 2006).
Koçi Bey, *Koçi Bey Risaleleri*, ed. Zuhuri Danışman and Seda Çakmakçıoğlu (Istanbul, 2008).
Kömürcüyan, Eremya Çelebi, *İstanbul Tarihi. XVII. Asırda İstanbul*, trans. and ed. Hrand D. Andreasyan (Istanbul, 1952).
Köprülüzade Mehmet Fuat, *Eski Şairlerimiz. Divan Edebiyatı Antolojisi* (Istanbul, 1934).
Kreutel, Richard F. (ed.), *Haniwaldanus Anonimi'ne Göre Sultan Bayezid-i Veli (1481–1512)*, trans. Necdet Öztürk (Istanbul, 1997).
Kritoboulos, *History of Mehmed the Conqueror. By Kritovoulos*, trans. C. T. Riggs (Westport, 1954).
Kuntay, Midhat Cemal, *Üç İstanbul* (Istanbul, 1998).
Kütükoğlu, Mübahat S. (ed.), *Osmanlılarda Narh Müessesesi ve 1640 Tarihli Narh Defteri* (Istanbul, 1983).
'Lütfi Paşa Âsafnâmesi (Yeni Bir Metin Tesisi Denemesi)', in *Prof. Dr. Bekir Kütükoğlu'na Armağan* (Istanbul, 1991), pp. 49–99.
La Croix, Sieur de, *Mémoires du Sieur de la Croix cy-devant secretaire de l'ambassade de Constantinople*, 2 vols. (Paris, 1684).
Lacroix, Frédéric, *Guide de voyageur à Constantinople et dans ses environs* (Paris, 1839).
Lane, Edward William, *An Account of the Manners and the Customs of the Modern Egyptians*, 2 vols. (London, 1836).
Latifi, *Evsâf-ı İstanbul*, ed. Nermin Suner (Pekin) (Istanbul, 1977).
Leyla (Saz) Hanımefendi, *The Imperial Harem of the Sultans. Daily Life at the Çırağan Palace During the Nineteenth Century*, trans. Landon Thomas (Istanbul, 2001).
Lithgow, William, *The Totall Discourse of the Rare Adventures, and Painefull Peregrinations of Long Nineteene Yeares Travayles, from Scotland, to....* (London, 1623).
Loenertz, R.-J. (ed.), *Demetrius Cydones' Correspondence*, 2 vols. (Vatican City, 1956, 1960).
Lucas, Paul, *Voyage du Sieur Paul Lucas, fait en MDCCXIV...*, 2 vols. (Amsterdam, 1720).
Machiavelli, Niccolò, *Il Principe e Discorsi sopra la prima deca di Tito Livio, con introduzione di Giuliano Procacci*, ed. Sergio Bertelli (Milan, 1960).

Marion-Crawford, Francis, *1890'larda İstanbul*, trans. Şeniz Türkömer (Istanbul, 2006).
Mayer, Georg, *Türk Çarşısı. Şark'ta Ticaretin Püf Noktaları*, trans. Yusuf Öztel and ed. Rıfat N. Bali (Istanbul, 2008).
Mehmet Enisi, *Bir Denizcinin Avrupa Günlüğü – Avrupa Hatıratım*, ed. N. Ahmet Özalp (Istanbul, 2008).
Menavino, Giovanantonio, *I cinque libri della legge, religione, et vita de'Turchi: et della corte, et d'alcune guerre del Gran Turco: di Giovanantonio Menavino Genovese da Vultri* (Venice, 1548).
Méry, Joseph, *Constantinople et la Mer Noire* (Paris, 1855).
Mihailović, Konstantin, *Memoirs of a Janissary*, trans. Benjamin Stolz (Ann Arbor, 1975).
van Millingen, Alexander, *Constantinople* (London, 1906).
'Mimar Sinan'ın Hatıraları', *Hayat Tarih Mecmuası*, no. 5 (June 1966), pp. 4–11.
'Mimar Sinan'ın Hatıraları: 2, Kırkçeşme Sularını Nasıl Getirdim', *Hayat Tarih Mecmuası*, no. 6 (July 1966), pp. 42–9.
Mintzuri, Hagop, *İstanbul Anıları (1897–1940)*, trans. Silva Kuyumcuyan and ed. Necdet Sakaoğlu (Istanbul, 1993).
Montagu, Lady Mary Wortley, *The Turkish Embassy Letters*, ed. Malcolm Jack (London, 1994).
Murad Efendi, *Türkiye Manzaraları*, trans. Alev Sunata Kırım (Istanbul, 2007).
Musahipzade Celal, *Eski İstanbul Yaşayışı* (Istanbul, 1946).
Mustafa Sait Bey, *Avrupa Seyahatnamesi*, ed. Burhan Günaysu (Istanbul, 2004).
Müneccimbaşı Ahmed Dede, *Müneccimbaşı Tarihi*, 2 vols., trans. İsmail Erünsal (Istanbul, n.d.).
Nabi, *Nabi'nin Surnâmesi. Vakaayi'-i Hıtân-ı Şehzadegân-ı Hazret-i Sultan Muhammed-i Gaazi Li Nabi Efendi*, ed. Agâh Sırrı Levend (Istanbul, 1944).
Naima, *Târih-i Na'îmâ*, 4 vols., ed. Mehmet İpşirli (Ankara, 2007).
Neşri, *Čihannüma die Altosmanische Chronik des Mevlana Mehemmed Neschri*, ed. Franz Taeschner (Leipzig, 1951).
Kitab-i Cihan-nüma, 2 vols., ed. Faik Reşit Unat and Mehmet A. Köymen (Ankara, 1949, 1957).
Nicolay, Nicolas de, *Dans L'empire de Soliman le Magnifique*, ed. Marie-Christine Gomez-Géraud and Stéphane Yérasimos (Paris, 1989).
Oğulukyan, *Georg Oğulukyan'ın Ruznamesi. 1806–1810 İsyanları. III. Selim, IV. Mustafa, II. Mahmud ve Alemdar Mustafa Paşa*, trans. and ed. Hrand D. Andreasyan (Istanbul, 1972).
Orga, İrfan, *Portrait of a Turkish Family* (London, 1950).
Orhonlu, Cengiz (ed.), *Osmanlı Tarihine Âid Belgeler. Telhîsler (1597–1607)* (Istanbul, 1970).
Oruç Bey, *Oruç Beğ Tarih*, ed. A. Nihal Atsız (Istanbul, 1972).
Özcan, Abdülkadir (ed.), *Anonim Osmanlı Tarihi (1099–1116/1688–1704)* (Ankara, 2000).
Özcan, Tahsin (ed.), *Fetvalar Işığında Osmanlı Esnafı* (Istanbul, 2003).
Özön, Mustafa Nihat (ed.), *Namık Kemal ve İbret Gazetesi* (Istanbul, 1997).
Özpalabıyıklar, Selahattin (ed.), *Türk Edebiyatında Beyoğlu* (Istanbul, 2000).
Öztürk, Necdet (ed.), *Anonim Osmanlı Kroniği (1299–1512)* (Istanbul, 2000).
Öztürk, Said, *Askeri Kassama Ait Onyedinci Asır İstanbul Tereke Defterleri (Sosyo-Ekonomik Tahlil)* (Istanbul, 1995).

Pachymeres, *George Pachymérè Relations Historiques IV. Livres X–XIII édition, traduction française et notes*, ed. Albert Failler (Paris, 1999).
Pardoe, Julia, *The Beauties of the Bosphorus* (London, 1838).
Pedani-Fabris, Maria Pia (ed.), *Relazioni di ambasciatori veneti al senato*, vol. XIV, *Costantinopoli Relazioni inedite (1512–1789)* (Turin, 1996).
Pertusi, Agostino, *Testi inediti e poci noti sulla caduta di Costantinopoli. Edizione postuma a cura di Antonio Carile* (Bologna, 1983).
(ed.), *La caduta di Costantinopoli*, 2 vols. (Milan, 1999).
Pertusier, Charles, *Picturesque Promenades in and Near Constantinople, and on the Waters of Bosphorus* (London, 1820).
Piloti, Emmanuel, *L'Égypte au commencement du quinzième siècle d'après le Traité d'Emmanuel Piloti de Crète (incipit 1420)*, ed. P.-H. Dopp (Cairo, 1950).
Quiclet, *Les voyages de M. Quiclet à Constantinople* (Paris, 1664).
Rado, Şevket (ed.), *Yirmisekiz Mehmet Çelebi'nin Fransa Seyahatnamesi* (Istanbul, 1970).
Ramsay, Sir W. M., *The Revolution in Constantinople and Turkey. A Diary* (London, 1909).
Rashid Rida (Reşid Rıza), *İttihad-ı Osmani'den Arap İsyanına*, trans. and ed. Özgür Kavak (Istanbul, 2007).
Recaizade Mahmud Ekrem, *Araba Sevdası* (Istanbul, 1985).
Roccatagliata, Ausilia, *Notai Genovesi in Oltremare. Atti rogati a Chio (1453–1454, 1470–1471)* (Genoa, 1982).
Rochebrune, A. de, *Dilber Kethy'nin Bursa ve İstanbul Hatıratı*, trans. Mahmud Sadık (Istanbul, 2007).
Roe, Sir Thomas, *The Negotiations of Sir Thomas Roe in his Embassy to the Ottoman Porte from the Year 1621 to 1628 Inclusive (Containing…)*, (London, 1740).
Rycaut, Paul, *The History of the Present State of the Ottoman Empire* (London, 1675).
Sadri Sema, *Eski İstanbul Hatıraları*, ed. Ali Şükrü Çoruk (Istanbul, 2002).
Safi, *Mustafa Sâfî'nin Zübdetü't-Tevârîh'i*, 2 vols., ed. İbrahim Hakkı Çuhadar (Ankara, 2003).
Safveti Ziya, *Salon Köşelerinde*, ed. Nuri Akbayar (Istanbul, 1998).
Sahillioğlu, Halil (ed.), *Topkapı Sarayı Arşivi H.951–952 ve E-12321 Numaralı Mühimme Defteri* (Istanbul, 2002).
Sanderson, John, *The Travels of John Sanderson in the Levant 1584–1602*, ed. Sir William Foster (London, 1931).
Sandys, George, *Sandys Travailes* (London, 1658).
Saraçoğlu, Ahmed Cemaleddin, *Eski İstanbul'dan Hatıralar*, ed. İsmail Dervişoğlu (Istanbul, 2005).
Sasani, Han Melik, *Payitahtın Son Yıllarında Bir Sefir*, trans. Hakkı Uygur (Istanbul, 2006).
Schiltberger, Johann, *The Bondage and Travels of Johann Schiltberger, a Native of Bavaria, in Europe, Asia and Africa, 1396–1427*, trans. and ed. Commander J. Buchan Telfer (London, 1879).
Schweigger, Salomon, *Ein newe Reyssbeschreibung auss Teutschland nach Constantinopel und Jerusalem* (Nuremberg, 1639).
Sultanlar Kentine Yolculuk 1578–1581, trans. S. Türkis Noyan and ed. Heidi Stein (Istanbul, 2004).

Selaniki Mustafa Efendi, *Tarih-i Selânikî*, 2 vols., ed. Mehmet İpşirli (Ankara, 1999).
Sevilen, Muhittin, *Karagöz* (Istanbul, 1969).
Seyid Vehbi, *Sûrnâme (Üçüncü Ahmed'in Oğullarının Sünnet Düğünü)*, ed. Reşad Ekrem Koçu (Istanbul, 1939).
Simavi, Lütfü, *Son Osmanlı Sarayında Gördüklerim. Sultan Mehmed Reşad Hanın ve Halifenin Sarayında Gördüklerim*, ed. Sami Kara and Nurer Uğurlu (Istanbul, 2004).
Smith, Albert, *A Month at Constantinople* (London, 1851).
Solakzade, *Solak-zâde Tarihi*, 2 vols., ed. Vahid Çabuk (Ankara, 1989).
Spandounes, Theodore, *On the Origin of the Ottoman Emperors*, trans. and ed. Donald M. Nicol (Cambridge, 1997).
Spataris, Haris, *Biz İstanbullular Böyleyiz! Fener'den Anılar 1906–1922*, trans. Iro Kaplangı (Istanbul, 2004).
Spon, Jacob and George Wheler, *Voyage d'Italie, de Dalmatie, de Grece, et du Levant fait aux années 1675 et 1676*, 2 vols. (Amsterdam, 1679).
Sunata, İ. Hakkı, *İstanbul'da İşgal Yılları* (Istanbul, 2006).
Şahin, İlhan and Feridun Emecen (eds.), *Osmanlılarda Divân-Bürokrasi-Ahkâm. II. Bâyezid Dönemine Ait 906/ 1501 Tarihli Ahkâm Defteri* (Istanbul, 1994).
Şerafeddin Mağmumi, *Bir Osmanlı Doktorunun Seyahat Anıları, Avrupa Seyahat Hatıraları*, ed. Nazım H. Polat and Harid Fedai (Istanbul, 2008).
Tacizade Cafer Çelebi, *Mahsure-i İstanbul Fetihnamesi*, İstanbul Üniversitesi Kütüphanesi, T 2634.
Tahsin Nâhid and Şahâbeddin Süleyman, *Ben... Başka!*, ed. Sibel Ercan (Istanbul, 2004).
Talu, Ercümend Ekrem, *Geçmiş Zaman Olur ki. Anılar* (Ankara, 2005).
Tavernier, Jean-Baptiste, *Nouvelle relation de l'interior du serrail du Grand Seigneur* (Amsterdam, 1678).
Les six voyages de Jean Baptiste Tavernier Ecuyer Baron d'Aubonne, en Turquie, en Perse, et aux Indies (Paris, 1679).
Taylesanizade, *Taylesanizâde Hafız Abdullah Efendi Tarihi: İstanbul'un Uzun Dört Yılı (1785–1789)*, ed. Feridun M. Emecen (Istanbul, 2003).
Tekeli, İlhan and Selim İlkin (eds.), *Mimar Kemalettin'in Yazıları* (Ankara, 1997).
Tevfik Fikret, *Rübâb-ı Şikeste*, ed. Kemal Bek (Istanbul, 2007).
Thévenot, Jean de, *Voyages de Mr de Thevenot tant en Europe qu'en Asie et en Afrique*, 3 vols. (Paris, 1689).
Thomas, G. (ed.), *Diplomatarium Veneto-Levantinum*, 2 vols. (Venice, 1890–99).
Topçular Katibi Abdülkadir Efendi, *Topçular Kâtibi 'Abdülkādir (Kadrî) Efendi Tarihi (Metin ve Tahlil)*, 2 vols., ed. Ziya Yılmazer (Ankara, 2003).
Topuzlu, Cemil (Paşa), *İstibdat-Meşrutiyet-Cumhuriyet Devirlerinde 80 Yıllık Hatıralarım* (Istanbul, 2002).
Tournefort, Joseph Pitton de, *Relation d'un voyage du Levant*, 3 vols. (Paris, 1717).
A Voyage in the Levant (London, 1718).
Tursun Bey, *Tarih-i Ebü'l-Feth*, ed. Mertol Tulum (Istanbul, 1977).
The History of Mehmed the Conqueror by Tursun Beg, ed. Halil İnalcık and Rhoads Murphey (Minneapolis and Chicago, 1978).
Ubeydullah Kuşmani and Ebubekir Efendi, *Asiler ve Gaziler. Kabakçı Mustafa Risalesi*, ed. Aysel Danacı Yıldız (Istanbul, 2007).

Ubicini, [J. H.] A., *Letters on Turkey: An Account of the Religious, Political, Social and Commercial Conditions of the Ottoman Empire* (London, 1856).
Ubicini, J. H. A., *1855'de Türkiye*, trans. Ayda Düz (Istanbul, 1977).
Ulunay, Refi' Cevad, *Eski İstanbul Yosmaları* (Istanbul, n.d.)
al-'Umari, 'Notice de l'ouvrage qui a pour titre Masalek alabsar fi memalek alamsar, Voyages des yeux dans les royaumes des différentes contrées (ms. arabe 583)', in E. Quatremère (trans.), *Notices et Extraits des mss. de la Bibliothèque du Roi* (Paris, 1838), XIII, pp. 334–81.
Uşaklıgil, Halid Ziya, *Saray ve Ötesi* (Istanbul, 2003).
Ünver, A. Süheyl (ed.), *Fâtih Aşhânesi Tevzînâmesi* (Istanbul, 1953).
Ülker, Hikmet (ed.), *Sultanın Emir Defteri (51 Nolu Mühimme)* (Istanbul, 2003).
Walsh, Robert, *Constantinople and the Scenery of the Seven Churches of Asia Minor* (London and Paris, [1839?]).
Wratislaw, A. H., *Adventures of Baron Wenceslas Wratislaw of Mitrowitz* (London, 1862).
Baron W. Wratislaw'ın Anıları, '16. Yüzyıl Osmanlı İmparatorluğu'undan Çizgiler', trans. M. Süreyya Dilmen (Istanbul, 1981).
Yücel, Yaşar and Selami Pulaha (eds.), *I. Selim Kanunnameleri (1512–1520)* (Ankara, 1995).
Zarifi, Yorgo L., *Hatıralarım. Kaybolan Bir Dünya İstanbul 1800–1920*, trans. Karin Skotiniyadis (Istanbul, 2006).
Zeynoub Hanoum, *A Turkish Woman's European Impressions*, ed. Grace Ellison (London, 1913).

Secondary sources

Ahmet Refik, *Kafes ve Ferace Devrinde İstanbul*, ed. Tahir Yücel (Istanbul, 1998).
Akgündüz, Ahmet, *İslâm Hukukunda ve Osmanlı Tatbikatında Vakıf Müessesesi* (Istanbul, 1996).
Akın, Nur, *19. Yüzyılın İkinci Yarısında Galata ve Pera* (Istanbul, 1998).
Aktepe, M. Münir, *Patrona İsyanı (1730)* (Istanbul, 1958).
'XVIII. Asrın İlk Yarısında İstanbul'un Nüfus Mes'elesine Dâir Bâzı Vesikalar', *İstanbul Üniversitesi Edebiyat Fakültesi Tarih Dergisi*, 9/13 (1958), pp. 1–30.
'Kâğıdhâne'ye Dâir Bâzı Bilgiler', in *Ord. Prof. İsmail Hakkı Uzunçarşılı'ya Armağan* (Ankara, 1988), pp. 335–63.
And, Metin, *Tanzimat ve İstibdat Döneminde Türk Tiyatrosu (1839–1908)* (Ankara, 1972).
Türk Tiyatrosunun Evreleri (Ankara, 1983).
Asiltürk, Baki, *Osmanlı Seyyahlarının Gözüyle Avrupa* (Istanbul, 2000).
Aykut, Nezihi, 'Osmanlı İmparatorluğu'nda XVII. Asır Ortalarına Kadar Yapılan "Sikke Tashihleri"', in *Prof. Dr. Bekir Kütükoğlu'na Armağan* (Istanbul, 1991), pp. 343–60.
Aynural, Salih, *İstanbul Değirmenleri ve Fırınları. Zahire Ticareti (1740–1840)* (Istanbul, 2001).
Barkan, Ömer Lütfi, 'The price revolution of the sixteenth century: a turning point in the economic history of the Near East', *International Journal of Middle Eastern Studies*, 6/1 (1975), pp. 3–28.

Başaran, Betül, 'III. Selim ve İstanbul Şehir Siyaseti (1789–1792)', in Noémi Lévy and Alexandre Toumarkine (eds.), *Osmanlı'da Asayiş, Suç ve Ceza 18.–20. Yüzyıllar* (Istanbul, n.d.), pp. 116–34.

Boyar, Ebru, 'Engelhardt from censorship to icon: the use of a European diplomat's history in Ottoman and Turkish historiography on the *Tanzimat*', *Eurasian Studies*, 3/1 (2004), pp. 91–7.

'The press and the palace: the two-way relationship between Abdülhamid II and the press, 1876–1908', *Bulletin of the School of Oriental and African Studies*, 69/3 (2006), pp. 417–32.

Ottomans, Turks and the Balkans: Empire Lost, Relations Altered (London and New York, 2007).

'Profitable prostitution: state use of immoral earnings for social benefit in the late Ottoman empire', *Bulgarian Historical Review*, 1–2 (2009).

Breathnach, Teresa, 'For health and pleasure: the Turkish bath in Victorian Ireland', *Victorian Literature and Culture*, 32/1 (2004), pp. 159–75.

Çelik, Zeynep, *The Remaking of Istanbul. Portrait of an Ottoman City in the Nineteenth Century* (Berkeley, Los Angeles and London, 1993).

Dankoff, Robert, *An Ottoman Mentality. The World of Evliya Çelebi*, with an afterword by Gottfried Hagen (Leiden and Boston, 2004).

Faroqhi, Suraiya, *Subjects of the Sultan. Culture and Daily Life in the Ottoman Empire* (London, 2000).

Fleet, Kate, 'Italian perceptions of the Turks in the fourteenth and fifteenth centuries', *Journal of Mediterranean Studies*, 5/2 (1995), pp. 159–72.

European and Islamic Trade in the Early Ottoman State (Cambridge, 1999).

'Early Ottoman self-definition', in Jan Schmidt (ed.), *Essays in Honour of Barbara Fleming*, I, Special Issue, *Journal of Turkish Studies*, 26/1 (2002), pp. 229–38.

'Power and economy: early Ottoman economic practice', *Eurasian Studies*, 3/1 (2004), pp. 119–27.

Goodwin, Geoffrey, *A History of Ottoman Architecture* (London, 1992).

Imber, Colin, *The Ottoman Empire 1300–1481* (Istanbul, 1990).

'What does *ghazi* actually mean?', in Çiğdem Balım-Harding and Colin Imber (eds.), *The Balance of Truth. Essays in Honour of Professor Geoffrey Lewis* (Istanbul, 2000), pp. 165–78.

The Ottoman Empire 1300–1650. The Structure of Power (Basingstoke, 2002).

Işın, Ekrem, *İstanbul'da Gündelik Hayat. Tarih, Kültür ve Mekan İlişkileri Üzerine Toplumsal Tarih İncelemeleri* (Istanbul, 1999).

İnalcık, Halil, *The Ottoman Empire: The Classical Age 1300–1600* (London, 2000).

and Donald Quataert (eds.), *An Economic and Social History of the Ottoman Empire*, 2 vols. (Cambridge, 1994).

İpşirli, Mehmet, 'Osmanlılarda Cuma Selâmlığı (Halk-Hükümdar Münâsebetleri Açısından Önemi)', in *Prof. Dr. Bekir Kütükoğlu'na Armağan* (Istanbul, 1991), pp. 459–71.

İrtem, Süleyman Kâni, *Abdülhamid Devrinde Hafiyelik ve Sansür. Adülhamid'e Verilen Jurnaller*, ed. Osman Selim Kocahanoğlu (Istanbul, 1999).

İskit, Server, *Türkiyede Neşriyat Haraketleri Tarihine Bir Bakış* (Istanbul, 1939).

Kaplan, Mehmet, *Türk Edebiyatı Üzerinde Araştırmalar. 1* (Istanbul, 1976).

Kayaoğlu, İ. Gündağ and Ersu Pekin (eds.), *Eski İstanbul'da Gündelik Hayat* (Istanbul, 1992).

Koçu, Reşad Ekrem (ed.), *İstanbul Ansiklopedisi*, 11 vols. (Istanbul, 1958–1971).
Aşk Yolunda İstanbul'da Neler Olmuş (Istanbul, 2002).
Tarihte İstanbul Esnafı (Istanbul, 2003).
İstanbul Tulumbacıları (Istanbul, 2005).
Kuban, Doğan, *Kent ve Mimarlık Üzerine İstanbul Yazıları* (Istanbul, 1998).
Kunter, Halim Baki, 'Türk Vakıfları ve Vakfiyeleri Üzerine Mücmel Bir Etüd', *Vakıflar Dergisi*, no. 1 (1938), pp. 103–29.
Kuran, Aptullah, 'A special study of three Ottoman capitals: Bursa, Edirne, and Istanbul', *Muqarnas*, 13 (1997), pp. 114–31.
Mantran, Robert, *Istanbul dans la seconde moitié du XVIIe siècle* (Paris and Istanbul, 1962).
Murphey, Rhoads, 'Provisioning Istanbul: the state and subsistence in the early modern Middle East', in Rhoads Murphey, *Studies on Ottoman Society and Culture, 16th–18th Centuries* (Aldershot, 2007), no. V.
Necipoğlu, Gülru, 'Challenging the past: Sinan and the competitive discourse of early modern Islamic architecture', *Muqarnas, Essays in Honour of Oleg Grabar*, 10 (1993), pp. 169–80.
Necipoğlu-Kafadar, Gülru, 'The Süleymaniye complex in Istanbul: an interpretation', ed. Oleg Grabar, *Muqarnas*, 3 (1985), pp. 92–117.
Ocak, Ahmet Yaşar, *Osmanlı Toplumunda Zındıklar ve Mülhidler (15.-17. Yüzyıllar)* (Istanbul, 1998).
Orhonlu, Cengiz, *Osmanlı İmparatorluğunda Şehircilik ve Ulaşım Üzerine Araştırmalar*, ed. Salih Özbaran (İzmir, 1984).
Ortaylı, İlber, *Tanzimat Devrinde Osmanlı Mahallî İdareleri (1840–1880)* (Ankara, 2000).
Örik, Nahid Sırrı, *Bilinmeyen Yaşamlarıyla Saraylılar*, ed. Alpay Kabacalı (Istanbul, 2006).
Özön, Nijat, *Karagözden Sinemaya. Türk Sineması ve Sorunları*, 2 vols. (Ankara, 1995).
Sakin, Orhan, *Tarihsel Kaynaklarıyla İstanbul Depremleri* (Istanbul, 2002).
Shaw, Stanford J. and Ezel Kural Shaw, *History of the Ottoman Empire and Modern Turkey*, 2 vols. (Cambridge, 1977).
Şehsuvaroğlu, Bedi N., *İstanbul'da 500 Yıllık Sağlık Hayatımız* (Istanbul, 1953).
Tanpınar, Ahmet Hamdi, *Beş Şehir* (Istanbul, 2001).
Tugay, Asaf, *İbret. Abdülhamid'e Verilen Jurnaller ve Jurnalciler. Jurnalcilerin Tam Listesi* (Istanbul, n.d.).
Uzunçarşılı, İsmail Hakkı, *Osmanlı Devletinin Merkez ve Bahriye Teşkilâtı* (Ankara, 1988).
Ünver, A. Süheyl, *İstanbul Risaleleri 1*, ed. İsmail Kara (Istanbul, 1995).
İstanbul Risaleleri 2, ed. İsmail Kara (Istanbul, 1995).
Vatin, Nicolas and Gilles Veinstein, *Le Sérail ébranlé. Essais sur les morts, dépositions et avènements des sultans ottomans XIVe–XIXe siècle* (Paris, 2003).
Yediyıldız, Bahaeddin, *XVIII. Yüzyılda Türkiye'de Vakıf Müessesesi. Bir Sosyal Tarih İncelemesi* (Ankara, 2003).
Yoldaş-Demircanlı, Yüksel, *İstanbul Mimârisi İçin Kaynak Olarak Evliya Çelebi Seyâhatnâmesi* (Istanbul, n.d.).
Yüksel, Hasan, *Osmanlı Sosyal ve Ekonomik Hayatında Vakıfların Rolü (1585–1683)* (Sivas, 1998).
Zachariadou, Elizabeth A., *Studies in Pre-Ottoman Turkey and the Ottomans* (Aldershot, 2007).

Index